"*The Dance of Innovation: Infrastructure, Social Oscillation, and the Evolution of Societies* is a very impressive work. The fusion-fission dynamic integrates a lot of complex processes into a workable model. I don't think I've seen an analysis of social change with this kind of scope, integrating the evolution of material and cultural infrastructures along with the evolution of humans both physically and mentally. The continuities in mechanisms from infra-human life-forms are striking. The book reminds me somewhat of the work of [classical sociologists], but with 150 more years of scientific knowledge accumulated, and a superior theoretical arsenal."

Randall Collins, *Professor of Sociology Emeritus at the University of Pennsylvania, is a world-renowned sociologist*

"*The Dance of Innovation: Infrastructure, Social Oscillation, and the Evolution of Societies* is unlike any book written in recent history in sociology. It advances a critical idea that is often lost in sociology – the central force of infrastructures. Human institutional systems and, indeed, all dimensions of the social and economic world do not exist nor function without viable infrastructures. Everything that humans do in building up societies is linked to technologies or knowledge about how to build infrastructures, that is, the sustaining foundations of human societies that allow their dynamic processes to operate and evolve. Another central idea is an old one but stated in a novel new way – the notion of oscillations around patterns of fission and fusion. Societies and, indeed, all social systems at all levels of human organization, are built up only to disintegrate at some point in time as nothing lasts forever. Such has always been true for human social evolution but has been particularly the case over the last 10,000 years where infrastructures have allowed humans to build large, complex societies filled with disintegrative tendencies, thus accelerating oscillation of patterns of social organization on a much more rapid and grand scale. This book is one of the most original contributions to sociological analysis in many decades; and even though it is highly theoretical, it is written in such an informal style that it is a pleasure to read."

Alexandra Maryanski, *Research Professor of the Graduate Division in Sociology, University of California, Riverside*

Sociologists need to incorporate an evolved human actor into their models of emergent social processes, and McCaffree does so here, admirably so. He notes that it is the distinctly human evolved capabilities for cooperation and symbolic communication that enable humans to create social groups of a size not seen in the animal world. At the same time the constant dissolution and recombination of those social groups is an important source of knowledge innovation and cultural change. McCaffree particularly highlights the important role of the development of both the knowledge and structures of physical infrastructure (the infrastructure that supplies vital functions such as the supply of clean water) in making the mass societies of the modern world possible.

Rosemary Hopcroft, *Department of Sociology, University of North Carolina*

The Dance of Innovation

Few of us, amidst our daily chores and responsibilities, consider how mundane infrastructure—from electrical grids to sewage systems—have developed over millennia in ways that enable everything we cherish, from democracy to technological innovation to individual liberty. But what drives the evolution of this infrastructure? And why is infrastructure so critical to human flourishing? In this book, the most innovative and interdisciplinary study of cultural evolution ever produced, new concepts are explored, new histories are brought into contact, and new groundbreaking insights are defended. What makes creativity unique in human societies is not only our capacity to generate and modify our diverse individual intuitions about the social and physical world, but also our capacity to form and leave groups fluidly in a dancing rhythm of oscillation across the expanse of history. This book walks the reader carefully through these processes, with clear concepts and an approachable writing style.

Kevin McCaffree is Assistant Professor of Sociology at the University of North Texas. He is the author or co-author of five books, coeditor of *Theoretical Sociology: The Future of a Disciplinary Foundation*, and series editor (with Jonathan H. Turner) of Evolutionary Analysis in the Social Sciences. In addition to these works, he has authored or co-authored more than 20 peer-reviewed journal articles and handbook chapters published on a variety of topics ranging from cultural evolution to criminology to the sociology of empathy.

Evolutionary Analysis in the Social Sciences

A series edited by Jonathan H. Turner and Kevin J. McCaffree

This new series is devoted to capturing the full range of scholarship and debate over how best to conduct evolutionary analyses on human behavior, interaction, and social organization. The series will range across social science disciplines and offer new cutting-edge theorizing in sociobiology, evolutionary psychology, stage-modeling, co-evolution, cliodynamics, and evolutionary biology.

Published:

Cultural Evolution: The Empirical and Theoretical Landscape by Kevin McCaffree (2022)

The Dance of Innovation: Infrastructure, Social Oscillation, and the Evolution of Societies by Kevin McCaffree (2022)

The First Institutional Spheres in Human Societies: Evolution and Adaptations from Foraging to the Threshold of Modernity by Seth Abrutyn and Jonathan Turner *(2022)*

For a Biosocial Science: An Essay on Evolutionary Theory, Human Nature, and Social Life by Alexander Riley (2021)

On Human Nature: The Biology and Sociology of What Made Us Human by Jonathan H. Turner (2020)

Mechanistic Criminology by K. Ryan Proctor and Richard E. Niemeyer (2019)

The New Evolutionary Sociology: New and Revitalized Theoretical Approaches by Jonathan H. Turner and Richard S. Machalek (2018)

The Emergence and Evolution of Religion: By Means of Natural Selection by Jonathan H. Turner, Alexandra Maryanski, Anders Klostergaard Petersen, and Armin W. Geertz (2017)

Forthcoming:

The Evolution of World-Systems by Christopher Chase-Dunn

Maps of Microhistory: Models of the Long Run by Martin Hewson

The Dance of Innovation

Infrastructure, Social Oscillation, and the Evolution of Societies

Kevin McCaffree

Routledge
Taylor & Francis Group
NEW YORK AND LONDON

First published 2022
by Routledge
605 Third Avenue, New York, NY 10158

and by Routledge
2 Park Square, Milton Park, Abingdon, Oxon OX14 4RN

Routledge is an imprint of the Taylor & Francis Group, an informa business

Library of Congress Cataloging-in-Publication Data
A catalog record for this title has been requested

ISBN: 978-1-032-20941-8 (hbk)
ISBN: 978-1-032-20939-5 (pbk)
ISBN: 978-1-003-26602-0 (ebk)

DOI: 10.4324/9781003266020

Typeset in Garamond
by Taylor & Francis Books

Contents

Introduction viii

1 Humans' Genetic Unity and Ape Ancestry 1

2 Fission–Fusion as the Central Sustaining Mechanism of Organismality, Part 1 52

3 Fission–Fusion as the Central Sustaining Mechanism of Organismality, Part 2 66

4 Intuitive Information-Processing 101

5 On the Important Distinction between Tools and Infrastructure 141

6 The Tools and Infrastructure of Fossil Fuel Societies 169

7 Cities Drive the Metabolism of Societies 197

8 An "Oscillation-Infrastructural" Theory of Cultural Evolution 218

References 249

Index 281

Introduction

"Civilization enables us constantly to profit from knowledge we individually do not possess ... The great problem is how we can all profit from this knowledge, which exists only dispersed as the separate, partial, and sometimes conflicting beliefs [of all people]."

Friedrich Hayek, The Constitution of Liberty

In this volume, I present a theory of cultural evolution drawn, as always, from a synthesis of the work of others. When I set out to write a book on any topic, I never have any intention other than to create a new mosaic. The scientific study of culture is complex enough, with many quite dedicated and quite brilliant minds focused on the task. Important innovations and next steps will come not as manna from heaven, dropping utterly unexpected into our laps. It will, rather, come from new angles and new insights resulting from radically rearranging and reconceptualizing existing concepts and insights. It is pure mythology that scientific advancements are made from some lone thinker typing away in a dark room, utterly disconnected from their contemporaries. This book is, therefore, an attempt at a novel and creative amalgamation, blend, coalescence; it is a theoretical alloy.

One central argument I make in this book is that the most important structures in cultural evolution are infrastructures, which are the proximate material means of extracting, processing, and/or distributing energy throughout societies. Infrastructures are the "units of evolution" in cultural evolution, and the engineering principles associated with their construction are the "units of selection." Too many of my contemporaries focus on norms, laws, institutions, and other sociocultural formations. These are all quite interesting, surely, much more interesting than waste treatment plants. But they are not, emphatically, I insist, *not* more central to cultural evolution than infrastructure. Any changes to ideas, groups, norms, and so on are epiphenomena of accumulated modifications to core infrastructure. By the end of this book, I hope to have made this argument cleanly and clearly.

I also hope that this book inspires serious consideration of constructional and civil engineering among social scientists who, currently, all but ignore these fields. Social scientists must refrain from droning on and on about norms and institutions and cooperation and so on as though these were disconnected from the infrastructures that fundamentally undergird them. We need more engineers to become sociologists, and more sociologists to appreciate what it is, exactly, engineers (and their collaborators) do. The next time you hear the hum of electrical wires overhead, or see gushing water from a broken main, consider that you are seeing the highly evolved structures that connect our society with all societies that have existed and will exist.

A second, and related, argument is that human societies are novel in the animal kingdom because of the flexibility of their fission–fusion social organization. People fuse (i.e., share attention or intention) and fission (disaggregate their attention or intention) more fluidly and more openly over time with the rise of particular institutions and urban ecologies. It is not only individuals that think but groups as well, and groups "think" by oscillating between fission and fused states. The contents of our mind, our subjectivities, are mere probability distributions associated with shifting group commitments, responsibilities, and periods of freedom from both. As the rhythm of fission–fusion oscillations flows over the broad expanse of history, group boundaries become more porous and the potential for innovation and creativity rises, allowing for the creation of more accessible and efficient infrastructures.

We have a lot of ground to cover in this book, but I assure you that our journey will be enlightening, challenging, and enjoyable. I will be intentionally modifying established concepts from outside of sociology like "eusociality"; I will be advocating for more mainstream use of new concepts like "organismality" or "alloliving"; I will be introducing wholly new concepts like "fission–fusion oscillation"; and, as I said, I will be insisting on the centrality of infrastructural shifts over deep history. We will take our time on this journey, so that what emerges by the end is an illuminative, useful, and novel take on cultural evolution.

Here is a somewhat more specific roadmap of where we'll be headed: first, I'll introduce a sketch of "human nature," or the particular components of human physiology, psychology, and social organization that set humans apart (only by degree) from other animals. In some cases, I will be highlighting relevant similarities between humans and other animals that too many social scientists ignore (for example, our organizational similarities to eusocial insects). Next, I will introduce the two central forms of information processing in human societies: individual and group information processing. Our individual information processing, I argue, occurs mostly as an expression of our, often misleading, intuitions. Our group information processing, on the other hand, occurs as varying forms of fission–fusion oscillation. It is this group information processing that harbors the potential to modify our intuitions about the physical and social world and, in doing so, unleash a nonlinear, deep-historical process of technological and infrastructural innovation. Finally, we will take a careful, detailed, tour of the evolution of infrastructure from the earliest human societies up to the present moment.

It is my hope that, upon finishing this book, the reader can appreciate not only the role of infrastructure in expanding our collective potential, but also how the openness of humans' group information processing will determine how much such potential will increase in the future.

The book you now hold in your hands—or that you are now reading on a screen—is the follow-up to *Cultural Evolution: The Empirical and Theoretical Landscape.* Ideally, the two volumes should be read in tandem, but each volume is a standalone work that can be enjoyed separately. If you are particularly interested in an overview sketch of social change and development over the last 12,000 or so years, along with the most prominent theories currently offered to explain such change, I recommend that you read *Cultural Evolution: The Empirical and Theoretical Landscape* as well. Another significant benefit of that book is its framing of existing theories of cultural evolution in a way that is consonant with (though conceptually different from) biological evolution.

With this general introduction aside, let's take our first step on this journey and consider just what makes humans uniquely capable, by degree, of infrastructural evolution.

Chapter 1

Humans' Genetic Unity and Ape Ancestry

At the level of DNA (deoxyribonucleic acid) base pairs (the molecules that, together, form the DNA double-helix), human beings are about 99.9% identical.[1] Granted, even if human beings are 99.9% identical from a genomic standpoint, a rough estimate suggests that in a genome of 3 billion base pairs, this would still leave 3 million that might vary between people. Still, this variance is minimal compared to the sharedness of our genes. This is one reason why, in order to make money, genetic-testing companies such as 23andMe (a reference to the 23 paired chromosomes in the typical human being) strive to present human beings as distinct from one another.

But our distinctness from each other should not be overstated. We cannot ignore the fact that the average genetic difference between people amounts to 0.1%; humans are perhaps more genetically similar to one another than is any other ape species (Barbujani et al., 2013; see also Maryanski 2018).

And this brings me to my second point, which is that human beings are, in fact, great apes. The origin of the primate line dates to around 50 million years ago, and the first primates, which are today called "Old World" monkeys, lived in trees within tropical forests. So-called "New World" monkeys became reproductively isolated from Old World monkeys after the tectonic plates comprising South America broke off from the plates which now sit beneath Africa. Old World monkeys, who stayed behind in Africa would, over branching evolutionary time, give rise to various species of apes by around 25 million years ago.

These ape species include gibbons, orangutans, gorillas, chimpanzees, and bonobos. The ape evolutionary line that would eventually become human beings broke off from the chimpanzee line around 6–8 million years ago. This means that chimpanzees and human beings share a common ancestor that lived around 6–8 million years ago. This is about the time when bipedalism seems to have emerged.

Across the ensuing years, various species of hominins would emerge and disappear, with humans outlasting the rest. For example, the species

DOI: 10.4324/9781003266020-1

Homo habilis emerged around 2.5 million years ago but went extinct after about a million years on the planet. *Homo rudolfensis* was alive a little more than 2 million years ago but went extinct rather quickly. The species *Homo erectus* also emerged around 2 million years ago, though it too was extinct by around 100,000 years ago. *Homo heidelbergensis* emerged around 1 million years ago but went extinct around 200,000 years ago. The *Homo sapiens* line—us—is typically regarded as emerging sometime around 200,000–300,000 years ago, and, thus far, we've not yet gone extinct (see Schlebusch et al., 2017 for methods of dating modern human genetic divergence).

All of these species of *homo* were very highly genetically related, so much so that many human beings alive today contain identifiable *Homo neanderthalensis* ("Neanderthal") genes within them. The entire *homo* line is so closely related that it makes sense to call all these species "humans," though they were not identical to us in terms of brain or body structure. Yet, what is clear is that the *homo* line of animals that was evolving during this period was struggling to survive, and that all these species, save us, went extinct. This is a mystery worth figuring out, because it takes us to the heart of what makes modern humans human.

1.1 What Facilitates Humanity's Apparent Uniqueness?

When thinking about interspecies comparisons, we must consider *behavioral* similarities also, not just genetic similarities. After all, human beings are genetically very similar to chimpanzees, but they are not always behaviorally similar!

Chimpanzees live in dominance hierarchies that contain less variation in strictness/tightness than the hierarchies humans live in, which seem to be relatively less strict and more fluid. Or consider that chimpanzees in the wild appear to share food with known conspecifics, but not with unknown conspecifics (i.e., they share and cooperate with friends or family or acquaintances, not with strangers). Also, for chimpanzees, engagements with unknown conspecifics along community borders seem to more often result in violent clashes than they do in human societies (i.e., male immigrants are almost always treated skeptically and often violently in chimpanzee societies, but less often in human societies). It is true that human hierarchies and group boundaries can become quite strict and quite hierarchical—but, critically, if we are looking at the social conditions within which human beings evolved (small groups of foragers), it is undeniable that the hierarchies and boundaries humans formed were more porous, more open to trade, more tolerant, and more symbolically complex than those created by chimpanzees or any other primates (Boehm, 1999; Mitani et al., 2002).

While chimpanzees live in small communities of known others, humans live in what have been variously been called "macro" (Machalek, 1992) or "mega" (Turner and Machalek, 2018) or "ultra" (Turchin, 2016) societies/colonies composed of millions, tens of millions, hundreds of millions, or more. In this way, human beings are more to ants, bees, or termites than they are to chimpanzees. As Richard Machalek has argued, groups, as such, are not rare in the animal kingdom—we've all heard about prides of lions, gaggles of geese, parades of elephants, packs of dogs, or schools of fish. What *is* rare is the ability to associate, even cooperate, with strangers. Only humans and eusocial insects do this on a scale unmatched in the animal kingdom.

And why might this be? Why might human beings be more capable of scaling their population numbers compared to other apes (or, for that matter, other mammals)? Old World monkeys, New World monkeys, apes, and humans all live in hierarchies and all are adept at foraging for food. Yet, only humans live in societies of tens of thousands, hundreds of thousands, and beyond. What makes humans different? Put another way, what is it about humans that enables them to live in massive colonies much more similar in size to insect colonies than to ape communities? Ants, bees, and termites, for example, have features of their societies—coordinated divisions of labor, active commodity economies, collective food-sharing and caring for young, distribution chains, and waste disposal systems—whose only equivalent is to be found in human societies (Crespi, 2014; Moffett, 2019).

What, then, facilitates humans' (relatively) more sociable outlook toward strangers and tolerance of difference?

1.1.1 High Genetic Relatedness, Reciprocal Altruism, and Entitativity

As I've mentioned, human beings share about 99.9% of their DNA in common with one another; humans' genetic similarity is higher than we find in any other ape species. This genetic similarity has important implications for social organization. Work in evolutionary biology clearly shows an altruistic tendency among animals when they are related to each other—this is perhaps most visible in the care that parents give to their children, but it can also be detected in preferential care for siblings, cousins, and so on. I will argue that, in humans, this kin-concern extends quite a bit further, but that, unlike the genetically hard-wired eusociality of insects, human eusociality has co-evolved with our capacity for symbolic expression and self-identity.

Allow me to explain.

W. D. Hamilton's (1964) well-supported theory of kin selection in biology predicts that biological altruism (the sacrificing of one's reproductive fitness for purposes of enhancing the reproductive fitness of another) will be most common between parents and offspring (who share, on average, 50% of their genes), and between siblings (who share, on average, 50% of their genes on account of sharing the same parents). The strength, or frequency, of this altruistic behavior would then be followed by care for aunts and uncles (who share around 25% of their genes with their nieces and nephews), cousins (who share on average 12.5% of their genes with one another), great-great-grandparents (who share on average 6% of their genes with their great-great-grandkids), and so on down the line.

Altruistic behavior toward kin is thus said to be "selected for" across evolutionary history: individuals with a genetic propensity for kin-based altruism preferentially sacrificed themselves for others who were likely to have similar genes, thus increasing the copies of these genes in the next generation. So, during an attack by a predator, an animal is more likely to attempt to save its offspring than its nieces or nephews (though it may attempt to save both), because offspring have more copies of the parents' own genes than do nieces or nephews. By the same mathematical logic, the animal would be expected to prefer saving three of its cousins over one of its uncles, because three cousins likely share more of the animal's own genetic material than does one of its uncles. This "evolutionary logic" is of course wholly intuitive to animals and not some conscious mathematical calculation. It is simply the case that animals that behaved in these ways, over evolutionary time-scales, were more likely to pass on their genes than other animals, and so the genes producing this altruistic behavioral phenotype spread across populations as well.

The question of why humans appear capable of living in large, cooperative societies thus hinges, in part, on how related humans are genetically to one another. The more genetically similar members of a species are to one another, the greater, in principle, the scope of kin selection—that is, the more generalized kin-selective effects will be in a population.

Another interesting parallel between eusocial insects and human beings involves the process of forming an abstract identity. Argentine ants, for example, appear to identify with their entire colony, treating other ants in their midst—even those they are personally unfamiliar with—as nestmates. These ants do not identify with kin per se, but with any ant in their colony who shares specific chemical/pheromone markers. Humans, as well, seem capable of identifying with the colony ("society," "nation," "culture") at large—as Mark Moffett (2019) points out, every time you walk into a coffee shop and order coffee from an unfamiliar person working the cash register, you are interacting with someone you do not know simply on the basis that they share an interpretable worker identity and a colony membership ("coffee barista in America") and are therefore expected to cooperate with you. While all mammals seem to form cooperative relationships here and there, only eusocial insects—and humans—seem capable of forming a colony-wide identity. Doing so enables a scale of cooperation unseen in other animals.

Yet, humans are not eusocial in the same sense that these insects are eusocial—humans do not have "queens" who do all of the reproducing, or genetically determined "workers" who are sterile but contribute to the economy. Rather, humans exhibit a capacity for *eusocialness* because they are, (a) compared to other apes, highly genetically related to one another; and (b) can construe relatedness symbolically with articulated speech and cognitive abstraction, as when two close male friends call each other "brothers" (or close female friends call themselves "sisters") despite being from different families. The combination of (a) and (b) is a major reason why humans have coffee shops but, despite being quite intelligent, elephants do not.

Regarding (a), humans are not genetic clones as in eusocial insects, but they are highly genetically related, moreso than other primates, making them unusually capable of eusocial*ness* or elevated prosociality. Regarding (b), the construction of fictive kin is likely made easier due to a higher proportion of shared genes, and thus a convergence of phenotypes. Still, humans do not form colony-wide identities only on the basis of identical genomes or chemical/pheromone signatures. Rather, colony identities in humans are more symbolically construed, and thus more porous and flexible than they are in other eusocial animals. As an example of this porousness, consider that human beings frequently trade goods between tribes, ethnic groups, and societies, whereas eusocial insects maintain strict chemical boundaries between colonies. The capacity for intersocietal trade is unique in human beings, and results from a more symbolic, abstract, and therefore flexible eusociality.

Biologists will be frustrated by my use of the term "eusocialness" to describe humans' tendency to cooperate with strangers or unfamiliar others. For biologists, eusociality is typically defined descriptively as what certain species of insect or mammal *do* in order to reproduce successfully. And, the answer for bees, termites, ants, some wasp species, and naked mole rats is that there are reproductive "castes," which are genetically hard-wired and which determine whether or not an individual will be capable of reproduction. There is, in other words, a division of labor at the reproductive level, with some members of the species being born sterile and dedicating their daily energies to taking care of the fertile members of their colony (Wilson, 1971; 1975). For these reasons, many evolutionary biologists would bristle at my use of the term "eusocialness" to describe human beings.

I suppose there is, arguably, at least one analog in human society for reproductive "castes"—female humans after menopause, who are sterile and thus able to tend to the offspring of their children (and others' offspring) without the possibility of reproducing themselves. This is the so-called "grandmother hypothesis" of human eusociality (Hawkes, 2014). Indeed, there are other intelligent, social animals, such as whales, who also become sterile after menopause, suggesting that menopause, and its eusocial implications, exists in mammals other than humans (Johnstone and Cant, 2010). Moreover, sterilized castes of humans in early state societies—"eunuchs"—were often employed to tend to young sons and daughters of aristocrats (Betzig, 2014.) And, some psychologists have argued that the tendency toward suicide in human beings (greater than in most other apes and mammals) might represent a pathological expression of a genetically eusocial tendency to sacrifice oneself for the group (Joiner et al., 2016).

Still, the human brain is very flexible and reliant on a significant degree of social learning in order to develop. This leads me to hesitate in over-committing to a view of human beings as eusocial in the "hard-wired," genetically determined sense that it seems to be in bees, termites, wasps, ants, and naked mole rats. Evolutionary psychology is a fantastic field, one I continue to learn from. Yet, evolutionary psychologists, sometimes by their own admission, overlook the degree to which social learning can stretch the variability of human belief and behavior. I'd like to not make this mistake. As the "cultural" evolutionary psychologist Cecilia Heyes (2018) reminds us, compared to other ape species, the human brain develops for so long outside of the womb, and is so much larger relative to our body size (especially in tissues dedicated to learning and remembering), that we have a unique capacity to form "cultural gadgets" (theory of mind, literacy, numeracy) that are not determined by our genome and on which we depend for navigating our social environments.

There is some debate within biology over whether the term "eusociality" should be more broadly defined (e.g., Crespi and Yanega, 1995; Sherman et al., 1995). I think we should distinguish between *genetic eusociality* and the eusociality characteristic of human beings, *behavioral eusociality*. This distinction should be viewed along a continuum, with some animal species being closer to the genetic/intrinsic end (e.g., the haplodiploidy found in eusocial insects) and other species being closer to the behavioral/learned end (e.g., human beings). Paper wasps rely on highly genetically determined pheromones and facial structures to tell who belongs to their colony (see Sheehan and Tibbetts, 2011); humans use scent and physical appearance as cues as well, but they can also prioritize symbolic and linguistic understandings of peoples' identity and group membership.

On the more genetically hard-wired end of the continuum, animals like bees will be determined by birth to either reproduce or aid in the reproduction of others. Some members of the species will be sterile, others fecund. Due to this situation, genetic relatedness will be high, the animals will perceive one another as chemically and/or behaviorally similar, and they will thus cooperate and sacrifice for one another. This cooperation and sacrifice would be a direct function of shared genes; this is classical kin selection.

On the behavioral end of the continuum, animals, like humans, that are highly genetically related (but not clones of one another or systematically sterile) as well as capable of greater executive cognitive functioning and emotionality should also exhibit high levels of altruism, cooperative breeding, and symbolic communication (i.e., language) relative to animals in the same genus (e.g., chimpanzees) that are less genetically related to one another or who have less developed prefrontal and subcortical neural tissue. These differences will be matters of degree, not kind. And, the capacity for emotion and symbolic communication can be bootstrapped for other purposes when necessary as, for example, when ancestral hominins engaged in cooperative large-game hunting or developed symbolically extended kinship categories so that nearby tribes could be traded with or intermarried with.

Let me be clear: humans *are* genetically determined at conception (absent complications and assuming minimally adequate nutrition and stimulation) to grow a larger cerebral cortex than, for example, chimpanzees. And, aspects of the functionality of this cerebral cortex can be leveraged to construe social relationships abstractly so as to include members of a distant tribe as members of one's "family" even if there is no literal, direct, family relation. Yet, I don't think that we should refer to humans as *genetically* eusocial, because there is nothing about the evolution of the cerebral cortex in human beings that necessitates colony sociality or high levels of colony altruism and pro-sociality. Rather, it is that the cortical and subcortical tissues can, over the course of development and socialization, be molded so as to adopt norms around group fairness, group sacrifice, and group loyalty. Thus, while humans have unique genetically determined properties that predispose them to develop the capacity for abilities like abstraction and language and complex emotionality, it is the *leveraging and cultivation* of these properties via socialization and culture that makes them "behaviorally" eusocial. So, it is not that genes play no role in humans' behavioral eusociality, rather, it is that socialization and social learning play a larger role in human society than in more genetically eusocial species such as insects and naked mole rats.

While sociologists such as Alexandra Maryanski (2018) have pointed out humans' high genetic similarity to one another relative to other apes, it is not often clear *why* humans are more genetically similar to one another than, say, chimps are to one another or gorillas are to one another.

It seems that the high genetic similarity in human beings is due to a series of genetic "bottlenecks" throughout hominin, and later human, history. These bottleneck effects would have significantly reduced the genetic variance of the species' gene pools. One major bottleneck resulted from a climatological shift, beginning around 12 million years ago during the mid-late Miocene, that led to a cooling of the global temperature and a receding of the tropical forest habitat that had been home to humans' ape ancestors (Turner and Maryanski, 2015). During this period, dozens of ape species died—they were poorly adapted to living on the open African savannah with its large predators, given that there were fewer and fewer trees to scamper up for safety. I will return to this issue shortly, but suffice it to say that climatic changes in the Miocene seemed to have reduced the gene pools of animals that were ancestors of modern human beings.

Second, it seems that another bottleneck occurred when some members of our species left sub-Saharan Africa and migrated to West Asia and Europe sometime between 50,000 and 70,000 years ago (Campbell and Tishkoff, 2008; Amos and Hoffman, 2010). Today, there is greater genetic diversity among humans living in sub-Saharan Africa, compared to humans who can trace their recent ancestry to countries in Asia or Europe. This appears to be due to the fact that only some groups of people migrated out of Africa all of those millennia ago, and many died on their migratory journey, thus winnowing the genetic diversity of those who survived the trek.

A third bottleneck may have occurred around 74,000 years ago with the volcanic eruption of Mount Toba in Indonesia, one of the largest eruptions known to the historical record. This eruption would have produced a decade-long volcanic winter and could have led to a substantial loss of human life, thus reducing the genetic diversity of human beings even further (Gibbons, 1993; Harpending and Rogers, 2000; Kelly, 2016).

A fourth important bottleneck actually results from a set of behavioral propensities of human beings, in particular their polygynous sexuality (a trait they seem to share with other ape species), their socially constructed rules about who is allowed to marry who, and their tendency for large-scale intergroup warfare and conquest. While polygyny is rarer in societies today, it appears to have been quite common in the sedentary hunter-gatherer, horticultural, and agrarian societies of history. Polygyny is the practice of one man having more than one wife, and typically this is a man of high prestige and influence who can afford to support more than one wife. However, the practice of polygyny throughout our species' history likely reduced genetic variation to a significant degree.

For example, consider William Loughlin's (see Flannery and Marcus, 2012) anthropological account of the Alaskan Eskimos of the Anaktuvuk Pass who, at the time, were led by a man of high status known for his caribou-hunting talents. Loughlin's biological analysis of group heredity determined that this *one man* had fathered or grandfathered 20% of the group. This sort of polygyny would have been fairly common in historical human societies; even today, studies of extant hunter-gatherers reveal that high-status men (typically skilled hunters) father more children and thus transmit a greater number of their genes into the next generation (Smith, 2004; Apicella, 2014).

Marriage rules within human societies also played a significant role in reducing genetic diversity. Humans in foraging societies did not usually mate indiscriminately with members of their (small) groups. Rather, they often mated and had children with those deemed appropriate by elders or by tribal rules, and typically this mating occurred with known, familiar others, leading to high rates of inbreeding. For example, an analysis of human skeletal remains found in the HaYonim Cave in northwestern Israel, dating to around 10,000–13,000 years ago, revealed a specific congenital abnormality (missing third molars in the mandible) consistent with a "history of inbreeding" (Smith, 1973, pg. 70).

This inbreeding would have been common especially in the form of cousin marriage (Kelly, 2013). After all, estimates of the typical band size for extant hunter-gatherers, across environments, ranges between only 10 and 30 people. Robert Kelly also notes, following H. Martin Wobst (1974), that a foraging group size of around 25 might be sufficient to enable optimal hunting and foraging success without causing any significant congenital disorders due to inbreeding. This number also assumes some degree of contact with other geographically local, but not family-related, foraging groups with whom people interbred. Hunter-gatherers commonly traded with other local bands, and this intergroup contact, when it led to occasional intergroup marriage and child-rearing, plausibly maintained reproductive viability. Research on contemporary hunter-gatherers also clearly shows that most individuals in residential groups are not biologically related family members (Hill et al., 2011), so there would have been sufficient genetic variation to avoid serious birth defects.

Nevertheless, in addition to the reduction in human genetic diversity wrought by widespread polygyny and often restrictive in-group marriage rules, consider the many conquering warlords of history, such as Genghis Khan, who, along with their troops, fathered large numbers of children during their conquests (Zerjal et al., 2003; Balaresque et al., 2015). These conquering groups, across human history, served to further reduce the genetic variation of human beings.

The number and severity of population bottlenecks affecting human genetic diversity is understudied (Amos and Hoffman, 2010). There is no consensus in the research literature about how many bottleneck events—or behaviors—affected ancestral and/or archaic human populations. All that can be known for sure is that the degree of genetic variability in humans today is, relatively speaking, low.

What do these bottlenecks and the resultant high genetic similarity among humans mean? It means that humans, the world over, are uniquely similar to one another compared to other ape species. Given this, we might expect human beings to share a suite of cognitive mechanisms (e.g., Tooby and Cosmides, 1990) and to be quite similar to one another in terms of personality and social attitudes. Indeed, Paul Hanel and his colleagues (2019) recently analyzed 22 variables in a large cross-cultural sample using the World Values Survey in order to assess how socially similar people are around the world. They note that, typically, researchers search for differences between groups, but that this approach skews our perception of the incredible convergent similarities across groups. In fact, across a number of variables and using a large sample (N=86,272), they found that peoples' moral attitudes, trust in strangers, trust in familiar people, valuing of benevolence, and respect for the elderly were remarkably similar across countries. While some attitudes showed greater divergences (e.g., moral attitudes toward sexual issues), overall, the degree of similarity between any two groups (e.g., highly educated groups in different countries compared to less educated groups in different countries) was over 90%. I quote their conclusion at length:

> The finding that similarities between various groups outweigh differences across a range of psychological variables might be considered as surprising given that most research claims to have found differences between groups. However, from a biological or evolutionary point of view this is less surprising: Well over 99% of our DNA is shared and every group or society needs to develop some shared standards of communication and action to function effectively … benevolence values (e.g., loyalty, honesty) are similar across countries because they guide human cooperation and supportive relationships. Universalism values (e.g., equality, broad-mindedness) are important in every society because they guide the commitment to outgroup members, with whom most groups and societies need to form some kind of relations either in schools or workplaces or, on a larger setting, when trading. Security is also highly valued across countries because in evolutionary terms there have often been threats from outgroup and ingroup members. The resulting similarities are manifested in many international agreements. For example, more than 190 countries belong to international crime police organizations (ICPO or INTERPOL), which indicates that they share at least some common policies regarding prevention of and responses to criminal behavior. Another example is the Universal Declaration of Human Rights, which has been signed by almost every nation and demonstrates that humans share a common system of values.
>
> (Hanel et al., 2019, pg. 558)

Humans are highly genetically similar; this means that a larger number of cognitive and behavioral similarities across groups than there are differences. This enables a greater degree of pro-sociality, altruism, and general "groupishness" relative to other ape species.

Next, let's turn to the concept of reciprocal altruism.

In addition to the kin selection discovered by Hamilton (1964), animals also prefer to cooperate with those who've been fruitful cooperators in the past, a tendency called "reciprocal altruism" (Trivers, 1971). In order for such a trait to be evolutionarily selected for, we would expect that animals that cooperated with other cooperators would be more likely to survive and pass on the genes underlying this phenotype, as compared with animals who attempted to cooperate with others without concern for whether those others would cooperate in return. That is, animals who cooperated with just anyone, including those who were unlikely to reciprocate, may have been less likely to survive compared to animals that attended to the probability of reciprocation before choosing to cooperate.

This adds an important social-psychological dimension to the sort of genetically based altruism discovered by Hamilton. In Trivers's conceptualization, yes, genetically related conspecifics will be more likely to cooperate than less genetically related conspecifics; *however*, animals will also willingly cooperate with conspecifics that are *not* genetic family members if those individuals are perceived to be cooperative and pro-social. In short, animals are genetically parochial, and prefer to benefit those related to them, but they are also interested in forming alliances with others outside their family, so long as those alliances are perceived to be cooperative and mutually beneficial. Thus, while kin selection is an important dynamic influencing animal behavior, animals also frequently form cooperative alliances and mutually beneficial "friendships" with nonkin.

The importance of reputation in human societies is indicative of this reciprocal altruism in human beings. People gossip a lot, and in doing so they exchange both positive and negative information about the character traits of others. Often, this gossip involves information about how trustworthy, helpful, or reliable other individuals have been and thus how cooperative or pro-social they are likely to be in the future (Wu et al., 2016a; Wu et al., 2016b; see also Simpson and Willer, 2015). That humans can construe their reputation symbolically, and assess it abstractly and linguistically with others, may indicate an unusually central role of reputation management in human beings relative to other primates. We care about our reputation because this is our means of facilitating cooperative relationships with others. If humans are more reputation-focused than other mammals, this would, as with all differences between humans and nonhumans, be merely a matter of degree.

Now, let's consider the concept of "entitativity."

Entitativity describes a very high level of cohesion between individuals; it is a sense of unity or oneness. It seems that entitativity is increased when animals engage in "rallies." Consider the example of gray wolves jumping on top of one another and playfully yipping and barking, or spotted hyenas jostling against one another excitedly with stiff, bristling tails (Moffett, 2019). This behavior serves to increase group cohesion, potentially for purposes of attacking prey or another group of conspecifics. It undoubtedly also serves to increase group cohesion because group cohesion is an end sought for itself in any animal that is born dependent on others—from birth, it feels good to be acknowledged, supported, and protected by one's group.

Humans engage in rallies (hereafter "rituals") as well, though the human version is often (not always) more symbolic and abstractly understood compared to other animals (Fischer et al., 2013; Rossano 2019). In human societies, rituals express a person's group identity, are often tied to ancestor, god, or society worship (consider rituals on Christmas or on the Fourth of July), and may involve complex, highly routinized steps (e.g., Passover *seder* in Judaism or a traditional coming of age ceremony) or less complex, less routinized habits (e.g., shaking a person's hand when you meet them or holding a door open for people behind you). Though sometimes more subtle and sometimes more complex than the rituals of nonhumans, human rituals nevertheless serve the same purpose as their nonhuman counterparts—namely, increasing individuals' sense of solidarity and oneness with others.

Conventional estimates place the emergence of distinctly human ritual behavior in the late Ice Age about 15,000 years ago with the "full-blown" emergence of art, music, and ornamentation (Flannery and Marcus, 2012, pg. 14). However, the fact that nonhuman animals also engage in (perhaps less complex) rituals suggests that rituals of some sort have always been a part of the evolution of hominins. In fact, more recent work is rewriting this conventional estimate of ritual emergence in humans; exotic raw materials and pigments were being used—likely for ritual ceremonies—at least 300,000 years ago in Kenya (Brooks et al., 2018). And, though speculative, the cranial capacity of *Homo erectus* and various subspecies, alive from around 2 million years ago to 500,000 years ago, strongly suggests proto-human ritualistic and symbolic abilities.

Regardless of the specific date of emergence, the time structure of human rituals seems to change as societies grow in population and density. People living in small, nomadic hunter-gatherer societies typically have unscheduled ritual behavior—whenever resources are plentiful, and conflict between bands or tribes is low, ritual celebrations will occur. But, if food is scarce or conflict is frequent, large ceremonial rituals will be put off. People living in sedentary farming societies, on the other hand, typically observe more scheduled rituals because, absent poor harvests, food is more plentiful and its supply more reliable.[2]

Whether particular rituals are highly routinized or not, scheduled or not, complex or not, people often engage in them regardless of whether they understand exactly *why* the rituals are important or *where* the idiosyncratic steps or rules of the rituals come from (Whitehouse and Lanman, 2014; Boyer, 2018). Rather, people often treat rituals as objective facts of their social worlds—this is what *we do*, and how *we do* it. Ritual practice of any complexity is socialized into children beginning at a young age; acknowledgment of and engagement in the rituals is considered a part of normative, correct behavior. This is true whether we think about the common, everyday rituals of human beings (e.g., greeting rituals when meeting someone for the first time) or we think about the complex rituals anchoring many religious traditions.

The most sophisticated theories of ritual behavior in sociology are Randall Collins' (2004) Interaction Ritual Theory and Edward Lawler and colleagues' (2009; Thye et al., 2019) Theory of Social Commitments. For Collins, physical co-presence with (nonthreatening) others increases the positive emotional energy circulating between individuals in an encounter. Insofar as this circulating emotional energy is directed toward a common focus of attention (could be music, could be a symbol, could be a team playing a sport), individuals will begin subtly synchronizing their behavior and physiological states, and this will lead to a sense of emotional entitativity. This emotional entitativity, or affective sense of oneness or groupishness, undergirds group cohesion and solidarity and will often be symbolized by group members in some external form (e.g., a band name, the cross in Christianity, a sports team logo). Individuals, moreover, will discuss these affectively entitative events with each other in conversation, or they'll don the logos/symbols of the group. In this way, their entitativity becomes a topic of group conversation, further reinforcing solidarity and cohesion and further directing attention to the group *as a group*.

For Collins, whether interaction rituals are maximally entitative (as when rituals are high in emotional arousal and highly routinized) or minimally entitative (as when rituals are low in emotional arousal and less routinized), what is important to understand is that they can still promote group cohesion. Entitativity in a society is enhanced, even if only subtly, if individuals know how to signal friendly intentions with any unknown person they might meet (say, with a handshake). And even if the sense of entitativity generated by superficial interaction rituals is lower compared to the routinized, highly emotional rituals of a strict religious tradition, remember that the handshake or hug or national song can integrate a larger number of people than the particularistic, idiosyncratic (if complex and emotional) rituals of a specific religious tradition. As a group gets larger, rituals typically become more abstract, less routinized, and perhaps less emotional, but no less important for group integration.

For Lawler and his colleagues, cooperative group interactions oriented toward shared goals can lead people to develop emotional attachments to *groups*, not just to the individuals composing the group. These person-to-group ties result from "task jointness" or the shared burden of labor that people shoulder in their pursuit of some collective goal, as well as the degree to which this task jointness produces a sense of shared responsibility, or shared fate, in the pursuit of said goal. The more a task is jointly (though not necessarily equally) contributed to by individuals, and the more a sense of shared responsibility emerges from this, the more individuals develop emotional and cognitive ties to the group itself as an entity. Rituals bind us together, as do joint tasks.

In broad summation, humans are highly genetically related, which facilitates cooperation and an easily extended, intuitive, sense of "kin." People are also, perhaps to a unique degree among animals, capable of interacting with others deemed cooperative, and do so according to a complex symbolic understanding of others' reputations across various spheres of life. Finally, the perhaps unique (in degree) capacity for ritualistic behavior and shared attentional allocation to tasks in humans further serves to reduce self–other boundaries and increase cohesion, group loyalty, and group sacrifice. High genetic relatedness and the associated behavioral capacity for *eusocialness*, along with the maintenance of social reputations and the capacity for ritual and joint-task-induced entitativity, are important reasons why humans have been able to scale their societies to numbers unseen in any other mammal species.

1.1.2 Cooperative Child-Rearing

Eusocialness and societal living in human beings seems to be, in part, an adaptation to the vulnerability of human infants. Human beings are born premature so that their large cranium can fit through the birth canal of their mothers. Infants, and their mothers, are thus highly vulnerable during the birthing and early child-rearing process. In fact, death in childbirth was common in the earliest human societies (Kelly, 2013). A human newborn's large cranium houses a very large brain—the average human brain is about three times the size of the average chimpanzee brain and contains at least twice as many cells in the cerebral cortex (Mora-Bermúdez et al., 2016). The cerebral cortex, and in particular the prefrontal cortex, of the human brain is centrally implicated in processing memory, impulse control, abstract thought, and theory of mind; these traits, together, comprise what psychologists call "executive cognitive functioning."

This enhanced capacity for memory, impulse control, abstract thought, and theory of mind (theory of mind being the capacity to consider and understand the mental states of others) in human beings facilitates social learning and enables the transmission of ideas and expectations for behavior ("norms") across generations. Yet, the vulnerability of human newborns and their mothers requires an existing social support system in order for vaginal birth to be a viable mode of reproduction. Succinctly put, in utero, a fetus "increases[s] a woman's energy needs *and* decreases here ability to meet those needs. Mother's need help, and the two sources are female relatives or friends and her children's father(s)" (Kelly, 2013, pgs. 191–192).

For these reasons, some have suggested that humans are unique in their "alloparenting" practices, that is, in their tendency to distribute the work of rearing (i.e., creating safe contexts for birthing, breastfeeding, and the provisioning of calorie-rich foods) and raising (i.e., the education and skills training necessary for becoming members of the group) children (Hrdy, 2011; Bentley and Mace, 2012). Extensive alloparenting, might have begun as early as 1.8 million years ago in *Homo erectus*, but it was being refined across ensuing species of hominins. Research indicates that the cranial capacity of Australopiths at birth, a hominin species alive 2–4 million years ago, was around 180 cubic centimeters (DeSilva and Lesnik, 2008). This is only a bit bigger than modern chimpanzees. However, *Homo erectus* babies had a cranial capacity of around 270 cubic centimeters. Babies' brains were getting bigger; babies were being born more and more prematurely to enable the continued growth of the cranium outside the womb, and they were, as a result, increasingly dependent on parents (and their group) for care.

The burdens and joys of childcare were shared by all members of the group in early human societies, as women on average may have been giving birth as frequently as once every four years (Kelly, 2013). Women helped care for other women's children in exchange for reciprocated helping in the future. As I mentioned above, some researchers also suggest that the evolution of menopause in human beings was adaptive because it motivated the care of offspring by grandmothers—after all, if human females were fertile throughout the life course, they might be less inclined to care for their grandchildren because they might still be raising children of their own into old age (Hawkes, 2003). It is notable that other animals heavily reliant on social learning and social coordination have evolved menopause as well (e.g., in whales; see Johnstone and Cant, 2010; Brent et al., 2015).

Of course, it wasn't just women doing the child-rearing, though they likely took on the brunt of it (Flannery and Marcus, 2012). Men, as well, would take on such tasks; in foraging societies, men curry the favor of, or repay debts to, other men and women by assisting in the child-rearing process (Kelly, 2013). In fact, the human brain is hypothesized to contain neural circuitry comprising a "parental care motivation system," that is measurable in both human males and females (Schaller, 2018). This evolved motivational system responds to youthful features in children and facilitates their nurturance and/or protection. Given the premature birthing pattern of human beings, as well as babies' utter dependency in early life, the evolution of this cognitive motivation system may have been the difference between the survival and death of offspring. Single motherhood or single fatherhood, especially in a dangerous ancestral environment, would have been a treacherous risk. It takes a village to raise a child, indeed. Though we cannot know for certain if a less-developed parental care motivation system in earlier *homo* species contributed to their extinction, what is more certain is that it has facilitated the survival of offspring in our own species.

Humans, then, distinct by degree from other primates, go through long pregnancies and give birth to babies whose brains are not yet fully developed. The capacity for social learning requires prolonged pregnancy and rearing, and prolonged pregnancy and rearing require extensive support from kin and nonkin. Evolved motivational systems, such as the parental care motivation system, would have helped human beings create cohesive "emotional groups" (Bader, 2017; see also Hrdy, 2011) inextricably linked to successful sexual (and thus community) reproduction. This is a cooperative child-rearing context that protects vulnerable mothers, aids in child-rearing, and continues throughout a prolonged period of community socialization of the child into adulthood.

1.1.3 Cooperative Hunting/Foraging and Defense

It is not just cooperative child-rearing—alloparenting—that, in large part, defined the evolution of humans as a species, but also cooperative resource extraction. The earliest form of this cooperative resource extraction was hunting and gathering, and this was the mode of life of every species of *homo* prior to human beings. Of course, this is the predominant mode of subsistence for all nonhuman animals, as well. To survive, an animal must either hunt other animals to eat, or forage for edible plants, nuts or other biomass.

The nutritive quality of an animal's diet significantly influences brain size and development, and this was especially true for ancestral hominid species (Hublin and Richards, 2009). Beginning around 4 million years ago, isotopic fossil evidence indicates that some apes ancestral to humans began consuming larger amounts of C4 and CAM plants (e.g., cactus, agave, sorghum, sedge seeds, tropical grasses), plants that chimps today still don't eat very frequently (Fahy et al., 2015; Schoeninger, 2018). These grasses are rarer in forested woodland areas, and more common on the African savannah, providing evidence that ancestral humans left the woodlands to attempt to brave life on the open savannah. Doing so not only required developing a new diet, but also a more emotional, intensive, form of social cohesion (see Turner and Maryanski, 2015).

Ancestral humans' consumption of a greater amount of C4/CAM plants, may have been, in part, because they were consuming more large game animals that persisted largely on diets of C4/CAM plants themselves (e.g., zebras, antelopes, buffalo). Given that the earliest stone tools (which seem designed for cleaving, butchering, and breaking the bones of large game animals) can be dated to between 2 and 4 million years ago, this fits well chronologically with what we know about the dietary shift of early hominids (Harmand et al., 2015; but see also Lewis and Harmand, 2016; Domínguez-Rodrigo and Alcalá, 2016). This is a disputed area of research, so I do not want to insist on the importance of the specific dating of stone tools. After all, monkeys have recently been observed flaking stone tools (but monkeys do not hunt large game animals), so there is no necessary relationship per se between evidence of stone tool use and the hunting of large game animals (Proffitt et al., 2016).

Still, regardless of what we can infer about the behavioral origins of stone tool use, it is more certain that cooperative hunting of large game animals facilitated the growth of brain tissue—and also the size of communities—in early species of *homo* (e.g., Laughlin, 1968). Chimpanzees enjoy eating colobus monkeys (and sharing the meat with friends), but colobus monkeys are small, and their nutritive value to a community would thus be lower than that of a woolly mammoth or buffalo. Also, eating raw meat can be dangerous, because flesh can be laden with pathogenic bacteria. We cannot, however, adequately talk about the practice of cooperative hunting without discussing the development of perhaps the first form of community infrastructure for food cooking and disinfection: campfires.

It is notoriously hard to date the emergence of fire used for cooking, warmth, and light—after a fire goes out, ashes just flit away in the wind and new soil eventually blankets over what remains. Even if fires were more archaeologically identifiable, how should we distinguish fires made by species of *homo* from fires that were started by some other means, such as sunlight beating down on dry brush? Typically, archeologists and anthropologists date the consistent use of fire for heating, cooking, and light at night to the Upper Paleolithic era (~10,000–50,000 years ago), though the controlled use of fire by *homo* in some form predates this period by thousands, perhaps millions, of years (Wrangham, 2009; 2017; Gowlett, 2016). Anne Delagnes and her colleagues (2016), for example, have uncovered evidence in South Africa of heat-treated silica rocks (which made them easier to shape) dating to the Middle Paleolithic era.

In addition to making meat more tender and less pathogenic, the use of fire for cooking would have broken down the cellulose in fibrous plants and tubers, making them easier to digest. Cooking food also allows it to be stored for longer periods, implying a tight-knit social grouping dedicated to maintaining and defending such stores (though storing food isn't much of a concern for mobile, nomadic foragers). Also, foragers likely used fire to clear grasslands so as to more easily see, and thus hunt, wild game (Kelly, 2013). Campfires and torches, because they could provide light and heat, would have also been a means of defense against predators. They also would enabled more socializing—discussion, debate, and storytelling—into the dark hours of the night.

Let's look more closely at the likely impact of diet on the evolution of brain tissue. Cooking on an open fire essentially "pre-digests" food before consumption, rendering fibrous plants and tough meat easier on the gut and more nutritious. Non-human primates with large intestinal tracts have rib cages that are bell-shaped, while humans have narrower, straighter rib cages; these large intestinal tracts in nonhuman primates are required to digest and draw nutrients from dense, uncooked, plant cellulose. Consider, as Kelly (2016) points out, that gorillas consume around 40 pounds of (uncooked) leaves per day! Most significantly, the caloric energy formerly dedicated to developing a longer intestinal tract could, upon the invention of campfires, be diverted to the development of the brain. According to Kelly:

> Cooked meat, even if it makes up only 10 to 20 percent of the diet, can have a perceptible effect on energetic efficiency … Your brain is an expensive organ; it makes up 2.5 percent of your body weight, but requires 20 percent of your energy. By cooking food, *Homo* diverted energy that had been spent on maintaining a massive gut to maintaining a large brain. This may be what helped drive another hallmark of humans, a brain that is large relative to our body size … Cooking made it possible to get more out of meat and tubers, and stone tools increased the ease with which tubers and hunted or scavenged meat were acquired.
>
> (Kelly, 2016, pg. 31)

Typically, estimates of Paleolithic-era diets in ancestral humans are inferred from the diet of extant human hunter-gatherers and the diet of these contemporary foragers ranges from 35% to 66% plants and 33% to 65% animal meat (Ben-Dor, 2018). However, these estimates obviously vary widely, in part, because extant human foragers probably vary more in their diet than did Paleolithic-era hominids. During the Paleolithic era, large mammals were being so frequently hunted that they began going extinct en masse. Beginning around 2.5 million years ago, the average bodyweight of mammals dropped from over 1,000 pounds to around 20 pounds in large part because the bigger animals were cooperatively hunted and eaten to extinction by hominins. The nutrition and satiation afforded by large game animals was simply unmatched: a Bison would have provided enough calories to last a 25-person foraging group for over a week (Ben-Dor, 2018). Not surprisingly, cooperative large-game hunting only intensified with time: beginning around 50,000 years ago, 90 genera of animals weighing over 97 pounds went extinct (Ben-Dor, 2018). This is why we cannot infer Paleolithic diets from modern hunter-gatherer diets: hominids had already wiped out all of the largest mammals, making vegetation more prevalent (it wasn't being eaten by large mammals any longer), thus skewing the diet of modern hunter-gatherers toward greater amounts of plant material, and less large game, than might have been true thousands or millions of years ago.

The legacy of this meat-eating can be found today in the fact that human beings are more carnivorous than any other ape species. This is revealed in characteristics that humans share with other carnivorous animals, such as the shortened digestive tract mentioned above (i.e., the large intestine in humans is 77% smaller by volume than would be that of a human-sized chimp) as well as in humans' higher number of fat cells and greater stomach acidity (Ben-Dor, 2018). The shortened digestive tract in humans likely co-evolved with the use of campfires for cooking, since a shortened digestive track requires that food be "pre-digested"/cooked before consumption in order for nutrients to be adequately absorbed (Milton, 1999).

The hafting of stone points into spears, a clear sign of group hunting in early *homo*, emerges ~500,000 years ago (Wilkins et a., 2012). And "spear-throwers" (a handheld lever that throws spears or darts or rocks; see Whittaker, 2016), which emerge later in *homo sapiens*, might be an even clearer indicator of cooperative hunting. Groups of ancestral humans, armed with spears or *atlatl*, would have been a formidable threat to any large land mammal (as well as a greater threat to one another, something I will return to later). The endurance-running characteristic of human beings (no other mammal has been witnessed running for as long as human runners), a shoulder skeletal structure adapted for throwing, and clearly higher fat reserves relative to other primates, strongly suggest that cooperative carnivorous hunting was a staple of human social life (Ben-Dor, 2018). We should not conclude from this information that humans are carnivores—we aren't. We are simply, by degree, more *carnivorous*. In order not to starve, foragers maintained diverse diets so as to leave them with options should any prior food staple become difficult to acquire (Hayden, 1981; Kelly, 2013).

Finally, I must underscore that cooperative hunting would have co-evolved with cooperative foraging, cooperative group defense and cooperative parenting because each would have increased the probability of survival of healthy infants and mothers. This suite of features, *allohunting, alloforaging, allodefense, and alloparenting*, constituted a proto–division of labor (people take on different roles in helping the group hunt, forage, defend itself, and raise children), as well as a proto–social safety net (even if one did not forage or hunt successfully, others will help provide) that would have been essential for the survival of a primate species with such long gestational periods and dependent offspring (see Figure 1.1).

In fact, as Matthew Dunn (2016) and others have recently argued, this four-pronged division of labor underlying forager social coordination may have made hominin, and certainly human, forager societies capable of a greater degree of entitativeness or "organismality" compared to other ape

allohunting and alloforaging	*allodefense*	*alloparenting*
Tasks associated with food procurement are distributed across the group. Successful hunters are encouraged to share; less successful hunters ask for help.	Tasks associated with self-defense are distributed across the group. Successful warriors are encouraged to protect more people.	Tasks associated with child-rearing and socialization are distributed across the group. Those who are successfuly rearing and raising their own children are encouraged to look after the children of others; less successful parents (or non-parents) are encouraged to ask for help, or to offer to provide it.

Figure 1.1 Social Mechanisms of Forager Group Entitativity/Organismality

species. I will return to this important issue of organismality below (see Queller and Strassmann, 2009).

1.1.4 Language, Symbolic Reasoning, and "Fictive" Kin

As Pascal Boyer has aptly pointed out: "The natural environment of human beings, like the sea for dolphins or the ice for polar bears, is information provided by others" (Boyer, 2018, pg. 67). Indeed, humans occupy informational niches, which we often call "cultures," and which co-evolved with humans' unique capacities for language and sociality (Pinker, 2010).

Language is a means of information extraction, processing, and distribution. All animals have the ability to communicate something about their physiological and emotional state utilizing gestures, vocalizations, or objects in the environment (Pepperberg, 2017). Yet it seems that the complexity and malleability of human language is, at least to some extent, unique among animals. And, once human societies developed pictographic and, then, alphabetic languages, they had a symbolic system usable by anyone willing to memorize particular symbols with particular meanings.

The complexity and malleability of human language facilitates the generation and transmission of mythologies, rituals, and social relationships. It is as though the ability to memorize, reflect on, and imbue emotions into symbols affords people a hallucinatory capacity—they can imagine and orient themselves to gods or royalty or cultural obligation. Sometimes the hallucinations afforded by language and imagination are bleak and hopeless (as when people feel stricken by witchcraft or condemned to hell), and sometimes they are utterly uplifting (as when people discuss their imaginings of a better society).

I don't intend to push the language-as-hallucination point too far, mostly because the stigma associated with the term "hallucination" distracts from my intended point. But, it is worth considering how the imagery and emotions triggered by linguistic expression can motivate people to mobilize for purposes of improving trade relationships or hunting strategy, or, to mobilize so as to better burn heretics or squander valuable resources. A chimp cannot convince another chimp to burn all pieces of fruit (or other chimps) in sight as an offering to the gods; only humans are capable of such abject lunacy. At the same time, no chimp can convince another chimp of their shared "chimpness" with others like them around the world.

But, let's take this back to the context of survival in small groups of foragers, because this is the context within which human language evolved. The necessary community rearing of vulnerable children and support of vulnerable families required the extensive transfer of information across generations; among other things, this would include information about the migratory patterns of game animals, about edible plant or nut seasonality, about predators, about threatening surrounding tribes, about cooperative trade partners, about relevant ancestors and rituals, and about the development of the social skills necessary to navigate small group relations. Without the symbolic transfer of information—via language—adults don't eat and children don't learn how to survive.

As I mentioned above in the opening paragraphs, all species of *homo*, save us, went extinct. Human beings do not have strong muscular bodies or large fangs or the capacity for rapid acceleration. Rather, humans have survived on account of their undeniable capacity for community- and colony-level sociality.

Work by Alexandra Maryanski (1986; 1994; 1995; Maryanski and Turner, 1992) has used a form of inductive theory construction called "cladistic analysis" to estimate the likely behavioral characteristics of the last common ancestor that human beings share with great apes. This analysis involves studying the social behavior of great apes (orangutans, gorillas, chimpanzees), discerning which characteristics these apes share in common, and inferring from these the likely characteristics of the ancestral primate from which modern apes (including humans) descended. Maryanski's method is similar to cladistic studies of ancient texts wherein similarities across disparate documents are used as indicators of the content of the original document(s) from which they were copied.

Maryanski's results suggest that the last common ancestor of contemporary great apes was behaviorally individualistic and highly socially mobile. This creature likely lived in dispersed communities of other conspecifics, interacting here and there with other members of its community. Community borders were likely monitored and enforced, but within the community most social ties were likely weak ties. Ties were likely weakest between adult females that dispersed to other communities at puberty, and they may have been weak-moderate among adult males prone to forming coalitions and to staying in their birth community past puberty (this is common in chimpanzees). And, according to her cladistic analysis, social ties were likely strongest between mothers and their offspring. Nevertheless, these ties, regardless of their strength, remained fluid, with ties strengthening and weakening across various individuals within a given community, albeit with the overall tie strength hovering around weak to moderate. Maryanski suspects that the evolution of the hominin line beyond this last common ancestor represents a "clear upward trend favoring a heightened sociality" (Maryanski, 2018).

But what led to this trend favoring heightened sociality, or entitativity, clearly evident in human beings today? In part, it may have been a result of directional selection on the genome of ancestral hominids to make them better adapted to living life on an open, dangerous savannah. Turner and Maryanski (2015) point out that between 5 and 12 million years ago, during the Late Miocene period, the globe's climate began to cool and the tropical forests that had been home to monkey and ape species began to recede. The receding of tropical forests left vast grassland savannahs in their wake.

This receding of forested habitat led to a growing competition over resources among primate species. Monkeys, as distinct from apes, live in very social, very strict, dominance hierarchies organized around female matrilines, and this group cohesiveness would have aided their survival on the open grassland savannahs. Being physically smaller than apes, monkeys could also maneuver more efficiently in what trees remained, and, moreover, they could digest unripe fruit (apes, including humans, cannot), making survival for ape species more and more precarious and difficult by comparison. Some apes, in particular those most related to modern-day humans, left the safety of the trees and took to the ground to forage for food and shelter.

Thus, the ape ancestors of modern human beings began to face a new set of problems between 5 and 12 million years ago: the climatic transition that produced a shift from forest to grassland habitats meant that apes were going to have a more difficult time finding trees to scale in order to stay safe from predators hunting on the ground. As Maryanski's cladistic analysis indicates, early ape species were likely quite solitary and most of their within-community ties to others were weak to moderate if not null. This tendency toward weak social ties would have left ancestral ape species vulnerable to competition for food with monkeys, as well as to predation from fearsome predators including large saber-toothed cats (*Machairodontinae*), hyenas (*Pachycrocuta brevirostris*), and crocodiles (*Crocodylus checchiai*).

These conditions, Turner and Maryanski (2015; see also Turner and Machalek, 2018) suggest, would have created a context wherein directional genetic selection might increase tissue and circuitry in the brain, facilitating group organization into dense social units in order for apes to more successfully fight off predators, find food, and survive as a collective in open-country grasslands. Turner summarizes the circumstances as follows:

> [Human nature] is, in essence, great ape nature, but a nature that was subject to intense selection as the hominin ancestors of humans had to leave the forests, in which all great apes evolved, and increasingly adapt to more open-country conditions on or near the African savannah. Only one ape can now live on the African savannah—H. sapiens ... Thus, the story of human nature is how the basic behavioral capacities and propensities of great apes were modified by Darwinian natural selection as it worked on great ape neuroanatomy to accommodate the demands of [open country habitats] ... and, eventually, to produce H. sapiens.
>
> (Turner, 2018, pg. 90)

Ape species over the millennia were whittled down in population numbers, dying off because they could not adequately adapt to these changing conditions. Yet, adaptive mutations and directional selection were gradually enhancing ancestral humans' capacity for survival. The increasing success of some species of *homo* on the savannah is well documented in the steady rate of extinctions of apex predators—ancestral humans were likely killing them all off, cooking them, eating them, and, in doing so, obtaining the fats, salts, and proteins necessary for the growth of neural tissue (Estes et al., 2011). Turner (2000; 2007; 2020), for example, provides evidence showing that the subcortical areas of the brain in humans (dedicated to generating emotions) are roughly twice the size of those in other apes. Moreover, it seems that the growth of these tissues dedicated to emotion-processing may have begun prior to the growth of the neocortex.

The brain size of the early *homo* species Australopithecine, alive around 4.5 million years ago, was not much larger than that of contemporary chimpanzees (who have an average brain case size of ~450 cubic centimeters). However, by around 2 million years ago, ancestral *homo* species have brain case sizes of around 500 cubic centimeters, and around half a million years ago *Homo erectus* have brain case sizes of ~1,150 cubic centimeters. Growth of the brain would continue across *homo* species, with modern humans revealing a brain case size of ~1,400 cubic centimeters (about 100 cubic centimeters fewer than Neanderthals, with whom humans interbred; see Villanea and Schraiber, 2019). *Homo erectus* may have been the first ancestral *homo* species to survive as allo-living hunter-gatherers, suggesting that an emotional-cognitive threshold had been reached allowing for highly integrated, cooperative social groups around half a million years ago (Leakey and Walker, 1976; Swedell and Plumber, 2012; Antón et al., 2016). In *Homo erectus*, half a million years ago, we have our first real glimpse of identifiably modern "human" social groupings.

It is also very likely that the origin of language rests at least partly in the capacity of early hominins to exchange subtle forms of emotional expression (Bechara et al., 2000; Damasio, 2001). This emotional expression would have been verbal and nonverbal—Giacomo Rizzolatti and Michael Arbib (1998), for example, note how important physical gesturing is to communication in monkeys (see also Fröhlich et al., 2019). And, if Turner's timeline is correct, an elaborated neurological emotional repertoire would have predated the identifiably human-like tongue, lips, larynx, and vocal tract which enable the fully articulated speech we have today. If so, the origin of language may be inextricably linked to the origin of musical expression—in fact, other researchers have posited "musilanguage" as a proto-form of articulated speech (Brown, 2001; Mithen, 2006).

It is hard to know for sure how this musilanguage developed, but it likely involved the intentional sharing, within a group, of synchronized, vocalized sounds following coherent themes (i.e., child-rearing, hunting, inter-tribal conflict, death of important band members) driven by the desire to communicate the experience of intense, complex emotional states. Those who could more precisely express their emotional states and tie these emotional states to particular events may also have garnered more status within the group and, therefore, experienced greater reproductive fitness. This "musilanguage," and the evolution of associated physiologies in early hominins (e.g., the lower position of the larynx in the vocal tract, the more fine-grained motor control of breathing, and so on; see Ghazanfar and Rendall, 2008), would have been a general foundation for the further development of both musicality and linguistic expression.

Since communities, not individuals, develop languages (and language conventions), the evolution of musilanguage, at some point, would have necessitated community socialization. Language is also fundamentally arbitrary, and thus socially negotiated, requiring, again, a significant level of community interaction (Luef and Pika, 2017).

Language and executive cognitive functioning enable the development of novel forms of tool development and use. Consider the following incisive point:

> Oldowan flake tools [dated to ~2.5 million years ago] don't require much forethought, but making an Acheulian hand ax [dated to ~1.5 million years ago] is a more language-like activity because the flint-knapper must think ahead, imagining how removing one flake will affect future flake removals so that he or she can arrive at the final teardrop-shape form. Language requires its speaker to do the same

> thing, using words and grammar that depend in part on what comes later in a sentence ... [considerations like these] suggest that language and tool manufacture might have coevolved.
>
> (Kelly, 2016, pg. 43)

Thus, an inextricable link between the evolution of emotionality, language, intelligence, tools and group bonding emerges (Turner and Machalek, 2018). A compatible theory is that of Daniel Dor (2015, 2017), who argues that language evolved as a technology of social intersubjectivity, one that could be used to intentionally adjust and/or influence the imaginations/understandings of the individuals communicating. Also, because language can be used to manipulate others, the constant, ongoing negotiation of in-group/out-group (i.e., trusted/distrusted) becomes increasingly important the more linguistic an animal becomes.

Rather than understanding language as just a physiological or cognitive ability, Dor encourages us to consider that the capacity for articulated speech evolved because of what it could *do* for primates desperately trying to organize themselves, and their relation to other groups, for survival. With language, animals can coordinate their emotions and abstract concepts, enabling increasingly intensive and/or nuanced forms of social integration.

Chimpanzees often verbally communicate to one another with "pant-hoots," which differ in "accent" from community to community (see Moffett, 2019, pgs. 148–152 for a discussion). This verbal communication very clearly serves purposes of within-community group coordination. More fine-grained, articulated, speech in early *homo* likely served similar purposes. However, a greater articulation of vocal sounds implies that community boundaries and groups were, themselves, becoming more complex, porous, and negotiated.

As group identity becomes more tied to vocalizations, it also becomes more abstract and flexible.

This process of construing unfamiliar or dissimilar individuals as important in-group members is often termed the creation of "fictive kin." What seems to make the creation of fictive kin in human beings unique (by degree) is that, unlike most animals, the human practices of hunting, parenting, trade, and defense all rely on expansive, extensive, coalitions between people who are often not family members and, in many cases, not very familiar at all with one another (Boyer et al., 2015).

I do not mean to imply that nonhuman animals fail to interact with anyone other than family members. On the contrary, for example, research shows that in chimpanzee societies friends are chosen on the basis of similarity in personality or behavior, not on the basis of genetic considerations alone, and that they trust their friends more than nonfriends (Massen and Koski, 2014; Engelmann and Herrmann, 2016).

Still, recall that chimpanzees, though social, are not societal. This is an important point that both Machalek (1992) and Moffett (2019) insist on. Chimpanzees and many other animals like dogs and cats are social, in that they can develop familiarities with others. That is, they can *familiarize* themselves with nonfamily-related others, and become more comfortable over time with those individuals (especially those who are also similar in personality). What makes an animal *societal*, though, and not only social, is their propensity to include unknown, unfamiliar others into their instrumental cooperative networks. Humans demonstrate their societal orientation every time they walk into a business or organization and interact pleasantly—*cooperatively*, even if only in an instrumental sense—with people they do not know, don't necessarily care to know, and may never see again.

Allow me to lead us into the next section with a final point about "fictive kin." It is of course true that humans have the ability to detect genetic/family relatedness, whether this includes physical resemblances, personality resemblances, or *in utero* acclimations to diet or vocal pitch/tonation (e.g., Heijkoop et al., 2009; Kaminski et al., 2012; Lee and Kisilevsky, 2014). Yet, we also know that "relatedness" can be construed abstractly, in a "fictive" way—as sharing a national identity, a political party, or a religious identity. Thus, anything that enhances an animal's capacity for abstraction, including language, the enlargement of subcortical tissue dedicated to emotion-processing and/or the enlargement of the cerebral cortex, will enhance their ability to construe relatedness. On account of humans' capacity for symbolic construals of relatedness, larger and larger groups of people can continuously fission and be fused under some salient symbol, so long as that symbol (or "totem") is tied to social emotions such as loyalty or appreciation (Durkheim [1912] 2008; Lawler et al., 2009). I don't need to know every particular fan of a certain basketball team, or every particular student of a college, for example, to identify with a "fan community" or "alumni community."

1.1.5 Abstract, Porous Hierarchies, and Negotiated Egalitarianism

Species of *homo* were so successful in their communicativeness, cooperative child-rearing, cooperative hunting, cooperative defense, and construction of fictive kin, in part, because of how hierarchies were managed. At least since the controversial work of Marshall Sahlins (1968; 1972), who termed hunter-gatherer society "the original affluent society," anthropologists have been interested in understanding how hierarchies might have been negotiated in the earliest human societies.

The conventional wisdom is that monkeys are typically very hierarchical, and that the primates most genetically related to human beings, chimpanzees, are quite hierarchical as well. Chimpanzee troops, the conventional wisdom says, are often dominated by a capricious alpha male leader.

But this picture of hierarchy among primates is incomplete. While monkey hierarchies may indeed be quite strict and ruthless, there are some signs that hierarchy in apes is more fluid and more socially regulated than in other primates or mammals. Some studies, for example, have found both chimpanzees and bonobos to have hierarchies more porous, more flexible, and less aggressively enforced than previously assumed (Paoli et al., 2006; Jaeggi et al., 2010; Boehm, 2012). Primatologists are now more careful to remind us that alpha male chimpanzees are at risk of being deposed—sometimes violently—by females and lower-ranking males if they become too aggressive or despotic (De Waal, 2019). So, do nonhuman apes maintain consistently strict, despotic, hierarchies or not? It seems that we must accept that research is mixed at this point, and that the true answer has a lot to do with whether one is studying captive apes or wild apes, as well as how resource-rich the environment is for the particular group of apes being studied.

Overall, however, a noncontroversial conclusion to be drawn from this research is that the last common ancestor to humans and other apes likely maintained relatively shallower and more egalitarian hierarchies compared to monkeys and other group-living animals (Boehm, 1999; Turner and Maryanski, 2015). This would seem to be at odds with the common sense observation that humans across history have created very despotic hierarchies. Yet, the actual anthropological evidence indicates that across human foraging societies, the prevailing form of social organization for at least 95% of human history, in-group social organization is mostly egalitarian. As Christopher Boehm (1999; 2012) argues, human beings, by virtue of their capacity for language, complex emotional experience, cooperative hunting, defense and long rearing/socialization period of youth, may be more capable of regulating their hierarchies than are other primates. And, in contemporary hunter-gatherer societies, individuals often simply leave bands or communities that are dominated by an egotistical or aggressive person—they "vote with their feet" (Kelly, 2013).

Of course, the reality is that humans have the capacity for both egalitarianism (demonstrated, depending on the study, by humans' closest living relatives: chimpanzees or bonobos), and they also have the capacity for despotism (also demonstrated, depending on the study, by chimpanzees and bonobos). However, as human communities scaled into the thousands, tens of thousands, and beyond, hierarchies would become more difficult to regulate interpersonally. In the small bands of hunter-gatherers where *homo* evolved, there would have been enough emotional face-to-face contact with familiar others to consistently regulate (or violently remove) those with inflated egos who were most desirous of power. Humans don't like bullies; neither do other apes. However, an enhanced capacity for language and emotional expression, along with a prolonged socialization period in childhood conducive to the internalization of fairness norms, likely increased ancestral humans' ability to regulate their hierarchies.

Let me make just a few more brief points.

First, the growth of the cerebral, and especially the prefrontal, cortex—facilitated by both cooperative hunting and the consumption of fat and protein in game animals—would have enhanced the capacity of ancestral (and modern) humans to think abstractly. And, as it turns out, the capacity to construe hierarchy in an abstract way may have facilitated the ability to regulate hierarchy. The greater the capacity to consider how hierarchies form and what their consequences might be for the group, the better an animal can decide when abuses of power within a hierarchy are likely to arise and harm group cohesion. In other words, insofar as ancestral (and modern) humans had a greater cognitive capacity to consider and reflect on hierarchical dynamics, we would expect on-the-ground hierarchies to be better regulated.

Second, an interesting possibility is that human alphas (male or female) are continuously monitored and made humble because the human capacity for abstract reasoning has enabled the contemplation of an *invisible* hierarchy, with sacred ancestors or natural spirits or gods occupying the top, most authoritative, positions and thus humbling everyone else in the forager group (even those with high status). A recent review of the anthropological literature concludes:

> When we look at hunters and gatherers, we see a dominance hierarchy as clear as that of chimpanzees. It is, however, a hierarchy in which the alphas are invisible supernatural beings, too powerful to be overthrown by conspiracy or alliance, and capable of causing great misfortune when disobeyed. The betas are invisible ancestors who do the bidding of the alphas and protect their living descendants from harm. *The reason human foragers seem … to have no dominance hierarchy is because no living human can be considered more than a gamma within this system.*
>
> (Flannery and Marcus, 2012, pg. 59; italics added)

As we will see shortly, the foraging societies documented by anthropologists often place great significance on relationships with ancestors. Human memory, emotionality, and language allow the construction of myths around sacred ancestors, many of whom are believed to have accomplished greatness in leadership while alive. It is possible, then, that these ancestors (along with even more powerful "spirits" or "gods") served to occupy the most elite positions in forager societies.

1.2 Socialization Processes

Lacking effective birth control or an acute understanding of the physiology of pregnancy, human hunter-gatherers typically have children every four years or so and rely extensively on infanticide and abortion to maintain population numbers below available resource thresholds. Once children are born, there are four key subsequent factors undergirding the socialization of children and young adolescents: (1) socially homogenous living arrangements, (2) multiple caregivers (alloparenting), (3) co-sleeping beyond infancy, and (4) few expectations for juveniles to contribute to the band or community economy (Boyette and Hewlett, 2018).

Regarding (1), the adults that children are exposed to in foraging societies tend to be similar to them in terms of a symbolic, superordinate, self-identity. For example, each adult in the band likely shares an ethnic identity or tribal identity and traces their biography to the same original set of ancestors. Presumably, this homogeneity adds legitimacy and context to the norms encouraging group loyalty, which children are expected to internalize (Lew-Levy et al., 2017).

For the most part, forager children are not "taught" how to behave, or what to believe, in the same way Westerners teach children in school today, with a list of facts or a list of skills that must be learned in specific blocks of time. Rather, children in forager societies typically learn informally from each member of the band; children play in mixed-age and mixed-gender groups and learn from a variety of adult "mentors." Their socialization is much more oriented toward integrating them into the habitus of daily life (Bourdieu [1980] 1990), or what Tuck-Po Lye (2004) has called an "embodiment" of culture, than it is oriented toward rote, decontextualized, instruction from a single "teacher." While certain complex skills related to tool manufacture (e.g., bows, spears, baskets) or certain rituals (e.g., sacred religious ceremonies) are sometimes taught to young bandmates in a more direct step-by-step manner as they get older, this constitutes a relatively small proportion of the total socialization experience of a young forager (Boyette and Hewlett, 2018).

Regarding (2), the distribution of socialization responsibilities across adults in the band and in the wider community provides a degree of flexibility to the norms taught to children. While certain norms are consistently found among foragers—norms for sharing, reciprocity, loyalty to the group, and so on—just *how* they are taught to young people varies depending on who is doing the instructing. If parents or grandparents fail to get the message across, it does not matter because other adults or older adolescents in the community might have more success. And, if an emphasis on any given norm shifts over time in response to environmental threat or tribal conflict, this change can be subtly and flexibly disseminated to youth across a variety of "teachers."

As for (3) above, forager parents sleep in close proximity with their children; they do not, like people in the modern West, sleep in distant, separate, rooms. This extended period of close parent–child contact, a perfect context for shared conversations and discussions, should be seen as contributing to the deep internalization of the wider community norms that children and adolescents learn loosely throughout the day from numerous others.

And, finally, (4), the fourth general factor underlying the socialization of children and young adolescents in forager communities, is a relative freedom from substantive economic contribution (Boyette and Hewlett, 2018). By "freedom," I do not mean that young foragers are discouraged from hunting or gathering, but only that their contributions are not assumed to be sufficient for contributing to band survival. Children and young adolescents tend to lack the patience, focus, and endurance necessary to successfully hunt large game or efficiently extract edible plants (e.g., digging up tubers); successful fishing is also beyond the grasp of most very young people, as it too requires significant skill and patience (Kelly, 2013). Forager children will often attempt to hunt rabbits or salmon for food, or gather firewood, but their contributions to the group is typically minimal.

Instead of feeling immediate pressures to produce and contribute, hunter-gatherer children are, more often, allowed an extensive period of exploration and learning. As they get older, stronger, and capable of greater patience and foresight, they will gradually be expected to contribute more, and will receive greater status/prestige as they do so. The obvious caveat here is that under conditions of famine, children from a young age may be encouraged to hunt or forage in a way that gleans substantive contributions. This is the outlying case, however; the mass extinctions of large fauna evidenced in the archeological record suggests that early nomadic foragers were very adept hunters and scavengers (Ben-Dor, 2018).

So long as the perception of threat is not too high, children learn to forage for food/materials and trade with others in the context of play. They interact with others in their band, residential grouping, and wider community. Children, like adults, roam freely throughout the day going from band to band within a given community (Boyette and Hewlett, 2018). Their play, and socialization generally, is thus supervised, but only in a loose sense. Play among forager children occurs in mixed-sex, mixed-age play groups, and is often collaborative. When disputes do arise, children often reach compromises amongst themselves, and this aids in their development of the autonomy and conflict-resolution skills necessary to eventually contribute to the maintenance of the wider forager community. An important part of this socialization process is sociality itself, that is, learning to be around others, cooperate with others, resolve conflict with others, and take instruction from others (Naveh, 2016). Our independent, perhaps even solitary, dispositional nature relative to other primates—which Maryanski (1986; 1994; 1995) locates in our last common ancestor with chimpanzees—is thus molded and bent toward group goals and cooperativeness.

Principally, children in foraging societies are socialized to appreciate the importance of sharing and of being humble, for example, when they contribute to a successful fishing expedition. Foragers begin learning how to trade and give gifts in early childhood, and the *act of giving or sharing* is typically valued more than the items shared or gifted (Kelly, 2013). Children learn to exchange with people of all ages, and all levels of group status, from their family/residential grouping to the larger ethnic/tribal collective. Sharing does not necessarily "come naturally" to children, but the strong inculcation of norms regarding sharing and reciprocity, linked to powerful group emotions associated with loyalty and selflessness, help motivate the sharing that is so necessary to small-group living. When resources are strained, when individuals get injured or incapacitated, or when prestigious individuals begin to grow large egos, the internalization of norms (at the individual and group level) supportive of demand-sharing helps maintain group cohesiveness.

Building a reputation as a cooperator who is willing to share with others also has downstream effects for child socialization in the next generation. Foragers with high social status (often, but not always, linked to hunting prowess) receive greater deference from others, more trade opportunities, and, perhaps most importantly, greater help in raising their children (Gurven and Hill, 2009). The intensity of alloparenting thus varies with the social status of the biological parents. And, plausibly, the more distributed the care for one's child, the more flexible and nuanced the socialization process. Regardless, the greater the alloparenting directed toward one's child, the greater the likelihood of child survival, increasing reproductive fitness. There is, then, a close connection between social status, generosity, and reproductive fitness in forager groups (Von Rueden and Jaeggi, 2016; see also Kelly, 2013, pg. 151 for a model of these complex relationships).

Now, I'd like to make a final point that will lead us into the next section: the freedom given to children in forager groups seems contingent on the prevalence of danger and conflict in the surrounding environment (Kelly, 2013). In areas where snakes, wolves, hyenas, or hostile people are prevalent, children will be kept close to the group or home base. Similarly, if the environment is hard to navigate or easy to get lost in, children will be kept close to the group. Even still, infant and juvenile mortality is very high in foraging societies; only about half of the babies born to contemporary foragers survive to adulthood, and this is mostly due to a high death rate before age five. Infectious diseases and parasites kill a large number of forager children—for example, in one tribe, the Dobe Ju/'hoansi, tuberculosis and malaria infections were responsible for 85% of childhood deaths (Kelly, 2013). In other foraging societies, measles, intestinal worms, diarrhea, and seizures account for a large proportion of childhood deaths.

So, while childhood in forager society was a "free-roaming" childhood for the most part, this was not without limits, and those children who grew up in dangerous ecologies would have their freedoms restricted. Since no forager ecology was totally devoid of threats, we must keep this in mind when discussing the social environment within which humans evolved.

1.3 Dangers and Threats

In a world devoid of modern medicine, science, or government, early humans (and their ancestors) would have lived precarious, often short, lives. Consider a Stone Age man, called "Ötzi," who died around 5,000 years ago only to be discovered mummified in the Italian Alps in 1991 (Kelly, 2016). Ötzi had a rough go of things, and there is no reason to believe that his life was unique in its harshness. He was five feet tall, weighed about 100 pounds, and was 45 years old when he died. He also had 50 tattoos, no doubt representative (as tattoos are today) of his attempts to form a self-identity and to internalize group memberships. His teeth were broken and flat from a diet of stone-ground wheat, he had multiple broken ribs, and he seems to have suffered from Lyme disease, arsenic poisoning, and other chronic conditions. He had been killed in the Alps with an arrow in his back followed by blunt force trauma to the skull.

Ötzi was roaming the countryside of northern Italy around 5,000 years ago, a mere blink of time in archeological terms. Still, Ötzi was a fully modern human, anatomically and neurologically. Consider another example, this time from a different but very closely related species of hominin, *Australopithecus afarensis.* This particular individual, Lucy, was found dead in a creek bed in Ethiopia in 1974. Lucy roamed the Earth around 3–4 million years ago, was about 3.5 feet tall, weighed around 60 pounds, and might have been 16 years old when she died. CT scans of her bones reveal severe life-threatening fractures of her ankles, knees, shoulder, hip, and neck (Kappelman et al., 2016). Archeologists speculate that Lucy fell out of a tree, possibly after attempting to flee a pack of hyenas or a saber-toothed cat. It is impossible to know for sure how Lucy died, but we can say with radiocarbon certainty that she died young and violently.

What dangers or threats seemed to be most prevalent for human beings and their hominin ancestors? Studies of extant hunter-gatherers reveal four general classes of threat (see Diamond, 2012): (1) inter-tribal/ethnic conflict (e.g., death by poison arrow), (2) dangerous plants and animals (e.g., poisonous snakes, spiders, or scorpions; predatory animals such as crocodiles; falling trees), (3) infections (e.g., infected insect bites or thorn scratches), and (4) accidental deaths and deaths from exposure (e.g., getting lost and starving, drowning, hunting accidents, serious burns from fire).

On top of these, Boehm (2012) points out that conflicts *within* a tribal or ethnic group can also lead to death, as when an individual steals food from others, sleeps with others' spouses or consistently violates a taboo and gets either speared to death or abandoned by their group. Some of the dangers affecting foragers are less familiar to us comfortable, ungrateful, urbanites: consider that, for example, attacks from jaguars and poisonous snakes account for almost a quarter (~22%) of all deaths among the Ache, an Indigenous forager society in Paraguay (Diamond, 2012).

Still, conflict within and between forager groups was as severe a threat as any in nature. While there are some forager societies that seem to experience little or no intra- or inter-group violence (e.g., the Paliyan of India; see Kelly, 2013, pg. 202), unfortunately most know warfare intimately (Pinker, 2011). Often, warfare seems to result from forager groups settling semi-permanently on a resource-rich strip of land (typically, it seems, near a body of water) and attempting to control or defend this turf from all comers. Also, because populations can grow larger the more reliable a resource patch is, sedentary forager groups often segment into subunits after reaching a certain size (~30–50 people). These community subunits can, themselves, fight over resources, thus increasing the homicide rate within an ethnic group (Kelly, 2013).

Warfare, when not an outright conflict, typically followed a tit-for-tat revenge-seeking logic: if you kill a member of my group, I will seek revenge by killing a member (any member) of your group. The transitivity of identity in human forager groups, as Moffett (2019) points out, means that any person sharing the offending tribe's identity is intuitively regarded as a fair target for revenge violence. There is, in other words, a common intuition about "group liability" (Kelly, 2013): if group A raids group B, and I am a member of group B, I will tend to assume that all members of group A have some group A-ness to them that I can fruitfully retaliate against. We are, it seems, intuitive essentialists; I will have more to say about this below. Foragers do not only start wars over resource shortages, there is also the ever-present risk of causing conflict over personal insults or accusations of witchcraft and black magic (Boehm, 2012).

The magnitude of violence in forager societies should not be underestimated. Forager societies are "stateless" societies, and, as such, they lack a bureaucratic system with a monopoly on violence; they lack the police, courts, and jails/prisons that in industrial societies serve as reasonably successful impartial arbiters of conflict between individuals (Weber, 1946; Pinker, 2011). Police, courts, and jails/prisons are the Hobbesian "Leviathan," influential throughout an entire society and available around the clock to enforce an (in principle) impartial legal system applicable to all. Of course, I am aware that policing in modern societies is concentrated in poor communities, and that minorities are disproportionately imprisoned. Plenty of sociologists writing different books will go on and on about this for you, if you'd like. But a focus only on the policy problems of the criminal justice system in modern societies misses the fact that having a phone linked to emergency dispatchers 24 hours a day can reduce the impact of violence and vengeance-seeking between communities. Criminal justice in modern societies is far from perfect, but insofar as it works, it works because individuals can (for the most part) rely on the state to intervene on their behalf to protect them from violence, retaliation, and vengeance.

Between 13,000 and 14,000 years ago, 58 people (including children) at the Jebel Sahaba "cemetery site," sitting along on the eastern bank of the Nile River in northern Sudan, were stuck with between 15 and 30 arrows and spears, and were left for dead in shallow graves (Wendorf, 1968; Judd, 2006). This was obviously a mass slaughter perpetrated by one forager tribe/ethnicity against another. There are numerous examples of such mass slaughter, which likely often took the form of ambushes—those in the shallow grave described above were found with their "hands to the face and body flexed" (Judd, 2006, pg. 53). These ambushes would have likely taken place in retaliation for perceived past indiscretions, and would have gone on for years between groups back and forth across generations, one mass slaughter after another.

Trade is a way that foragers from different tribes fuse together socially, facilitating the ever-present possibility of creativity and innovation in survival strategies. The more geographically distant the trade relationship, the more likely were interactions to involve discussion of places or people who might have seemed exotic or unconventional in their various goods and practices. I take this cross-pollination of ideas and experiences between forager tribes/ethnicities as equally a fact of life, alongside the fact of blood feuds, raids, and death; the former required only curiosity and optimism, the latter required an antidote: humility. Let me end this section with an anecdote about how the !Kung Bushmen foragers deal with successful hunters with growing egos (as recorded by anthropologist Richard Lee):

> "Why did you tell me the black ox was worthless, when you could see that it was loaded with fat and meat?"
>
> "It is our way," he said smiling. "We always like to fool people about that. Say there is a Bushman who has been hunting. He must not come home and announce like a braggard, 'I have killed a big one in the bush!' He must first sit down in silence until I or someone else comes up to his fire and asks, 'What did you see today?' He replies quietly, 'Ah, I'm no good for hunting. I saw nothing at all {pause} just a little tiny one.' Then I smile to myself," /gaugo continued, "because I know he has killed something big."
>
> (Lee, 1969, pg. 3)

1.4 Hierarchy and Leadership

Hierarchies are the metaphorical spinal cord of social collectives.

So many students today hear the word "hierarchy" and think "inequality." How sad; as though their only conception of hierarchy is of illegitimate or coercive hierarchies. In the real world (not the Marxist fever dreams of their professors), hierarchies are just the social means by which large groups are coordinated. They can be inequitable and cruel, or wonderfully mobilizing, purposive, and focusing.

Hierarchies organize the division of labor between individuals or subgroups, as well as the flow of resources, and, as such, hierarchies can reduce conflict and increase a collective's capacity for action. However, it is equally true that the perceived legitimacy and stability of a hierarchy is predicated on its continued capacity to mitigate conflict and adequately distribute valued group resources. Thus, while hierarchies are ultimately a mechanism that canalizes decision-making, behavior, and resource flow, the legitimacy and stability of hierarchies are also expressly contingent on their ability to accomplish these things. We shouldn't take for granted, therefore, that hierarchies are always helpful or always conducive to the health and well-being of those involved (Sapolsky, 2005).

Yet, without hierarchies, groups dissolve into their individual components. If the political leadership of a nation collapses, important political decisions will be made at the state or county level, and if leadership there collapses or is perceived to be illegitimate, decisions will be made by individuals in family groups, occupational groups, or community groups. If the leadership there collapses, individuals make decisions by themselves, or with just a few confidants. This would be a bleak situation, indeed. Unfortunately, this is a situation many refugees and diasporic people face and have faced.

When I use the term "hierarchy," I mean the *relatively* centralized decision-making apparatus organizing a group's goals and behavior. Hierarchies of people within groups can be, for various reasons, tight and rigid or loose and open (see Figure 1.2).

In particular, zoological and social-psychological research seems to suggest that hierarchies become more tight and rigid under conditions of threat or danger, when resources can be monopolized and/or during periods of increased competition within and between groups (Aktas et al., 2016; De Silva et al., 2017; Gelfand, 2019). Certain ecological conditions are also important as regards the tightness/strictness of a hierarchy: in geographic locales where dispersal is easier, or in social environments where other groups can easily be joined, hierarchies will find it more difficult to exert control over group members. Hierarchies also appear to loosen as resources become easier (vs. harder) to extract or as populations grow smaller or become more stable in their growth (vs. larger and more unstable in their growth). Moreover, hierarchies can be rooted in group-specific considerations (for example, the Hindu caste system, where people are understood only as essential members of groups), or they can be rooted

Hierarchy Closedness and Rigidity ⟷	Hierarchy Openness and Flexibility
• Growing Perception of Threat/ Danger • Valued Resources Can be Easily Monopolized • Growing Perception of Competition Within or Between Groups • Few, or Declining, Options for Alternative Group Membership • Roaming Range is Smaller/Space is More Confined • Growing Group Size • People Evaluated More as Members of Groups than as Individuals	• Declining Perception of Threat/ Danger • Valued Resources are Distributed around the Natural or Social Environment • Declining Perception of Competition Within or Between Groups • More, or Increasing, Options for Alternative Group Membership • Roaming Range is Larger/Space is Less Confined • Declining, or Stabilizing, Group Size • People Evaluated More as Unique Individuals

Figure 1.2 Influences on Hierarchy Closedness and Openness

in individual-specific considerations (for example, selecting any person to lead a group that best accomplishes a specific task).

Nomadic foragers, for the most part, tend to have loose, porous hierarchies composed of individuals with varying levels of status and prestige. Skilled hunters, medicine men/women, and elders tend to have particularly high levels of status, but all decisions made within a band or residential group are basically democratic, with all adults weighing in regardless of status or prestige (Kelly, 2013). Leadership, then, tends to take the form of group decision-making, and anyone with a big ego or exhibiting hints of despotism and authoritarianism is mocked mercilessly until they are humbled. Forager "alphas," insofar as they exist, enjoy their group influence only insofar as others deem them helpful and cooperative (Boehm, 1999; see also De Waal, 2019). Leadership in forager societies is "situational, contextual, easily disposable and highly functional" (Bastardoz and Van Vugt, 2019).

This pragmatism in leadership and hierarchy might be summed up like this: *if they're useful and skilled, as well as kind and humble, then this person's thoughts or behaviors should be granted greater importance*. Rather than a person serving as a designated "leader," forager life was a context where anyone fitting the profile of being trustworthy and helpful could have influence. Being pragmatic is your only option if you want to survive on an open savannah with dependent children and the elderly, alongside predators stronger and faster than any one of you. As Nicolas Bastardoz and Mark Van Vugt (2019, pg. 86) put it: "Humans faced adaptive pressures to pool risks by coordinating their actions on critical tasks including defense and hunting, and to cooperate via food sharing." To this, one should add cooperative parenting; this may have been the central concern driving coordination for defense, hunting, and food-sharing (see Quinlan and Quinlan, 2008; Hrdy, 2011; Bogin et al., 2014).

If foragers such as the !Kung or Eskimos are any indication, humor has long been an incredibly important component of hierarchy regulation and contestation (Flannery and Marcus, 2012). If a skilled (or, for that matter, unskilled) hunter, healer, or weaver begins to become verbose, overbearing, and coercive, they are ruthlessly mocked and made fun of (Boehm, 1999). This is a form of indirect aggression, in the more socially acceptable form of humor, which keeps everyone on the same page about what a schmuck so-and-so is being, and gives the schmuck himself (or herself) something to think about if they want to be in the group's good graces. This humor, though, is not typically mean-spirited or cruel. Rather, it is more like an occasional teasing to keep a person's ego from getting too big, and it prompts the narcissist to find honor and humility in conceded weaknesses and imperfections. When times are good, foragers maintain a light-hearted play-like environment that helps boost creativity and communication while at the same time reducing tensions and regulating hierarchy in ways that avoid conflict in close quarters (Gray, 2014).

If a forager group abandons a nomadic lifestyle to settle around a specific resource patch, they will tend to begin hoarding/accumulating more food and materials, which then need to be defended from outsiders. Leadership becomes more permanent under these conditions and has tended to lead to the formation of what anthropologists have called "Big Man" societies composed of a chief and his council (Turner and Maryanski, 2015). These chiefs tend to instantiate their rule by linking their biographies directly to salient gods, spirits, or ancestors, and they tend to try to pass on their ruling privileges to their offspring (Flannery and Marcus, 2012).

In an important sense, this is the first emergence of true systematic inequality, because chiefs tend to enjoy a heavily disproportionate influence over tribal decision-making, and tend to enjoy a disproportionate amount of food and material delicacies. To support their right to have such influence, they make specific claims about their unique ancestry, or unique connection to the gods, spirits, and ancestors. In doing so, the implication is that others in the tribe lack such illustrious connections, rendering them lower status by birth (Flannery and Marcus, 2012). The emergence of inequality, then, is a function of population size, density, resource-hoarding, and the emergence of chiefs or permanent leaders with allegedly unique and special connections to important ancestors or supernatural beings.

These "Big Men" or village chiefs often hold potlucks and feasts for their own tribe and other tribes, especially when such gatherings might reduce tensions within or between groups. If tensions are already too high, potlucks and feasts might only make things worse by aggregating people in a single location. But, otherwise, these feasts are joyous occasions filled with food and trade. Tribal chiefs will also attempt to compete with chiefs from other tribes to see who can be more generous in their offering of resources during these gatherings. This generosity can be seen as a hold-over of nomadic forager norms for leader humility, but, equally, it is a valuable, if costly, signal of the wealth and security of that chief and his tribe (Kelly, 2013).

Research suggests that individuals who are older, who best model group norms, and who are centrally positioned in the larger social network are most likely to become so-called "Big Men" or chiefs (Bastardoz and Van Vugt, 2019). These individuals are ambitious, skilled, and charismatic. When times are tough and threatening, chiefs might express a greater degree of dominance and hostility toward outsiders. These signals of formidability suggest that the leader might be successful in fighting off the source of threat. On the other hand, when times are good, chiefs may express more warmth, trustworthiness, and concern. Regardless, those who live under such an individual still tend to insist on norms encouraging humility—if and when the Big Man begins to act selfishly or coercively, people often expect the freedom to complain, ridicule, disobey, and, generally, vote with their feet.

In closing this brief discussion of the early forms of human hierarchy, I should mention some generic features of hierarchies that are likely operative in any society:

1. Cooperation and coordination are generally perceived to be beneficial under circumstances perceived to be threatening/dangerous or uncertain.
2. Leaders/leadership of hierarchies are chosen (formally or informally) according to their perceived personality traits (e.g., charisma), along with their human (talents, skills, credentials) and social (network contacts) capital.
3. Under conditions perceived to be relatively more threatening/dangerous, increasingly large constituencies of individuals will demand tough, aggressive, independent leadership.
4. Under conditions perceived to be relatively less threatening/dangerous, increasingly large constituencies of individuals will demand compassionate, passive/restrained, cooperative/collaborative leadership.
5. The cohesiveness and stability of a hierarchy is contingent on the magnitude of perceived threat, the perceived fairness of resource/task distribution, and the relevance of the leadership's human (talents, skills, credentials) and/or social (network contacts) capital.
6. The easier it is to leave one group hierarchy for another group hierarchy, the more often people will switch (perhaps not permanently), especially when hierarchy cohesiveness and stability is low.

7 Both the evolution of hominin psychology as well as the cultural development of group norms for humility and fairness contain mechanisms for regulating levels of inequality in hierarchies.

These are generic features of hierarchies; they are principles that emerge from the coordination difficulties facing all hierarchies. Followers need to be somewhat happy, or perceive no viable options for leaving, if they are to remain (voluntarily) in a hierarchy. Like their chimpanzee cousins, humans are emotional and independent, and prefer *the option* to leave groups that do not suit them (though, depending on the personality of the human in question, they may or may not frequently act on that option).

The above list is drawn from the work cited in this section (especially Bastardoz and Van Vugt, 2019). I wish also to integrate some of the insights of Max Weber (1964). With regard to Weber, even the most disorganized, loose, hierarchy might maintain itself if the leader is sufficiently emotionally persuasive or charismatic. And, though Weber focused way too much of his attention on bureaucracy, a very historically recent form of hierarchy, he nevertheless had several important insights about the general structure of group hierarchies. I'll mention them below, expanding our list:

8 Hierarchies involve impersonal obligations, that is, obligations to others that result from the position one holds in a hierarchy, not necessarily their personal preferences. Hierarchy is a *social* phenomenon, and its effectiveness in mobilizing people is contingent on the level of agreement between individuals regarding competencies and obligations.
9 Hierarchies involve communication about clearly defined roles, so that people can understand and behave in accordance with group expectations.
10 Roles in hierarchies are optimally (but not always) voluntary, such that one can be expected to (and often will actually) care about their roles enough to perform them.
11 Roles in hierarchies are optimally (but not always) filled according to competencies, which can be situational.
12 Resources often flow through hierarchies in ways that reward those in high-ranking positions, even though the individuals occupying these positions may or may not be objectively relevant, competent, or useful (people might occupy high-ranking positions in hierarchies for many reasons other than competence, such as social network connections or greater family income enabling more opportunities for advancement).
13 People closely identify with, and are often assumed by others to be defined by, their roles in various hierarchies, especially occupational.

Weber discussed more than just these, but these are important to set out. Also, it bears mentioning that George Ritzer (1964), perhaps more than anyone else, fleshed out Weber's work on hierarchy to show how the embeddedness of group hierarchies can make them increasingly rigid and overly deferential. Ritzer's paradigmatic (and overly modern) example of the "irrationality of rationality" is McDonald's, the hamburger chain: McDonald's is composed of local, regional, national, and international management-level supply chains composed of numerous sub-hierarchies. Rules of operation are written down and enforced. Efficiency, calculability, predictability, and centralized control are the dominant goals. Yet, despite all of this, McDonald's is often regarded as low-quality, tasteless, and not the most desirable place to work. Extensive hierarchy and regulation, in other words, is never synonymous with quality or outcome; rather hierarchy and regulation are *necessary but not sufficient* mechanisms for ensuring particular desired outcomes or improved quality.

Though it is totally unfair to focus on McDonald's and, no less, to argue that one of the most sophisticated and successful businesses in the history of the world is irrational or incompetent, Ritzer has nevertheless done so. His fundamental point is an important one, though: the more rigid, rule-bound, and deferential hierarchies become, the harder it will be for new or creative (and potentially very good) ideas to be shared and adopted because the circulation of people into and out of the group will be too restricted and because people will fear the social consequences of thinking differently.

1.5 Societies as Organisms and as Capable of "Organismality"

Human societies with their distinctive level of alloliving represent an unusual degree of group entitativity in the mammalian kingdom.

Now, I must begin to push this understanding further; I want to suggest that human societies are capable of becoming so intricately and fractally entitative that we must use a different, stronger term: human societies are capable of becoming, to greater or lesser degrees, *organismic*.

So-called "major evolutionary transitions" occur when biological organisms exhibit a new level of complexity that results from shifts in the organization and coordination of constituent, lower-level units (Szathmáry and Maynard Smith, 1995; Maynard Smith and Szathmáry, [1995] 2010; Calcott and Sterelny, 2011). Consider the difference in biological organization between single-celled organisms such as salmonella bacteria or slime molds and multicelled organisms such as cats, dogs, and humans. In each case, these organisms respond to environmental conditions, grow, and reproduce—each is alive. However, the level of organizational complexity differs: single-celled organisms consist of only one cell type, whereas multicelled organisms consist of different cells, functionally specialized for various purposes, working in concert with one another to facilitate the survival of the collective, emergent, animal.

Single-celled organisms (emerging around 3–4 billion years ago) predate multicelled organisms (emerging around 500–800 million years ago), suggesting that, at some point in the history of evolution on Earth, several individual cells aggregated as a colony and eventually specialized in their functions, creating a new, emergent, entity (Wolpert and Szathmáry, 2002; Pennisi, 2018). While no one knows for certain which organisms constituted the first multicelled organisms, it is nevertheless clear that lower-level groupings of different cells could have produced survival benefits beyond what each cell would experience on its own, leading to the eventual evolution of single biological entities—animals—composed of many different cells interacting with and complementing the capacities of one another.

This major evolutionary transition from single-celled to multicelled organisms involved, in short, a shift from individual entities composed of the same, cloned, cell to individual entities composed of numerous different, but molecularly "cooperating" (in the sense of some degree of information or resource transfer) cells. This cooperation is thought to have emerged as a result of cells' incremental specialization in specific survival-relevant functions. Once cells begin to specialize, they can no longer survive on their own, and are thus bound to their relationship to other cells specializing in complementary survival-relevant functions (Michod, 2007). These specialized cells (and there are, for example, around 37 trillion cells organized into at least 200 specialty functions in the human body) collaborate chemically to produce an emergent organism, an animal, which serves as a "survival vehicle" for all of its constituent cellular and underlying genetic components (Pennisi, 2018).

Once lower-level units are sufficiently organized, natural selection can operate on the higher, more complex, organizational level; that is, major evolutionary transitions introduce new "levels" of selection (Hanschen et al., 2015). The "fitness" of these new evolutionary units is, in turn, thought to be determined by a combination of reproductive frequency (fecundity) and/or survival (viability) (see Roff, 2002; Hanschen et al., 2017). As John Maynard Smith and Eors Szathmáry (1999, pg. 19) put it: "Entities that were capable of independent replication before the [evolutionary] transition could afterwards replicate only as part of a larger whole." In a human being, for example, selection occurs not only on particular cells (and their constituent genes), but also on the gene networks that constitute human chromosomes *and* on the gene networks undergirding the prokaryotic cell-networks (e.g., bacteria) which cooperate with human eukaryotic cells to maintain our (or any animal's) health.

Natural selection is constantly occurring across levels of life—biological individuals are, in fact, a "functional consortia of many species living, developing and evolving together" (Gilbert et al., 2017, pg. 305; see also Salvucci, 2016). This collaborative circumstance across emergent levels of life is wonderfully worded in the relevant literature; this is how microbiologists phrase it:

> The human oral cavity contains a number of different habitats, including the teeth, gingival sulcus, tongue, cheeks, hard and soft palates, and tonsils, which are colonized by bacteria. The oral microbiome is comprised of over 600 prevalent taxa at the species level, with distinct subsets predominating at different habitats ... The skin is [also] an ecosystem composed of 1.8 meters of diverse habitats with an abundance of folds, invaginations and specialized niches that support a wide range of microorganisms ... many of these microorganisms are harmless and in some cases provide vital functions that the human genome has not evolved.
>
> (Dewhirst et al., 2010, pg. 5002; Grice and Segre, 2011, pg. 244)

There's also a great deal of cooperative relationships between "bacterial" prokaryotic cells and "animal" eukaryotic cells happening within various organs, especially the gut, which in humans is home to *at least* 1,000 types of bacteria. These, and other related bacteria, have shared a co-evolutionary history with hominins for at least 200 million years (Lloyd, 2017). In fact, most of the genes that cooperate and, as a result of this cooperation contribute to the health of the animal they compose, are bacterial genes (Turnbaugh et al., 2007). When a human infant is born, a community of eukaryotic and prokaryotic organisms, communicating constantly with the world around them, has been born as well (Gilbert, 2014). Some of the genes for the bacteria living in the various niches of the mother's body are transferred to her offspring as it passes through the birth canal in true Lamarckian fashion (Lloyd, 2017).

Humans and other animals are *both* integrated, individually behaving entities *as well as* communities of prokaryotic and eukaryotic cells of "different sizes interacting at different developmental, ecological and evolutionary scales simultaneously" (Chiu and Gilbert, 2015, pg. 191). This cooperation between cell networks occurs because it increases the adaptive flexibility of the emergent organism—component entities can vary more, and change more quickly, than can the entities they co-constitute. The more different organisms, with different strengths and weaknesses, collaborate with one another, the better equipped they will be to respond to unpredictable environmental shifts and other dangers. Inter- and intracellular cooperation constitutes an "insurance policy" regarding the health and welfare of the emergent entity these cooperative relationships constitute (Yachi and Loreau, 1999; Lloyd, 2017).

Of course, cooperation is not a given—there is a greater potential for cellular conflict in a multicelled organism, because the genes responsible for different cells may be incompatible in the functional results of their expression (Wolpert and Szathmáry, 2002). Within the human genome, for example, even specific genes compete with one another by replicating at higher rates *within* the genome (Trivers, 2017). Mechanisms for suppressing conflict between genes that might code for proteins to build different cells are, therefore, an important requirement for the formation of multicellular organisms. Indeed, the suppression of conflict is important in any system composed of independent, constituent, subunits and predicated on cooperation between these subunits. For example, in a human society, the construction and maintenance of infrastructure necessary for group survival (roads, gaslines, waterlines, electrical grids) depends in part on taxation, and while some individuals cheat on their taxes, most pay them, and legal penalties exist for those who cheat.

Major evolutionary transitions have been happening throughout the history of Earth (Grosberg and Strathmann, 2007). While scholars differ with regard to the specific number of evolutionary transitions that are believed to have occurred, most agree that such transitions occurred:

1 when different independently replicating molecules cooperatively coordinated chemically and produced protocells;
2 when protocells cooperatively coordinated chemically and produced prokaryotic cells;
3 when prokaryotic cells cooperatively coordinated chemically and produced eukaryotic cells;
4 when eukaryotic cells (and prokaryotes) cooperatively coordinated and produced multicellular organisms;
5 when asexual, self-replicating multicellular organisms cooperatively coordinated chemically and behaviorally with other organisms to reproduce sexually; and
6 when insects and at least one mammal (naked mole rat) cooperatively coordinated genetically to concentrate reproduction in certain castes within large colonies.

Maynard Smith and Szathmáry (1999; see also Szathmáry, 2015) as well as others (e.g., Wilson, 2012) argue, albeit controversially (see Dawkins, 2012), that human societies—with their use of language, printing technology, and, more recently, the internet as sources of transmittable information—involve the coordination of lower-level units ("individuals") into integrated group wholes. As with the problem of genetic and cellular conflict within multicelled organisms mentioned above, human societies also require mechanisms of suppressing conflict between units, and these include everything from shared religious mythologies, egalitarian social norms, humor, and, in more recent human societies, police and courts.

Just as the genetic code might be understood as a molecular language, humans have the physiological and behavioral capacity for verbal language, and these are "two natural systems providing unlimited heredity" (Maynard Smith and Szathmáry, 1999, pg. 18). Genes can recombine to create many different biological structures just as language can be used to form various social structures including groups, subgroups, and societies. However, even the evolutionary transition from less linguistic/symbolic hominins to fully linguistic/symbolic humans presupposes still other, prior evolutionary transitions, such as the transition from animals without any nervous system (e.g., sea sponges) to animals with "nerve nets" (e.g., jellyfish) to animals with full central and peripheral nervous systems (e.g., rats, cats, chimpanzees, and people).

In sum, major evolutionary transitions involve cooperation between different units to such a degree that relations between these units become coordinated "subunits" of a larger cohesive structure (Clarke, 2014). Put another way, these transitions involve "the formation of a cooperative group and the transformation of the cooperative group into a more cohesive and integrated entity that can be considered a new level of individual (organism)" (West et al., 2015, pg. 10112). Cooperation between units (see West et al., 2015) involves:

1. some degree of communication/transfer of information;
2. division of labor/function;
3. mutual dependence; and
4. mechanisms to minimize conflict.

Of course, conditions of the environment (e.g., shifts in the magnitude and/or source of threats/dangers) will determine when cooperation is perceived (cognitively in humans or more chemically/molecularly in protocells, cells, or eusocial insects) to be mutually beneficial. An important implication here, which I will return to below, is that we should think about organisms not so much as entities but as continuums or waves, that is, as entities defined by their relative (see Figure 1.3):

communicativeness (*relative to* noncommunicativeness);
labor differentiation/asymmetry (*relative to* labor symmetry);
functional interdependence (*relative to* independence); and
capacity to minimize zero-sum and deadly interactions (*relative to* facilitating conflict between subunits).

Major transitions in evolution constitute shifts in organismality, which we should understand as operating along continuums (Queller and

Less Organismic		**More Organismic**
Individual Unit Isolation (units have no, or reduced, capacity to communicate across the system)	↔	Individual Unit Connectivity (units have the capacity to communicate across the system)
Functional Symmetry (units perform identical, parallel, tasks)	↔	Functional Asymmetry (units perform different, but compatible, tasks)
Functional Independence (units exist independently of other units in the system)	↔	Functional Interdependence (units depend on the activities of other units for survival within the same system)
Conflict Over Resources is Unregulated (interactions between units are more zero-sum)	↔	Mechanisms Exist for Minimizing Conflict (interactions between units are more positive-sum)

Figure 1.3 Social Continua Influencing The Extent to Which Entitative Human Groups Become "Organismic"

Strassmann, 2009; Díaz-Muñoz et al., 2016). When lower-level units are sufficiently integrated, they create higher-order levels of complexity, enabling natural selection to operate on multiple levels. Evolutionary transitions, then, are not (only) singular events that happen or do not happen, instead, *levels of life are constantly in flux, transitioning back and forth across degrees of communicativeness, labor differentiation, functional interdependence, and positive sum exchange.*

The important question facing us is, then, to what extent is the potential for integration/cooperation in human groups facilitative of something beyond minimal entitativity, but rathr something more *organismic?*

Before continuing on, let me add just a bit more color to this concept of organismicness or organismality. A good example is the Portuguese man o' war, which appears to be a single animal, in particular, a jellyfish, that floats around in tropical and subtropical seas pushed about by wind and ocean currents.[3] However, this animal, while operating as a unified entity, is actually a group of genetically identical, but individually specialized, animals who coordinate with one another to hunt and reproduce as a colony, which is called a "siphonophore." Some of the animals that, collectively, comprise the man o' war specialize in floating, others in capturing prey, and still others in feeding or reproducing. From afar, this entity appears to be a single animal, yet, it is in fact a physiologically and chemically integrated group of animals.

Or, consider the possibility that bee and ant colonies might vary in their organismality (McMullan and Brown, 2009; Stroeymeyt et al., 2010); some beehives are more integrated and reveal a greater degree of cooperation between individuals, making those hives relatively more organismic. In other words, the survival of individual bees might be so predicated on the infrastructure of the hive that we might be more accurate in saying that the hive itself is becoming an organism. While we might look at a Portuguese man o' war and see one animal, it is actually a colony of many animals; while we might look at a beehive and see many animals, it might also be understood as a (more or less) single organism. Our eyes betray us, because, depending on the level of analysis we take, we might see a single entity or the many constituent entities that comprise it.

1.5.1 Sociology and the Study of Organismality

When considering human societies, my suggestion is that we think of them not as "organisms," but as more (vs. less) organismic. The "organismic analogy" was quite popular in classical sociological theory, with Auguste Comte, Hebert Spencer, and Émile Durkheim variously employing the term to draw attention to how groups and societies (i.e., groups of groups) functioned as integrated units.

Comte ([1851–1854] 1975a; 1975b; 1975c), for example, argued that societies were cohesive only insofar as ties existed between spouses, between spouses and their children, as well as between families and local or national communities. For Comte, spouses co-cultivated a sense of *attachment/interdependence*, while cultivating a sense of *benevolence* in their dependent, needy offspring. Especially in late childhood and onward, kids may develop an increasingly intense sense of *veneration*, or humble thankfulness, for their parents' care.

Comte suggested that to the degree that spouses become more interdependent with one another and benevolent toward their children, and to the degree that children become more reverential toward their parents, each member of the family would have the capacity to exhibit some combination of attachment, benevolence, and veneration toward the larger community. Adults might build attachments to others outside the home, perhaps at work, or they might exhibit benevolence toward needy others, such as the homeless, or they might exhibit veneration for a well-functioning government. One of the central founders of sociology, then, was thoroughly *organismic* in his approach—the more attachment, benevolence, and veneration characterized ties within the family and between family and community, the more organismic was the society.

Comte puts his thoughts like this:

> I shall treat the social organism as definitely composed of the families that are the true elements or cells; next, of the classes or castes that are its proper tissues; and last, of the cities and communes that are its real organs.
>
> (Comte, A. [1851–1854] 1975d, pg. 429)

However, as the above quote shows, many classical sociologists took the analogy between societies and biological organisms too far—societies are not biological organisms in the same sense that a human body is a biological organism.

People (and scientists) have long struggled to see the world in continuums and in abstract forms of emergence. It is not easy to think like this; we gravitate so naturally to dichotomies or typologies or essences or some other category system.

A family is not a cell; a cell is a molecular aggregation of proteins, fluids, membranes, and so on. A family, obviously, is composed of people, albeit people composed of cells, but these people have additional relationships to other people and groups whose characteristics are best explained by reference to things like norms, ideas, or civil infrastructure, not to organelles and cytoplasm. We should be understanding evolution in a continual, abstract, fractal sense, not only in a specific sense, as with the evolution of specific structures like cells.

Thus, an animal isn't (only, necessarily) eusocial *or not*; rather, there are various ways in which animals can exhibit eusocialness; an entity isn't an organism *or not*; rather, there are various ways in which entities can exhibit organismicness; an entity isn't a unit of selection *or not*; rather, there are various ways in which entities can exhibit degrees of selection-proneness (depending on their materiality or discreteness).

So, no, Comte, families are not cells, classes are not tissues, and cities are not organs. They are something different; they are, as with the people themselves, new entitative forms capable of, and thus components in, larger aggregations varying in organismality.

Matt Dunn (2016) outlines three (bad) reasons that have led sociologists to ignore the idea of societal organismality. Let's look at each one in turn.

One was Weber's methodological individualism. Weber insisted that groups and societies, being composed of individuals, were actually nothing more than the cumulative actions of individuals toward other individuals. The problem here, of course, is that insofar as individuals act *as if* groups or societies are real superordinate entities, their behavior is better explained as acting in response to these entities they are perceiving (or imagining). For example, a president might initiate a war with another country for political legitimacy, even if they personally have no particular conflict with any individual from that country. The notion that other people constitute a "country" is what allows the president to declare "a war" against it. I'm applying W. I. Thomas' principle: if animals perceive that groups exist distinct and emergent from the individuals that comprise them, then they will behave *as if* these groups are real. Once an animal can construe or imagine that collectivities exist and act *as collectivities*, their behavior can shift in response to this perception.

So, was Weber right to think that groups and societies are ultimately composed of individuals? Well, yes. But, his thought was incomplete. I would agree that groups and societies are composed of nothing more than individual humans; yet, individuals act on the basis of a belief that they are responding to groups as groups, or to institutions as institutions.

Consider the problem another way. Are groups or societies composed of single individuals? Well, it depends. Single human beings in aggregation, yes, but, as it turns out, single human beings are not single entities; rather, single human beings are in part comprised of consortiums of microbiota and other cellular networks. It depends on what "individual" we want to recognize, be it the individual microbes, the individual constituent person, or the individual aggregation of human beings. If the prokaryotes and eukaryotes are sufficiently integrated, what emerges is a person; if people are sufficiently integrated, what emerges is a (more vs. less) coordinated group. This is how evolution works, via the "teamwork" of various degrees of "teamness." Not all consortiums of living organisms constitute a new entity, just as not all aggregations of human beings constitute a group or society.

A second reason why the organismic analogy fell out of favor in classical sociology is due to the influence of Karl Marx and, more generally, of what came to be called "conflict theory." For those who espoused this theory, social life is best understood as a field of unending conflict between opposed groups, some of whom enjoy more wealth, status, or power than others. No doubt, social life is rife with exploitation and inequality, beginning especially with the hoarding of resources in the horticultural and agrarian societies of history. Still, there is more to life than conflict and, indeed, if one looks close enough, there is a shocking amount of cooperation in even the most conflictual settings—consider an aggrieved family whose loved one has been murdered, sitting emotionally but calmly in a courtroom watching court proceedings to determine the guilt of the accused.

We do not need to choose between a theoretical perspective that construes the world in terms of conflict and one that construes it in terms of cooperation. Rather, we simply need to observe, for example, that the greater the conflict between subunits the less organismic will be the emergent entity. Or, the lower the conflict between subunits, the more organismic any emergent entity will be. Human beings, on account of their intelligence and emotionality, have the ever-present (if not often realized) *capacity to become relatively more (or less) organismic in their aggregations.*

A third reason why the organismic analogy became less popular in sociological theory is due to the "biophobia" that has stricken the discipline of contemporary sociology (Van den Berghe, 1990; Ellis, 1996; Marshall, 2018; Takács, 2018). Being mostly motivated by their personal politics, many sociologists now regard disciplines such as biology as irrelevant at best, and potentially dangerous, at worst, because they worry that biology will suggest some constraints to human nature, thus limiting the viability of the utopian political world they seek. As a result, contemporary sociologists—much like religious fundamentalists who also harbor a constant desire to push utopian politics—regard evolutionary theory with great skepticism.

Richard Machalek and Michael Martin, in their assessment of the situation, conclude that "consequently, most sociological inquiry today proceeds apace absent any connection to biology" (Machalek and Martin, 2004, pg. 456). The reality is that sociologists, today, receive no training in biology or in evolutionary theory, which leads them to question their relevance to social life. Then, to justify their ignorance, they assert that biological approaches to social life are somehow immoral ("what of the eugenics movement 100 years ago!" they often assert bizarrely, as if some short-lived and ill-advised political movement disproved entire fields of science) or unnecessary ("humans have culture, so they are not bound to evolution or biology!" they often assert confusedly). It is an embarrassing state of affairs indeed, but not one that we must indulge.

Despite sociology's modern hesitancy to think of societies as entities varying in their organismality, outside of sociology this point of view is starting to gain traction (for a source of this resurgence, see Queller and Strassmann, 2009). Many of those I've mentioned above have argued, in various ways, that human society represents a major evolutionary transition, but *how* exactly this happened and *what* exactly has transitioned is the subject of much debate. Claes Andersson and Petter Törnberg, for example, write:

> We propose that human evolution is best understood as an evolutionary transition in individuality that combines evolutionary patterns familiar from earlier [transitions] but in a radically new type of substrate. ... The proposed hominin [transition] would have begun in early [hominin] communities [beginning around 2.6 million years ago], with large game carnivory, we argue, as the kernel around which the initial mutualistic system of traditions coalesced ... We see human evolution as fundamentally about the emergence of evolution

> on a new level of organization, and the evolution of a new set of basic evolutionary mechanisms for heredity, storage, development, and organization.
>
> (Andersson and Törnberg, 2019, pgs. 86–87)

For Andersson and Törnberg, hominin communities likely started out very similarly to the communities that chimpanzees have today, where socializing *within* a community occurs frequently throughout the day depending on individual preferences. On the other hand, interactions *between* communities would have, more often, been violent and territorial.

At some point, likely after a group grew to greater than 100–150 emotionally bonded hominins, it fissioned into two subgroups, with these subgroups each sharing the norms and mythologies of the original fused group. This split community, though now fissioned into distinct subgroups, was not totally differentiated because each group still shared a superordinate ethnic or tribal identity, norms, rites of passage, and associated mythology. So, even if subgroup members stop physically interacting (which is unlikely), their "fitness interests are aligned," insofar as each subgroup engages in the same eating, sleeping, hunting, and child-rearing behaviors on account of their sharing of norms and culture (Andersson and Törnberg, 2019, pg. 88).

As the aggregate community continued to increase in total size (containing more and more subgroups), complex cooperative relationships could have brought larger and larger benefits to collective child-rearing, food/resource extraction, and defense from predators or hostile neighbors. While chimpanzee communities sometimes fission, they've only been observed doing so twice in the wild (apparently observed once by Jane Goodall, once by Takeshi Furuichi), and did so slowly over the course of about a decade (Feldblum et al., 2018). Early hominins, on the other hand, were developing increasingly unique (by degree) capacities for abstract symbolic reasoning and articulated speech, which would have allowed for a more fluid construal of group boundaries that would be easier to define and redefine as circumstances required. In my terms, hominin groups were developing the neurological ability to engage in more fluid, more complex, forms of fission–fusion oscillation.

Some of these subgroups would have become more isolated than other subgroups, for example, in situations where roaming ranges were expanded or new territories were established. In these circumstances, some of the more isolated subgroups might have developed slightly varying traditions, norms, or mythologies. Andersson and Törnberg (2019) suggest that it is likely that, in some cases, this variation in belief and behavior between increasingly geographically distant subgroups might have (1) conferred a greater competitive or survival-relevant edge to some subgroups over others; (2) facilitated trade or openness to innovation; and (3) facilitated the development of more flexible understandings of the ecology (i.e., not only tied to specific plants or animals that might be less prevalent in other localities). Any fissioned subgroup, then, which becomes sufficiently isolated from the group it descended from (but where some level of cooperation is maintained), might develop beliefs and behaviors that confer new survival benefits, facilitate greater innovation, and are more useful across a greater number of contexts.

While it is, of course, impossible to know for sure what sort of constellation of beliefs and behaviors kickstarted a degree of organismality in ancestral hominins, a good guess is a combination of "tool-assisted cooperative carnivory" (Andersson and Törnberg, 2019, pg. 91) and, I would add, increasing ideological and behavioral pressure to engage in alloparenting, alloforaging, and allodefense. After all, the evolution of the brain and the needs of highly dependent infants imposed a significant caloric and time demand on ancestral humans. These demands would have been high enough to inextricably link the biological survival of offspring to the social maintenance of cohesive, resource-provisioning subgroups composed of kin and fictive kin.

Some subgroups would have enforced this allodefense, allohunting/foraging, and alloparenting differently—and, sometimes, more effectively—than other subgroups. My argument, then, is not for some creation moment when humanesque alloliving sparked into existence. Rather, what seems to have happened is that the capacity to fission and fuse in more complex and task-specific ways—facilitated by numerous evolved capacities such as those for abstraction, impulse control, and emotionality—allowed for more flexible social-role responses, norms, and hierarchies regarding the shared burdens of parenting highly dependent offspring and surviving on an open savannah filled with predators.

Notes

1 http://humanorigins.si.edu/evidence/genetics

2 People in farming societies typically have less diverse and less nutritious diets: for much of human history, people in such societies subsisted largely on wheat, barley millet, corn, and a few other crops. Compared to the more diverse diets of hunter-gatherers, replete with various proteins, nuts, tubers, and fruits, farming society diets were more monotonous, but notably more reliable and more easily mass produced. And this reliability and mass production of food enabled the more scheduled, rigid, and complex rituals we see in agricultural societies.

3 https://oceanservice.noaa.gov/facts/portuguese-man-o-war.html

Chapter 2

Fission–Fusion as the Central Sustaining Mechanism of Organismality, Part I

> "The free individual is not one who already knows absolutely what he wants, but one who has incomplete preferences and is trying by means of interior deliberation and dialogue with others to determine precisely what he does want"
>
> (Manin, 1987, pg. 364).

A society isn't only a single entity, it is also a fractal-like aggregation of subsocieties. Fission–fusion is a general mechanism operating in animal (and human) societies that allows for and maintains such aggregations. When individuals and subgroups oscillate between fission–fusion states in an open (i.e., accessible to symbolic outsiders) system, collectives becomes increasingly behaviorally and ideationally complex and thus more flexible in their ability to adapt to changing circumstances.

Relatedly, attitudes and values are not so much singular beliefs held by people. Rather, the contents of each individual person's mind are shifting probability distributions. When survey researchers or qualitative interviewers ask people about their attitudes or values, they often get singular responses. So, it seems as though individuals "have" particular attitudes or values. Yet, this conclusion would be a seductive mistake. Depending on the degree to which an individual feels subjectively integrated into one or more social groups, or subjectively distant from said groups, or feels that they are *becoming* relatively more integrated or *becoming* relatively less integrated (and all of this can in principle vary second to second, day to day, year to year, generation to generation), the probability distribution associated with their likely response in any given moment will shift. People, obviously, look like independently acting agents, but the contents of their minds are better understood as shifting probability distributions associated with relative changes in their perceived level of fission or fusion with the groups in their lives.

Quantitative and qualitative research rarely, if ever, account for this, and even longitudinal research often assumes that only elapsed time and various life experiences are relevant to changes in attitudes or values. But this is wrong. Elapsed time is important, so are life experiences. However, the

DOI: 10.4324/9781003266020-2

shifting probability distributions of individuals' stated attitudes or values responds, ultimately, to their perceived location in the oscillating fission–fusion dance between salient social groups. We are not aware that the contents of our subjectivities can be so variable; indeed, we are often also not aware that stability in our responses might be owed to stability in oscillations over time.

Let's now begin our deep dive into just what, exactly, fission–fusion oscillation involves.

Fissioning occurs when individuals in groups (or subgroups embedded in superordinate groups) disband or separate relative to a prior state. Fissioning is reduced co-presence and/or reductions in joint/collective attentional allocation. Fissioning, then, refers to a state of relative *reductions in co-presence or joint/collective attention.* Fission states give individuals the freedom to experience new events or locales, to have new thoughts, and to try new behaviors that might otherwise be discouraged or seem unnecessary in a more fused, group context. Relative to a more closed and norm-enforcing fused state, fission states will be more conducive to novel (and potentially disorganized) experiences, ideas, and behaviors.

Fusion is a state different from fission only by degree—it occurs when individuals (or subgroups) aggregate or intermix to an increased extent. Specifically, fusion is increased co-presence and/or an increase in joint/collective attentional allocation. Fusion, then, is a state of relative *information retention, integration, and coordination facilitated by increases in co-presence or joint/collective attention.* The fusion of individuals into a group, or of subgroups into a supra-group, can, under certain conditions that we will be discussing, improve decision-making capacity. In short, these conditions occur when group boundaries are open/porous and when people of different demographics *and* experiences *and* worldviews can more freely circulate in and out. This is because in an open, circulating, group errors of individual perception or unrepresentativeness of experience can be drowned out by a more detailed, and thus potentially more accurate, group consensus (Merkle et al., 2015; Muthukrishna and Henrich, 2016).

Porous group boundaries, along with the ability to enter and exit groups freely, provides an avenue by which individual brains can become better information-processors. Collectively, as groups, the information-processing improves as well.

Consider it this way. Throughout their life-course, individuals develop beliefs and expectations about other people and their worldviews. Some people and some worldviews might be regarded as dangerous, odd, or immoral and consequently stigmatized and avoided. By contrast, other people and their worldviews might be admired or respected. Now, thanks to our ubiquitous confirmation bias (Nickerson, 1998), that is, our tendency to seek confirming evidence for what we already believe is true, we may preferentially remember negative experiences with stigmatized outgroups, or regard such experiences as fully diagnostic of "people like that." However, in a context of fission–fusion oscillation with porous boundaries, people will, over time, be exposed to a greater number of opportunities for positive, productive interactions with stigmatized outgroups. Additionally, there will be more opportunities, over time, for negative or conflictual interactions to occur with admired, respected outgroups. Both positive interactions with stigmatized outgroups and negative interactions with admired ingroups constitute "expectancy incongruent" experiences, potentially spurring increases in cognitive flexibility and creativity (Meleady et al., 2019).

Thus, fission–fusion oscillation is a mechanism by which groups can process information more creatively and accurately, increase their flexibility in response to environmental changes, and therefore potentially increase adaptiveness. Optimal fission–fusion oscillation facilitates the spread of information (in the form of emotions and body language or in the form of verbally/symbolically articulated experiences or ideas) and resources (organic and material goods; energy sources). But, the determining factor is the oscillation between the two states. Individuals and/or groups that are too fused/overintegrated will tend to absorb less new information because communication will be too rote, regulated, or habituated. Individuals or groups that aren't fused enough/underintegrated, will absorb less new information because interpersonal contact will not be sustained long enough for a useful or memorable communication to transpire.

Generally, the perception of threat causes individuals or subgroups to fuse (Gelfand et al., 2011; Gelfand, 2019) in order to better internally coordinate for purposes of threat-response and mobilization.

Circumstances that are perceived to be relatively less threatening will lead to relative increases in fissioning. After all, when the adoption of new (potentially unhelpful) beliefs and behaviors is less costly to life and limb, people will feel relatively unconcerned about acting and behaving independent of group norm consensus. Under conditions perceived to be threatening, however, the consolidation and enforcement of normative beliefs and behaviors will take (relative) precedence.

Fission–fusion oscillation is a generic property of societies—it is the fundamental mechanism of group organization and continuance. There are aspects of fissioned states that motivate relative increases in fusion, and aspects of fused states which motivate relative increases in fissioning. The mechanism is a hydraulic feedback loop that serves to, among other things, ascertain and distribute information, release social tension and build social rapport, defend against threats, and seek out novelty.

2.1 Fission–Fusion in Animal Societies

It was Hans Krummer (1971) who first used the concept of fission–fusion to describe behavioral subgrouping in animals, particularly chimps, baboons and geladas. For Krummer, fission–fusion was defined as the tendency of an animal to alter group composition depending on the availability and distribution of resources.

Geladas (Old World monkeys), for example, can organize themselves into two tiers, a larger superordinate troop or smaller subgroups (Krummer, 1971). Some of these subgroups contain one male ("harems") while other subgroups contain all males who share an alliance. During certain periods, or in certain locations where resources are scarce, the troop splits up into a greater number of small subgroups that live and forage for resources independently of one another. Conversely, during periods, or in locations, of relative resource abundance, gelada subgroups begin to fuse, and the acquisition and dissemination of resources happens more at the troop level. This provides out first hint that fission-fusion oscillation responds not only to threat levels, but also to the need to acquire and divide up resources.

Or, consider chimpanzees:

> Chimpanzees, for example, live in an open society in which large, well-defined groups have not been identified. The parties of a wide area meet and recombine in a constant process of reorganization. This seems to be an ecologically ideal fusion-fission system, providing group sizes and compositions for every conceivable context.
>
> (Krummer, 1971, pgs. 90–91)

Much the same could have been written of humans. Although under conditions of resource deprivation, high population density, or when resource patches are especially defensible, forager societies might become territorial and hostile to foreigners, there is clearly a capacity—and great interest—in roaming a territory unencumbered and establishing new trade or social relationships (e.g., marital bonds) between societies.

Chimps (and other animals) often do fuse into defensive alliances. Perhaps the simplest form is when young male chimps compete with other young males to display physical dominance—an isolated male is far more likely to lose to an allied team of males, and for this reason, if for no other, males often create alliances with one another and hang out in small groups (Wrangham and Wilson, 2004). Yet, lacking articulated speech and certain cortical and subcortical neural tissues makes it more difficult for chimpanzees to modify their group memberships as flexibly as humans can. While we can only speculate as to the ultimate source of human–chimp differences, it is plausible that leaving the tree canopies to try to survive on the savannah rendered early hominins highly vulnerable to predators, and that this motivated a novel form of fusion—the creation of defensible, alloparental, "home bases" in which to sleep, converse, and care for others.

Fission–fusion oscillation in mammals has most commonly been observed among primates (including humans), dolphins, bats, spotted hyenas, and elephants (Aureli et al., 2008). I suspect, however, that fission–fusion behavior is much more common than it seems. Prairie dogs, wolves, lions, and elephants, for example, temporarily aggregate in various places as required by resource availability or defense against predators (see Moffett, 2019 for other examples). This behavior can be quite complex too, as when a lion takes a moment to sneak away to another group (or lion "pride") in order to establish some familiarity and rapport before defecting (temporarily or permanently) from its current group. It also occurs when animals aggregate for purposes of capturing large prey, stealing from neighbors, enhancing defense, or just to keep warm at night (i.e., thermoregulation) before dispersing to roam a range freely during downtime (Krause and Ruxton, 2002).

Across species of animals, five common dimensions of fission–fusion emerge: (1) high vs. low variation in spatial cohesion among group members; (2) high vs. low variation in total group size; (3) high vs. low variation in subgroup size; (4) high vs. low variation in party composition; and (5) high vs. low variation in tie strength / emotional bondedness.

With regard to (1), under some conditions, animals will aggregate more closely and take up less space, for example, to huddle around a rare, valuable resource. Under other conditions, group members will spread out more widely, for example, when food sources are patchy and distributed around an ecosystem. Regarding (2) and (3), animal groups will shrink and swell in size in response to resource availability and distribution as well as in response to threats (from other animals or from the environment). Regarding (4), which individuals belong to which groups (or which groups belong to which collectives) varies—individual animals (and groups) sort themselves along dimensions such as personality, skillsets, and social status (known as "resource holding potential"; see Briffa and Lane, 2017; Dong et al., 2017; Žampachová et al., 2017; Wright et al., 2019; Crawford et al., 2020).

Finally, regarding (5), ties between subunits can be more or less emotional, more or less anxiety-inducing, more or less comforting. Emotionality, perhaps especially in humans, can in various ways motivate fissioned or fused states. For example, emotions such as fear, puzzlement, and surprise might motivate temporary dispersal in order to search for information to help understand and better respond to whatever has caused these emotions. Or, fear, puzzlement, and surprise could motivate a desire to aggregate with others in order to mobilize for defense or to monitor others' actions.

As well, some aversive emotions associated with experiencing new, unfamiliar people or ideas—annoyance, anger, or disgust, for example—can motivate a decreased search for new information and a desire to further embed oneself into existing collectives (Buckels and Trapnell, 2013; Reicher et al., 2016). Or, feelings of annoyance, anger, and disgust might come from being overintegrated into a collective and thus motivate dispersal. The same emotions felt in different contexts can drive people to disperse in some cases or aggregate in others. And, when intense positive or negative emotions are experienced with others, a process of identity fusion can occur, stimulating a sense of oneness or "we-ness." This subjective sense of oneness or "we-ness" can, in turn, motivate individuals to sacrifice their time and effort (or, potentially, sacrifice themselves in acts of martyrdom) to further the goals of the group (Jong et al., 2015; Whitehouse et al., 2017; Kavanagh et al., 2019).

The five dimensions above also implicate time decisions and space decisions, or, in other words, decisions about when interaction should occur and where (Sueur et al., 2011). These decisions may be implicit, following emotional intuitions, or they may be more abstractly or symbolically represented (in animals with large prefrontal cortices). In either case, decisions made about when to interact and where will tend to involve calculations (implicit or otherwise) about resource availability, threat assessment, and the degree of pre-existing familiarity between group members.

Varying combinations of (1)–(5) can also facilitate community monitoring, because when individuals are relatively fissioned (moving in isolation or in relatively smaller subgroupings) they can more freely and openly evaluate how others in their community access, consume, and store resources, and, when they are relatively fused, this information can be transmitted to others in various ways. Varying combinations of (1)–(5), in other words, facilitate the foraging of information about the state of the environment and the state of others in that environment. And, better information, especially during times of scarcity or danger, can be the difference between survival and death.

The probability of a superordinate group fissioning into subgroups, is, primarily, a function of the number of groups in a collective, or of individuals in a group. With regard to humans, as cognitive psychologists (e.g., Pinker, 2015), anthropologists (e.g., Kelly, 2013; Dunbar, 2016), and sociologists (e.g., Durkheim [1893] 2014; Turner, 2016) have all shown, it is difficult to maintain close bonds with very large numbers of individuals because emotional bonds can be cognitively taxing, and because these bonds take time to form and maintain. In order to manage this cognitive load and time demand, individuals segment themselves into subgroups and, especially in humans, rely on larger abstractions (e.g., ethnic identity, national citizenship, organizational affiliation) to categorize and relate to unknown or unfamiliar others who belong to one's larger, superordinate "ingroups."

As I've suggested above, human groups fission for a lot of other reasons; a central reason is because people prefer to fan out and explore new resource niches when threat/danger is (relatively) low and/or when resources are variously distributed throughout an environment. This acquisition of new resources might be in the form of pieces of firewood or ideas or money and everything in between. Another reason why groups fission is to manage in-group social tension, namely, conflict or anxiety about roles, obligations, or disputes over resources. Or, sometimes groups fission because individuals enjoy pursuing and experiencing novelty and new experiences separate from their particular group obligations. And, of course, sometimes groups fission because individuals' personality traits, ideologies, goals/hobbies, or particular life-course experiences are too distinct from one another to communicate effectively about group coordination (Seebacher and Krause, 2017).

I have also mentioned above how human groups fuse for a lot of reasons; centrally, they fuse so as to facilitate the dissemination of resources, to behaviorally mobilize in response to the perception of threat or to integrate new information. Additionally, fusion might occur as a result of individuals sharing personality traits, ideologies, goals/hobbies, or certain experiences—people prefer to associate with those similar to themselves, and such association can help them feel more comfortable and confident (McPherson et al., 2001; Kossinets and Watts, 2009; Grant and Hogg, 2012).

Animals engaged in more complex forms of fission–fusion tend to be highly intelligent in the sense of having a sophisticated capacity for detecting and reasoning about social cues (Aureli et al., 2008; Ramos-Fernandez et al., 2018). This seems to be the case because fission–fusion oscillation creates more complex demands on social cognition than does prolonged fission or prolonged fused states. Fission–fusion oscillation is cognitively demanding because time spent temporarily in isolation or in smaller groups facilitates a freedom of movement that can lead to experiences, and thus cognitions, that differ from those of the larger group. Also, time spent in different groups (or subgroups) might alter the skillsets or dispositions of constituent members. Thus, animals using the mechanism of fission–fusion will need to have good enough memories so that they can track changes in individuals' abilities, interests and group memberships over time.

Indeed, animals engaged in fission-fusion oscillation may develop greater capacities for *inferential reasoning* (to track relations between individuals on account of assumed group/subgroup membership), *analogical reasoning* (to track ways in which groups/subgroups are similar to or different from one another), and "*equivalence classes*" (to conceptualize individuals as representative of some shared group trait), all of which can be cognitively demanding (Aureli et al., 2008). In animals engaged in patterns of fission–fusion oscillation, these forms of reasoning are often represented via sound, vocalization, scent, or behavior (as they are in humans, though humans are unusual in their additional use of abstract symbols and articulated speech).

Both African and Asian elephants, for example, use "snorts, barks, grunts, trumpets, cries, and even imitated sounds" to communicate between elephant groups and subgroups (Barcus, 2014). These elephants have been found to respond behaviorally to the alarm calls of familiar others, but not to the alarm calls of elephants in unfamiliar herds, indicating that group alliances are tracked via subtle differences in emitted sounds (O'Connell-Rodwell et al., 2007). In fact, on the basis of findings like these and others (e.g., Poole et al., 2005; Stoeger and Manger, 2014) researchers now argue that elephant group/subgroup socialization relies on vocal learning. So-called "combination calls" in such elephants—for example, an elephant emitting a combination of high-frequency "roars" and lower-frequency "rumbles"—appears to communicate particular circumstances, such as being separated from a group (Pardo et al., 2019).

And, as I mentioned above, coordination within a fission–fusion community relies on emotional intuitions—the more various and complex are subgroupings, the more animals can reduce cognitive burdens by relying simply on the way others make them feel. Consider the emotional components of "equivalence classification," for example: if a conspecific from subgroup Y refused to reciprocate grooming or resource-provisioning in a prior encounter, an animal might feel avoidant or anxious with regard to future interactions with any individuals from subgroup Y.

However, self-control over one's emotions and behavior will also be an advantage (if not a prerequisite) for organizing into more complex fission–fusion communities (Aureli et al., 2008). Insofar as group composition changes fluidly over time, animals will need to be able to inhibit their hostility and/or anxiety so as to respond cooperatively to shifts in group membership. If one individual leaves a group, or another joins, animals can rely on emotional intuitions to determine how to respond, but they may need to inhibit their response long enough to gather relevant social or environmental information so as to respond in a way that maximizes the benefits of cooperation and minimizes conflict.

2.2 Oscillation as Calibration

A varying rate of oscillation between fissioned and fused states can be adaptive on account of fissioned states encouraging informational or resource foraging, and fused states encouraging coordination, mobilization and information/resource integration (Miramontes et al., 2016; Falcón-Cortés et al., 2019).

However, it is nevertheless possible for this oscillation mechanism to halt in a prolonged period of either fission (i.e., social separation) or fusion (i.e., social aggregation). If, for example, contact between groups becomes severely disrupted, perhaps due to prolonged conflict or geographic isolation, then fusion becomes increasingly difficult. Or, even if individuals continue to occasionally circulate between groups, if circulation is not frequent enough, new group members may be viewed with suspicion as "outsiders" who do not think or behave in ways similar enough to those of other group members.

Prolonged periods of fissioning will tend to occur when perceived threats and dangers are few and/or when resource quality, quantity, or accessibility vary widely (Sueur et al., 2011). However, the longer individuals have been foraging in relative isolation, or in smaller subgroup units, the more accustomed they will tend be to self-directed thought and behavior and, thus, the more averse they may be to adopt obligations imposed on them by larger superordinate collectives.

Generally, individuals will not aggregate into groups (and groups will not aggregate into superordinate groups) when the following three conditions hold (see Olson, 1965; Wallis, 1991): (1) when individuals (or subgroup leadership) perceive greater costs to participating in an aggregate than benefits; (2) when group goals can be accomplished (or are perceived as able to be accomplished) without the efforts of all constituent members; and (3) when benefits accruing from the achievement of group goals are shared with (or accessible to) others regardless of their group membership or their involvement in the task. In short, fusion tends not to occur when no, or few, benefits to such aggregation are perceived, when aggregation is unnecessary to accomplish a particular goal, and when the fruits of group effort can be enjoyed without group membership. A limitation of existing research is that (1)-(3) are highly instrumental and pragmatic considerations; individual people (and subgroups) may still aggregate purely out of emotional reasons—to avoid feeling lonely, insignificant, or wayward, or to bolster a sense of drive or motivation or to enjoy the feeling of contributing to coalitional competition between groups (Clark et al., 2019).

There are several risks inherent to prolonged fission periods. Fissioned individuals who are either isolated from one another or in relatively smaller subgroups will be more vulnerable to predation and attacks from other groups, or, simply, more vulnerable to periods of scarcity such as famines or, in contemporary societies, unemployment or recessions. By contrast, individuals fused into larger superordinate groupings can mobilize a more substantial defensive response to attacks or a more substantial support network for periods of disadvantage and scarcity. Fission states in general, and certainly if prolonged, can render individuals more vulnerable to outgroup threats, environmental dangers, and/or economic vicissitudes because fewer others can be relied on for provisioning or defense.

It is, however, important not to be alarmist about fission states—animals in a group, especially humans, can easily stay in touch with one another even if they are not immediately co-present. Anyone who has ever lived near an area full of coyotes knows the telltale shrieking yips when one group has something important to communicate with surrounding coyotes that are not immediately co-present. Many animal species do this; the evolved "logic" seems to be: fan out in groups of varying size to explore the area, but stay in touch. Of course, if animal subgroups (or individuals) wander too far out of earshot or smellshot, communication can become difficult. This is less a problem for humans with our sophisticated communication technologies, whether it is foragers using smoke signals to communicate across vast distances or people in industrial societies using the internet to video chat or send text messages.

Still, the important point is that animals can communicate with one another, even when they are not co-present. Moffett puts it this way:

> In even the most dispersed fission-fusion societies, animals usually have some means to check in at intervals with those who aren't too remote. Spotted hyenas whoop and holler at any provocation; chimpanzees stay in touch by loud pant-hoots; lions roar; wolves howl. As long as lines of communication exist, individuals aren't completely cut off.
>
> (Moffett, 2019, pgs. 40–41)

This point is especially true for humans—perhaps more than any other animal on Earth, humans can maintain *very* subtle, minimalistic fused states.

In a way similar to how superordinate group memberships become more general and abstract the larger society becomes, allowing for a low-level fusion even when one is alone or disbanded into subgroups, so too do formal institutional/bureaucratic rules become more general and abstract the larger society becomes, allowing for a similar degree of low-level fusion at all times. At a certain societal size, with sufficiently generic identities, roles, and values, simply construing oneself as a "national citizen" simultaneously ties you to potentially millions if not billions of other people, but does so in an extremely generic, vague way. The same is true when two people share a societal membership and reflect upon the formal rules governing a given institutional bureaucracy (for example, two people might discuss, in extremely generic terms, how "colleges," or "prisons" or "hospitals" operate). The larger societies become, the more vague our shared culture becomes, but with the benefit that more and more individuals can be thus fused, even if only at a low level of intensity or specificity.

On the other hand, individuals (or sub-groups) fused (i.e., co-present or aggregated) for prolonged periods may become behaviorally and ideologically very similar to one another (see, e.g., Sunstein, 2002). As a result, they may respond too slowly or too inflexibly to changing circumstances involving new, as opposed to old, threats and dangers. Prolonged fusion states, then, are not *necessarily conducive to defense against threats*. Such states can also render individuals more vulnerable to outgroup threats and environmental dangers to the extent that unhelpful beliefs or behaviors are maintained in the group due to conformity pressures. Conformity to group ideals, norms, and rules will be especially costly to individuals' lives and opportunities when enemies/competitors adopt new attack or mobilization strategies or to the extent that social or environmental conditions change in unforeseen ways (e.g., shifting demographics, economic disruptions or climate change / natural disasters).

Prolonged fused states can also produce social conflict—sustained co-presence can lead to disputes over resources, disputes over responses to threats, or disputes over how groups and subgroups should be organized (i.e., disputes over hierarchy and status). This is *especially* true when resource quality, quantity, and accessibility become more difficult to rely on or obtain, because this will make it easier to accuse some people/subgroups of hoarding resources or taking advantage of group resources without contributing (i.e., free-riding).

Social conflict is a perennial logistical hurdle in fused groups, though it can be addressed via periodic fissioning, which allows group members to go their own way (or mingle in their own chosen subgroups) for a while. Fissioning thus mitigates the costs of conflict that emerge during prolonged periods of fusion (Sueur et al., 2011). If a fused group experiences too much conflict, without a period of separation, any disaggregating that eventually does occur may be permanent due to the magnitude of perceived grievances experienced while fused.

Fused groups can become "stuck" in a fused state, just as fissioned groups can become "stuck" in a fissioned state. In the case of a group in a "stuck" fused state, individuals (or subgroups) may perceive few or no opportunities for dissent, critique or rebellion because in-group boundaries are so strictly monitored or because anticipated punishments for dissent are so severe. In this situation, even temporary movement to another group or abandonment of the present group may appear dangerous or risky (Sueur et al., 2011). And, generally, where gathering new information is more difficult / less reliable, individuals will tend to rely on the group's average preference, or on the knowledge of those deemed credible by surrounding group members (Sueur et al., 2011).

Ultimately, it seems that fission–fusion states calibrate themselves to the environment by oscillating. Prolonged fissioning provides few opportunities for adaptive group-level benefits, and the same is true for prolonged fusing. A natural question to ask, then, is: what is an "optimal" oscillatory rate?

Well, there is no one answer for this, since natural and social environments can differ considerably. But, we *can* say, roughly, what it is that calibrates the oscillating dynamic. What calibrates the dynamic is the (1) length of time that can elapse before dispersed group members become vulnerable to (perceived) dangers, (2) the length of time that can elapse before aggregated groups become inflexible, rigid, or fatigued in their efforts to coordinate/mobilize, and (3) the length of time that can elapse before individuals or subgroups become uncertain or confused about their group roles and obligations toward others.

2.3 Decision-Making and Disagreement

In circumstances where degrees of fissioning occur less often, group members will need to focus more of their attention on coordinating their behaviors and beliefs vis a vis others, resolving conflict, and promoting cooperation (Aureli et al., 2008). Conversely, during periods when fissioning occurs more often, group members will need to focus more of their attention on framing and negotiating periods of separation, developing strategies for re-establishing relationships, and reducing stress and anxiety during reunions.

Variations in group composition, in addition to larger group size, can make reaching a group consensus more difficult—the more individual group members differ in their skillsets, experiences, or personalities, the more differences of opinion and intuition may arise (Casari and Tagliapietra, 2018). At the same time, variation in skill, experience, or personality can also generate novel solutions and new collaborative insights. So, communication and cooperation are key: insofar as groups vary in their members, and can facilitate cooperative interactions, new adaptive solutions, insights, or behaviors are increasingly probable.

Having said this, the more frequently a group fissions, the more individuals (or subgroups/subunits) will tend to have dissimilar experiences or develop skillsets or competencies in isolation from one another, which can result in conflicts during group decision-making (Merkle et al., 2015). Conflict over group decisions can generate new options for subgroup membership (when sufficient discord leads to the formation of new subgroups) and/or when individual people (or group subunits) cannot come to a consensus. Conversely, conflict over group decisions might lead to greater fusion, as when such conflict provides a context for domineering or powerful individuals to direct or manipulate the decision-making process, and/or when such conflict provides a context for entrepreneurial leadership that organizes opinions into consensus attitudes/goals. Where contestation over the legitimacy of group hierarchy is high, small subgroup "mobs" (starting with perhaps two to four people; see Abbink and Doğan, 2019) may emerge to further coercively canalize group attitudes and goals. Such mobs will vary in their self-interestedness: sometimes a mob will direct its behavior toward manipulating other group members to maximize the mob's personal gain, while at other times a mob will more pro-socially direct its behavior toward redressing abuses of power (as when mobs of chimps or humans depose authoritarian leaders; see Boehm, 1999; 2012; De Waal, 2019).

It is, of course, always possible that a group will disperse into its individual components due to high levels of disagreement, a lack of emergent leadership, or because individuals' skillsets and experiences do not align adequately to justify group-level decision-making. Individuals (or subgroup units) may also refrain from cooperating with superordinate collectives on account of hoping to monopolize valued resource niches at a more local level (Merkle et al., 2015).

Past states of relative fissioning can increase the quality/accuracy of decision-making during subsequent fused states (Surowiecki, 2005). As I've discussed, this is because fissioned states allow individuals (or group subunits) relatively more freedom to reflect upon and analyze behaviors and ideas they have adopted from others. Put simply, relative periods of fissioning can "[preserve] dissent and prevent groupthink" (Shavit et al., 2017, pg. 205). Even the anticipation of disagreement or dissent, if it increases attention to one's argumentative strategy, can improve the quality of deliberation and debate (Lloyd et al., 2017).

The effectiveness of fissioned states, or of longer fissioned periods, in increasing collective decision-making accuracy will depend on how normatively constrained thought and behavior tend to be when fused, how open to experience constituent individuals are, their range of movement, their range of exploration of new locations, and potentially, the nature of individuals' other group memberships. So long as constituent individuals (or subgroup units) have relatively distinct experiences/information, and to the degree that this experience/information is efficiently and democratically aggregated and assessed, the accuracy and adaptiveness of supraordinate group decision-making will increase (Surowiecki, 2005).

Communication in fission–fusion groups is also important because there is typically more than one group fissioning–fusing in a given society. So, for example, while one group is in a relative state of fissioning, requiring less time or resources from an individual, another group might be in a relative state of fusion, requiring more time or resources from that same individual. Given this, individuals (or subgroups) may glean useful information, resources, or protection by becoming relatively more fused to a new group and relatively more fissioned from an old one. This variable capacity to relate to different groups in different ways (or, to understand one's group membership obligations as varying depending on the context) facilitates group-level decision-making in changing resource environments (Aureli et al., 2008; Merkle et al., 2015; Falcón-Cortés et al., 2019).

Due to the complexity of fission–fusion dynamics, group consensus can be difficult to achieve. Luckily, there are many ways of achieving it. As mentioned above, consensus might be achieved organically, when temporarily leaders emerge due to their ability to interpret and express collective desires. Or, consensus might be achieved in a more coercive manner, as when domineering individuals or mobs pressure people to express particular points of view. Consensus might be regarded as "active" in situations where people express their views openly, or more "passive" in situations where people simply refrain from objecting (Shavit et al., 2017).

Interestingly, people may share a consensus view and not even be aware of it. Yet, the existence of the agreement acts as a check to prevent conflict from escalating. That this is the case has been made clear in modern social scientific surveys of people who share opinions but do not realize it. For example, political conservatives and liberals in the United States, often regarded in media as highly polarized, agree on a lot more then they often realize—for one example, self-reported liberals estimate that only about 50% of conservatives have favorable attitudes toward immigration, when in reality 90% of conservatives report favorable attitudes (for other examples, such as gun control, see Yudkin et al., 2019). Clearly, then, there is a distinction between consensus attitudes and fused coordination: the case of liberal–conservative "polarization" in the United States shows that when arbitrary membership boundaries and politicized identities discourage co-presence or interaction, a consensus can be shared yet lead to little or no coordination toward common goals. The perception of disagreement, even when there is actually substantial underlying agreement, can stall productive interaction and decision-making.

Chapter 3

Fission–Fusion as the Central Sustaining Mechanism of Organismality, Part 2

Fission–fusion oscillation operates fractally.

Fissioning individuals can, in principle, retreat to smaller and smaller subgroups *ad infinitum*. Sure, a small aggregate of people might simply scatter, but even scattered individual people are, themselves, a consortium of microbiota. In a literal sense, life is always only a collaboration of aggregates. Aggregates divide fractally into sub-aggregates; they also embed fractally into supra-aggregates.

Consider the example of a pandemic or of hostile wartime invasion. In either situation, individuals will retreat from the habits of their daily life—they may leave or lose their jobs, they may stop wandering too far outside their neighborhoods, they may leave or lose the ability to attend schools. In such threatening circumstances, individuals limit their social obligations and territory-roaming so as to form tight-knit aggregates comprised of only the most trusted individuals in their lives.

As many have pointed out (e.g., Tainter, 1988), even when an entire society collapses, people rarely scatter individually in all directions; instead, they restrict their movement and interactions to subgroups in small villages and settlements outside of the city center. Collapsed societies and societies in crisis balkanize; they rarely typically become atomized. As conditions improve, people begin expanding their roaming territories and rebuilding acquaintanceships in metropolitan city centers. Groups reaggregate and re-embed in superordinate groups amidst a new rhythm of arriving and leaving. Life goes on.

It is important to keep in mind that the mechanism of fission–fusion is only discernible as a relative effect. A social system will experience states of *relative* fissioning, which is not necessarily dispersal in the sense of people abandoning their group commitments. For example, even those in very tight-knit groups (think of a religious cult), where people cooperate behaviorally and share worldviews and goals, will still experience relative states of fissioning, such as times when people eat on their own, sleep, shower, or read. In highly fused groups, it might just be noninteractive co-presence that constitutes relative fissioning. Even people who spend a

DOI: 10.4324/9781003266020-3

great deal of time together physically are not always together subjectively, that is, they are not always *sharing a focus of attention or intentionality*.

Just the same, individuals who are quite dispersed from their fellows (e.g., they live alone, they do not work, they are not married, they have no kids) are nevertheless incidentally co-present with others if they go to the store or take a walk in town. Navigating a busy street corner, a crowded mall, or the aisle of a grocery store requires a quite minimal degree of shared attention with others, but there still must be some degree of shared attention or individuals would not be able to coordinate their bodies in space to avoid colliding! This is minimal fusion, but it is still worth noting.

When one sees an aerial shot of a New York City or Chicago crowd during a parade, there is indeed some degree of fusion happening there even if we were to suppose that no one in the crowd actually "knows" each other. The logistical and motor complexities inherent in aggregation require that individuals note the placement of other people as they walk by them, for example, or form and maintain some sort of single-file line leading to a necessary resource (like the bathroom). This shared focus of attention, and/or intention, is a telltale sign that individuals (or groups) are fusing, even when such fusion is very minimal and, potentially, inconsequential to belief or behavior. Yet, even where fusion is minimal, the rate of interactions is likely to rise and we shouldn't underestimate the potential for so-called "serendipitous encounters" to spark unexpected friendships and collaborations.

If fissioning involves a relative decrease in shared attention or intention, it will tend to produce a relative increase of variation in peoples' (or subgroups' average) beliefs or behaviors. Symmetrically, if fusion represents a relative *increase* in shared attention, or intention, this may produce, over time, decreased variation in peoples' (or in a subgroup's average) beliefs or behaviors. And, because people in a society (of any size) also rely on the extraction, processing, and distribution of energy to survive, fissioning is likely associated with relative increases in the variation of energy sources or of energy access (e.g., food, fuel, electricity, water). Symmetrically, fusion is likely associated with relative decreases in the variation of energy sources or of behaviors associated with energy access.

In short, a fission state is not necessarily, or only, mere physical dispersal when it comes to human beings—it is also a state of relative dispersion of beliefs, behaviors, affiliations, and sources of / forms of access to energy. Similarly, a fusion state is not necessarily, or only, mere increases in physical co-presence—it is also a state of relatively higher correlations between beliefs, behaviors, affiliations, and sources of / forms of access to energy.

3.1 Network Dimensions of Innovation in Oscillating Fission–Fusion Systems

As mentioned above, fission states represent opportunities for individuals (or subgroups) to obtain forms of information or to experience events distinctly from the larger group or subgroup. Physical dispersal increases the probability of nonshared experiences, behaviors, or ideas; as well, a reduction in the correlation of belief and behavior among group members reduces the strength of peer pressure and the demand for conformity. Fusion states, on the other hand, represent relative increases in opportunities for information-sharing and information integration into the group's "collective brain" (Muthukrishna and Henrich, 2016). However, aggregation and higher rates of interaction can cause or exacerbate interpersonal disagreement and conflict, or, they can lead to an increasing desire for novelty or for nonshared resources and experiences, all of which may then motivate relative fissioning.

What I'm suggesting is that the physical (or virtual) act of dispersal and reaggregation, with periods of dispersal or aggregation sometimes lasting great lengths, has the potential, over time, to introduce variation and efficient modifications into cultural practices. And the more of an open system (I will return to this modifier in a moment) the fission–fusion mechanism operates in, the more individuals (or subgroups) can contribute to the potential for innovation by drawing on their pre-existing differences in belief, behavior, or experience.

From a sociological perspective, the formation and maintenance of weak-tie relationships is an important driver of innovation (Rogers, 1962; Granovetter, 1983). Weak-tie relationships, in the sense used here, are not necessarily emotionally weak (though they often are), but rather weak in that the ties connect socially distant people of different subgroups. While strong ties within our most salient subgroups (friends, family) can be comforting and supportive, they are mainly sources of redundant information that can stifle innovation (Ruef, 2002). Typically, you know what your friends and family believe, how they behave, and what other groups they care about. However, an acquaintance or friend from a new group might harbor new insight or engage in behaviors that are less familiar.

So, while human social networks are typically composed of an assortment of both strong and weak ties, weak-tie connections to those in less familiar groups can be an important source of novelty. This is important to note because it suggests that, during fission states, innovation is not only a function of relative independence from the collective, but also a function of aggregation or association with less familiar, weak-tie contacts from other groups. Novelty might result from individual (or subgroup) "foraging" for information or experiences, but more commonly in human beings, novelty results from weak-tie contacts with individuals who have (at least somewhat) different strong-tie networks, different group commitments, and different experiences. When an individual returns to their associations with ingroup strong-ties after being exposed to novel forms of culture via weak-tie associations, this novelty can be subsequently integrated and leveraged for ingroup innovation.

Some sociologists have begun conceptualizing network gaps between groups as "structural holes," and conceptualizing these holes as sites where people (or new subgroups) might become "brokers" of information transfer and, thus, innovation. Robert Burt explains this concept lucidly in his article "Structural Holes and Good Ideas":

> The hypothesis in this article is that people who stand near the holes in a social structure are at higher risk of having good ideas. The argument is that opinion and behavior are more homogeneous within than between groups, so people connected across groups are more familiar with alternative ways of thinking and behaving, which gives them more options to select from and synthesize. New ideas emerge from selection and synthesis across the structural holes between groups … For example, consider four levels of brokerage … The simplest act of brokerage is to make people on both sides of a structural hole aware of interests and difficulties in the other group … Transferring best practice is a higher level of brokerage. People familiar with activities in two groups are more able than people confined within either group to see how a belief or practice in one group could create value in the other and to know how to translate the belief or practice into language digestible in the target group. A third level of brokerage is to draw analogies between groups ostensibly irrelevant to one another. People who recognize that the way other groups think or behave may have implications for the value of operations in their own group will have an advantage over those who do not … Synthesis is a fourth level of brokerage. People familiar with activities in two groups are more likely to see new beliefs or behaviors that combine elements from both groups.
>
> (Burt, 2004, pgs. 349–350, 355; see also Burt, 1992)

As Burt explains, surface contact between different groups (whether distant subgroups of the same superordinate group, or subgroups in separate superordinate groups) might increase awareness of differences in organizational culture, which may stimulate new insight. Even the ability to observe interactions between two outsider groups might lead to the adoption of norms or policies deemed to be especially effective and relevant to one's own group.

Another possibility Burt notes is that individuals partaking in the activities of two different groups might come to recombine (or watch others recombine) these activities, incidentally or intentionally. The more a person splits their time across different groups, the more their attention is directed toward ostensibly different ideas or behaviors that they might integrate, or see others integrate, into new cultural forms.

However, there is more to the story than just weak ties as sources of novelty or innovation in the context of fission-fusion oscillation. Weak-ties have a downside, namely, that they are weak.

Because weak ties span potentially quite distinct groups, weak-tied people (or subgroups) may experience a "lack of trust, an unwillingness to share benefits, or a limited ability to understand one another" (Larson, 2017). Others have pointed out that if the rate of interaction is lower between weak-tie contacts, relative to strong-tie contacts, less total information will tend to be transmitted in the former compared to the latter (Aral and Van Alstyne, 2011). The fidelity of this transmission may be lower as well, because individuals may fail to communicate their group's behaviors or ideas in a way that seems relevant to their weak-tie friends.

For Sinan Aral and Marshall Van Alstyne (2011), a low rate of interaction and a low fidelity of information transfer are more likely in weak-tie relationships because these tend to be more demographically or ideologically diverse relative to strong ties. They call this the "diversity-bandwidth tradeoff": as differences between people increase, trust and mutual understanding become harder to establish and maintain, and thus the bandwidth (i.e., total amount) of transferred information is often smaller. Weak ties, then, while potentially great sources of creativity and novelty, may actually be low-bandwidth channels of information if individuals (or subgroups) believe themselves to be too distinct from one another behaviorally or ideologically. Strong ties might transmit redundant information over time due to high rates of exposure, but they also transmit a lot of total information. The tradeoff is that, though weak ties will tend to transmit less redundant information, they may also tend to transmit less total information across interactions.

Overall, weak ties will tend not to be generative of creative insight or innovation when opportunities for cross-group interactions are few in number or when people are parochial in their information-sharing (as, for example, in social environments with a high level of historical conflict between groups). Nevertheless, if individuals are motivated to associate and interact with outgroup members, weak ties are indeed a key ingredient in the stimulation of novelty and creativity (Larson, 2017).

I have spent my time here discussing the group-level drivers of innovation, but we mustn't lose sight of the reality that individuals are, in the end, the ones *expressing* innovative insights, even if the engine generating such insights is the fission–fusion oscillation of which the individuals are a mere part. How can we, then, understand these dynamics using the language of individual expression? We would do it thusly: the subjective contents of individuals' minds are arrayed along a probability distribution, what physicists might call a "wave function" of fluctuating probabilities. Good (/helpful/insightful/adaptive) innovative ideas will be rarer than noninnovative ideas or bad innovative ideas, but there is still some fluctuating probability associated with any one individual expressing a good innovative idea. What, then, raises the probability of good innovative ideas being expressed? Perhaps, given what we've discussed so far, the answer is now obvious: the probability distribution associated with an individual expressing a good innovative idea is determined by the existing (at t_0) probabilities associated with that individual expressing a particular attitude, value, or behavior weighted by that individual's rate of fluctuation into relatively fused states (or trajectory toward fused states) and fissioned states (or trajectory toward fissioned states).

In other words, innovative potential at the individual level is a function of a person's existing subjectivity and the degree to which that subjectivity is challenged or reinforced within groups as well as reflected on and changed when free of group influence. This dancing oscillation in open-system fission–fusion systems facilitates the breaking apart, rejoining, and discarding of the components of individuals' subjectivities. Of course, even still, the possibility of innovation is low, since this breaking apart, rejoining, and discarding of subjective states is always and only probabilistic, and probabilities, by their nature, do not favor rare outcomes however beautiful or needed they might be.

3.2 Combination, Recombination

We might say that *combination* is what occurs when individuals who are not familiar (i.e., people who do not know one another, people who do not have a pre-existing rapport with one another) and/or not similar (people who do not share behaviors or cognitive representations) aggregate or share attentional allocation with one another for a period of time. *Recombination* is the opposite—recombination occurs when people who are familiar or similar to one another reconvene or reaggregate.

Fusion states, then, are some admixture of combination and/or recombination. Combination and recombination, as discussed here, are, of course, theoretical ideal types; in practice, one existing group member with similar characteristics to others in their group might bring a friend to join, who is unfamiliar to the others and perhaps different in their worldview. This would constitute an mixture of recombination (the existing group member reconvening with their groupmates) and combination (the existing group member's friend who comes to a group event, despite being unfamiliar and, perhaps, dissimilar to other group members).

Combination and recombination are different forms of fusion; they are analytically distinct, even if they occur together often in practice. Recombination is most common in small-population, homogeneous environments (i.e., a rural town), where people know one another and share worldviews. Combination is most common in larger, heterogeneous environments (i.e., an urban metroplex), where people might gather for a public event despite not knowing one another, or having various worldviews. However, even in a large, heterogeneous environment, there will be spaces defined with strict boundaries—even in a cosmopolitan metroplex a person can attend a private gym or private school, which will ensure that more recombination than combination occurs.

Relative to recombination, combination may be a greater generator of innovation, on account of the fact that people who are unfamiliar or dissimilar are aggregating and interacting. This unfamiliarity and dissimilarity can be a source of perceptual novelty, uncertainty, and unpredictability in interactions that, while potentially taxing individuals' cognitive load, are optimal for the production of new insights, compromises, and innovations. Recombination, by contrast, harbors relatively less potential for innovation, because the individuals aggregating are already to some extent similar or familiar with one another's behaviors or ideas; interactions and conversations are more likely to be redundant if, albeit, potentially more comfortable and easier to engage in.

Now, if it is the case (as it seems to be) that heterogeneous interactions tend to have lower information bandwidth, because human beings have preferences for homophily, then this simply means that innovation (particularly, beneficial forms of innovation) will be unusual and rare. Yet, even if information bandwidth is low among dissimilar or unfamiliar interaction partners, the probability of innovation can still rise if societies become increasingly interlinked/globalized and urbanized, given that social networks in such societies will reflect this pluralism (Bruce, 2011). Does this mean that inter-societal exchanges and the growth of cities will cause peoples' social networks to be composed more and more of weak ties (and only highly curated strong ties)? This would be my contention, but more on this later.

Let's look at how these combinatory/recombinatory processes might operate. First, we need to specify the constituent components of a fused state. To do so, I integrate work on the "core design principles" of cooperating animal groups (Wilson et al., 2013) with work specifying the "design constraints" of large colony-esque "macro"-societies (Machalek, 1992; Turner and Machalek, 2018). To begin, let's consider the combinatory and recombinatory processes operating in fused groups, of any size, before considering such mechanisms at the macro-societal level.

The real challenge, and the most fundamental requirement, of maintaining a fused state is *managing a common pool of resources* that individuals (or subgroups) have access to by virtue of their group membership. A common pool of resources is important for sustaining the group *as a group*, yet, being resources, they are valuable and thus must be apportioned in a way that is not frivolous. Humans (and to various degrees, other social animals) accomplish this by forming and maintaining the following (adapted from Wilson et al., 2013):

1 defined, albeit often porous, group boundaries and autonomous (or, at least, semiautonomous) group-level decision-making;
2 formal or informal rules specifying rewards and punishments;
3 formal or informal rules facilitating communication between group members about the organization of the group; and
4 formal or informal rules associated with the resolution of conflict.

When I say that (1)–(4) are formed and maintained so as to sustain group coordination, I do not necessarily mean that they are formed and maintained consciously, as a result of some formal committee. This may be the case, especially in very large societies reliant on bureaucracies. Typically, the formation and maintenance of (1)–(4) will result from a mix of overt collective intentions, shared intuitive habits or routines, and, potentially, direction from charismatic high-status individuals in the group.

With regard to (1), a basic prerequisite for fusion into a group is that constituent individuals (or subgroups) delineate that a group, in fact, exists, with (potentially porous) boundaries. This delineation of "we-ness" or "groupness" subsequently enables influential individuals or leadership to express decision-making at the group level, as what "the group" wants or needs as distinct from what particular individuals (or subgroups) might want and as distinct from what superordinate groups might demand.

When people with pre-existing familiarity or who share physical or ideological similarities re-establish group boundaries (i.e., "recombination"), they may draw on their existing symbolic repertoire of worldview, behavior, or appearance, in order to make group boundary establishment easier. For example, when a group of individuals who were part of a hiking club disperse during the winter season because it is too cold to hike, when they reconvene in the summer, they may still be wearing similar gear (i.e., hiking shoes or backpacks that they all bought together) and can draw on past shared interactions (i.e., the experience of a particularly tough overnight hike) to re-establish the sense of "we-ness" marking group boundaries.

In contrast to the situation of recombination, in cases of combination, individuals (or subgroups) may not be able to draw as readily on similarity or familiarity to establish group boundaries. In this case, people will need to interact with one another directly (face to face or virtually) to determine what aspects of others' identities, personalities, experiences, or other group affiliations are most salient in the aggregate, and from which a new, composite, group boundary might be drawn.

Let's return to the hiking group example, but imagine it as a case of combination instead of recombination. Suppose that an online post specifies the time and place for the first meeting of a new proposed hiking group. The person posting online has no idea who will show up, though they can be reasonably certain that whoever shows up has some interest in hiking (though we cannot take even this for granted—people quite out of shape or quite uninterested in hiking might show up out of pure curiosity or due to a lack of awareness of their own interests). At this inaugural meeting, people will need to interact with one another to establish a sense of what identities, personalities, experiences, or other group affiliations are common among those who showed up, which will lead to Bayesian inferences (likely made subliminally) about what this new aggregate has in common, and what they might not. If there is insufficient overlap in peoples' identities, personalities, experiences, or other group affiliations, a collective focus of attention on the goal of "forming a hiking group" might not be sustained; in this case, no sustained fusion occurs. On the other hand, if there is sufficient overlap in peoples' identities, personalities, experiences, or other group affiliations, then individuals will be more likely to maintain a collective focus of attention on delineating the group boundary "we-ness" of a new hiking group. The longer the collective focus of attention on creating a new hiking group, the more likely certain group exemplars are to emerge who can take on leadership roles that help further define the particular beliefs and behaviors associated with the establishment of this new hiking group.

What influences the degree to which people perceive one another as similar? A sense of similarity to others might be perceived on account of the pre-existing distribution of resources in a society. In particular, individuals who share demographic similarities (e.g., race, sex, age, formal educational attainment, income) may be more likely to also share worldviews and expectations about what belief and behavior is correct / socially acceptable or incorrect / socially unacceptable. This is due to the fact that demographic characteristics in society, particularly large societies, are often highly correlated with economic outcomes (Blau, 1986; 1994; Blau and Schwartz, 1997) and because the perceived availability of economic opportunity constrains how people learn to value or appreciate different forms of art, food, entertainment, politics, and other forms of culture (Bourdieu, 1977; 1984; [1980] 1990). For example, if racial categories are correlated with income or wealth in a country, this will constrain where individuals are likely to live, what foods they enjoy eating, what music they enjoy listening to, or what "feels true" in political life. In short, people's intuitions about what cultural forms are "good" or "bad" are shaped, in part, by their existing demographic or subgroup locations in the larger superordinate society.

A shared "habitus," to borrow Pierre Bourdieu's ([1980] 1990) term referring to the embodiment of culture (e.g., the correlation between economic class and intuitions about which music is believed to "sound best" or what food is believed to "taste best" or what political configuration "works best," and so on), will aid a group in the establishment of all points (1)–(4) above. Sharing a habitus can facilitate agreement between fused entities with regard to (a) what symbols, beliefs, or behaviors ought to delineate group boundaries, (b) what beliefs and behaviors are acceptable/good or unacceptable/bad and how the former can be incentivized and the latter disincentivized, (c) how people should communicate with one another in the group, and what forms of communication (e.g., up or down hierarchies) are appropriate, and (d) how disputes should be resolved.

In short, shared location in the economic structure of a larger society confers similarities in intuitions about culture, which can facilitate the re-establishment of a group among familiar people or the establishment of a new group among demographically similar but unfamiliar people. These shared intuitions about culture might be expressed in various ways: as beliefs, intentions, behaviors, emotions, group affiliations, languages/jargon, adornments, and other material goods, past experiences, or personalities (Goffman, 1959; Collins, 2004; Turner, 2010).

With regard to point (2) above, compared to combining groups, recombining groups may have less interpersonal disagreement to manage when it comes to collective decision-making about what group behavior is acceptable and unacceptable. The tradeoff, though, is that combining groups may, as a result, develop clearer and more flexible conflict-resolution mechanisms. Norms specifying rewards and punishments may, therefore, be more efficient or less damaging in combining groups relative to recombining groups—this is akin to the distinction between inefficient, damaging retributive punishment and more flexible and efficient restitutive punishment described by Émile Durkheim ([1893] 2014).

With regard to points (3) and (4) above, any aggregation of individuals will reveal inequalities in power (ability to coerce others) or status (prestige associated with skills/occupation or identity). Given that individuals (and subgroups) have general preferences to align themselves with others who are socially influential (Carr et al., 2014), and given that those higher in power or status often serve as information and resource brokers in networks (Emerson, 1962), this means that communication will be canalized—influential people will tend to be in greater demand as communication partners relative to less influential people.

In recombining groups, then, norms facilitating communication between group members up and down power and status hierarchies may be re-established more easily, on account of past acknowledgments of differences in status and power between individuals (or subgroups). Insofar as individuals in the group share cultural intuitions, there may also be easier agreement about what "counts" as an important skill or whether powerful (i.e., coercive) individuals ought to be adhered to.

Put differently, recombining individuals (or sub-groups) may be more willing to put up with coercion from ingroup leadership because, though nobody likes being coerced, the logic/justifications used by the coercive person may seem more plausible/intuitive/understandable in groups that are already familiar or otherwise aligned demographically or ideologically. In more diverse or less familiar collectives, on the other hand, people may feel more comfortable dissenting or disagreeing about values, goals, relevant experiences, and, perhaps especially, the structure of the ingroup hierarchy—in these settings, the identification of individuals with plainly valuable skills can confer greater influence (and canalize communication more effectively) than will an individual attempting to coerce others who do not know them, or who do not share their particular demographics our outlooks. Nevertheless, even in highly familiar or similar groups, coercion will have its limits—humans enjoy their autonomy and are sensitive to the distribution of resources and influence within a group—so if other groups are available to be joined that appear less coercive, individuals may jump ship.

Large human groupings, such as societies, are not easy to sustain because they require interaction and, sometimes, collaboration with others one does not know personally. Accordingly, combination and recombination in larger groups, as opposed to smaller groups, rests on additional factors:

1 "Individuals must be able to engage in interpersonal cooperation with strangers";
2 "Individual members of society must be divided among distinct (potentially overlapping) categories, each of which engages in a specialized activity"; and
3 "Individuals at each point in the division of labor must be integrated into a larger social whole" (Turner and Machalek, 2018, pg. 409; see also Machalek, 1992).

These factors become particularly important when familiarity drops away and we consider how individuals (and subgroups) can coordinate with others socially when they know them only as "members of my society" in an abstract sense. The problem for very large groups, like societies, is: how do individuals (or subgroups) facilitate fused states with completely unfamiliar but symbolically similar others (*recombination*) as well as with completely unfamiliar and symbolically dissimilar others (*combination*)?

As Mark Moffett (2013; 2019) explains, chimpanzees are quite unlike human beings in that they struggle (in the wild) to interact with complete strangers without becoming emotionally overaroused and violent. The clearest example of human uniqueness (relative to chimps), for Moffett, is our ability to walk into a coffee shop and interact with a number of anonymous others (people waiting in front of you in line, the cashier, the person making your coffee) in a way that is quite cooperative, even if only in an instrumental sense (you want coffee; they want your money). It's also possible that you strike up a conversation with the cashier, come to find out you are both students at the same university, and decide to keep in contact.

The point is this: unlike most other animals, people in a society rarely fear those they do not know. They certainly can—consider wartime scenarios when a soldier from one country trespasses into the defended territory of his enemies—but this example simply highlights the salient point that humans can form themselves into aggressive tribes/platoons/groups under conditions of threat and uncertainty. Yet when conditions of threat and danger are lower, people can also decide to extend their symbolic understandings of "we-ness" to those who are unfamiliar, thus including them in a shared superordinate group, reducing anxiety and the potential for conflict (Machalek, 1992; Moffett, 2013).

Justin Lane (2018) distinguishes between *relational ties*, which exist between familiar others who've shared experiences, and *conceptual ties*, which involve internalizing a symbolic representation of who belongs in one's group writ large, including potentially unfamiliar, anonymous others. The former relies on episodic memory (i.e., recalling past, shared, emotionally salient experiences), whereas the latter relies more on semantic memory (i.e., recalling what symbolic identifiers mean or what group norms are important).

The human brain has difficulty processing social obligations to more than about 150 people (Dunbar, 2014), but because humans can group others according to their symbolic identifiers (e.g., as citizens or as members of this or that occupation), the number of actual people who can be considered members of the same society is potentially infinite (Dunbar, 1993; Moffett, 2013). For example, insofar as I have an understanding of the marker "American," and some set of civic criteria and symbols/behaviors for what counts as "American," this identity can be extended to hundreds of millions of people and beyond. Identities and ideological or behavioral cultural markers need not be complex—in fact, the more diffuse and vague they are, the more effective they will be (up to the point that their broadness confers no meaning at all) in integrating mass numbers of people—they need only to serve as symbolic placeholders designating superordinate group membership.

There are of course many, many identity "markers" circulating in a society. I focus below, somewhat arbitrarily, on what I regard to be the most salient to humans' capacity to interact with unfamiliar others in very large, anonymous societies: a national identity and an economic identity, both of which contain presumed (broadly shared, course-grained) ideologies and behaviors. A national identity signifies the largest possible superordinate group membership, that is, the most generic possible shared beliefs or behaviors. People can be members of multiple nations insofar as they allocate the attention necessary to adapt their beliefs and behaviors to the prototypical norms of the new cultures. And, the actual content of a national identity can be minimal; what is it that I, for example, share with other people I regard as American? Not much. I can maybe presume they are proficient in English (but not necessarily), I can perhaps presume they will know to shake my hand if I extend it, that they know what a hamburger is, and so on, but, if nothing else, I can presume that they harbor no hostility or ill will toward me by virtue of my nationality.

Economic identities signify, again in the broadest sense, what it is a person (or subgroup) *does* in terms of contributions to society—the clearest examples are occupational role identities. A shared national identity implies some degree of shared access to some group resources, whether these are parks, museums, community centers, schools, county hospitals, or other public spaces. A broad occupational role identity immediately, and with maximal abstraction, contextualizes an individual (or subgroup) relative to their contribution to the "resource commons" of society (Ostrom et al., 2002; an idea found in Durkheim [1893] 2014). It is no coincidence that, in polite conversation, the query "what do you do for a living?" is so ubiquitous and incessant. It is, in fact, a primary means of coordinating with one another in massive anonymous societies.

National and economic identities are examples of how humans symbolically represent a fused state of "we-ness" in a maximally abstract sense. The anonymous individuals around us, those we talk to getting coffee, or walk past on the sidewalk, or sit next to on the train, or interact with in class are individuals we assume to be members of our society(ies) and current (or potential) workers who, at least to some extent and even if only indirectly, contribute to the common pool of resources we rely on. With these basic assumptions, enough preliminary "culture" is shared to reduce anxiety and the potential for conflict, raising the degree of opportunity and motivation for sustained attention and interaction among unfamiliar, anonymous, individuals (or subgroups).

3.3 Fusion Occurs across Levels of Contact

In order to further theorize these processes, we should distinguish between the levels of contact that individuals (or subgroups) might experience. We can specify three levels of contact: awareness, surface contact and mutuality (Finkel et al., 2015). Figure 3.1 depicts these levels of contact.

Consider first, awareness. Awareness, I suggest, comes in two subtypes: "focused" and "unfocused" (here, I am drawing from, and modifying slightly, Goffman, 1961). Focused awareness occurs when an individual (or subgroup) directs their attention to certain others in their environment but does not interact with them. This might happen on a bus when a man sits

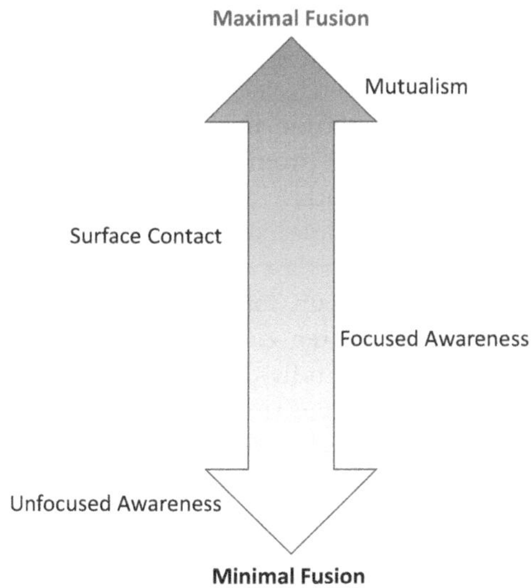

Figure 3.1 Continuum of Fusion and Emotional Energy

across from another man or woman that he eyes, but does not speak with. At a group-level, this might occur when one group gathers information about another group but does not interact with members of that group. In an internet context, focused awareness might occur when an email/message is sent, and read by another party, but not responded to; another example would be noticing a new person on a group video chat, but not interacting with them.

Unfocused awareness, on the other hand, occurs when people register only co-presence, but do not attend much (if at all) to others around them, and do not at any point interact. This would happen on a crowded bullet train, where you can feel or see people around you, but do not stop to allocate attention to any one person. In a group context, this might involve becoming aware that there are various hiking (or art, exercise, etc.) groups in the neighborhood, but not inquiring further about the structure or particular interests of any particular group. In an internet context, this might involve scrolling through the authors or titles of opinion articles, but not clicking on any one link to any one article.

The distinction I want to make between focused and unfocused awareness is that of the degree of attentional allocation. Attentional allocation to others is, by definition, relatively lower in encounters with unfocused awareness than in encounters with a more focused awareness. But, "awareness," both focused and unfocused, accounts for much of our experience with totally anonymous, unfamiliar individuals on a daily basis.

The next level of contact to consider is surface contact. This is an elaboration of focused awareness—if attentional allocation is sustained long enough for an actual interaction to occur, we have surface contact. This might involve a casual conversation between individuals, an invitation to attend a business meeting sent from one group to another, or a set of exchanged emails/messages. Surface contact varies in its level of intimacy—conversations, for example, can be more or less emotional and personal. Surface contact might last for a train ride, a week, a year, or indefinitely—people can maintain long-term relationships at merely the level of surface contact. We often call these acquaintanceships, and sustained surface contact between individuals or groups can be understood as a common form of weak-tie connection (Aral and Van Alstyne, 2011).

If surface contact is maintained, and individuals share salient similarities in goals, personality, identity, worldview, behavior, or other group affiliations, then we might see the third level of contact: mutualism. This level of contact, as I am using it here, is akin to Edward Lawler's "joint productive exchanges," where individuals (or subgroups) work toward a common goal larger than each could easily achieve on their own (Lawler et al., 2008; Lawler et al., 2009). Mutualism can be found, to varying degrees, in partnerships, alliances, teams, and task groups.

Fused states constituted by no more than co-presence, or mere awareness, are very common occurrences in human societies and very fundamentally important for the maintenance of cooperation and cohesion. They are constant, small, reminders that others around us, whom we do not know, harbor no malicious intent. I mention this here because this form of interaction will become very important when we consider, later, the rise of urbanization, mass transit, and other ways that humans aggregate in large anonymous numbers. The point is that *not all fused states are intentional groupings*. A mass of people moving about on 5th Avenue in Manhattan are fused in the sense of being co-present and/or allocating (some level) of attention to one another (otherwise, they'd walk into each other constantly on the sidewalk!). This is, admittedly a nascent state of fusion, one which requires very little from people. But, it is a state of fusion nonetheless, and making fine-grained distinctions in possible fusion states is expressly the purpose of this section.

Fused states constituted by surface contact are also very common; think of everything from short conversations to the consistent, if intermittent, comingling of employees from different companies at biannual conferences. Depending on how long the surface contact is maintained, the individuals (or subgroups) involved may come to define themselves with certain labels or symbols, or think of themselves as a group or collective.

A sense of "we-ness" will be far more common, however, in fused states constituted by mutualism. Mutualism occurs when individuals interact with one another cooperatively to accomplish a goal that would be difficult or impossible to accomplish by one's (or one's subgroup's) efforts alone. As Lawler and his colleagues have shown experimentally, mutualistic exchange with others, wherein individuals—or subgroups—jointly contribute to a collective goal, can produce positive emotions which are then attributed to the collective (Lawler et al., 2000; Thye et al., 2019). What happens is that, assuming sharedness of contributions is high enough, individuals (or subgroups) begin to have a hard time distinguishing their personal contribution to collective goals goods from the contributions of others, and, over time and as a result of this, individuals (or subgroups) begin attributing any positive emotions associated with progress toward goals/goods to the group (or group collective) itself, as opposed to one or another of its constituent members.

Fused states, then, can occur at the level of awareness (both unfocused and focused), surface contact, or mutualism. Given this, we cannot only think of fusion in terms of intentional, goal-oriented groupings of individuals; fusion is more than mutualism. Just as important, we must conceptualize combination and recombination in terms of successive levels of contact. Any combining or recombining of individuals (or subgroups), regardless of how familiar they are with one another or how demographically or ideologically similar they are with one another, will tend to move successively through these levels of contact.

Consider, for example, a pair of individuals who have not seen one another in a long time, but have built a rapport with one another in the past, and who share a lot of political views in common. If these individuals recombine into a grouping, they will, of course, have to first become aware of the presence of one another (the awareness level), engage in some sort of shared attention and interaction (the surface contact level), and, potentially, begin synchronizing their behavior in a way that generates shared group resources or makes progress toward shared goals (the mutualism level). Just the same, individuals (or subgroups) who've never met or interacted in the past and who share few if any demographic or ideological traits will still need to pass successively through levels of contact if they are to fuse into an intentional group—they will need to become aware of one another, attend to and interact with one another, and, potentially, coordinate and synchronize behaviors in pursuit of resources and group goals.

There will still be unique challenges associated with successively passing through levels of contact in cases of combination (relative to recombination). When parties to an aggregation are more similar or familiar, movement from the level of awareness, through surface contact, to mutualism may occur quite quickly. Interactions may be easier to initiate when entities are homophilous because cognitive resources are less taxed with the need to (a) process presumed (or actual) differences between people (or subgroups); and (b) adjust to perceived expectations or assumptions regarding the belief or behavior associated with these differences (Kilduff and Krackhardt, 2008).

In combining groups, the more individuals (or subgroups) differ from one another, or are less familiar, the more they will rely on stereotypes and intuitions to guide social interactions (Macrae and Bodenhausen, 2000), and this can increase the potential for conflict and dissolution insofar as these stereotypes are untrue or discriminatory (for a suggestive analysis, see Marineau and Krishnakumar, 2014). Difference and unfamiliarity increase the total amount of social information to be processed, and so the brain tends to shift to a more heuristic/stereotypic processing of interactions with others, "because under conditions of cognitive load less resources are available to reflect on a decision, which makes analytical processing more difficult and leads to using cognitive shortcuts" (Samson and Kostyszyn, 2015).

Sometimes this can be efficient, for example, when stereotypes are accurate (Ryan, 2003). But often, especially in a highly diverse social ecology, reliance on stereotypes will lead to rote, short, uncomfortable interactions. The mere presence of difference or unfamiliarity, to the degree that it increases the brain's processing burden, will also decrease performance of the social skills necessary to sustain attention or interaction (Samson and Kostyszyn, 2015). We can expect this effect to be even more substantial when people perceive their outside natural or social environment to be threatening, because concern about threat is itself taxing to our cognition and nervous system. Thus, social unfamiliarity or dissimilarity in a threatening circumstance is maximally burdensome to the brain's information processing capacities, leading to even greater overreliance on heuristic/stereotype shortcuts and a substantial risk of conflict.

Also, as a compliment to the (potential) progression from awareness to surface contact to mutualism, we should consider the opposite progression from mutualism to surface contact to awareness for those groups that are fissioning. The complement to combination and recombination processes are *disaggregating processes* whereby individuals (or subgroups) gradually or suddenly reduce their rate of co-presence or shared attentional allocation. Disaggregating processes might run from awareness to surface contact, back to awareness, to lack of any awareness (think of a person who has a short conversation with an anonymous person at a bar before getting up and walking away). Or, they might occur more slowly, as when individuals (or subgroups) move from awareness through to a sustained collaborative mutualism that becomes interspersed with increasingly long periods of mere surface contact (think of two companies collaborating full-time on a project, but only nine months, then six months, then three months out of the year). Groups combine and recombine, but they also disaggregate (both physically and attentionally), and they do so at varying speeds and for varying durations. If disaggregation occurs for long enough and the beliefs and behaviors of individuals (or subgroups) become sufficiently distinct from one another, *there may be little possibility of recombination*.

3.4 Open and Closed Fission–Fusion Oscillation

Fission–fusion oscillation can occur in relatively more open or relatively more closed contexts.

Open contexts are those with more porous, or flexible, boundaries. In open contexts, group membership is either easy to obtain or open to be negotiated. Closed contexts are those with more restricted or policed boundaries. In open contexts, the flow of people and information into and out of the group will be less restricted and regulated. In closed contexts, the flow of people and information will be more restricted and regulated.

Oscillation in more open contexts slows the rate at which constituent units will perceive familiarity and similarity, but, over time, these contexts tend to contain more diversity, novelty, and potential for innovation. Familiar, homogeneous groups, then, are both an outcome and an indicator of a closed context. Heterogeneous groups are both an outcome and an indicator of an (relatively more) open context.

And, similar to the process of combination discussed above, in more open contexts group deliberation and decision-making is likely to be more complex, require more self-control, and contain more conflict because of the relatively higher rate of circulation of potentially unfamiliar and dissimilar individuals moving into and out of the group. Open contexts facilitate what Ayelet Shavit and colleagues (2017) call "pluralistic deliberation," which, again, generates greater novelty and adaptive problem-solving, but comes with a greater potential for disagreement and fissioning due to frustration or conflict. Conversely, and similar to the process of recombination discussed above, in more closed contexts group deliberation will tend to take place between people who are (relatively) more familiar or similar and, thus, closed contexts will tend to be less culturally complex and will tend to contain individuals (or subgroups) more reliant will tend to contain individuals (or subgroups) more reliant on intuitions about appropriate ideas and behavior stemming from participants' shared habitus.

Past work in sociology suggests that the more familiar and similar members of a group are, the more likely they are to have closed or restricted boundaries (e.g., Iannaccone, 1994). This is because shared worldviews, and the behaviors associated with those worldviews, may make outsiders appear *too* different and therefore potentially threatening (Collins, 2016). Symmetrically, this suggests that the more unfamiliar or dissimilar members of a group are, the more likely they are to develop porous group boundaries. In groups characterized by "pluralistic deliberation," outsiders (and their possibly unusual opinions) will not appear as threatening and may be more often valued as potential contributors to the group's decision-making processes.

3.5 Fission–Fusion Symmetry

There is a certain geometry to the fissioning–fusing process. When a group fissions, it is not necessarily the case that each constituent member (be they individuals or subgroups) disperses to an equal degree—that is, groups do not necessarily fission symmetrically. In the case of a pandemic, a country might quarantine some districts, but not others, effectively fissioning off some areas from the broader collective. Or, as another example, a business strained financially might lay off only some, but not all, of its workers. In both cases, fissioning is asymmetrical, with some individuals (or subgroups) dispersing but others remaining in relative states of aggregation. Or, consider that migrant assimilation into a country is always uneven—those migrants with more network contacts in the host country may be more easily absorbed into the host country's economy (Facchini et al., 2015; Vacca et al., 2018; see also Pescosolido, 1986). In this latter case, it is the fusion into the group that is asymmetrical.

When I describe "fission states" or "fusion states," I am describing increasing or decreasing variation in proximity, attention or intention—no perfectly symmetrical state of fusion or fission is implied. In a state of fusion, some will be more co-present than others, or will share more attentional allocation than others. Similarly, in a fissioned state, some will be less co-present than others or will share less attentional allocation than others. Consider two people in a relatively fissioned state: one might engage in more surface contact with certain others, despite being temporarily disaggregated from the larger collective. Or, consider two people in a fused state: one might engage in less surface contact with certain others, despite being aggregated.

While fused states are defined by relative increases in co-presence or attentional allocation, this does not imply that all entities party to a fused state are necessarily equal in co-presence or attentional allocation. And, while fissioned states are defined by their relative decreases in co-presence or attentional allocation, this does not imply that all dispersed entities are necessarily equally dispersed (physically or attentionally).

3.6 Fission–Fusion and the Perception of Threat/Danger

I am intending to follow a large body of work (e.g., Spencer 1897; Staw et al., 1981; Baumeister et al., 2001; Turner, 2010a; 2010b; Gelfand et al., 2017; Gelfand, 2019; Collins 2004; 2016) when I interpret the relationship between threat perception and fission–fusion oscillation. I touched on this issue in the last chapter, but now it is time for a bit more depth.

The perception of threat is influential to human behavior because when people perceive survival or flourishing to be more challenging, they will tend to be more motivated to embed themselves in groups as a means of effective defense or offense. If people feel threatened, but do not feel their survival or opportunities to self-actualize are in jeopardy, they might just be waiting in line to ride a scary roller coaster, or about to watch a horror movie. Fear of survival and reduced opportunities for flourishing (self-understanding, self-expression, upward mobility, etc.) are where the theoretical rubber meets the road. This point of view presumes that the brain and body are evolved to be sensitive to changes in the likelihood of survival and in opportunities for (individual or group) flourishing. In keeping with evolutionary theory, I further presume here that, specifically, the most influential forms of threat perception will involve concerns that basic economic, reproductive, or childcare conditions are changing in ways that seem either survival-threatening (extreme cases) or nonoptimal (less extreme cases).

Threats can be exogenous or endogenous to a group. Generally, if the source of threat is identified as exogenous to the group, support for ingroup leadership and hierarchy rises, and individuals (or subgroups) experience greater pressures for conformity (Staw et al., 1981). On the other hand, if the source of threat is attributed to dynamics (or individuals) internal to the group, the leadership/hierarchy may become unstable and individuals will feel less pressure to conform to group norms, leading the group to fission. See Figure 3.2 for a depiction of some of these endogenous and exogenous sources of threat.

The threats depicted in Figure 3.2 are not exhaustive of the possible threats perceived to be bearing down on people. Figure 3.2 does, however, depict some of the most important threats, and the point is that these threats vary in their exogeneity and endogeneity. Some threats originate (more or less) from within a society, such as the breakdown of infrastructure and technology used for extracting resources from the natural environment. Other basic internal concerns include population size and density, civil rights abuses, civil war deaths, and levels of inequality.

Other threats originate (more or less) externally. Threats such as those stemming from natural disasters (hurricanes, tsunamis, earthquakes, droughts), communicable disease (plague, smallpox, malaria), or from international military conflicts originate at least partially outside of the operations and activities of a single society. Though Figure 3.2 depicts a two-by-two typology, we should not be wedded to the mutual exclusivity of each category—"exogenous" disease, for example, might not be *caused* by the activities of societies, but disease may well spread and become

	Ecology	Social System
Exogenous	(a) Natural disaster (b) Disease (c) Climate change	(a) International military deaths (b) International Trade disputes/sanctions (c) Foreign occupation (d) Immigration/ refugee rate
Endogenous	(a) Natural resource availability (b) Protein supply (c) Fat supply (d) Air quality (e) Water quality	(a) Population size (b) Population density (c) Market crashes (d) Human rights violations (e) Civil war deaths (f) Violent crime rate (g) Infant mortality (h) Inequality (GINI)

Figure 3.2 Commonly Perceived Threats Facing Human Societies

damaging on account of the internal dynamics of a society (e.g., poor water purification leading to cholera outbreaks).

Mobilization under threat involves increasing levels of group integration marked, for example, by (1) relying on information drawn from past experiences (instead of seeking new experiences), (2) reduced attention to peripheral/weak network ties, and (3) an increased tendency to give stereotyped or habituated responses to social stimuli (Staw et al., 1981). These responses are arguably a result of peoples' motivation to habituate to beliefs and behaviors conferring predictability, order and stability (Jost and Hunyady, 2002; Kay et al., 2008; Hogg and Adelman, 2013; Landau et al., 2015).

While there will sometimes be a strong correlation between the perception of a threat and the actual objective existence of that threat, there will not always be much of a correlation—for example, people in the contemporary United States are far more concerned with violence and terrorism than they are with high blood pressure, though the latter is a much more realistic threat for most people. This imbalance in threat perception is due to several factors: death from physical violence often happens more quickly and painfully than does the long-term damage of high blood pressure, and perhaps as a result, journalists disproportionately report on violent relative to nonviolent health risks (see Ritchie, 2019). In trying to understand fission–fusion oscillation, what matters is peoples' *perceptions* of threat more than the actual objective threat. Skewed media (and academic/intelligentsia) portrayals and peoples' own abject ignorance will reduce the accuracy of people's perceptions, yes, but it is these perceptions that nevertheless motivate fusion responses.

Also, the environmental and social conditions (including media reporting) of the recent past, as regards threat perception, will tend to be more emotionally salient due to a pervasive processing bias in human cognition known as the "recency bias." This bias in information-processing is theorized to be a component of a larger processing structure known as availability heuristics, which influence what information is processed in the brain during decision-making tasks. Recency bias in particular appears to occur because "the piece of information that is the last in being presented is also the most easily remembered, and therefore it is usually weighted more heavily than other pieces of information, which can lead to serious errors in many domains" (Blanco, 2017, pg. 4). This means that levels of threat perception at t_{-1} disproportionately influence threat perception at t_0, which, in turn, constrains perception at t_{+1} and so on. This also suggests that even if social or natural conditions become objectively less dangerous, behavioral responses will still be calibrated to past perceptions of threat.

Charles Hermann's (1963) classic analysis specified some conditions under which a threat might be more acute, becoming, as he termed it, a "crisis." A crisis occurs when the threat to survival is substantial and unanticipated and when the time horizon available to act is small. Under crisis conditions, fusion will occur at a much more rapid rate. By contrast, when threat perception is rising more slowly over a longer period, the degree to which individuals (or subgroups) fuse will occur more slowly (especially to the extent that the fusing group is dissimilar or unfamiliar).

Fission and fused states (as with any behavioral states) can, over time, habituate peoples' expectations. The expectations people have about future interactions, after all, develop in accordance with their prior experiences (Berger and Wagner, 2016). As a result of habituation, a shift in oscillation from a period of a certain degree of fissioning to a period of relative fusion might be perceived as threatening because it forces individuals (and subgroups) to navigate changes in personal distancing and attentional demands. Just the same, transitioning from a sustained period of relative fusion to relative fissioning can be seen as threatening—people may experience a sense of being without a home or community (Berger et al., 1974; Bellah et al., 1985). The point is that *the perception of threat can emerge endogenously from the process of fission–fusion oscillation itself*: (1) individuals (or subgroups) habituated to fused states may, especially if they are materially or psychologically vulnerable, be threatened by reductions in co-presence or shared attentional allocation; and conversely (2) individuals (or subgroups) habituated to relative fissioned states may, especially if they are materially or psychologically advantaged or comfortable, be frustrated or angered by social pressures for co-presence or shared attentional allocation.

Let's consider, now, the extremes of threat perception. The perception of very high levels of threat or very low levels of threat has paradoxical effects on fission–fusion oscillation. The relationship between threat and fusion, for example, appears to be curvilinear such that increasing threat perception motivates a relative shift to a fused state, but if threat is too pervasive, unexpected, and overwhelming (like Hermann's crises mentioned above), individuals may not even want to waste time mobilizing a coordinated response (i.e., an "every man/woman for themselves" scenario).

The relationship between fission–fusion oscillation and threat perception is thus curvilinear: at *low* levels of perceived threat, individuals will tend to prefer relative fissioning, while at *moderate–high* levels of threat individuals will tend to prefer relative fusing. However, at *very high* levels of perceived threat, there will be a steady rise in fissioning ("every man/woman for themselves") when the perceived benefits of group coordination are lower than the perceived benefits from pursuing idiosyncratic responses to a crisis. These are conditions that would be regarded as socially hopeless because seeking a coordinated response with others seems, in principle, incapable of adequately addressing the threat.

But what if the perception of threat is very low? There may be persistent negativity and threat biases in the brain's processing of information (even in a utopia, people would clamor on about small slights and injustices; see Baumeister, 2001), but this does not mean that threat will always be perceived as equally imminent, severe, or widespread. Under prolonged conditions of very low threat perception, we would not expect individuals to remain (relatively) fissioned indefinitely. Humans are emotional and tribal, and they're prone to represent reality in terms of good, moral ingroups and bad, immoral outgroups. They construe the world in these terms especially under conditions of threat or uncertainty, but this tribalistic tendency, reliant as it is on persistent, evolved cognitive mechanisms (see Clark and Winegard, 2020), will not simply disappear when threat abates. Rather, it seems that during periods of low threat perception, when individuals (or subgroups) do fuse into aggregates, they will do so only if such groupings require relatively few obligations and little investment from members.

So, under conditions of low threat perception, when people do fuse, they will often aggregate into low-obligation, low-commitment, groupings because during periods of relative resource abundance, stability, and safety there will be less concern for free-riding.

I must make one final point before closing out this section. Institutions and their embedded organizations constitute a "field," or a series of encounters where interpersonal relationships form around explicitly or implicitly shared goals (Martin, 2003). Neil Fligstein and Doug McAdam (2011; 2012; see also Kluttz and Fligstein, 2016), for example, argue that "fields" depend on a set of shared understandings between individuals (or subgroups) about what's at stake, who occupies what position(s), and the rules guiding acceptable beliefs/behaviors. There can be threats to each of these components of an organizational/institutional field. Also, depending on how organizations within institutions dispense resources or opportunities for membership, demographic groups may perceive inequality threats associated with their participation in the organization.

John Martin (2003, pg. 28) describes the social "field" as an "organization of forces" that both facilitate and constrain individual (or subgroup) behavior. Unsurprisingly, the forces I regard as most salient to explaining the emergence and content of culture in institutional and organizational fields are those operating during fission–fusion oscillation. But the particular institutions (and suborganizations) that I regard as most important to the maintenance of a society—that is, the most important fields—are those related to defense and social regulation (modern examples include police, fire, courts, jails/prison), reproduction (e.g., maternal medical care, childcare, schooling), foraging (e.g., occupation, schooling), and recreation (e.g., parks, recreational businesses). I highlight these "fields" because these seem to be core components to the "life-world," to borrow Jürgen Habermas's (1984; 1987) and Alfred Schutz and Thomas Luckman's (1973; 1989) term, of human foragers as well as of ancestral hominins and other primates.

Obviously, organizations within institutions associated with defense and social regulation, reproduction, foraging, and recreation will take on different forms and develop different formal and informal rules. For example, the goals of defense and social regulation (safety, enforcement of cooperative behavior) overlap with, but are not the same as, goals associated with reproduction (childcare, child socialization), which overlap with, but are not the same as, goals associated with foraging (income, resource extraction, occupational attainment), which overlap with, but are not the same as, recreational goals (self-development, play). Consequently, the particular ways that individuals (and subgroups) symbolically represent the transition to fissioned or fused states may differ depending on the field at issue. Threat experienced in the reproductive field, for example, might be represented using different symbols, and may be perceived relative to different goals, than threat experienced in recreational fields. Yet, in either case, moderate-high threat will tend to motivate relative increases in aggregation for purposes of mobilizing a coordinated response.

3.7 Attentional Allocation Does Not Require Physical Co-Presence

It is especially worth noting in the modern era of the internet that the aggregation of attention or intention can occur virtually, not only physically. I have tried, thus far, to make a distinction between aggregation that results from physical co-presence and aggregation that results from shared attentional allocation. This is important, because communication technologies from Morse Code to virtual reality allow non-co-present individuals to attend to the same computerized facsimiles of one another, enabling interaction and, potentially, collaboration across geographic space.

It is possible that face-to-face, physical, co-presence produces a level of emotional energy and anxiety that virtual shared attention does not. Contemporary theorists in sociology mostly theorize in-person interactions. Perhaps best among them is Randall Collins (2004), who draws on Durkheim's ([1912] 2008) concept of "collective effervescence" to describe how sustained co-presence often involves some degree of interaction that, even in the form of conversation, relies on behavioral synchrony (gestures, verbalizations, tones). This synchrony can produce a euphoric anxiety that feels energetic and positive. Behavioral synchronization with others also reduces the neurological encoding of self–other boundaries (Paladino et al., 2010), and if self–other boundaries are consistently reduced in the context of cooperative goal-seeking, a sense of moral community and collective identity—an entitative "we-ness"—can emerge (Lawler et al., 2009).

Yet, becoming a member of a moral community is exciting whether it happens in person or online, and, for that matter, online interactions can also be synchronous and emotionally energizing. I suppose euphoric anxiety, metabolic energy expenditure, and attentional allocation may be higher during face-to-face interactions; Susan Pinker (2015) makes a compelling case about the cruciality of face-to-face contact for social learning and emotional communication.

But there are other aspects to think about. For example, interaction with unfamiliar or dissimilar people might elicit less dysphoric anxiety (for those fearful of certain outgroups) when it is computer-mediated relative to the greater intensity of in-person, face-to-face interaction. On top of this, virtual forms of fusion may involve more and more accurate simulations of physical co-presence as artificial intelligence and the engineering of computer processors and circuits becomes more advanced. It is not inconceivable that computing technology advances to a point where facsimiles of an individual's full physical likeness and sensory stimuli (e.g., smells associated with a person) are projected remotely and virtually.

Assuming a society is materially secure and politically stable, the promiscuous sociality enabled by social media may seem exciting or interesting to people. I may have a hard time making one real, in-person, friend every day, but I can get 50 followers in a single day on Twitter if I am witty (or insufferable) enough. The sort of social-informational promiscuity facilitated by the internet and social media might seem destabilizing to those more familiar with profound economic or social uncertainty. But, for kids growing up today—who will inherit some of the richest, most stable nations thus far known to humankind—the buzzing, blooming excitement of being able to read/view *almost anything* and attempt to communicate (through text, call, or perhaps posted videos) with *almost anyone* via the internet is a delicacy unknown to most humans who've ever lived.

No longer do young people need to go looking for a job—now, they can develop some skill in makeup, videogames, or whatever, post videos of themselves demonstrating the skill, and draw an income from viewers around the world. Or, they can post products they've made to websites like Etsy or Instagram, which serve as more direct virtual marketplaces. I suspect the major flaw in existing sociological theory is to assume that face-to-face contact is always necessary for a genuine sense of social support or belonging. In egregiously rich, comfortable modern nations (compared, of course, to the horticultural and agrarian empires of history), people are more at risk of obesity and boredom than starvation or violence. It is these people who will find promiscuous internet socializing / information-foraging to be distracting, gratifying, and useful; and, being mammals, they'll also tend to forage in groups.

I will be returning to this issue throughout the book. For now, I just want to point out that fusion states needn't necessarily be physically co-present states. The more fundamental criterion is *shared attentional allocation*, which requires the development of sophisticated technological innovations to occur without co-presence.

3.8 Visualizing Fission–Fusion Oscillation as Superimposed Longitudinal and Pseudo-Transverse Waves

Before I offer some abstract visualizations of the fission–fusion process, I want to briefly point out that fission–fusion oscillation can be analyzed cross-sectionally, in periods, or longitudinally.

Cross-sectionally, we can think of a group as being in a relative state of fusion or in a relative state of fission and assess the causes or effects of this state on individual or group information-processing. Regarding period effects, we can think of a group as experiencing spans of relatively consistent (or inconsistent) states. For example, a group may be more likely to fuse or fission for a given stretch of time even if it also experiences intermittent states of both. In this circumstance, we might say that for any time point between period x and period y, individuals (or subgroups) spent 10% more time in a relative state of fusion (or fission) compared to the baseline rates for that group or society.

We might also think of fission–fusion oscillation longitudinally as the overall tempo of the mechanism across time as it affects a group or a society. A longitudinal view of fission–fusion differs from a periodic view only by degree: a periodic view assess cohorts during specific periods, whereas a longitudinal view might assess the entirety of the period of a group's or society's existence (to the extent that available data permit analysis of such a long period). To say, then, that the fission–fusion mechanism operates in terms of cross-sectional, periodic, and longitudinal time scales is just to say that we can consider a specific snapshot of a group's or society's fissioned or fused state or short-term change over blocks of time, or the overall, long-run, average states that a group or society has experienced. In this critically important sense, fission-fusion oscillation is a nested process, having long-run historical effects, potentially punctuated period effects and acute effects.

Now, let's turn to some visualizations that I hope will be helpful. Figure 3.3 through Figure 3.9 represent attempts to visualize the fission–fusion dynamics thus far described. These are not mathematical or even necessarily substantive theoretical models. Rather, they are conceptual models, that is, attempts to visualize general processes to aid sociologists in their particular substantive applications.

In order to visualize these processes, I will be borrowing some helpful terms from physics. I only do this to help us better conceptualize the phenomenon at issue, not because I think sociology should necessarily aspire to be like physics, or that all physical models are useful for modeling social behavior (though some have been found to; check out Bain and Bartolo, 2019). I only borrow some general language and concepts from physics to aid us in conceptualization.

First, let me define a few terms. Below, I will be visualizing fission–fusion in terms of waves. Waves are a very widespread, generic natural structure. We can see them in the ocean, of course, but also in the traveling of sound or light. Most, if not all, forms of energy can be conceptualized as *either* a group of particles (e.g., light photons) or as a wave (e.g., a "beam" of light). Also, some waves must travel through matter, like waves in ocean water, while other waves travel independently of any medium, like light waves.

Waves, then, are a common naturally occurring structure of energy transfer, which (a) often, but not always, rely on a form of matter for their conduction; and (b) sometimes, but not always, manifest themselves in terms of the organization of particles into waves.

There are commonly considered to be two broad types of waves: longitudinal waves (note: different use of the word longitudinal here) and transverse waves. Longitudinal waves are composed of particles revealing different rates of "compression" (particle concentration or increases in

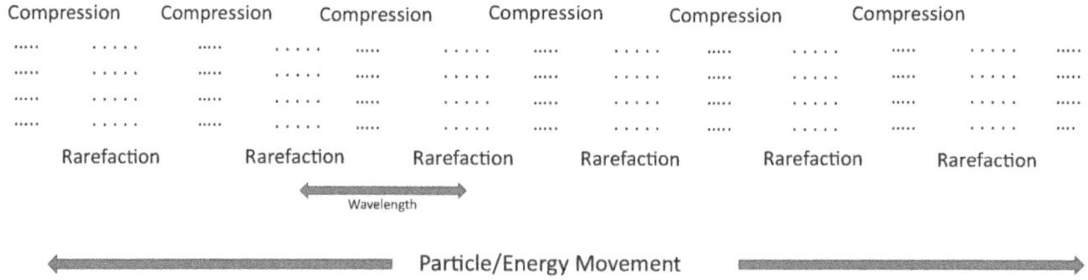

Figure 3.3 Depiction of a Longitudinal Wave

particle density) and "rarefaction" (particle dispersion or decreases in particle density). Figure 3.3 depicts a longitudinal wave visually: particles travel via oscillating compression and rarefaction in one direction or another. Longitudinal waves also have amplitudes (calculated as the maximum increase or decrease in particle density) and wavelengths (calculated as the distance between compressions or rarefactions).

Transverse waves, by contrast, move differently. Whereas particles move in one direction or the other, back and forth, in longitudinal waves, in transverse waves particles are dispersed perpendicular to the flow of energy. Figure 3.4 visualizes an example of a transverse wave. As you can see in the figure, transverse waves have peaks and troughs. This perpendicular, up and down, dispersal is measured in physics as an "amplitude." The distance from peak to peak, or from trough to trough, is the "wavelength."

Now, consider the structure of a longitudinal wave superimposed on a transverse wave, as depicted in Figure 3.5. While longitudinal waves contain particles that only vary in their displacement parallel to the direction of energy flow, I've arbitrarily violated this assumption in the figure and depicted some of the "particles" in the longitudinal wave as

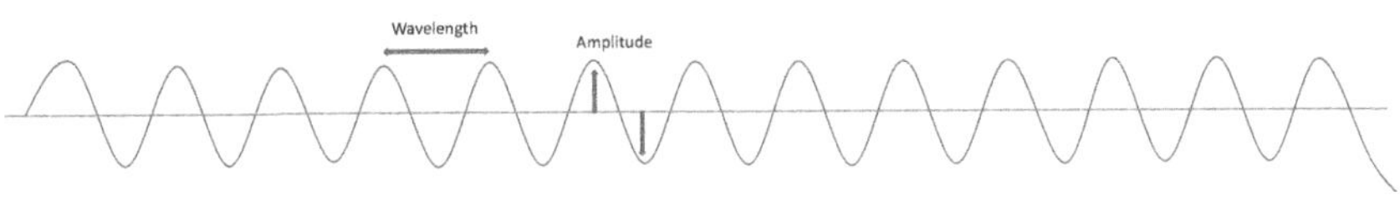

Figure 3.4 Depiction of a Transverse Wave

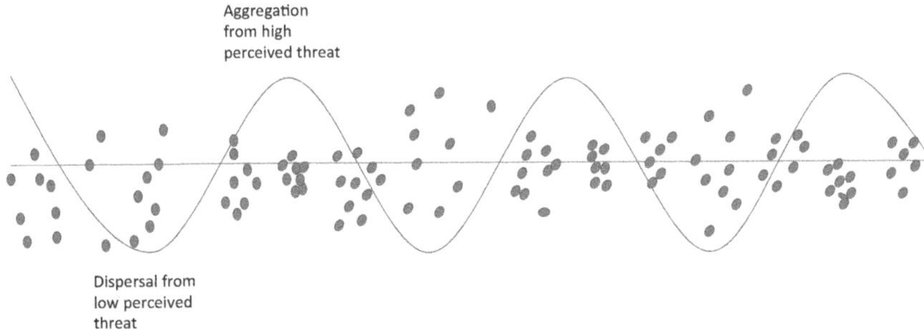

Figure 3.5 Fission-Fusion Mechanism Depicted as Superimposed Transverse and Pseudo-Longitudinal Waves: The Example of Threat Perception

having perpendicular amplitudes. This is because I hope for you to conceptualize the particles here in terms of individual people or subgroups. As depicted, the fused ("compressed") particles vary in two-dimensional space to represent the practical reality that not all fused individuals in a group (or subgroups in a supergroup) are equally co-present or equally attending to one another.

The superimposed transverse/longitudinal waves depicted in Figure 3.5 can help us visualize a couple of important aspects of the operation of the fission–fusion mechanism in human societies.

For one, as I said above, fission (/fusion) states do not imply a symmetry of reduced (/increased) co-presence or attention; some individuals in fission (/fusion) states are more (/less) co-present, or collectively allocating their attention, than others. Just as not all groupings are equally "groupish," not all people acting independently are equally isolated. Second, the transverse wave in Figure 3.5 can help us visualize varying perceptions of, for example, existential threat or inequality threat. Suppose the troughs of this figure represent periods where the perception of threat is low. Under these conditions, physical or attentional dispersion will rise, as denoted by the greater spacing between "particles" (i.e., individuals or subgroups) in the figure. Alternatively, suppose the peaks of the wave in the figure represent periods where the perception of threat is relatively high. Under these conditions, physical or attentional dispersion will lower, as denoted by the greater concentration of "particles."

Let's now consider something a bit different. For both longitudinal and transverse waves, wave "speed" is the distance a wave travels in a specific amount of time. Wave "frequency" is measured by the number of waves that occur in a specific amount of time. Take a look at the high-frequency, high-speed, low-amplitude transverse wave depicted in Figure 3.6. This wave is moving along pretty quickly, covering a lot of space in each wavelength, but the amplitude (dispersion from the bisecting equilibrium line) is very small.

Now, my hope is that this visualization will aid you, the reader, in conceptualizing how perceptions of, for example, existential (physical danger, threats to physical survival) or inequality threat (inequality in income, credentials, housing) might change over time in a society. *Groups do not only fuse*

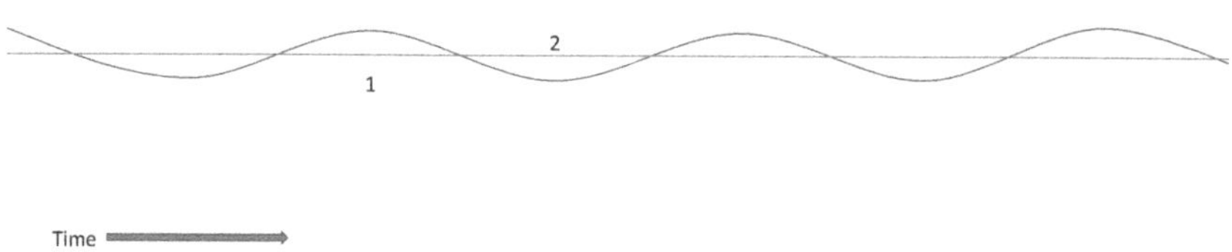

Figure 3.6 Depiction of a High Frequency, High Speed, Low Amplitude Transverse Wave

because of rising perceptions of threat; they also fuse because resources or tasks have become concentrated in space (and therefore require group negotiation and coordination to acquire), and/or because of a desire for intergroup contact as with trade relationships, to share information or to foster emotional bonds. However, I will focus here on the case of fusion under conditions of perceived threat, just to offer a clear example.

So, with this in mind, let's return to the high-frequency, high-speed, low-amplitude transverse wave depicted in Figure 3.6. These figures are simplifications, ideal types, of possible wave forms. But let's suppose the wave in this figure is a depiction of changes in the on-average perception of threat over time. The low amplitude exhibited by point "1" on the figure represents a slight increase in the perception of threat relative to the baseline or average perception of threat in a group of individuals. This amplitude is going to be a function of changes in the average group perception (weighted for higher status individuals) of threat conditions. A low-amplitude increase implies either that the perception of threat, though rising, is small relative to the baseline perception (resulting in little need for increased collective coordination), or that the threat is predictable/expected (resulting either in learned helplessness or an already prepared response).

If conditions are changing in ways that are perceived as threatening, but only slightly more threatening or less predictable than normal, then the fusion response will be slight—group boundaries will become slightly more rigid and defined, hierarchies become slightly more strict, punishments for deviance become slightly stronger, and synchronization and mimicry of behavior within the group becomes slightly more coordinated. All in all, little effort is needed, and little is expended, in responding to changing circumstances. At point "2" in the figure, however, perception of threat is decreasing, or the threat is coming to appear more predictable and controllable. Consequently, the group's boundaries will become slightly less clear, hierarchies slightly less strict; punishments for deviance slightly less strong; and synchronization and mimicry of behavior within the group will become slightly less coordinated. In sum, the wave depicted here in Figure 3.6 represents a slight and stable fission–fusion oscillation over a moderate-long period of time in response to conditions that are perceived to change little or are perceived to be predictable.

Now, consider the high-frequency, low-speed, high-amplitude transverse wave depicted in Figure 3.7. In this wave, dispersion from the baseline or equilibrium point is significant. This wave symbolizes a perception of threat or instability that differs dramatically from period to period and would result in a fission–fusion oscillation that would be very unstable: combination/recombination would take place over a short span of time and would involve the attempted imposition of strong norms by intolerant hierarchies. During less-threatening or more stable periods,

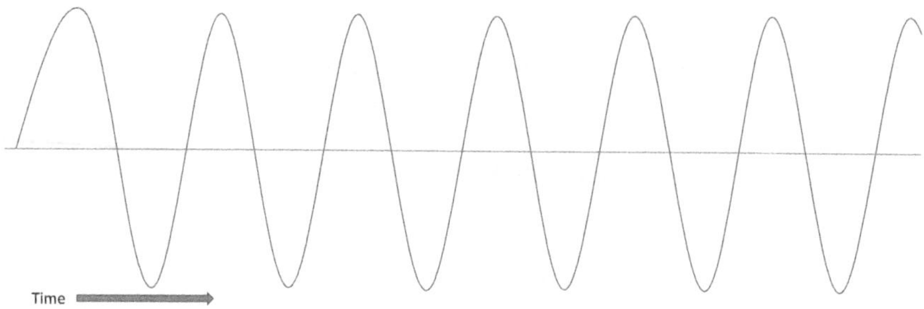

Figure 3.7 Depiction of a High Frequency, Low Speed, High Amplitude Transverse Wave

fissioning would happen quickly (no doubt motivated by the suppression of individuality and suffocating normative restraint stemming from the prior strong fused state) and would involve individuals (or subgroups) pursuing goals or experiences regarded as quite distinct from one another.

A society fusing and fissioning so intensively will be strongly reliant on individuals sharing pre-existing experiences, ideas, or behaviors in common, as this will both facilitate combination and recombination during transition to a fused state as well as facilitate dispersal without risking isolation and alienation from superordinate group identities. The sort of oscillation depicted in Figure 3.7 would be hard for people to manage emotionally, especially with a population diverse in pre-existing experiences, beliefs, or behaviors. The wave depicted in this figure encourages us to consider how societies and states might fail/collapse because the oscillating response to threat is too extreme or not extreme enough, leading to an erratic pendulum effect.

Next, take a look at Figure 3.8, which depicts a low-frequency, low-speed, high-amplitude transverse wave.

As you can see in Figure 3.8, I cannot even depict the full wavelength; oscillations are too few, the wave is too slow. As applied to fission–fusion oscillation in human societies, this wave represents slowly changing perceptions of threat and consequently long, slow transitions from fissioned to fused states and vice versa. Amplitude is high, though, symbolizing large overall changes in the perception of threat/instability over time. Yet, because perceptions are changing slowly, the available time to negotiate group boundaries, hierarchies, and shared goals during combination or recombination is greater. This rate of oscillation may therefore be less prone to conflict and competition relative to the high-frequency, low-speed, high-amplitude transverse wave depicted in Figure 3.7.

Finally, consider the more complex wave depicted in Figure 3.9.

This wave has asymmetric amplitudes. I offer this as a way of beginning to consider the reality of fission–fusion oscillation—rarely in any group or

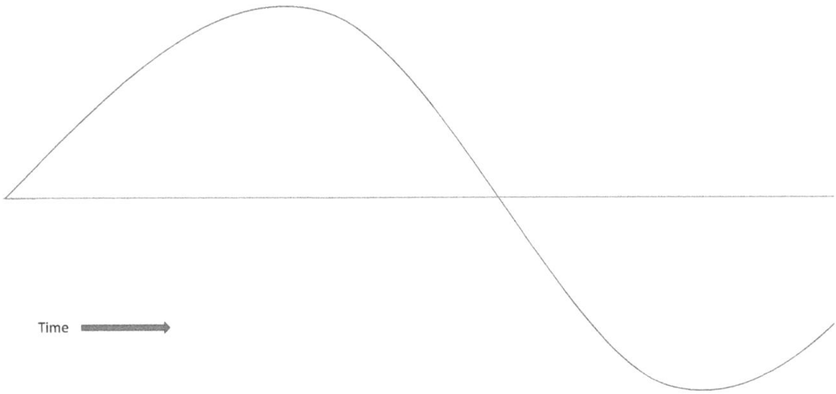

Figure 3.8 Depiction of a Low Frequency, Low Speed, High Amplitude Transverse Wave

society is it symmetrical over long enough stretches of time. Given habituation, coupled with the recency bias, periods where threat perception declines dramatically and groups fission to a significant extent (point "1" on the figure), may be associated with a slowed, lagged response to the perception of threat and subsequent fusion in the future (point "2" on the figure). Subsequently, any damaging consequences that result from this lagged response to the perception of threat may result in a slight over-perception of threat in the future (point "3" on the figure) and so on. Obviously, the particular threat dynamics and fission–fusion oscillation that results will be specific to whatever society we are examining, but the point I want to make here is that, in reality, threat perception (or perception of available trade partners, or of resources, or of

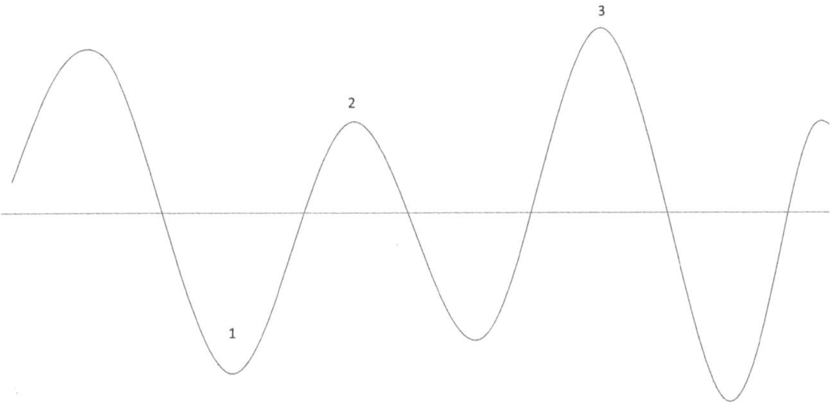

Figure 3.9 Depiction of Asymmetrical Amplitudes in a Transverse Wave

opportunities for identity verification or of available information) rarely if ever changes symmetrically over time, and thus oscillation between fissioned and fused states is rarely symmetric either.

Finally, I want us to return to a point that opened this chapter: how the attitudes, values, beliefs, and intended behaviors of individuals or the (*on-average*) attitudes, values, beliefs, or desired policies of members of groups or societies are, in fact, probability distributions dependent on the relative degree of fusion or fission across a variety of groups.

Depending on how fused or fissioned (defined as the peak or trough of a given wave) an individual perceives themselves to be in any given moment with (or from) any given group, the probability of their expressing a particular attitude, value, belief, or intended behavior will fluctuate. When relatively fused with a particular group, attitudes, values, beliefs, or intended behaviors associated with that group will be more likely to be expressed; when relatively fissioned from a particular group, attitudes, values, beliefs, or intended behaviors associated with that group will be less likely to be expressed.

In this way, the contents of our individual subjectivities are a result of numerous probability distributions associated with our oscillating into and out of fused or fissioned states across groups. When we are explicitly asked about our particular opinions or attitudes (e.g., marital intentions, religiosity, political affiliation) in a survey or interview, our brain will sample our feelings of affiliation or disaffiliation with the various groups in our life and we will spit out an answer. This is why it seems as though people "have" particular attitudes, values, intended behaviors, and ideologies—when directed to provide a response, our brain is a sufficiently complex processor to allow for seemingly precise estimates of our feelings or intentions, though the reasons why we feel as we do, or intend as we do, are often more opaque and simply explained away as "just what I thought in the moment" or "what any decent person would say." And, given people's preference for homophily, predictability, and stability, our perceived levels of fusion or fission into or from this group or that group will not necessarily always be wildly in flux, and from this reality results the apparent stability in our responses. However, if an individual leaves a salient group, or finds themselves increasingly on the outskirts, or, conversely, begins forming a new group or finding themselves gravitating toward a new group, the contents of their subjectivity may change. Again, however, the reasons for our shifting subjectivities may remain opaque to us, and we may simply shrug our shoulders and say "I don't know, I guess I just changed my mind."

Something similar might be said for the aggregated subjective states of whole societies. Societies have more or less common, *on-average*, attitudes, values, beliefs, or desired public policies. Groups themselves in societies, after all, become more or less fused or fissioned with other groups across institutions. Put another way, groups across institutions oscillate in their degree of embeddedness or disembeddedness from other, superordinate groups, and this oscillation may influence group members' *on-average* perception of the desirability of particular attitudes, values, beliefs, or desired public policies.

Lastly, it is important to note that the particular oscillations associated with individuals' (or groups') relative fusion with, or fission from, various groups or (superordinate groups) might create interference patterns. Waves, after all, tend to do this: consider what might happen in a pond when stones are dropped in separately—the waves associated with the drop of one stone interfere with and modulate the strength of the waves associated with the drop of the second stone. For our purposes, we must keep in mind how interactions between individuals, groups, and societies might modulate the probability of any given entity expressing (as an individual or *on average*) the attitudes, values, beliefs, or behaviors (/desired policies) associated with a particular level of perceived fusion with, or fission from, a group or superordinate group; the fusedness or fissionedness of others are inputs to our own assessment of our desire to fuse or fission. For example, imagine person 1, who is highly fused with group A, meets a new person, person 2, who is rather fissioned from group Z. Now imagine that person 1 and person 2 happen to meet in the context of a newly forming group M. Person 1's desire to affiliate with and/or adopt the emerging consensus attitudes, values, beliefs, or behaviors associated with group M might be attenuated on account of person 2's expressions (vocal or behavioral) associated with their lack of integration into group Z.

In other words, a person who is relatively fused to a particular group might be less motivated to become fused to a new group if, in the midst of group formation, it becomes clear (consciously or subconsciously) that one or more members of the new group are not particularly fused to the other groups they associate with (perhaps they imply a belief that group commitments are a burden, or a hassle). Of course, this might go the other way too, if the newly forming group is in some way predicated on some members renouncing their old group affiliations. Similar dynamics might hold for two (or more) groups seeking to form a third group, where one reveals a different *on-average* perception of embeddedness with an outside group. This might hold also for entire societies seeking to form an intersocietal system or council, where the members of some societies perceive *on-average* differences in global economic, political, or social embeddedness. The purpose of this theoretical investigation is not to outline all possible interference patterns. I will pursue this in future works. My point here is merely to suggest that the oscillating waves associated individual, group, and societal fission–fusion dynamics may produce interference patterns with one another, changing the probability distribution associated with expressing any given (individual or *on-average)* attitude, value, belief, or intended behavior.

Chapter 4

Intuitive Information-Processing

> "Intuitive theories help us *get by*. Scientific theories, on the other hand, help us *thrive*. They furnish us with fundamentally more accurate conceptions of reality and thus fundamentally more powerful tools for predicting it and controlling it."
>
> (Shtulman, 2017, pg. 16)

In this chapter, I will discuss research on peoples' intuitions about the world. The study of peoples' intuitions about the social world was first pursued by Lawrence Hirschfeld (1994) in anthropology as the study of "folk sociology." Today, this work is pursued across disciplines, from cognitive psychology (e.g., Boyer, 2018) to sociology (e.g., Turner and Machalek, 2018). If fission–fusion oscillation is how groups generally process information, it is intuitive social-psychological heuristics that influence how individuals generally process information.

The brain relies on intuitions when interpreting the world because intuitions reduce the complexity of incoming stimuli by relying on certain rote modes of interpretation (Kahneman, 2011). For example, when we see several people in leather jackets bearing the same insignia riding motorcycles on the freeway, we don't need to know the particular relationships they have with one another, rather, we can deploy the social categorization "biker gang," and feel as though we've learned something about who "those people" are. Reliance on heuristics is most common when interpretations or decisions are made with minimal reflection, under pressure, and/or with little information. Education and social learning can help people identify and attempt to reduce their reliance on heuristic information-processing, but education and social learning do not necessarily remove the tendency to rely on such heuristics despite our best intentions (Shtulman and Valcarcel, 2012).

Our intuitions about the world arise from innate cognitive circuits that are present from birth in nascent form and that become refined, calibrated, and elaborated to varying degrees over time via social and experiential learning (see Gelman, 2003; Carey 2009; Bloom, 2013; Rhodes and

DOI: 10.4324/9781003266020-4

Chalik, 2013; Bian et al., 2018; Boyer, 2018; Tomasello, 2019; Kim and Spelke, 2020). Given that the actual neurology of the circuits generating intuitions about social life is still poorly understood, I'm assuming here that human intuitions about social life (1) exist cross-culturally, (2) emerge very early in life (i.e., infancy or childhood), (3) are capable of calibration in response to social and experiential learning, and (4) are present in some form in (at least) genetically similar species (e.g., chimpanzees).

It would seem that the neural circuitry underlying our intuitions about the world, albeit in highly plastic/malleable form, is inborn in most human beings, constituting a component of "human nature." However, when I use the term "human nature," I do not intend it to be understood only in an exclusively genetic or neurological sense—human nature is what it is because certain pre-adaptations for group living inevitably interact with, and develop in accordance with, the actual social structures people find around them in their environments. Evolved neurological mechanisms, in other words, are dependent for their functioning on stimuli from the social and natural environment (Sperber, 2019).

The social worlds that humans are born into contain structures that are not strictly determined by their genes—things like demographic distributions, marriage rituals, trade relationships, and various organizational cultures. All human societies have these social structures, though the forms they take differ. It is the interaction of pre-adapted neurology with these common social structures that shape and mold the expression of intuitions (see Turner, 2020).

Consider some of the findings from developmental psychology. Children assume that they have an intrinsic obligation to other ingroup members, but that obligations to outgroup members (even obligations not to cause harm) are contingent on the existence of an explicit rule (Rhodes and Chalik, 2013). Also, by preschool, children appear to assume that individuals belonging to the same social category are automatically friends with one another and share social norms (Rhodes and Chalik, 2014).

For example, even if a girl chose not to play with a doll in a past encounter, other young children will often assume that she will play with a doll in subsequent encounters because of an essentialist intuition that "this is what girls do." The categorization into an essential "type" of person (in this case, a girl) drives intuitions about who this person is likely to be friends with, and their likely behaviors and ideas. By age 6–7 at the latest, children also seem to find it intuitive that individuals prefer others who share their social category membership (Rhodes and Chalik, 2014). Also, while normative complexity may be lower in chimpanzee communities, chimps express the very same tendency to categorize individuals as members of either ingroups or outgroups, and to patrol and regulate these boundaries (Moffett, 2019).

Children (and other primates), "can thus use social categories to predict elements of social structure—how people will interact with each other, what relationships they will form, and toward whom they will direct harmful behaviors" (Rhodes and Chalik, 2013, pg. 1003). Though perhaps more complex or flexible in humans, the very tendency to draw conclusions about a person's probable social network, ideas, and behaviors on account of their social category membership seems to be an evolved intuition. These intuitions simplify the actual complexity of social life; they are an energy-saving shortcut. Such energy-saving shortcuts are likely to have evolved given the brain's dependence on, well, energy—the human brain constitutes about 2.5% of an average person's bodyweight, but requires at least 20% of our caloric energy (Kelly, 2013).

We see the expression of such intuitions in adult humans, of course, not just in children. These intuitions are developmentally stubborn, rooted as they are in our evolved psychologies. Let's consider some general intuitions that anthropologists have discerned. In their survey of the research, Kent Flannery and Joyce Marcus (2012) identify several "first principles" followed by most all adults living in small-scale foraging societies around the world. Paraphrased, these principles are:

1. People are animated by invisible forces (souls);
2. Particular identities, places or material items are special/set apart/sacred;
3. The morality of friends and family is important: kindness, fairness, and generosity are central moral values;
4. People who come later to something (e.g., a territory, idea, occupation) should defer to, or attempt to learn from, those who came earlier; and
5. Our beliefs and behaviors are superior to those who believe and behave differently from us.

(1)–(5), though prevalent among foragers, are also prevalent among people all over the world today living in a variety of different societies. These are good examples of intuitive sociological and social-psychological heuristics that adults (and children) use regularly to interpret their world. They are available to all people, regardless of educational attainment or class position. Let me say just a bit about each.

Regarding (1), many adults all over the world believe in souls. Many cognitive scientists regard belief in souls as "maturationally natural," because people's thoughts *appear to be* immaterial and, thus, people often infer that the thinker of thoughts (the soul of a person) might be capable of surviving the death of their material bodies (McCauley, 2011; Chudek et al., 2013). This is intuitive to many people in all societies, though, again, learning and culture can incentivize people to try and reflect on and override these intuitions. After all, in case it needs saying, there is no evidence whatsoever for some nonphysical "soul stuff" in the human body. The brain, banal as it might sound, is a wonderfully complex processor made of nothing more than electricity, chemistry, and tissue. But, this is not how it feels intuitively.

Regarding (2), since Émile Durkheim's ([1912] 2008) theory of totemization, researchers (see Lawler et al., 2009) have considered how certain identities, places, and items can be suffused with the emotional authority of a group. A country's flag, for example, though literally a piece of cloth, is also a symbol of the ties that bind people together and is therefore treated as something more than the sum of its threads and fibers. The same is true for a wedding ring, or the location where a wedding took place. Human beings, perhaps uniquely in the animal kingdom, can construe identities, places, and items abstractly, as signifiers that capture the positive emotions—the "collective effervescence"—of groups. All societies have identities, places, and items considered sacred and set apart. Here's Ralph Linton's classic account of the development of a sacred identity among a regiment of the US Army:

> [Consider] the 42nd, or Rainbow, Division. The name was arbitrarily chosen by the higher officials and is said to have been selected because the organization was made up of units from many states whose regimental colors were of every hue in the rainbow. Outsiders usually addressed division members as "Rainbow," and to the question "What are you?" nine out of ten enlisted men would reply "I'm a Rainbow." This personal use of the name became general before any attitude toward the actual rainbow was developed. A feeling of connection between the organization and its namesake was first noted in February, 1918, five to six months after the assignment of the name. At this time, it was first suggested and then believed that the appearance of a rainbow was a good omen for the division. Three months later it had become an article of faith in the organization that there was always a rainbow in the sky when the division went into action. A rainbow over the enemy's lines was considered especially auspicious, and after a victory, men would often insist that they had seen one in this position even when the weather conditions or direction of advance made it impossible. This belief was held by most of the officers and enlisted men, and anyone who expressed doubts was considered a heretic and overwhelmed with arguments.
>
> (Linton, 1924, pgs. 296–297)

In this case, it was a rainbow that came to symbolize the positive emotion generated by support from ingroup members. Instead of a complex (energy-intensive) reflection on past instances of group support and group interaction, members simply use the moniker "rainbow," or the symbol of a rainbow, to immediately generate these pro-social feelings.

It isn't just regiments in the US Army that develop identities and other symbols regarded by group members as beyond reproach, special, and sacred. Consider sports fans and their team "totems," music fans and the symbols or places associated with their favorite bands, or political partisans and the iconographic imagery associated with leaders of their political parties. And, of course, in more recent times, the rainbow image has come to be used by people identifying with the empowerment associated with LGBTQ activist communities. Humans, being such symbolic creatures, can crystallize the emotional power of group-belonging into various images, identities, or locations, thus generating and regenerating these powerful emotions at will.

Regarding (3), Jonathan Haidt's (2012) research clearly shows that human moral attitudes emphasize certain common factors, factors like (ingroup) loyalty, (ingroup) fairness, and avoidance of harm. Haidt's work in particular suggests that, while US conservatives place a greater emphasis on some factors, like deference to authority, than do US liberals, both conservatives and liberals see moral value in concerns about harm and fairness (though each may define harm or fairness differently depending on the political issue at stake). Anthropologists such as Donald Brown (1991) have been documenting these common, shared moral concerns for decades and, most recently, Oliver Scott Curry and his colleagues (2019) have developed a general theory of "morality as cooperation" that integrates prior research. They argue that evolution has equipped human beings with the ability to express at least seven modes of cooperation, many, if not all, of which are exhibited by other mammals. These modes of cooperation likely evolved because they facilitated care of infants and cooperative hunting (perhaps especially in human beings, but in all mammals to greater and lesser degrees).

The first mode of cooperation identified by Curry and his colleagues is kin selection or a preference for highly genetically related others like biological mothers and fathers, brothers and sisters, aunts and uncles, and cousins over strangers (Hamilton, 1964). The second is mutualistic coordination, which benefits all parties involved (albeit not always equally). The third is reciprocal exchange—or what I referred in Chapter 1 using Trivers's (1971) original term "reciprocal altruism," though, in human beings who can represent kin symbolically/fictively, the best term really is "reciprocal exchange" (see Emerson, 1981; Molm, 2003). This reciprocal exchange results from an undeniable reality of social life—"much of what we need and value can be obtained only from others" (Molm, 2003, pg. 12). Whatever it is—from job opportunities to coffee to childcare—we often rely on others for it, and the people we most prefer to help are those who've helped us in the past. I will scratch your back, if you scratch mine.

The fourth and fifth modes of cooperation that appear to be (nearly) universally valued by human beings are heroism/courage and respect/humility (Curry et al., 2020). When people act courageously or respectfully, they do what they believe is best for the group, even if this comes at a personal cost. Courage can cost a person their life or reputation by leading to bold action; respect and humility can do the same in complimentary fashion (e.g., respect for and deference to one's country has caused many people to die in war). Courage is the individual pursuit of noble group goals, while respect and deference are the steadfast commitment to such goals above and beyond individual desires.

The sixth mode of cooperation Curry and his colleagues (2019; 2020) have discerned statistically is fairness or equality. This is best exhibited in human foraging societies, where small group numbers require that everyone pitch in to improve the chances of survival and, consequently, that everyone should be taken care of and looked after. While there are many possible modes of cooperation implied in this egalitarianism, reciprocal exchange might be the most important (Apicella et al., 2012). The seventh mode of cooperation discerned by Curry's work is respect for property. While this might not seem as though it were a form of cooperation, it most certainly is—though individuals might want what others have, their resistance to stealing it ensures that everyone can possess and use things in accordance with the best interests of the collective. Who, for example, would buy a plot of land on which to build a hospital if they could not be reasonably certain that this land would not be stolen?

Regarding (4) above, there is widespread evidence across human societies of the tendency to respect wise, experienced people over less experienced novices. Human beings, relative to other extant apes, show a tendency to excessively imitate the behaviors of others, and skilled people, in particular, are preferentially mimicked (Whiten et al., 2009). Imitating others is not some juvenile trait, either; adults may mimic others as much, if not more often, than children do (McGuigan et al., 2011). The tendency to learn from and imitate those with more experience or wisdom is critically important for the intergenerational transmission of knowledge. What makes human culture seemingly unique is its "ratcheting" or cumulative development over generations. Were humans not so capable of communicating with, and learning from, more experienced others, they would not be able to adopt existing cultural practices in order to innovate and improve on them for subsequent generations (see Dean et al., 2012; Chopra et al., 2019).

Finally, regarding (5) above, it is interesting to note that most, if not all, foragers adopt names for their tribes that roughly translate to "person" or "human" (for examples, see Flannery and Marcus, 2012). The implication is that all other groups are less human or differently human. While this obviously didn't impact the formation of trade relationships between societies too severely—trade has been common in humans for the entirety of our existence—we also should not downplay how intuitively intolerant of outgroups humans and other animals can be.

Humans tend to think of their particular local ingroup (e.g., family, friends, hobby groups, work groups) and supergroups (e.g., national identity, political identity, religious identity, or ethnic identity) as somehow superior to others in terms of behavior or belief. This has an analogous counterpart to our perceptions of ourselves as above-average on most all characteristics relative to other individuals—in either case, we often intuitively construe the beliefs or behaviors of our groups (and ourselves in particular) as superior to the beliefs or behaviors we attribute to other groups (and to other individuals) (Hargis et al., 2020). Expression of this tendency has been termed the "minimal group effect" because it is precisely that; minimal, arbitrary differences between people (everything from eye color to clothing to minute political differences) often motivate the construal of group boundaries according to which "we" are better / more ethical than "them" (Tajfel et al., 1971; Dunham et al., 2011; Dunham et al., 2013; Otten, 2016). In collectivist societies, this might take the form of communal narcissism, whereas in more individualistic societies this might look more like individual narcissism.

The ultimate evolutionary reason why animals, and especially humans, are so emotionally bonded to their ingroup is due to their dependence on others from birth (almost always mom, but often a community of others) (Churchland, 2011). Humans in particular are born into groups composed of emotion-laden norms, many of which, across our evolutionary history, were not shared by other groups. Group boundaries have always been salient in our species, precisely because norms are an essential requirement for in-group coordination. However, an information-processing problem arises due to the reality that these norms vary between groups. So, the brain likely evolved mechanisms to determine what norms ought to be learned and maintained and which ought to be ignored or disdained. These mechanisms include a homophily bias to associate with others who seem physically or symbolically similar to us, a familiarity bias to learn from those we're most comfortable with, a prestige bias to learn from those who have high status in our ingroup, and so on (see Henrich, 2017).

If someone from another group wears or eats or believes differently, this may, even if the difference is only arbitrary, be perceived as a signal of their lower willingness to cooperate, that they share fewer experiences, or perhaps that they adhere to different moral values. To put it as Jonathan Turner, Alexandra Maryanski (Turner, 2020; Turner and Maryanski, 2015), Robert Boyd and Peter Richerson (2005), and others have argued: humans' capacity for emotion and abstraction allowed for the adoption of emotion-laden group rules and norms that facilitated ingroup cooperation and survival (along with outgroup competition and tribal conflict). Our endowment from evolutionary selection processes is a brain prepared to understand, and emotionally commit to, our group's norms (Tomasello, 2019).

The tendency to believe in the superiority of the beliefs and behaviors of one's own group, as against those of other groups, is a widespread regularity in all human beings from children on the playground to scientists in the lab (Haidt, 2012; Moffett, 2019; Clark and Winegard, 2020). Of course, this tendency to construe ingroups and outgroups is just a pre-adaptation; depending on social learning and experience or idiosyncratic genetic propensity, some people will be more prone to beliefs about group superiority than others. In particular, prior research suggests that the people most motivated to construe outgroups as inferior are those who score highly on tests of "social dominance orientation," and those who are frustrated or anxious about intergroup competition (Kteily et al., 2011; Hochschild, 2016; Stephan and Stephan, 2017).

Perhaps it also needs saying that, for those of us who consider ourselves liberals and who believe ourselves to be utterly free of irrational intolerance, I am sorry to say that our irrational intolerance is just invisible to us, as it is to many who are convinced of their moral superiority (see Conway et al., 2020).

This is not to say that the tendency cannot be overcome. More on that in a moment.

4.1 Core Components of Humans' Intuitive Sociology: Groups, Power, Norms

Pascal Boyer (2018) provides some—albeit speculative—detail about the sociological intuitions that people all around the world tend to develop early in life and express into adulthood (see Figure 4.1). The first is that *groups are like big people*. That is, we construe groups of people as though they act in lockstep, according to homogeneously shared intentions. That village did X, or immigrants do Y, or Apple (the tech company) is pursuing Z. We intuit "the government," or "the rich," or "the police," or "society" acting as though each were a singular conscious unit, with uniform intentions, desires, and goals, as though big groups were simply big

Groups	Big groups are like big people
Power	A coercive substance leading/forcing others into zero-sum exchanges
Norms	Constraining external objects/homogenously-shared opinions

Figure 4.1 Core Sociological Intuitions*
*Adapted from Boyer (2018)

people. I cannot tell you how many times I've heard an otherwise bright student or colleague tell me what society "wants" from them or how society is "manipulating" them or what society "thinks" about this or that. In case it needs saying, I do not exempt myself from making similar errors!

In reality, groups are composed of a variety of different individuals, many of whom differ in behavior and belief from others that we arbitrarily categorize as being in the same group. These intuitions are popular in political discourse—how many social scientists, journalists, and political elites can be overheard blathering on ignorantly about what "people of color" want or don't want, as though a Caribbean construction worker, a Brazilian bank CEO, and an African American computer engineer all share some basic essence that unifies them. Or, how many political pundits can be overheard ruminating about what a particular "country" is seeking in a trade agreement, or what "conservatives" or "liberals" believe, and so on? Or, in our daily lives, consider how often we regard a particular "group" or "collective" or "committee" or "department" or "family" as believing this or trying to do that. We can find such intuitions in the smallest foraging societies and in the largest postindustrial nations.

For example, Boyer describes people's intuitions about "the government" as follows:

> In the same way groups or social categories are often mistaken for quasi-persons, the state is described as an entity that has knowledge and intentions. This description is of course misleading. ... Rather, there are vast numbers of interactions between individuals, the complexity of which greatly exceeds our cognitive capacities. ... So the human mind is placed in a situation in which unfathomable processes (the complex reality of decision making in a modern state) result in people actually doing things, such as bureaucrats distributing benefits, tax officers demanding payment, police officers arresting people, and so forth. The easiest way for a human mind to explain what is done by many human actors in a complex set of interactions is to summarize all this complexity as the doing of one generic or single mind, the mind of the state.
>
> (Boyer, 2018, pg. 212)

The intuition that groups and governments are singular entities, essentially just big people, satisfyingly reduces the actual complexity of social life. Instead of (1) considering that groups might share goals or attitudes only on average, or (2) considering that many people simply go along with their group out of a sense of obligation, or disinterest, instead of actually endorsing or agreeing with their group, or (3) considering that people that we categorize as members of a group might outright disagree with what others similarly categorized are doing or saying, people often instead just treat groups as monolithic, intentional agents.

A second core component of humans' intuitive sociology identified by Boyer (2018) is the assumption *that power/influence is a substance that people "hold," "lose," "gain," or "give" to others.* The common metaphor of the wealth "pie" perfectly encapsulates this, insofar as wealth is a proxy for power. The metaphor is incorrect because the pies we eat, once baked, do not expand in size indefinitely! Thank goodness. But economies can, in principle, expand indefinitely *if* successively more efficient, successively more renewable, energy sources are used to fuel core infrastructure. Since 1600 and especially since 1800, the wealth "pie" of the world has begun to expand in total size; this is the reason why poverty has been declining globally, but inequality seems to be growing. There is more wealth to go around and, thus, more wealth to be hoarded by elites.

But, nevertheless, the intuition is stubborn, whether it regards power itself or proxies for power like wealth. Because sociological intuitions are neurologically reliant on more evolutionarily ancient intuitions about the physical world (more on this in a moment), power is often intuitively conceived of as a forceful substance. Foragers often use the concept of *mana* to describe peoples' capacity to influence others, and this is similar to Max Weber's ([1922] 1978) recognition of charismatic authorities in contemporary societies. We often say that so-and-so is "in" power, and this reveals our intuition that power is a sort of substance that "moves" people around.

"Power," being processed cognitively as a forceful substance, is assumed to have push–pull effects on others. Intuitively, power is a substance that "pulls" people toward certain positions, or, "pushes" them out. People "withstand" or "resist" or "repel" power. Conversely, people "give in to," "submit to," or "yield" to power. We live in a world of hierarchies, forms of leadership, and social networks that are imbalanced in terms of the influence some have on others; thus, genuine, constant, reflection on the (1) litany of ways in which people express influence over others, (2) the many reasons why people might enjoy this influence, endorse this influence, regret, undermine, or hate this influence, and (3) the many ways in which power "holders" can be impotent or ineffectual, would be an overbearing information-processing burden on the brain. We might reflect, here and there, about the actual particular psychological, sociological, and historical dynamics that determine which people have influence, and in which contexts, but, for the most part, we rely on our intuitions to reduce our cognitive load. Whether it is a horticulturalist hearing that a chief has defended their village from foreign invasion, or an industrialist hearing that a larger corporation has "swallowed" up a smaller company, the intuition is the same: power repels and engulfs.

Even as I write this chapter, I find myself wanting to write sentences that feel clear but that, in fact, reveal my own unhelpful or incomplete intuitions. Again, I do not exempt myself from these simplistic, flawed ways of understanding social life. The point is our common proneness.

A quirk of our intuitive conception of power as a forceful substance is that we often assume relationships between entities deemed "powerful" and entities deemed "powerless" will be zero-sum—the powerful take, the powerless give, and the more the powerful gain, the more the powerless lose. This intuition is particularly strong when powerful parties to an exchange are poorly understood and highly influential—clearly, foragers can appreciate the benefits of trade with one another, but it is harder for us to understand trade with/between major corporations or countries as this didn't occur in our ancestral past.

Companies, businesses, and large nations are relatively new "inventions" arising from massive increases in population, and our intuitive theories of the world struggle to interpret their presence and role in exchange relationships. Economic exchanges involving large entities are understood, intuitively, in terms of winners (the powerful) and losers (the powerless). We are "intuitive mercantilists," who doubt the plausibility of win–win exchanges (Johnson et al., 2020). It seems intuitive that the powerful parties to an exchange will maximize payoffs and that the less powerful parties to an exchange will experience only losses. If some CEO made 50 million dollars last year, this means that some group of people, somewhere, must have lost 50 million dollars, right? The wealth "pie" is fixed, right?

Consider some other examples of our intuitions about economic exchange (see Boyer and Petersen, 2018). Entire subfields of modern journalism and social science have cropped up to discuss, *ad nauseam*, how international trade and globalization are having negative impacts on people, relegating them to poverty and oppression (e.g., Davis, 2006; Castellanos, 2018). Relying on our intuition that complex aggregates are like big people, we might think it sensible to talk about what capitalism "wants" or "needs," or how the economy "doesn't care" about us (Forstmann and Burgmer, 2018). And, often, these intuitions are misleading because power is not a single coercive substance and because economies are not, in fact, big people (Leiser and Shemesh, 2018). The typical well-socialized, and consequently badly misinformed, social science "academic" or journalist is only too happy to drone on about how capitalism and globalization are rendering the world poor and sick—meanwhile, in reality, global poverty continues to decline as worldwide markets provide people more and more opportunities to leverage their skills and wares for pay (McCloskey, 2016; Rosling et al., 2018; and for continuously updated data on declining poverty rates, see Roser and Ortiz-Ospina, 2020). Fewer and fewer people around the globe are still beholden to the fertility of the soil around them for survival—now, for example, anyone in the world with internet access can open an online business and sell their products to anyone interested. Yet, the actual facts of the matter are often less important (albeit also harder to discern) than our emotional intuition that large-scale economic processes produce big winners *and* big losers.

As for why academics and journalists so eagerly rely on their intuitions about exchange relationships in the economy, a good possibility is that becoming an academic or journalist requires many years of schooling but pays relatively little in salary. So, the people writing articles and books on the economy have a personal axe to grind—they've been in school for decades but make less money than those CEOs we all love to hate, so certainly *something* must be amiss, and they assume their intuitions must be correct. But, if these academics and journalists actually bothered to ask poor farmers in China or India whether they hope to move to a nearby city so they can access a globalized economy and a better life, they'd often be surprised by the answer. I am emphatically *not* saying that globalization always, or even usually, favors the worker or the downtrodden farmer; rather, what I *am* suggesting is that the intuition that globalized economies always enrich transnational businesses at the zero-sum expense of impoverishing workers is not accurate despite *feeling* like it makes sense.

Consider some other examples that might better make the general point (again, see Boyer and Petersen, 2018)—political conservatives and the working poor in various countries have often complained, throughout history, that immigrants "steal jobs," despite the fact that, on balance, immigrants fill positions that no one else wants and often work for cheap, thus enriching their new home countries. Or, some of the same people might be heard complaining that immigrants or racial minorities abuse the welfare system while neglecting the fact that people are typically on welfare only for short periods, and that this aid often helps people bridge periods between jobs. Though "liberals" (whose economic intuitions tend, only on the average, to make them skeptical of markets, profit-seeking, and transnational corporations) and "conservatives" (whose economic intuitions, only on the average, make them skeptical of welfare policies or extensive immigration) might differ in the substance of their intuitions, their tendency to essentialize others and regard exchanges as zero-sum seems to be a commonality.

In reality, exchanges are rarely zero-sum, with one individual (or group) monopolizing the resources of others. Most of the time exchanges are positive sum, even if they are unequal, and this reality is important for understanding our modern world (Wright, 2001). When we look around us, we see a lot of inequality and need, but if we look closer we see that amidst inequality and need there is a growing standard of living (measurable in so many ways: per capita GDP, life expectancy, infant mortality, access to technology) all around the world, albeit to greater and lesser degrees (Pinker, 2018; Rosling et al., 2018). We rarely take a moment to consider that our laptops, cars, indoor plumbing, electricity, ovens, dishwashers, and so on are forms of wealth that haven't always existed. Rather, we take these life-saving and life-enhancing items for granted and focus our attention only on what we are lacking relative to others; we focus on the threats and ignore the improvements.

I agree that inequality is a legitimate moral concern and that the powerful are advantaged in market negotiations, but relying on our zero-sum intuitions about exchange and power blinds us to the fact that cumulative economic growth (especially in the context of middle-class markets; see McCloskey, 2016) has benefitted everyone, albeit not equally.

The benefits of exchange are hard to track, because they vary so widely, and because they would overwhelm our cognition if tracked with any exactitude across a whole society over long stretches of time. Consider the complexity of just a two-way national exchange:

> Instead of focusing on country A receiving payment from country B for product K, we [might] have to consider also country A obtaining payment from country B for product L, and moreover realize that by obtaining payment for K from country B, and by doing so comparatively cheaply, [country] A is able to shift production from K to L.
>
> (Leiser and Shemesh, 2018, pg. 34)

This is how economies actually work: increasingly complex feedback loops composed of indirect effects and aggregated variables over time between multiple exchange partners with varying interests. Cognitively taxing, indeed, but often positive sum in consequence.

So, instead of reflecting on the complexities at hand, we often just rely on our intuitive economic sociology: exchanges are zero-sum and powerful/advantaged entities ruthlessly exploit weaker/disadvantaged entities. This intuition, in particular, was probably a key psychological motivator for foragers to regulate their hierarchies, ridicule those with big egos, and insist on collective decision-making. Indeed, the evolved inference system we often rely on to generate intuitions about economies and exchange relationships is calibrated to (1) detect free-riders (i.e., those who are taking advantage of others while providing little if anything in return); (2) evaluate exchange partners (i.e., in terms of their fairness, honesty, or work ethic); and (3) track coalitional affiliations (i.e., who is likely to pursue shared goals) (Boyer and Petersen, 2018). In both small groups of ancestral foragers and in more recent postindustrial economies, (1)–(3) would have been important, and adaptive, concerns. However, modern economies are much larger, contain many more moving parts, and are influenced by entities (e.g., corporations) and dynamics (e.g., mass immigration) that did not exist in our ancestral environment, and this is why intuitions that evolved to help us navigate small-group foraging life can often lead us astray when we rely on them to interpret our modern world.

A third core sociological intuition discussed by Boyer (2018) is that *norms (i.e., patterned collective behaviors) are constraining objects in the world.* This intuition, as with the others, can be discerned very early in child development and is culturally universal. By preschool, for example, children regard the arbitrary rules of a game as existing somehow outside of the subjective opinions of individuals. Children taught the rules to a new game will protest and become upset when newcomers violate these rules, as though the rules existed as externally discernible objects that obviously must be navigated and acknowledged. Even if children make up the rules to a game themselves—once made, there is an intuition that the rules are objective and external (Hardecker et al., 2017).

Adults are no different, regardless of how arbitrary the rules might be. If memos in an office are habitually sent with a certain header and introduction, and an employee begins sending memos without this header or introduction, many in the office may begin to act as though some external aspect of reality is not being acknowledged or understood (office management might exasperatedly insist that "this is just how a memo must look!" as though there were some kind of objectively existing Platonic ideal about office memos). This response would come even if the header/introduction convention is unnecessary, pointless, or counterproductive—people will often endorse unhelpful or pointless norms because they are worried about their social reputation and because they want to be held in good esteem by others (Taylor, 1982; Willer et al., 2009).

Here is a splendid example of the intuitive externality of norms among ancient Sumerians:

> In the language of every society there are abstract terms that underlie many of the logical premises … the Sumerians had *me* … *Me*, sometimes translated as "order," referred to the rules that the gods had established so that society would run smoothly. In the words of epigrapher Benno Landsberger, *me* "emanated from gods and temples in a mystic manner, was imaged as a substance, was symbolized by emblems, and could be transferred from one god to another."
>
> (Flannery and Marcus, 2012, pg. 481)

This intuition was described by Durkheim in his concept of "social facts." Social facts, for Durkheim, are regularities that are emergent from the interactions of many individuals and are not, thus, attributable to each individual themselves. In Durkheim's words:

> When I perform my duties as a brother, a husband or a citizen and carry out the commitments I have entered into, I fulfill obligations which are defined in law and custom and which are external to myself and my actions. Even when they conform to my own sentiments and

> when I feel their reality within me, that reality does not cease to be objective, for it is not I who have prescribed these duties; I have received them through [social learning] ... The system of signs that I employ to express my thoughts, the monetary system I use to pay my debts, the credit instruments I utilize in my commercial relationships, the practices I follow in my profession, etc., all function independently of the use I make of them ... Thus there are ways of acting, thinking and feeling which possess the remarkable property of existing outside the consciousness of the individual.
>
> (Durkheim [1895] 1982, pgs. 50–51)

For John Searle (1995; 2010), informed as he is by Durkheim's early work, social norms are "ontologically subjective but epistemologically objective." By this, Searle means that the content of norms exists in our mind (they are ideas about collective behaviors), but, being commonly held, they also constrain and pressure our own behavior even if we don't like them or wish to behave differently.

A particular form of "social fact" that Searle discusses is that of a "status function declaration," which occurs when people with institutional status make (or write) decrees stating the existence of new social conditions. Marriage officiants, or county clerks, declare that two people "count" as married; a bill prescribing or proscribing a certain behavior, once signed, "counts" as a law; a young person after obtaining a certain number of course credits, receives a piece of signed, embossed paper, and now "counts" as a high school graduate. Once our imagination begins playing along, regularities emerge, and we can begin to talk about rates of patterned behavior called "marriages," or "crimes," or "graduations."

Institutions are primate dominance hierarchies (see Korsgaard, 1996; 2009), in which those occupying top hierarchy positions are imbued with the capacity to make status function declarations. Indeed, institutions, themselves, are a kind of status function declaration—consider when a new building is determined to "count" as a "school" according to the bureaucratic filing, and approval, of an educational license. Across human history, individuals in leadership positions across institutions have been making status function declarations about who "counts" as connected (in this way or that), or what "counts" as a site of a certain activity (i.e., recreation, education, medicine, business), or which behaviors "count" as appropriate, inappropriate, and so on. The accumulation, interaction, and dissolution of these declarations over time are the ebb and flow of culture.

In actuality, as Searle points out, these status function declarations are just collective agreements about how to symbolically represent patterned social behavior. Being collective, it is a "fact" above and beyond the opinions or actions of any one of us (or any one group of us). This does not mean that, for example, rules or social obligations cannot change, but it means that they will only change insofar as the legitimacy of leadership, and associated hierarchies, are themselves challenged. And, less acknowledged by Searle, Durkheim's point is that any collective behavior exhibited with regularity begins to feel like a force guiding (or coercing) our behavior, whether or not it is "declared" as a component of social reality by someone in an institutional leadership position.

Reflecting on the complexity of the countless "agreements", implicit and explicit, made between people about how to pattern their ideas and behaviors would be a massive burden on our cognitive information-processing. We can do so, on occasion, as you are doing now in reading his book. But it is cognitively difficult and tiring. It is much easier to simply rely on the intuition that norms and institutions are objects "out there" that we must navigate or conform to (or, for the rebellious of us, resist).

Since the word "norm" has so many contested definitions—norms can be explicit or implicit, codified or assumed—perhaps it will help make the point to understand that ideas, generally, are intuitively understood to be objects. We consider ideas as being big or small, we seek to explore ideas, lose ourselves in ideas, confront ideas, add one idea to another, burst ideas, watch ideas collide, "touch on" the ideas of others, feel close to or far from an idea, claim ideas are circular or square or represent a field, and regard ideas as uneven, balanced, or cluttered (Tversky, 2019).

We use the language of physical objects when we discuss ideas, and the norms these ideas represent, because we rely on a similar inference system to understand both the physical and social world. Our physical inference system is evolutionarily ancient, but the brain recycles and repurposes inference systems for new challenges, such as the challenge of cooperative foraging and child-rearing. Our social cognitions are rooted in our neural processing of the spatial world.

And, when we rely on our intuitions that norms and ideas are external canalizing structures, we feel pressured by this or that institutional practice, "crushed" by this or that tradition, "restrained" by certain societal expectations, or desire to "break free" from the "constraints" imposed by this or that law. We can talk about changes in, or rates of adoption of, a certain norm, or we can agree that a collection of bricks and windows and wooden seats is a thing called a "school" wherein certain patterned activities can be assumed to take place.

As I've suggested above, humans often rely on their intuitions because of how much they can reduce the cognitive-processing burden associated with the complex stimuli that make up social life. But this is not the only reason. The intuitions discussed above also help people coordinate their behavior with one another. Political leaders construe entire nations as having wants or desires so as to negotiate alliances or trade relationships; children in the schoolyard construe groups as agents sharing intentions (the "nerds" or the "jocks") so as to better sort themselves and interact with others. Similarly, implicitly construing norms as external, guiding objects might help a person feel confident that they will know how to behave (and can expect others to behave) when attending a funeral or wedding or music concert or sporting event. Our intuitions about groups, power, and norms are imperfect approximations that "provide a convenient shorthand for coordination processes that would be exceedingly difficult or cumbersome to [achieve] otherwise" (Boyer, 2018, pg. 237).

Our intuitions are, of course, flexible, and we are certainly capable of reflecting on them in an effort to modify them. Our intuitions about this or that group or norm or exchange relationship can be detached from one context and applied to others. Humans can accomplish this feat of abstraction because of the plasticity of our brain's neuronal networks and the degree to which our brain can absorb and process social information.

Mice, for example, exhibit a "conjunctive coding" of neural activation when processing, for example, information about a piece of cheese sitting on a table in front of a window (Quiroga, 2019). This conjunctive coding indicates that when mice are confronted with a piece of cheese on a table, they represent the cheese on the table, and might not consider that yesterday they saw cheese on a bed, or on a sidewalk. In any given situation, a mouse encodes the object they see only in that specific context. Humans, on the other hand, exhibit an "invariant coding," meaning that their "neurons [do not necessarily] activate in response to a person AND a place, or a person AND a task," but are rather activated more flexibly, independent of other contexts or associations (Quiroga, 2019, pg. 1389). Humans appear better capable of mentally construing "cheese" (or "table" or "group member" or anything else) as a concept distinct from the particular immediate context.

Monkeys, by comparison, exhibit a "mixed coding" that falls somewhat in between the information-processing of mice and humans. In monkeys, neurons activate differentially depending on the context, but their neurons also maintain consistent patterns of firing (i.e., processing cheese on a table in front of a window vs. cheese on a table in front of a blank wall—in either case, cheese is paired with the presence of a table, but some aspect of the context has changed). Evidence like this appears to support contentions that humans are uniquely capable of mentally representing their concepts abstractly. Yes, mice and monkeys have concepts like "cheese," but the neural processing of these concepts is more involuntarily tethered to features of the environment or context, while in humans these concepts are more easily processed independently of these considerations.

This capacity for abstraction and flexible contextualization is the reason why humans can express their intuitions about groups, norms, and power in new ways if populations begin to grow larger or social complexity increases beyond small foraging groups.

A major underlying reason why we rely on simplistic intuitions when thinking about complex systems like economies, social hierarchies, norms, groups, and power relations is that the human brain does not easily grasp the notion of "emergence." Consider that, in reality, heat is an emergent property of the movement of particles in a material or substance and, yet, our intuition is that heat is an essence that a material either "has" or "does not have," making it difficult for us to understand the reality of the situation. Or, consider how traffic is an emergent process of many individual choices to transport oneself to correlated locations, yet, we talk of "traffic" as though it were a singular phenomenon that can be "high" or "low."

Emergent processes have three unique characteristics that make them hard for our brains to grasp (Chi, 2005; Chi et al., 2012; Shtulman, 2017): (1) they do not have clear cause and effect explanations but rather result from system-wide interactions, (2) they result from an equilibrium(s) of many interacting components, and (3) they represent continuums of change and do not necessarily have a set beginning point or endpoint. Continuums of numerous interacting components across equilibrium-seeking systems are difficult to reflect on in any sustained manner, and are thus tiring and overwhelming for any individual to grasp succinctly with any regularity. Thus, we fall back on the misleading certainty of our intuitions.

It is very important, at this juncture, to point out that our sociological intuitions *are not genetically determined or inevitably expressed in identical ways across individuals and cultures.* Depending on the cultural context, some intuitions will be reinforced more than others. For example, in a culture where immigration policy is closely aligned with particular political parties, those in support of parties opposed to immigration may double down on their intuitions, while those who align with parties in favor of immigration may reflect on and suppress the expression of their intuitions.

Or, for example, individuals living in countries where access to tertiary education is more limited may be more prone to rely on their intuitions about the homogeneity of outgroups, whereas individuals living in countries where access to education is more widespread might be more motivated to reflect on and suppress their intuitions about the homogeneity of outgroups (assuming, of course, that professors themselves are not wildly indulging their own intuitions). We must keep in mind that any implicit "bias" in human information-processing will be calibrated to the particular conditions of an individual's cultural environment. Intuitions may be evolved mechanisms for rapidly and efficiently processing complex information, but the *calibration* of these mechanisms is context-specific.

While research on the cultural calibration of evolved intuitions is scant at best, there are a few illuminating case studies. I'll describe one here to (hopefully) make the larger point. People the world over seem to have intuitions about the shape of the Earth. Some people express an assumption that the Earth is a hollow sphere, some say the Earth is disk-like, and others say the Earth is a solid sphere with a flat top. However, research suggests that these intuitions are strongly influenced by culture. Andrew Shtulman (2017), for example, notes that Samoan children typically presume that Earth is shaped like a ring, and that this ring-shape corresponds closely to the actual arrangement of Samoan houses and markets, which are themselves arrayed in rings around a courtyard (in the case of homes) or an open plaza (in the case of markets). "Accordingly," Shtulman writes, "Samoan children project this structure, ubiquitous in their built environment, onto the Earth itself" (Shtulman, 2017, pg. 101).

This general insight about the cultural calibration of our intuitions was foreshadowed 100 years ago by Durkheim and his nephew Marcel Mauss, who both noted that hunter-gatherers and horticulturalists often developed intuitions about group origins or sacred myths that corresponded in subtle ways to the physical structure of their environments and/or the patterns of their social interactions (Durkheim and Mauss [1903] 2009).

4.2 The Psychological Foundations of Sociological Intuitions

People all around the world, to varying degrees, demonstrate a tendency to presume that those they are interacting with (typically ingroup members) are being honest (Levine, 2014). Though more cross-cultural work is needed to establish just how universal this tendency is, it stands to reason that a "truth-default" would be adaptive, given humans' dependence on social learning for survival. Humans imitate those around them (particularly those who are similar or familiar, those with high status, and/or those representative of majority opinion) constantly, beginning very early in life, and this has long been an important means for transmitting strategies of tool use, childcare, group coordination, and other survival-relevant concerns (Nagel, 1993; Churchland, 2011; Tomasello, 2019). According to prior research, even when study participants are prompted to think critically about the information they're receiving from others, participants still assume the truthfulness of 58%–88% of the messages they receive from others (Clare and Levine, 2019).

If people have a clear or exigent motivation to lie, they often will. But, in most contexts, this motivation isn't present and, consequently, the assumption that others in one's ingroup are telling the truth is usually efficient and helpful (Verschuere and Shalvi, 2014). This is not to say that people are necessarily credulous or gullible. People won't often trust information from others they deem incompetent, who've lied in the past, whose information is unusual or unbelievable, or who are assumed to have ulterior motives (Mercier, 2017; 2020). Rather than regard humans as gullible, it would be more accurate to think of humans as prone to trust those who are familiar, similar, and/or who have good reputations (Mikolajczak et al., 2010). This trust is the glue that enables people to be socialized into the beliefs and behaviors of their ingroup.

Nevertheless, though the combination of our truth-default bias and our proneness to believing in the superiority of our ingroup's normative beliefs and behaviors accelerates social learning, it can also lead to between-group conflict or outgroup avoidance. Even if the avoidance of outgroup contact does not lead to conflict, it can still lead to a lack of innovation, creativity, or cognitive flexibility. In other words, our psychological and sociological intuitions can conspire to create a closed fission–fusion system instead of a more open fission–fusion system.

This brings me to a second, very important, psychological bias to consider: essentialism. By the time they are nine-months old (and possibly sooner), infants begin attributing a fundamental nature, or essence, to things (Gelman, 2003). For example, an object that makes a goofy noise when turned upside down will be logged in memory, and any object that looks similar will be expected to have this characteristic when turned upside down. Another example: a child who picks up a pinecone, and who mishears her mother call the object a "pine comb" will attempt to run it through her hair, as if all "combs" had a similar property regardless of their appearance (Gelman, 2003).

Children also ascribe essential characteristics to animate living things. For example, showing children a drawing of a racoon turning into a skunk leads to children concluding, even at the midpoint of transition, that the animal is either a racoon *or* a skunk; it cannot be both (Keil, 1992). Children assume racoons have an immutable essence that makes them what they are, and this is distinct from the immutable essence that makes skunks what they are. Cactuses have the property of "cactusness," blue whales have the property of "blue whaleness," and so on. Though a baby blue whale might be different in size or behavior from an adult, it is still assumed by children (and, typically, adults) to have the essential characteristic of "blue whaleness."

Consider another example: by at least four years of age, children report the intuition that a kangaroo adopted by goats would not develop any of the behaviors of goats (because it has the essence of "kangarooness"). Similar studies show that five-year-olds, on average, assume that if a child is adopted at birth by parents who speak a language different than that of the child's biological parents, the child will nevertheless grow up to speak the language of the biological parents, as though birth confers an unchanging essence (Gelman, 2004). Not surprisingly, given its prevalence, there are certainly times when this essentialist bias results in accurate beliefs—for example, when children intuit that a lemon seed will result in a lemon plant even if the seed is placed in an orchard of orange trees (Shtulman, 2017).

Lest we conclude that this is only a psychological bias in children, the tendency to essentialize living things is also why it is difficult for adults to understand Charles Darwin's theory of evolution. The presumption that animals are unchanging "kinds" (as opposed to constantly varying temporary aggregations of genes) was the default explanation for biodiversity for much of human history (Bloom and Weisberg, 2007; Shtulman, 2017). A particularly amusing example of a taxonomy of animals prior to the development of evolutionary theory comes from Jorge Louis Borges's (1966) description of an ancient Chinese encyclopedia called the *Celestial Emporium of Benevolent Knowledge*:

> The following is a taxonomy of the animal kingdom ... animals are divided into (a) those that belong to the Emperor, (b) embalmed ones, (c) those that are trained, (d) suckling pigs, (e) mermaids, (f) fabulous ones, (g) stray dogs, (h) those that are included in this classification, (i) those that tremble as if they were mad, (j) innumerable ones, (k) those drawn with a very fine camel's hair brush, (l) others, (m) those that have just broken a flower vase, (n) those that resemble flies from a distance.
>
> (Borges, 1966, as quoted in Tversky, 2019, pgs. 179–180)

It is as if the human mind cannot resist imposing categories onto the world, and oftentimes drawing these categories around perceived intrinsic essences. People apply this categorical essentialism to other humans as well, for example, when they insist that the wants and needs of all men and boys (having "maleness") are distinct from the wants and needs of all women and girls (having "femaleness"). The judgments we make about the character and motivations of people we've grouped into social categories, being intuitions, occur to us very rapidly, perhaps 30–40 milliseconds after seeing their face (Todorov, 2017). Once a category of animal, plant, or person has been established, all members of that category are presumed to be born with a motivating essence, and when we categorize other humans, this motivating essence is often morally or emotionally laden, as when "groups" in society are regarded as violent or conniving. Categories of living things are assumed to share underlying uniform properties, and we apply this to our own species, not just to plants and animals (Gelman, 2004).

When people group others into social categories and ascribe an essential quality to those in these categories, they are treating groups of people as though they were members of another species of human being, different from oneself in immutable ways—people in a group are "like this" or "do that" or "believe this," on account of "who they are." Consider all of the essentialist categories that laypeople and social scientists alike rely on—categories like race, ethnicity, occupation, or class. Upon reflection, it would be hard to maintain the assumption that all people of a certain race, or occupation or social class share some underlying, unchanging similarity (because, in reality, they don't), but the intuition is strong.

Whether it is a Marxist sociologist discussing "class consciousness" or "white privilege," or a republican voter discussing the ingenuity of "the rich," humans find it obvious that we should be talking about broad social categories as though these were usefully informative. This tendency to essentialize human groups can lead to the development of discriminatory stereotypes and between-group distrust and conflict, especially given the tendency for people to regard their own group as superior to outgroups. The developmental psychological research suggests that children begin applying essentialist stereotypes to outgroups by the time they are six years old (and possibly earlier) (Pauker et al., 2010). For example, studies show that by seven years old, children will report that people of different social categories (e.g., Arab or Jew, rich or poor) are only slightly more similar than animals of different species (see Shtulman, 2017).

It is also important to keep in mind that this tendency to essentialize is not, in and of itself, malicious. Indeed, we very often essentialize *ourselves*. Regardless of how old they are, people tend to report that their current beliefs or preferences are more stable (that is, more likely to persist into the future) than were our past beliefs or preferences (Quoidbach et al., 2013; Shtulman, 2017). We recognize that we are different today than we used to be, but stubbornly assume that who we are today more approximates our "real" or essential self. It is as though, as we age, we feel that we approximate a "true self" more and more (despite the fact that beliefs and preferences continue to change across the life-course).

Relatedly, when we or other members of our ingroup err in some way, we tend to conclude that it was the environment or situation that is to blame; on the other hand, when those in an outgroup err, we conclude that they are prone to mistakes and improprieties simply on account of the type of people they are. This "attribution bias" emerges because we treat members of our ingroups as earnest individuals with agency but more often presume that members of outgroups are morally questionable automatons (Duncan, 1976; Hewstone, 1990; Sherman et al., 2005). So, for example, when I or someone I love gets arrested, it is because of all of the stress in life we are experiencing, or because those police officers were out to get us, but when "those people" get arrested it is because they are just lazy, dangerous, or incompetent. Plausibly, this tendency to essentialize outgroups and to regard their behavior as a result of stable dispositions is also implicated in how humans think about societies regarded as distant or foreign. "We" do things in our country because of tradition, or necessity, or social pressure, but "they" do things in their country because that is the kind of people they are.

Outgroup essentialism and ingroup superiority beliefs are sustained via low intergroup contact (Pettigrew and Tropp, 2006; Blau and Schwartz, 1997). We interact more often with, and were exposed more growing up to, some groups than others. Interaction rates may differ because our occupation, neighborhood, or daily routine exposes us to some people more than others, or because our parents' socioeconomic status or their income influenced how (and whether) we were exposed to various groups in society. Intergroup contact can mitigate the rigidity of these socialization experiences: the more we interact with individuals categorized as members of a group, the less we see them as identical to all other members of their group. In other words, the more we interact with "members" of a group, the more we see them as individuals and the less we see them as automatons acting according to some group essence.

The "outgroup homogeneity effect," or the tendency to think all outgroup members look, behave, or think the same way, diminishes the more people interact with, or learn about, particular members of that outgroup (Kite and Whitley, 2016). People, of course, vary in their belief and behavior, and do not monolithically conform to some imagined group essence—this reality becomes clearer the more we interact with people from groups we believe to be different from our own. Intergroup contact, because it may be perceived as more difficult or more fraught with potential conflict, is often less preferred than intragroup contact; to make matters worse, we are also raised in a certain social *habitus* that prepares us to construe some groups as more reliable and trustworthy than others. The consequence is that, the more we rely on our intuitions about the homogeneity, inferiority, and essential difference of less familiar "groups," the lower the likelihood of interaction and thus empathy, creativity, and innovation (Hodson et al., 2018; Bagci et al., 2019; Meleady et al., 2019).

Humans' tendency toward essentialist explanations is a result of the more general tendency to categorize the world around us. All animals do this, although some use more abstract conceptualizations than others. Nevertheless, our tendency to see the world in terms of categories often leads to inferential errors because the world is not, in fact, composed of categories of things but, rather, is composed of continuums of change and interaction. Continuums, however, are complex and do not admit of easy discussion. We'd rather, for example, think of someone as "having" or "not having" a mental illness rather than think about mood instability, depression, or psychopathy as a distribution of many traits present to varying degrees in any one individual. Similarly, instead of tracking all of the ways chairs or weddings differ from one another we just hold a general concept of "chair" or "wedding" and ignore, for the most part, all of the many variations of these things in the world. As with the sociological intuitions discussed above, our psychological intuitions exist for the same general purpose: to reduce the complexity of information in the world, to help us make decisions easily, and to facilitate cooperation with those in our ingroup.

Human beings (and likely other animals) also show a "confirmation bias," that involves selectively perceiving (or remembering) confirmations of pre-existing assumptions and selectively misperceiving (or forgetting) experiences that contradict pre-existing assumptions (Nickerson, 1998). This bias may also lead people to selectively expose themselves to circumstances likely to confirm, rather than challenge or undermine, their prior assumptions. Confirmation bias most often takes the form of seeking to confirm beliefs or attitudes consistent with those of our ingroup (Mercier, 2017). While the underlying reasons for the existence of confirmation bias are debated, an implicit preference to maintain cognitive consistency (i.e., reduce cognitive dissonance) and to bolster social support from others for already adopted worldviews are plausible.

This ubiquitous tendency to seek confirmation of our pre-existing worldviews and prior experiences can lead to the "spontaneous" formation of hierarchies, such as when people in a fused state share a pre-existing assumption that men (or women) are better leaders and, therefore, become more willing and able to perceive good leadership qualities in men (or women) (Correll and Ridgeway, 2006). The expectations that people have about individuals in various social categories can canalize perception, and thus behavior, in ways that potentially reproduce inequalities and/or discriminatory patterns of behavior (Ridgeway, 2011).

People are also biased toward perceiving and responding to threatening stimuli: this is variously called a "threat bias" or "negativity bias" (Baumeister et al., 2001). This attentional bias is presumed to have been adaptive evolutionarily—individuals more attentive to dangerous or negative stimuli would have been more likely to survive and reproduce relative to individuals less attentive to such cues—and is therefore a bias likely to exist not only in humans but across species. However, the combination of threat sensitivity and confirmation bias may produce circumstances where individuals develop absurd and irrational concerns about outgroups. To the degree that an individual, or group of individuals, has developed assumptions about the negative or dangerous traits of others, these assumptions might be maintained via selective exposure to (or selective remembering of) circumstances that confirm these assumptions. For example, if a person suspects that "white people" (and their "whiteness") are dangerous, they might prefer news shows that confirm these suspicions, or better remember negative (rather than positive) interactions with "white people" (see, for example, Knobloch-Westerwick et al., 2020).

Across studies, people have also been found to express an intuition that the social conditions that exist have always existed, or ought to exist; this is variously known as a "status quo bias," "existence bias," or tendency toward social "system justification" (Tversky and Kahneman, 1991; Jost et al., 2004; Eidelman et al., 2009). The particular "status quo" in question might correspond to the existing perceived normative order in the larger society, or it might correspond to an individual's particular subgroup norms. People tend to default to what they are familiar with (i.e., the status quo) when they are confronted with making a decision among a broad range of possibilities or alternatives, or when they are uncertain and worried about the outcome of a decision. For example, if people are told that a business has been around for 100 years, or that an organizational policy is 100 years old, people often demonstrate a preference for them relative to newer businesses and policies (Eidelman et al., 2009; Eidelman et al., 2010). Note that this preference emerges irrespective of the objective value, usefulness, or rationality of a particular business or policy—rather, if it has been around a long time, the intuition is that there must be something good about it. A moment's reflection will reveal that this intuition isn't always accurate—a business might persist, even if its product is useless, just because it has a low operating cost—but it is nevertheless and intuition that often comes effortlessly.

Uncertainty and worry moderate the strength of this effect: those who are more economically or socially vulnerable, perhaps paradoxically, are often more likely than people with higher socioeconomic status to justify or rationalize existing social hierarchies and organizations. Working-class individuals, for example, are often more likely to justify existing social hierarchies than are economic elites (Jost et al., 2008; Jost, 2017). This motivation to defend the status quo appears to be related to the relationship between economic distress (and/or institutional marginalization) and the likelihood of experiencing "aversive levels of uncertainty, insecurity, and social exclusion [along with a palliative] desire for long-term stability and security that is consonant with … thrift and self-reliance, as well as law and order" (Jost, 2017, pg. 74).

4.3 Humans' Intuitive Sociology and Psychology Rely, in Part, on Intuitions about the Physical World

In the above section, I described how our sociological intuitions about groups, power, and norms are predicated, to some extent, on psychological intuitions. Here, I hope to make the case that both our sociological and psychological intuitions are premised—to a substantial extent—on even more evolutionarily ancient intuitions about the physical world.

Evolutionary processes are nothing if not pragmatic and energy-saving (except, of course, in cases of runaway sexual selection, such as the classic case of the peacock's tail). Evolutionary processes appear to, if possible, work on existing structures, modifying them slightly over time. Sometimes, a random genetic mutation can confer rapid survival/reproductive benefits and spread throughout a population quickly. This, however, happens more rarely, because biological organisms are very complex fractal systems and random changes to such complex systems are much more likely to disrupt essential processes, or have no impact at all, than to have synergistically positive effects on survival or reproduction.

Thus, to the degree that cognitive inference systems about physics aided survival and were available for selection, evolutionary processes would have bootstrapped the existing neural structures responsible for these physical intuitions to create new neural networks dedicated to interpreting group life. Put bluntly, if ancestral primates couldn't avoid boulders and cliffs and long drops, they wouldn't survive long enough to symbolically represent, and respond to, collective behavioral patterns in their environments.

Consider some of our intuitions about the physical world. Beginning in infancy, cognitive inference systems develop to help babies, for example, understand that objects exist continuously and will not disappear after passing out of sight, that objects have solidity and will collide with one another, and that objects will fall if not supported (Hespos and van Marle, 2012; Shtulman, 2017; Boyer, 2018). In adulthood, when norms, or powerful individuals, appear to be influencing our behavior, we say that we can feel their "force" or "weight" impinging on us—we generate intuitions about the social world by recruiting intuitions that evolved for interpreting the physical world.

Many more examples might be given (see Tversky, 2019). Consider that, when we look at a group of things (geese, baseballs, barbecues), and they are far away from us, they look clumped together and homogeneous. This is also a convenient inference to make about social groups that we perceive as distant from us emotionally or in terms of our worldviews or identities—those groups "far" from us emotionally or symbolically are assumed to contain individuals who are "all the same," and whose traits and attitudes blur together. Or, as discussed above, physical objects in our environment, like trees or rocks, are grouped easily and essentialized if we don't develop too much of a familiarity with them. However, people more familiar with these objects, such as an arborist or a geologist, would cringe when hearing about how nonchalantly these terms "tree" and "rock" are thrown around—*what species* of tree, the arborist might ask, or *what mixture* of minerals, the geologist might ask.

We distinguish minute differences between our family members and friends because we are familiar with them, but we make little if any distinctions between, for example, those we regard as our political enemies. The physical intuition is that distant items in the world can be grouped for ease of information-processing and decision-making, and our social intuitions bootstrap these neural networks to provide us with the intuition that people we're not very familiar with can be easily grouped as well.

4.4 Fission–Fusion and Intuition

If it is not clear already, *social intuitions are inextricably linked with fission–fusion processes.* Intuitions enable and constrain fission–fusion oscillation; fission–fusion oscillation can also suppress or exacerbate our intuitions.

Fusion, to a large extent, relies on the ease with which we intuit, and enjoy pursuing, group cohesiveness and normative compliance. This should not surprise us—it merely reveals to us that how *groups of brains* process information (i.e., fission–fusion oscillation) depends on how *individual brains* process information. Symmetrically, how *individual brains* process information depends on how *groups of brains* process information. For example, if it didn't feel intuitive that those we've seen in the past might be seen again (see Krasnow et al., 2013) or that norms were external objects to be navigated, it might be harder for groups to disaggregate or reaggregate physically or attentionally. These intuitions about social life, then, should not be read as somehow distinct from fission–fusion oscillatory processes. Rather, these intuitions are part and parcel of them.

Just the same, however, our intuitions can undermine the rhythm of fission–fusion oscillation. This might occur when prejudices or stereotypes reduce peoples' comfortability with porous group boundaries. Sarah-Jane Leslie (2017), for example, describes the tendency for people to overgeneralize about the behavior of those we are less familiar with. If one person from some group acts in a particular way, we often hasten to assume that all members of that group will act similarly. Consider how many Americans grew fearful of Muslim immigrants after 9/11 (despite very few Muslims being terrorists) or how many Americans have grown fearful of police violence toward minorities (despite very few police officers acting unlawfully during arrests). The less familiar we are with a particular group, or the less similar we perceive ourselves to be to members of that group, the more quickly we overgeneralize about their supposed traits. Obviously, this can make open-system fission–fusion oscillation more difficult to establish with any rhythm. And, as I described above, a more closed fission-fusion oscillatory process will generate and integrate creativity and innovation at a lower rate because exposure to people with different experiences or different beliefs and behaviors will be more unusual.

There are also specific sets of intuitions likely to be stimulated by a fissioned, or fused, state. I call these "sets" of intuitions in the sense that they are composed of correlated, though analytically distinct, intuitions. They are correlated because fissioned, or fused, states involve complex behavioral repertoires and are thus supported and motivated by more than just one or two intuitions. Specifically, social organization that is "tighter" (i.e., more fused), relies on and facilitates different forms of (1) attentional allocation, (2) reasoning, (3) attribution, (4) self-understanding, (5) emotion, and

(6) motivation compared to "looser" (i.e., more fissioned) states (Varnum et al., 2010; Gelfand, 2019).

With regard to *attentional allocation*, relative fused states facilitate "field-dependent" attentional allocation, that is, attention to the emotional and physical cues of others, along with particular features of the immediate environment and social context. This attention to others and to the immediate environment helps coordinate behavior and belief with others in a given setting. As examples, we might think about how fusion at the level of mere awareness—say, navigating a busy sidewalk in a large city, or squeezing into a bustling subway car—might be facilitated by attending to the immediate moment-to-moment movement of others. Or, we might consider the need to attend to ingroup members' idiosyncratic needs and abilities when discerning how to extract, process, and distribute a valuable natural resource.

On the other hand, a relatively more fissioned state will facilitate more "field-independent" attentional allocation. The more individuals are freed from the obligations and demands of the collective, and the less restricted and monitored their movement, ideas, and behaviors, the more people can begin to think abstractly, daydream, and generate new (perhaps heretical) thoughts and behavioral patterns. Similarly, the less restricted or confined an individual's movement in space, the less relevant the details of any one location are to deciding where to move next. In a fissioned state, peoples' attention can be reallocated to non-immediately relevant social concerns and/or to multiple possible locations in time or space.

In short, when coordination with others is paramount, attentional allocation must be at least somewhat restricted to the immediate setting and to other group members; conversely, when coordination with others is relatively less important, attention is easier to detach from any particular group member or setting.

With regard to *reasoning styles*, fused states motivate and rely on intuitions about the validity/legitimacy of norms, traditions, and practicality (Varnum et al., 2010). This is true almost by definition—fused states are defined by their greater co-presence and/or shared attention, all of which, over time, reify certain habits and ideas/behaviors. The reification of shared behaviors or ideas is what we call a "tradition" or a "norm" or what seems "practical" in any given situation. By contrast, relative fission states allow for violations, critiques, or challenges to the status quo. This means that fission states enable, and to some extent rely on, reasoning that is more analytical, critical, or abstract.

In a fused state, belief and behavior can be monitored and policed by other group members more easily. In a fused state, individuals will also more likely self-monitor their beliefs and behaviors so as not to invite group reprisal. In a fissioned state, however, because co-presence and/or shared attention is relatively lower, individuals are (relatively) unbound from acting or believing in ways reified as necessary or practical or traditional by others. In addition, and equally important, the accumulation of critical or abstract reflections on reified group practices can itself justify fissioned states: the more individuals (or subgroups) come to regard co-presence and/or shared attention as stifling to creativity or independence (or, perhaps, simply unnecessary), the more prolonged fission states will be and the more likely fission states will be in the future.

With regard to *attribution styles*, relative fused states motivate more situational explanations for peoples' behaviors and beliefs, whereas relative fission states motivate more dispositional explanations for peoples' behaviors and beliefs (Varnum et al., 2010). This occurs separately from the flattering psychological tendency to assume that others' poor or inadvisable behavior is due to who they are (disposition), whereas our bad actions result from situational or environmental circumstances beyond our control (situational). The attributional intuitions that stem from fusion–fission do not necessarily involve attempting to blame others for their bad behavior while striving to absolve ourselves of blame for our own such behavior. Rather, the attributional intuitions stemming from fission–fusion dynamics result from the greater field-dependent attentional allocation (mentioned above) in fused states. When people are attending (even minimally) to others, their intentions, or the immediate setting, they will often recruit their observations about the embeddedness of others in a context when attempting to understand why others behave and/or believe as they do.

In a fissioned state, there are fewer people (or subgroups) paying attention to one another, and so features of the setting are less available to use as explanations for others' actions. On average, then, the more fused people are with one another (either physically or attentionally), the more intuitive it will seem that the beliefs and/or behaviors of others are due to features of the immediate, shared, setting. Conversely, the less fused people are with one another (either physically or attentionally), the more intuitive it will seem that the beliefs and/or behaviors of others result from specific attributes that they have as individuals (or independent subgroups). The same goes for self-attributions: greater fusion with others will tend to increase our intuition that our own behaviors and beliefs result from features of shared situations, whereas greater fissioning will tend to motivate intuitions that our behaviors and beliefs result from our own personality traits, personal experiences, particular genetic propensities, and so on.

With regard to *self-understanding*, fused states will tend to motivate construals of oneself as interdependent and other-directed. Conversely, fission states will tend to motivate self-construals as independent and self-directed (Varnum et al., 2010). Another way of saying this is that fused states motivate collectivist self-understandings (i.e., boundedness to others, indebtedness to others, deference to others), whereas fission states motivate individualistic self-understandings (i.e., independence from others, distinctness from others, superiority to others).

This is consistent with work done by Harry Triandis (1995), Richard Nisbett (2004), and others showing that people in "tighter" (i.e., on average more fused) cultures around the world interpret themselves, their goals, and their actions relative to the presence, desires, or expectations of others much more so than do people in "looser" (i.e., on average more fissioned) cultures. People in more fused cultures consider context and the relationship between people more when forming their identities and when making decisions; people in more fissioned cultures consider context and the relationships between people relatively less when forming their identities and making decisions. Typically, this research compares individuals in East Asian countries with those living in Western (usually North American) countries, and finds that construals of self are more interdependent in the former and more independent in the latter (De Oliveira and Nisbett, 2017). Some work, however, helpfully shows that these construals vary also *within* "Western" and "Eastern" countries (both of which, of course, contain subcultures and geographic locales that are more fused than others), not only *between* "Eastern" and "Western" countries (e.g., Varnum et al., 2008; see also Gelfand, 2019).

While emerging work in this area is showing that these differences in interdependent vs. independent self-orientation are stable across demographic characteristics like age, gender, or educational attainment within countries (e.g., Kitayama et al., 2019), we should not be persuaded by an essentialist account of cultures as intrinsically distinct from one another, however tempting this might be. More plausibly, so-called "collectivist" cultures are those that have had lower *per capita* incomes for longer periods and have relied more on farm labor in recent years; thus, people in such societies depend more on proximate community-embeddedness for survival. It seems that, as societies anywhere become richer and more urbanized, the people within them become more independent and self-directed in their orientation to the world (see Morris, 2015; Inglehart, 2018).

With regard to *emotion*, individuals in relatively fused states will tend to express a greater proportion of "socially engaging" emotions, whereas individuals in relatively fissioned states will tend to express a greater proportion of "socially disengaging" emotions (Varnum et al., 2010). The sort of socially engaging and socially disengaging emotions that facilitate fused or fissioned states can come in positive and negative forms (Kitayama et al., 2006). Positive socially engaging emotions might include respect, humility, awe, empathy, or friendliness/affability; negative socially engaging emotions might include guilt, indebtedness, shame, or fear of outgroups. These emotions, positive or negative, motivate people to pursue co-presence or shared attention with others.

On the other hand, socially disengaging positive emotions characteristic of a shift to relative fissioning might include feelings of personal pride, superiority, efficacy, increased sense of self-esteem, or feeling as though one were "on top of the world" (Kitayama et al., 2006). Negative socially disengaging emotions might include frustration (toward the ingroup), anger (toward the ingroup), or annoyance (toward the ingroup). These lists of emotions are certainly nonexhaustive. The point I'm hoping to make is that there are always emotional components to the motivation to aggregate or disperse and that these emotions will feel intuitive to those headed toward a fused or fissioned state.

Finally, with regard to *motivation*, in fused states individuals (or subgroups) will tend to be explicitly motivated by group (or supergroup) achievement and provide assistance to ingroup members. By contrast, in fissioned states entities will tend to be explicitly motivated by personal achievement and self-actualization (Varnum et al., 2010). These will be experienced as intuitions—the more fused a context is, the more it will seem obvious and clear that group achievement and assistance to others are paramount and overriding concerns. It will seem similarly obvious in a relatively fissioned context that self-expression and the pursuit of personal goals are paramount and overriding obligations.

In the above discussion, and to some extent throughout this manuscript, it may seem as though I am juxtaposing two discrete states: fusion vs. fission. But, just read more closely—I am most definitely not intending to do this. Fusion states phase, often smoothly, into fission states and vice versa. To fission is often to be fused to a smaller grouping. As I stated earlier, fission–fusion is a fractal dynamic. Within a fused collective, some individuals (or subgroups) are more independent than others, and during fissioning some individuals (or subgroups) remain more co-present and collective in their intentions.

If it seems that I am discussing fission and fusion as though they were entirely discrete, separable states, this is only because it is immensely difficult to discuss the dynamics of each relative state while also properly emphasizing their overlap. Certainly, someone sitting alone in the wilderness is fissioned from others and not merely part of a smaller fused group. But, how many of us sit alone in the wilderness for any length of time? Most importantly, how many of us could survive like this for any length of time? Moreover, when we are sitting in the wilderness alone, our wandering thoughts invariably relate to experiences we've had with others or ideas we've learned from collectives of various sorts. And, even if we entirely quieted our thoughts through some sort of disciplined meditation while out in the wilderness, the physiological functioning of our bodies would remain a testament to the fusion of communities of bacteria on our skin, in our gut, and in virtually every organ of our bodies. So, please keep in mind that I am trying to draw theoretical and analytical distinctions between the intuitions relatively more or less present in fissioned vs. fused states not because fissioned states are always distinct in any definitive sense from fused states, but because our emotions and cognitions do in fact differ, often in subtle ways, depending on our proximity (physically or attentionally) to others.

4.5 Reflection on and Suppression of Intuition

Intuitions are the fodder for conceptual and emotional change. Intuitions are the starting points from which we adjust; they are our baselines for change. Intuitions appear obvious, come to mind easily, and reduce the complexity of experience into actionable understandings. Sometimes, intuitions are often profoundly unhelpful misconceptions (such as the intuition that groups are like big people); other times, intuitions help groups coalesce (such as the intuition that group goals should supersede individual concerns). And, sometimes intuitions help motivate changes in our forms of social organization (e.g., when the emotions of annoyance or frustration toward the ingroup lead to relative fissioning).

We might try to unlearn our intuitions, but researchers in this area have provided evidence suggesting that this isn't possible. We cannot unlearn our intuitions, but we can become aware of them and work to override them when they aren't rational or helpful. Shtulman (2017), who I've leaned heavily on in this section, says as much:

> While we can learn new, more accurate theories of a phenomenon, we can't seem to *unlearn* our intuitive theories. They continue to lurk in the recesses of our minds long after we have abandoned them as our preferred theory. Intuitive theories are always there, influencing our thoughts and behaviors in subtle yet appreciable ways. As we acquire [more accurate] theories of the world, our intuitive theories are never completely erased from our minds.
>
> (Shtulman, 2017, pgs. 13–14, italics in original)

Shtulman is in large part correct, both on empirical and theoretical grounds. Empirically, children and adults reveal similar intuitions, though adults are often educated and patient enough to reflect on the legitimacy of their intuitions in a way that children cannot. Theoretically, intuitions are the reliable outputs of cognitive inference systems that evolved to reduce informational complexity so as to motivate decision-making. Intuitions are, therefore, probably impossible to "erase" from our minds.

But, as far as I'm concerned, some intuitions are more easily adjusted or reflected on than others—intuitions that power is a forceful substance that people "carry," or that exchanges are zero-sum, or that demographic groups harbor certain essences are all capable of adjustment upon reflection in a way that, for example, feeling lonely, and thus desirous of co-presence with others, is not. This is because, in many important ways, groups really aren't like big people, but when I am lonely, I really do want to be around others. Both might be intuitions, but the former is much closer to a mere factual inaccuracy than the latter.

Researchers have discerned several successful methods that can help people address their more irrational or unhelpful intuitions. One method involves encouraging people to think more in terms of continuums than categories. Instead of considering only homogeneous categories (e.g., "the rich" and "the poor," or "white people" and "people of color," or "citizens" and "immigrants," etc.), we might reflect upon how rich people might differ from one another, or how the poor might differ from one another, and so on. In other words, we can begin to think more accurately, and less intuitively, if we consider how individuals vary *within* essentialized categories instead of only pitting one essentialized category against another as though each were a homogeneous monolith.

Another helpful strategy is much more straightforward: just teach people about the nature and structure of their intuitions. This seems to be the biggest advantage (some) scientists have over the lay public—ideally, scientists, in the course of their professional education, learn to reflect upon and mitigate their intuitions when attempting to discern truths about the world. This is certainly not true of all scientists. Physicists, for example, are far more cognizant of their false intuitions about matter and motion than, for example, sociologists are about their false intuitions that groups are like big people or that exchanges are zero-sum. This may be because physicists study entities more remote from personal experience, like atoms, compared to sociologists, who study entities regularly experienced, like economies. Perhaps, the more remote a phenomenon is from personal experience, the easier it is to become aware of, and check, our intuitions. Regardless, simple awareness of the sometimes fallacious nature of our intuitions can help motivate reflection and adjustment.

Another method that seems helpful is to have people write out mechanistic explanations for relationships between entities (Shtulman, 2017). This exercise can help people see that they do not really understand what they think they do, and that they are, actually, just relying on intuitions. For example, many people think they understand what weather or clouds or rainbows or cars or economies are, but if they were to sit down and write out a diagram explaining how, for example, sunlight and refraction produce rainbows or how the various components of an engine interact in a car or how economies produce inequities, they would quickly come to see that they do not, in fact, understand what is going on. Such a humbling experience might motivate people to reflect on the intuitions that led them to believe they understood more than they did. People cannot simply be told that they do not understand what they think they understand—they will stubbornly insist they understand things perfectly well (because their intuitions feel so obvious and informative). Rather, people need to go through the exercise of attempting to actually write out a detailed mechanistic explanation that specifies relationships between variables (*not* a narrative explanation relying on vague jargon) before their own confusions will become apparent to them.

Having said all of this, it seems that our intuitions are best overcome not by individual willpower or individual reflection, but rather by the institutionalization of norms that require and reward such reflection. Specifically, the institutionalization of scientific experimentation, peer review, and replication incentivize people to examine their intuitions in light of data, evidence, and experimentation, and it is these institutionalized incentives (in terms of prestigious jobs, status hierarchies, and societal influence) that best motivate the dispelling of those intuitions that are least helpful and most prone to inaccuracy (Bronowski, [1958] 2011; Deutsch, 2011; Pinker, 2018). Incentives to examine and reflect on our intuitions must be formalized institutionally in order to ensure that such reflection and examination are undertaken with any regularity—"science" as an occupation, with all its flaws, has done more to dispel unhelpful intuitions than any other arena of human behavior.

Even still, while the institutionalization of scientific endeavors has aided in dispelling some of our more unhelpful intuitions, this certainly does not mean that scientists never err or that the public necessarily trusts the findings of scientists. Indeed, scientists themselves constantly struggle to overcome their own fallacious intuitions, and, even when they have done so with some success, they struggle to disseminate their research to a public quite content to rely entirely on their own intuitions.

Hugo Mercier and his colleagues (2019) have run some experiments to determine how effective exposure to scientific expertise is for dispelling layperson intuitions. They've found that when people are provided answers to a question by those acting as "experts" on the topic, most adopt the provided answers. In other words, when an expert gives direct information to someone that turns out to be helpful, that person tends to accept the advice. Yet, when the nonexpert attempts to transmit this information to others, fewer than 50% remember to say that the information came from an expert, thus reducing the likelihood that others will follow the advice. Also, Mercier and his colleagues found that if people are merely advised of another person's expertise, instead of seeing it for themselves, they are far less likely to defer to the ostensible expert. Thus, regardless of how successful scientists are in dispelling their own unhelpful or inaccurate intuitions, getting the public to follow along with their discoveries is often difficult absent direct interaction and demonstration.

4.6 Intuitive Physics, in Greater Depth

I tried above to describe what appear to be general human intuitions about the social world. But these are not the only intuitions that social scientists should take seriously. Intuitions about the physical world are also important not just to mention briefly (as I've done above) but to actually center in this discussion. The reason why I need to draw your attention to our inaccurate intuitions about the physical world is because, as I argued in *Cultural Evolution: The Empirical and Theoretical Landscape* and will argue in the next chapters, engineering infrastructure is the "unit of evolution" in cultural evolution (for the distinction between units of selection and units of evolution, see Maynard Smith, 1987).

The reason why sophisticated engineering infrastructure has developed so slowly in human beings—consider, for example, the gap in time between the use of fire and the use of electricity—is partly because our false perceptions of the physical world are stubbornly intuitive. Yet, technological innovation that expands the efficiency of a society's infrastructure is critical in determining the sorts of lives people can live and the opportunities that will shape their values and worldviews.

So, here, let's consider in more detail some of our intuitions about the physical world, keeping in mind how inaccurate or unhelpful intuitions might slow our capacity to build a better world through more innovative and efficient engineering.

When we think of matter or energy, we easily call up an image or idea of "stuff," that can be used and depleted. However, trained physicists and chemists would insist otherwise: matter and energy cannot be created or destroyed, only transferred. This principle is today known as the "conservation of matter." This is not intuitive to us, nor is it intuitive to the physicists or chemists who study it. Physicists and chemists have to constantly reflect on and try to effortfully control their intuitions about matter and energy (Shtulman and Valcarcel, 2012). It *seems* as though evaporated water has disappeared (when, in reality, it has just been converted to a gas/vapor); it *seems* like a burning log disappears (when, in reality, the log's matter was converted into heat). The molecular composition of matter, and the ways this composition can be converted, is not obvious to us. The mechanistic process of conversion is, literally, invisible to the naked eye. All we see—all natural selection required us to notice—was the brute form of logs (or fire) or of water (or vapor). So, we notice that where water or a log once was, it is no more, and we intuit that the matter and energy contained in these things has disappeared as well.

We can see the emergence of this intuition in childhood—classic experiments by Jean Piaget showed that, when preschoolers handle two clay balls of the same size and weight, they correctly report that both balls contain the same amount of clay and are the same weight. Yet, if the experimenter then flattens one of these balls with their hand into the shape of a pancake, children will report that the flattened clay now has a different weight and a different amount of clay than its balled-up counterpart. Another experiment revealed that when children are presented with two glasses that both contain the same amount of water, one short and wide and one tall and thin, young children will often conclude that the tall glass contains more water (even when they can see the same amount of water being poured into each). These intuitions are stubborn in children until around middle school, at which point they begin learning to override their intuitions in order to conclude that matter has been conserved and that, though the pancake-shaped clay, or water in a tall glass, may look larger, they do not in fact contain more clay or water.

Shtulman (2017) suggests that human beings do not easily perceive weight or volume; rather, they perceive what he calls *heft* (how heavy something feels) and *bulk* (how big something looks). In an ancestral environment, assessing the heftiness and bulkiness of various items—rocks, people, baskets—would have been sufficient for organizing group labor or transporting particular resources from point A to point B. The problem is that our intuitions about "heft" combine what are actually two distinct properties of matter: the weight of matter and its density. A five-pound clump of cotton may feel lighter than a five-pound bar of lead, on account of lead's higher density, despite both being the same weight. Relying on this intuition may cause us to not notice or reflect much on things that have weight but low density, such as dust or air. Relatedly, we might think a small rock is more likely to float than a large ship, since the former has such little bulk and heft. Yet, this intuition would lead us astray—what matters more is the density of the object, not its weight.

Similarly, our intuitions about "bulk" combine our perception of the volume of matter with its surface area. Spilled milk may cover a larger area of the floor than milk contained in a carton, but this does not mean that there is more milk on the floor than there was in the carton. Relying on this intuition may cause us to not notice or reflect much on the fact that all matter has volume, but may not take up much space, such as steam. While it is obvious to us that rocks and water and logs and leaves and dirt are made of matter, it is consequently far less obvious to us that steam or clouds or oxygen are made of matter. Air, for example, does not intuitively seem like it is composed of matter because "it has volume that cannot be seen (no bulk) and weight that cannot be felt (no heft)" (Shtulman, 2017, pg. 24).

Another way to think about these tendencies is to understand that humans (and animals generally) evolved to perceive matter in terms of tangibility. Matter that is not tangible would, by definition, have been difficult to see or taste or touch, and thus difficult to use or manipulate. It follows that the evolutionary processes honing our perceptual systems would ignore the prevalence of intangible forms of matter. Easily sensed and manipulated objects would appear to contain matter—things like bricks, stones, trees, and tools—while other things such as steam (matter as vapor) or ideas (electrochemical reactions in our brain) would be regarded as not having matter. Ideas (and norms) are a special case, indeed. We clearly perceive them, but they are not tangible. So, we regard them as immaterial objects. This intuition underlies our beliefs about souls and ghosts and gods; in fact, however, our intuitions are just leading us astray once more. Ideas, like bricks, are composed of matter. The material substrate of ideas is imperceptible to us, not necessarily because it is so small and particulate (as with steam) but because it resides in the imperceptible darkness of our own skulls. Our intuition, absent an understanding of neurology, is to regard ideas or norms as canalizing, but immaterial, objects external to us when they are, in fact, a socially calibrated by-product of electricity and chemistry flowing through tissues in our skull.

Even accounting for education, experience, and reflection, our intuitions are stubborn (Shtulman and Harrington, 2016; Shtulman, 2017; Young et al., 2018). For example, when asked to rapidly classify entities as either material or immaterial, adults only correctly classify ink, perfume, and air as being composed of matter between 75%–85% of the time. Adults correctly classified thunder as matter only about 35% of the time while, also, classifying light as matter 37% of the time, despite the fact that because light has no mass it cannot be considered matter. With the naked, uninformed eye, it is impossible to distinguish the plasma electrons composing thunder, which have mass, from the photons composing light, which have no mass. Shtulman (2017) also points out that we make intuitive errors so commonly that they become figures of speech—it makes no sense to ask if a glass is half empty or half full, because all glasses are always full of either water or gas (i.e., oxygen).

Humans tend also to conflate heat with temperature. Historians assume that this was a common misunderstanding at least until around 1761, when Scottish chemist Joseph Black found that adding heat to a bucket of ice water did not raise the temperature of the water until all of the ice had melted. What Black had discovered was that the movement of particles in the heated water did not increase until the movement of the much slower moving particles (comprising the ice) began to increase (i.e., until the ice melted). Though Black had added heat to the ice water, the temperature lagged behind, because our measures of temperature capture only the average energy of a substance.

Upon some reflection, it is obvious that heat is distinct from temperature. Imagine you open the door of a car when it is 110 degrees Fahrenheit outside—the synthetic leather (really, just plastic) covering on your steering wheel might scald your hands, as will the metal seat buckle. But a cotton t-shirt in the back seat or a pillow you use for your lower back won't burn you at all. This difference is due to the fact that some materials, on account of their composition, conduct heat better (or worse) than others. As this example shows, the temperature of a car is distinct from the movement of particles within the materials inside the car. The metal seat buckle, for example, contains delocalized electrons that vibrate and move more freely, generating more heat, which can then burn your hand.

Heat is just the energy resulting from increased movement of molecules in a substance. We cannot "trap" heat or "transfer" heat or let heat "escape." We can simply note increases in the movement of molecules comprising a substance, with increased movement denoting greater energy and, thus, heat. Increases in heat are increases in energy along a continuum. There is no point at which "heatedness" is attained as a distinct construct from "coldness," other than from our own subjective perception. Heat is not a "substance," with essential properties. Rather, heat is an emergent process, a by-product, of the increased movement of particles in a substance or material.

But, organisms did not evolve to accurately perceive heat-as-energy. Rather, organisms evolved to avoid getting burned. So, when we touch our fingers to a stove, we recoil, and claim that the stove is "hot," even though what we've actually registered is not the rapid movement of particles but, rather, how fast our skin was transferring heat from the stove. The faster the heat transfer, the greater the pain and cellular damage—so we recoil. As Shtulman (2017) points out, if it was an accurate reading of temperature that we were responding to, we would recoil our hand from the hot air of an oven as quickly as we would if we touched a hot pan inside the oven. But, we don't. We can reach inside an oven because air is a poor conductor of heat, but we cannot touch the pan inside the oven with our bare hands because the metal of the pan is a much better conductor of heat. In either case, our mind is not accurately perceiving the relationship between heat and temperature, or between the movement of particles and heat/energy, but is rather registering, in a vague way, how well heat is transferring from the outside environment to our skin, and when this transfer is fast, we remove our limbs from danger.

Like heat, vision is also assumed to be a sort of substance. Eyesight is intuitively perceived to be a substance emitted from our eyes. Superheroes, for example, with "x-ray vision" are depicted as emitting some sort of rays from their eyes that can see through walls. It is as though our eyesight involves two spotlights shining out into the world, making the world visible to us. Famous thinkers from Plato to Leonardo Da Vinci (along with many of us today) relied on this intuition.

It is perhaps not surprising why this intuition about vision exists. It certainly seems as though we open our eyes to extract an image of the world external to us. It does *not* seem as though the light reflecting off this world is being registered by the cells in our eye and calibrating the rods and cones within it to generate a mental image. Even when adults are explicitly instructed as to how light entering the eye generates visual imagery, they still revert three months later to an intuition that something is being *emitted from* the eyes to generate visual imagery (Shtulman, 2017). How vision *seems* to work, how it *feels*, drives our perceptions of how vision really operates mechanistically. Once again, our intuitions, though sufficient for survival and reproduction, lead us astray from the goal of accurately understanding reality.

As with heat and vision, so too do we intuit that electricity is an essentialized substance in the world. The reality is that electricity, as with heat and vision, is an emergent property, or by-product, of interactions in nature, and is not itself a substance containing a discrete essence. Electricity, in particular, emerges from the movement of electrons through circuits, and this understanding seems to have begun with the experiments of Italian physicist Alessandro Volta in the 1800s (more on this later). Children and adults alike, even those adults with PhDs in physics, nevertheless easily revert to relying on their intuitions about electricity; the intuition is usually that electricity is a substance ("juice") that flows from an outlet into a television or toaster or hairdryer (Shtulman, 2017).

In reality, electricity does not flow down a wire as water might flow down a pipe. Rather, turning on a wall switch or plugging a device into a wall outlet serves to complete a circuit, allowing copper wires to transfer the electrons that can power our devices. The wires comprising a circuit simply conduct the transfer of electrons (already floating in the atmosphere) between the wall of your house and the device you want to turn on. Just as roads canalize and direct the emergence of traffic, so do wires comprising a circuit canalize and direct electrons—it is no more accurate to intuit that electricity is a substance than it would be to intuit that traffic is an essentialized substance. Electricity and traffic are emergent properties in nature, not substances with essences.

The intuition that emergent properties are intrinsic components of objects is also often extended to our understanding of gravity and motion. We do not easily perceive how the mass of objects, and their relationship to one another in space, can create a gravitational field. Rather, we perceive the heft of objects, and conclude that heftier objects must fall faster than less hefty objects because they are heftier. It is not obvious to us that the Earth is, itself, a quite heavy object, and that its mass is sufficient to draw objects toward it, on account of its distortion of what Hermann Minkowski (1909) conceptualized as the "fabric" of space-time (following Albert Einstein's lead; see Einstein, 1905). Space and time are, it seems, a "fabric" revealing a certain curvature resulting from the mass of the objects in it. The Earth's mass bends the curvature of space-time, causing smaller objects to fall into this curvature. This is what we now call gravity, despite few of us actually understanding the full complexity of the physics behind it (myself included).

Our intuitions that objects have an essence that includes weight, and that heavy objects fall down because they are heavy, are easier to understand than complex theoretical physics. They're also fully sufficient for navigating the world long enough to survive and reproduce. Natural selection, being an oft-efficient process, wouldn't have produced brains that intuit an accurate picture of the physical world, but would rather stop once cognitive processes were sufficiently complex to ensure survival and reproduction.

The same is true for our understanding of motion. Intuitively, we presume that objects move because they were pushed. After all, when we push objects with our bodies, they move. This intuition is certainly sufficient for dragging boulders and stones around our landscape to create pyramids, Stonehenge, or the large buildings that today house our institutions. "Force," then, is intuitively assumed to be something that is transmitted between entities, as when we push a gasless car toward a gas station. Physicists today, however, understand motion as something continuous, adjusted only by the degree of friction in the environment. In a frictionless environment (i.e., outer space), objects move continuously, indefinitely, smoothly along. On a road, or a dirt path, it seems as though an object at rest is not moving, and that we must push it to move it. We cannot see, from our immediate vantage point, that the object is moving, quite quickly—it is hurtling through space on the surface of the Earth!

As with our sociological intuitions, our intuitions about the physical world presume solidity, continuity, and cohesion where, often, there is none. Groups of people we are not familiar with are more easily thought of as cohesive, solid units of people all sharing beliefs, intentions, and behaviors, pushing one another along in unison. In reality, groups are often an emergent result of many interactions, and do not reveal fully shared beliefs, intentions, behaviors, or influences. Similarly, large companies or nations of people do not all think, or behave, alike. Groups, relationships, and norms are not essential substances "out there" in the world. Yet, the actual reality—groups, relationships, and norms are complex emergent processes containing various continuums—is too complex for any one person to accurately reflect on with any regularity. Only open-system fission–fusion oscillation can dissolve our intuitions in favor of shared experimentation, shared experience, and shared intellectual growth.

Chapter 5

On the Important Distinction between Tools and Infrastructure

Tools are an extension of an organism's nervous system. With tools, animals can reach further, eat more, and defend better. If tools can extend an individual organism's capabilities, then infrastructure (collectively utilizable tools) can extend a society's capabilities as well as its values and logic of operation.

Tools come in different shapes and sizes, and serve different purposes; tools vary along a number of continuums. However, I must direct your attention to a more hidden continuum: tools that emerge from and extend individual capacities and those that emerge from and extend collective capacities. This is a relative, not an absolute, difference. Some tools are *relatively* more likely to emerge from and provide benefits for individuals, other tools are *relatively* more likely to emerge from and provide benefits for collectives.

Consider the modern example of a wrench. A wrench is useful for individuals, and handing out wrenches to many people (or making them available for sale) improves the efficiency with which people can adjust nuts and bolts in any appliance or vehicle they have. However, any given single wrench is only a tool I can use or that someone else can use. It is not, per se, a tool *we* can use. Yes, many wrenches can be manufactured for the masses, making the same tool *I* use available to *you* as well. Yet, there is an important relative difference between a wrench and, say, a high-voltage power line providing electricity to anybody plugged into that particular electrical grid. A power line is very much a tool, but it is the sort of tool usable by anyone within range. A power line transmits electricity (for lighting or heating or powering devices) to many people simultaneously. You and I can, at the *same* time, use the *same* power line for different purposes.

Keeping with a modern example, imagine mechanics working in an auto-body shop. There may be several wrenches available for the mechanics to use, but each wrench is used by a particular mechanic in the context of a particular project (e.g., changing a tire). Yet, the electricity flowing into the shop is accessible, simultaneously, to any employee who decides to use it. You can turn on a switch in the shop's front office that illuminates it,

DOI: 10.4324/9781003266020-5

and, simultaneously, I can be using an electric drill plugged into a different wall of the same shop. Or, across the street in my home, I might be turning on my electric stove, totally unaware of the goings on at the auto shop but relying on the same overhead power lines. The infrastructure that makes the transmission of electricity possible is, compared to a wrench, a simultaneously usable "collective tool."

For the purposes of conceptual clarity, from here on out I'm going to be calling that which is used by individuals or small groups to extract, process, or distribute resources a *tool*. And, I will be calling that which is used by large collectives to extract, process, or distribute resources *infrastructure*. Relative to tools, which other mammals and primates use regularly, the creation of infrastructure requires a more concerted, more developed, "collective intentionality" (Tomasello, 2019) to build and would, to varying degrees, result in relatively greater collective utilizability. My claim is not that nonhuman animals necessarily lack infrastructure—beavers have dams, ants use plants as a form of collective housing and food, and so on. Rather, my claim is that human infrastructure is unique, only by degree (as it appears to us), in its collective construction, use, and modification over time.

This distinction between tools and infrastructure matters because *some level of group fusion is required to plan, direct, and construct infrastructure.* Laborers must be coordinated and synchronized in their construction of key components of infrastructure, and elites must be coordinated and synchronized in their planning, funding, and operating of infrastructure. If fusion among workers or elites is unattainable or not sustained, infrastructure decays, dissolves, or is never built, making the growth of the population or economy more difficult or impossible. Just as important, open-system fission–fusion oscillation is necessary for generating the creativity and innovation necessary for new infrastructures, or for improvements in infrastructural efficiency or infrastructural sustainability. The freedom of thought and experience afforded by relative fission states, and the relative integration of ideas afforded by fused states, drives the modification of our intuitions, and thus of our infrastructure over time.

Again, to be clear, no strict dichotomy should be read into my theoretical distinction between tools and infrastructure—infrastructure is composed of tools and tools are required to maintain infrastructural units. A Neolithic-era garden hoe is makable and usable by individuals; an ancient Greek cargo ship is much harder for an individual to make alone, and more than one person can use it at a time; undersea power cables and electrical grids are well-nigh impossible to develop oneself but are usable by millions and billions of people. The important point is not my arbitrary terminology of "tool" and "infrastructure"; rather, the important points are the dimensions of *collective development* (including associated novel innovations), *collective construction*, and *collective accessibility/usability*, with "tools" more on the end of individual construction and usage, while "infrastructure" is more on the end of collective construction and usage.

Figure 5.1 Conceptual Distinction Between Tools and Infrastructure

These distinctions are visualized in Figure 5.1. Each individual continuum distinction between tool and infrastructure is hardly without exceptions—the cell phone on the table or desk next to you right now is not collectively utilizable, despite being collectively developed by innovative research teams. This is why the continuum distinction between tools and infrastructure rests on *all three axes*: infrastructure is that which is relatively more collectively developed/conceptualized *and* more collectively constructed *and* more collectively accessible/usable.

Let's consider some examples of this continuum distinction between tools and infrastructure. In human foraging bands, spears are a valuable commodity. Though wooden sticks disintegrate with time, the sharpened stones presumably attached to these sticks are well-known to archeologists and suggest that humans have been using spears to hunt for at least a couple of hundred thousand years (Wynn, 2009). A group of spear-throwers is no doubt a formidable force. Yet, while the information required to make a (good) spear may be collectively held (i.e., many individuals in a foraging society might understand the steps necessary to haft a sharp stone or bone to a wooden shaft), the product itself, the spear, can be made by a single skilled artisan and is usable only by one person at a time.

Now, by contrast, consider campfires, which have likely been used by *Homo*, in some form, for millions of years. Anatomically modern humans were already using fire to improve their weaponry by the Middle Paleolithic period (Delagnes et al., 2016). As with the example of a spear, the knowledge of how to start a fire, stoke a fire, and put out a fire might be shared by many people within a foraging band. Campfires can also be started by a single person. However, a key difference is that, once a fire is started, anyone in proximity can use it for warmth, for cooking, for light, or for heating stone or wood to make better spears. The fire, itself, is relatively more collectively usable than the spear itself (even if the knowledge necessary to create both is, to some extent, collectively held). This is the sense in which a spear is more of a tool, and a campfire is more of an infrastructural unit.

Also, technologies generally (i.e., tools or infrastructure) are *material structures containing information*—they are information-containing structures. The information contained in technology can be discerned through reverse engineering, or by observing in detail the operation of technology. In other words, insofar as a piece of technology is perceived to be useful, someone can always attempt to observe *why* it seems to work better than other technologies and attempt to incorporate this information into future iterations of the technology.

Sometimes, we can simply look at a piece of technology and deduce how it was made, and what its intended purposes were. Think of a straw hat with a large brim as a tool to keep sunlight off one's face, neck, and shoulders. Simply looking at this device is sufficient for discerning roughly how it was made (e.g., woven plant fiber), and suggests a possible use (e.g., when put on one's head, a shadow is cast over areas of the body that would be exposed to light). At other times, the information and intent encoded into technology is less obvious—think of someone seeing an overhead power line for the first time.

Or, to use an example from the time period we will shortly be considering, think of a plow. Sometime between 3000 and 4000 BCE, people in Sumer and Egypt began using wooden plows to break up soil in order to make seed-planting easier. The plow would be attached by a harness to a draft animal, such as an ox, and dragged through the soil. If someone who'd never visited a farming village before came across a plow, its uses and construction might not be obvious. Certainly, a person could quickly figure out how a plow might be used, but the transparency of the information embedded in the object is arguably lower than for, say, a straw hat. The level of information transparency in an electrical generator is lower still, and by the end of this book, you'll know why: infrastructure evolves; it is the result of many cumulative modifications that produce a "hiddenness" of the specific information necessary for reconstruction.

I will be returning to these points in the next major section of this book. The important points I hope to make now, however, are: (1) technology contains information, revealed to varying extents in its operation and functioning; (2) some technologies contain more information, or more difficult-to-extract information, than others; and (3) some technologies—infrastructure—are more collectively developed, collectively constructed, and collectively utilizable than others.

5.1 Tool Use in Farming Societies

Human foragers have used tools for the purposes of hunting and gathering since the Paleolithic era. However, the use of tools for more explicit engineering purposes—levers, pulleys, ramps, screws, wedges, and wheels attached to axles—dates to the rise of Mesopotamian farming societies (Zhang and Yang, 2020). The ancient Egyptians, for example, used these "simple machines," along with massive amounts of slave labor, to build their majestic pyramids. But, it is the agricultural tools I'd like to focus on here. Though the pyramids and temples of the ancient world were engineering feats, they were less proximate to the more mundane and more necessary task of feeding people. Without fed people in dense numbers, there are no pyramids, temples, or anything else.

Many tools could be discussed. Threshing sledges, for example, were used in the earliest societies in southern Mesopotamia to separate edible grains from undigestible straw. These sledges were simply boards with sharp stones attached to one side that, when drug, tore the straw from the grain. An even more important tool in early farming societies was the plow, a tool so important that, according to an ancient Chinese text, "no king or ruler of a state could dispense with it" (as quoted in Smil, 2017, pg. 53). Without the use of a plow pulled by an ox, farmers must manually hoe the land themselves. Hoeing is monotonous, tiring, and slow. But without digging a hoe into the ground and breaking up and turning over the soil, seeds are harder to plant, soil is more difficult to aerate and fill around plants, and weeds cannot be dug up. Relative to the manual hoeing of soil, plows made the maintenance of large crop fields easier and more time efficient.

The earliest plows were "ard plows" and can be dated to Mesopotamia around 4,000 BCE (Smil, 2017). These plows were simple wooden devices attached to the back of oxen which then dragged a large sharpened stick through the soil as they walked. To properly aerate soil and dig out weeds before planting, farmers would march the ox across the field, with the trailing plow creating grooves in the soil called "furrows." Seeds and fertilizer could then be sprinkled by hand into these grooves, before the soil was smoothed back over. Ard plows were a farming "mainstay" in ancient Greece and Rome, and also common throughout the Middle East, Africa, and Asia.

Innovations of the ard plow were slow but steady over time, and many slight innovations have no doubt been lost to history. Perhaps the earliest innovation was the attachment of metal tips to the sharpened stick that draft animals dragged through the soil behind them—this prevented the sharpened stick from breaking or fraying. In Egypt around 3,000 BCE, for example, ard plows were being fitted with iron tips (Smil, 2017). Eventually, the entire plow was built from iron or steel instead of wood, which obviously increased its durability (but, also, its weight, meaning that oxen took longer to drag them and became fatigued more easily). Another important innovation was the attachment of a moldboard to the base of the plow. This curved plate guided the plowed soil to one side instead of the plowed soil heaping up haphazardly around the path of the sharpened end being drug through the soil. The first moldboards were just wood panels, but by the first century CE, the Chinese were using curved cast iron metal plates. The furrows created with moldboard plows were clearer, more organized, and thus easier to fill with seeds and fertilizer.

Just how the moldboard was constructed, and from which material, varied across regions. In medieval Europe (and elsewhere), for example, farmers used wooden moldboards but also attached "coulters," which were sharpened spikes, knives, or discs that helped break apart hardened soil ahead of the cutting edge of the moldboard (i.e., the "plowshare"). Coulters were essentially a secondary device for breaking up soil and were especially useful when the soil was so dry that the plowshare itself wouldn't adequately dig up and turn over the dirt. Harrows were (and are) another important tool for farmers. Harrows are square or rectangular panels attached with sharpened spikes, pegs, or knives that can be dragged through soil by draft animals (or, by humans, if resources are too scarce to support animal domestication) to help break up or spread out clumps of soil before or after tilling. The first harrows, "brush harrows," used thick sticks with sharp branches, which were dragged across the soil as needed. Later harrows used metal spikes instead of sticks because, of course, sticks broke much too easily. Conveniently, the harrow could be turned over (with spikes or sticks pointing upward) and subsequently dragged along the soil in order to smooth it over.

The farming innovations discussed above are common in some form around the world, but there are always exceptions. For example, some societies did not use plows pulled by draft animals. In some regions, resources were too scarce to feed both humans and domesticated animals, in which case humans pulled the plows. Or, in the case of Mesoamerican societies which did not have access to large hoofed animals that could be domesticated and used for labor, a foot plow was used (known as a *chaki taklla*) (Smil, 2017). This foot plow consisted of a large, curved, and sharpened wooden stick affixed with a crossbar that could be pushed down into the soil by the user's feet. The foot plow appears to have been most prevalent in regions of South America (in particular, the Andean region) with no domesticated draft animals, but they were also used in Europe and the South Pacific region where steep and stony mountain terrains made use of an animal-driven plow inconvenient or impossible.

Once soil was sufficiently furrowed, it needed to be seeded. So-called "broadcast seeding," which simply involves dropping seeds in furrows by hand, was, and is, common though it is rarely used today on large farms because it tends to be an inefficient use of seeds and leads to uneven growth (Smil, 2017). Innovations with regard to seeding have been documented beginning at least in 1300 BCE in Mesopotamia. So-called "seed drills" were pipe-like wooden devices with funnels at the top facing the user and were affixed with wheels or push-handles. Seeds were simply poured into the funnel and a "regulating device" such as a stick or wedge would be used to ensure that seeds were dropped from the device slowly into furrowed soil (Needham, 1984). Later, iron multi-tubed seed drills were developed in China in the second century BCE. Seed drills were often pulled by draft animals, but generally seeding was a physically easier task than plowing and thus more easily doable by humans. In some places, such as northern Italy in the 1500s, seeding drills were directly attached to plows, efficiently merging the aerating and seeding of soil.

Countless other innovations in farming tools might be recounted. Indeed, a discussion of innovations in draft animal harnesses, alone, could constitute an entire section of this book—from the double head yoke used to harness oxen in Mesopotamia, to the more comfortable single neck yoke that emerges in parts of Europe and East Asia, to the dorsal yoke used to harness horses. By the nineteenth century, horse harnesses had numerous components that had accumulated via innovation and experimentation over hundreds of years, components such as bits, collars, hames, back bands, belly bands, reins, and traces to say nothing of the variety of horseshoes that extended the working capacity of horses by protecting their hooves (Smil, 2017).

Or consider the sharpened stones used to harvest wheat, barley, rice, and other grains in early farming societies that gradually developed into sickles and then into a variety of different types of scythes (some better for grass-mowing, others better for harvesting grain) along with a bevy of supplemental tools used for straightening and sharpening (Smil, 2017). Each of these tools, indeed, each of any tool, underwent their own incremental process of adjustment and modification. Ancient southern Mesopotamian farmers in rapidly growing villages, for example, eagerly sought new methods of making sickles because the flint usually used was becoming harder and harder to obtain as plant cultivation became more widespread (Flannery and Marcus, 2012). The innovation hit on by potters and farmers was to overfire (i.e., vitrify) pottery clay to significantly sharpen it, and to use this sharpened clay to cut down wheat harvests. The downside was that, like glass, the overfired pottery broke easily. As this example shows, the development of tools (as with the development of infrastructure, discused shortly) was *not straightforwardly linear*, despite how we often think about it for the purposes of explanatory brevity. This innovation of the sickle improved the rate at which grains could be cut, but it came at a significant cost to durability. Increases in efficiency of one sort frequently come with tradeoffs—the contemporary examples we can all identify are the use of fossil fuels or noxious manufacturing chemicals and the externalities they pose to our environment.

Much more recently, in the 1830s, the mechanical reaper was invented independently by Obed Hussey and Cyrus McCormick, and this constituted a profound innovation over large groups of men swinging scythes. The mechanical reaper was a revolving set of blades attached to a platform pulled by draft animals. As the animals moved, the blades cycled and cut the crop, and as they completed their cycle, they shuffled the crop onto the platform where someone walking alongside the device could easily gather up the harvest. The mechanical reaper was three to four times more efficient than groups of men swinging scythes (Schlebecker, 2006). Needless to say, the mechanical reaper was an enormous success fairly quickly—from 1850 to 1860 the number of mechanical reapers being manufactured increased tenfold (Olmstead and Rhode, 1995).

Once the harvest was gathered, various tools were developed to separate chaff from grain, bundle and transport crops, grind grains into flower, or extract oil from seeds. Harvesting was itself an activity that, on farms of sufficient size, would require a large group. When a resource of sufficient plentifulness is discovered or cultivated, members of perceived ingroups will fuse in order to coordinate the extraction and distribution of this resource. This was particularly true *before* the advent of mechanical harvesting tools, when human labor was all that was available. On this, Vaclav Smil (2017) points out:

> Before the introduction of mechanical reapers … manual grain harvesting was the most time-consuming task, taking three to four times longer than plowing … comprehensive studies of China's traditional farming [have confirmed this]: planting and harvesting (between March and September) in China's double-cropping area used virtually all (average of 94–98%) available labor. In parts of India the two peak summer months required more than 110% or even 120% of actually available labor, and a similar situation prevailed in other parts of monsoonal Asia. This … could be overcome only if all families worked arduously long hours—or by relying on migrant labor.
>
> (Smil, 2017, pg. 64)

Farming, in particular harvesting, in traditional societies was thus a fusion-inducing event, and one that was potentially an open-system fusion allowing in immigrants who might come with different sorts of cultural capital and innovative ideas of their own.

In this section, I have attempted to discuss the sorts of innovations in tool use that emerged in farming societies. I must underscore, though, my proposed continuum of (relatively more individualistic) tool use and (relatively more collectivist) infrastructure use. What shaped the growth and economic expansion of farming societies was *not*, per se, these tool-level innovations discussed above. Rather, there were much more diffuse, shared, engines of growth that a focus on mere tool use obscures. I am not discounting the gains in efficiency wrought by innovations in tool use in early farming societies. Rather, in the next section, I want to direct your attention to other changes occurring underfoot in these societies, changes far more significant to economic growth, population growth, and eventual shifts in values and worldviews.

5.2 Infrastructure in Farming Societies

To reiterate, I want to suggest that the sorts of devices that human beings use to extract, process, and/or distribute energy from the environment can be classified along a continuum of relatively more individualistic development, construction, and accessibility ("tools"), and relatively more collective development, construction, and accessibility ("infrastructure"). In what follows, I hope to make the point that some innovations in farming were relatively more infrastructural than tool-related and that innovations in infrastructure undergirded and provided the context for innovations in tool use. Innovations in infrastructure, in other words, was and is a more fundamental precondition for societal change than innovations in tool use.

Try to keep in mind that when I am discussing infrastructures like irrigation and canal systems or roadways, I am thinking about how human beings have dug, carved, shaped, and built their landscape so as to facilitate the extraction, processing, or distribution of the energy necessary for the survival and growth of the collective *as a collective*. For example, the more water that is accessible to all people within a territory, by virtue of being in that territory and near a system of irrigation, the larger the number of people who are freed from the burden of finding water for just themselves, their families, or their land. And, in addition to the survival-relevance of water for drinking and crops, water is also *an essential form of energy* for societal growth.

To the extent that basic needs for survival are met by an infrastructural "commons" (Hardin, 1968), individuals can form values and goals independent of survival concerns (Inglehart, 2018). We must also keep in mind the basic zoological frame of reference, even if the infrastructure humans make is qualitatively more complex: "Humans, like beavers and termites, are vigorous practitioners of what biologists call 'niche construction': the active modification of their habitat, which can alter the selection pressures on behavior through feedback relationships" (Lansing and Fox 2011, pg. 927, as quoted in Wilkinson et al., 2015, pg. 398).

I'll discuss below the following forms of infrastructure: irrigation, waterways, and roads. This selection is totally arbitrary; there are some important forms of infrastructure that I won't discuss at all. Perhaps these omissions are egregious. But, this book is already set to be rather dense, and so I am limiting myself to a few examples. I trust the reader can extrapolate further from my initial sketch here.

The larger point is to center infrastructural systems (and their components) as the most relevant unit of cultural evolution. So, I will give some examples below, but I do not, and cannot, dwell on providing an exhaustive list of all infrastructure-like entities known to archeologists.

5.2.1 Irrigation Systems

Irrigation was probably the most important form of infrastructure in the large farming societies of history (as it is, still, today). In some cases, the need for water was satisfied by rainfall alone, but the more crops that need to be cultivated, and the more people and draft animals that need water to survive, the less rainfall suffices. Larger populations need more water, and historically this need was met by a centralized, bureaucratic, coordination of elites to mobilize labor for the building of irrigation systems (Wittfogel, 1957). Villages, towns, and city centers popped into and out of existence across the stretch of millennia, many of them in the valleys and basins where water at high elevation could be canalized toward crops, thirsty people, and thirsty animals. It is hardly controversial to suggest that, were it not for innovative irrigation systems, the first truly massive agrarian societies like the Sumerian region of Mesopotamia (circa 4,500–2,000 BCE)—which contained city-states of 50,000 people—would not have emerged.

Though I'm going to be focusing on the relationship between irrigation and access to water and food at scale, we have to remember that any large-scale elite-funded project was often, in practice, as much about asserting authority as it was about helping commoners and farmers survive. We can speculate that some rulers were simply benevolent, and hoped to provide water to their people, but we shouldn't be naïve enough to simply presume this. For example, discussing Ur-Nammu, king of the third Ur dynasty for nearly 20 years, Stephanie Rost writes:

> The motive as the provider of agricultural abundance features very prominently in Ur-Nammu inscriptions [and was] certainly designed to sanctify and legitimize his claim to power. It might have also been a strategy to create economic incentives that would attract labor and a population to rule and in turn increase agricultural production and state revenues … ancient water works were of pivotal importance to legitimize royal power and its self-perpetuation in the process of state formation. Massive diversion dams were a public spectacle of the king's ability to harness water [and to] create "verdant, visually striking oases that generated agricultural abundance."
>
> (Rost, 2017, pg. 12).

Whether built for reasons of agricultural productivity, or for the expression of elite power, the truth is that, via taxation, these are inextricably intertwined. The important point is that, once built, irrigation systems were, in principle, usable by anyone along their path.

Irrigation construction was predicated on two novel forms of group fusion—novel, that is, from the standpoint of fusion forms in nomadic foraging societies. The first was a relatively more closed-system fusion of elite planners and bureaucrats who determined where canals were to be dug and how labor would be recruited and paid. In ancient farming societies, enslaved people undertook much of the labor for these construction projects (David, 1997). "Payment" for such large-scale infrastructure-related construction projects in the ancient world was typically rations of beer and/or grain; evidence for rationed grain payments is suggested by the ubiquity of "bevel rim" bowls throughout ancient Mesopotamia (Sánchez and Fenollós, 2012). This laborer class—consisting mostly of captured slaves, but also of indebted peasants and immigrants—constituted the second form of fusion. This fusion of laborers was more of an open system than the fusion of elite planners. While family heredity, nepotism, and/or military glory were typically required for inclusion into the small centralized group of royal planners, laborers were drawn from the population at large including people from the countryside who sought residence in the boundaries of the kingdom.

The most ancient form of irrigation infrastructure is "gravity-fed." Gravity-fed irrigation required some reservoir of water (natural or human-constructed) sitting at a higher elevation than the village. A large main "conveyor" canal was dug into the soil at the bottom of the reservoir, and this then directed the flow of water into slightly smaller "branch canals," which weaved into farmland territory before emptying out into "distributary" canals that fed directly into farmers' crop fields (Rayne and Donoghue, 2018; Tianduowa et al., 2018). In fact, a single main canal could provide water to more than one village, via branch canals, and in the ancient world this would have enabled the simultaneous cultivation of food by people who may not have been too familiar with one another (not friends or kin) but who nevertheless relied on the same irrigation infrastructure.

Qanats were another form of canal system, dating to perhaps the 7th century BCE in Persia. In a *qanat* system, holes up to 300 feet are dug, in descending fashion, into the sloping side of a hill or mountain. Laborers would then scale down these holes with ropes in order to reach underground water basins, or aquifers, where they would go about excavating an underground main canal leading from the aquifer down the hill (Wulff, 1968). From there, the underground main canal empties out into any number of branching canals that flow into villages, city centers, and crop fields.

Qanats come with numerous benefits. For example, less water evaporates in a *qanat* system because water flows underground instead of above-ground, underground water tends to have less bacteria and fewer pollutants (because the soil acts as a filter when groundwater seeps down to the aquifer), and no system of water pumps or carriers are needed to keep the water flowing because the *qanat* is built directly into a sloping hill or mountain. H. E. Wulff (1968) conservatively estimates that the water sales and increased crop sales enabled by *qanat* construction constituted about a 10%–25% return on investment. This means more crops and more water for more people, all while increasing efficiency relative to individuals finding and acquiring water on their own.

Consider the following quote from archeologist Julien Charbonnier regarding *qanats* and how they might be the sort of technology I've defined above as "infrastructure":

> Construction of qanats is clearly beyond the scope of ordinary individuals or families as they require large investments, both in terms of labor and money and can therefore only be built by wealthy land-owners, communities or states. In the latter two cases, water from the qanats is shared among a group of people and requires rules for cleaning, repairing and sharing water: as such, a community of water users is born. Sometimes, this takes the form of a hierarchical system and an organization is set up to supervise the sharing of water and to maintain the canals. Apart from its physical aspect, the qanat system therefore has an intangible cultural element.
>
> (Charbonnier, 2018, pgs. 53–54)

Indeed, this "intangible cultural element" is the sharedness of the infrastructure and the beliefs and behaviors that it literally keeps alive in the people who adequately tend it. And what Charbonnier calls a "hierarchical system and … organization … set up to supervise the sharing [and maintenance of] the canals" took the form of fusion at the elite (land-owning monarchy, military, clerical classes) and laborer levels, the former to plan and fund, the latter to dig out, construct, and maintain the structure. Certainly not all *qanats* were expensive projects of huge agricultural states, but the largest, and most often used, were (Charbonnier and Hopper, 2018). For example, in the ancient Chinese city of Chang'an (the capital city of the Han Dynasty beginning in 206 BCE) archeologists have found evidence of continual, intergenerational, large-scale maintenance of reservoirs and canals. The following passage will give you a sense of the scale and planning of irrigation in Chang'an, and of the importance of such irrigation for the survival of the city:

> In the beginning years of [the] Han Dynasty, water-supply in Chang'an was adequate. [But], [the] Wu Emperor (7th emperor of Han) rapidly expanded the size of the capital. [The] water-supply then became insufficient. Therefore, the Kunming Reservoir was dug ... there was a stone tablet built at the point where [the] Jiaoshui River enters [the] Kunming Reservoir. The purpose of the tablet was for blocking/transferring water into the reservoir. In flood season, extra water from [the] Jiaoshui River could flow over the tablet into [the] Fengshui River, thus protecting [the] Kunming Reservoir from the flood. [The] Kunming Reservoir supplied water downstream through channels in the east side and the north side. The one in the east was called Old Kunming Channel, built specifically for supplying water to canals. The one in the north was called Kunming Reservoir Water, built specifically for supplying water within the city. There was another adjusting reservoir connected to [the] Kunming Reservoir Water before it enters the city. The water was divided into two distributaries after this: one to the north into the palace heading for [the] Weihe River, one to the northeast into the city ... At the end of [the] Han Dynasty, Chang'an was severely damaged due to numerous civil wars. The channels were also destroyed. Water in the city was not suitable for drinking due to salinization. This was one of the key reasons that [the] Sui and Tang Dynasties went seeking new locations for the capital.
>
> (Du and Chen, 2007, pgs. 175–176)

But, what of the very *idea*s of systems of underground *qanats*, aboveground canals, reservoirs, dikes, and dams? How can we understand their emergence as forms of innovation in extracting and distributing water to others? For this, we must look to the increasingly open-system fission–fusion oscillation occurring as individuals moved into and out of the relatively porous boundaries of emerging agricultural cities. In this way, irrigation efficiency, the sharedness of water that resulted, and the villages and barter-based markets that developed nearby provided a social space where peasants, immigrants, and others co-mingled, discussed, and exchanged ideas. Some would branch off on various work projects, some formed friendships, some moved in with others. This relatively open-system fission–fusion constituted a growing laboratory for innovation. Literacy, mass education, efficient large-scale transportation, and other innovations were still in the distant future but more and more people were aggregating in these villages and urban centers of early agricultural societies, and novel insights and practices were being generated.

Many other examples of irrigation systems could be discussed. Aqueducts, for example, required prolonged planning and more maintenance than the typical *qanat* discussed above. Perhaps the most well-known system of aqueducts are the Roman aqueducts, and although these were more sophisticated in terms of engineering compared to other irrigation systems, they nevertheless served the same basic infrastructural purpose as did more ancient systems. The Roman aqueducts were used and maintained for hundreds of years, and some, such as the Zaghouan Aqueduct in Tunisia, are still used today (Chanson, 2000).

The Roman aqueduct system consisted of lead pipes and stone canals built underground that emptied out into aboveground bridges stacked on top of each other to enable the water level to shift to varying heights, as needed, to carry water to fields and towns. These aqueducts carried water incredible distances, with some extending nearly 75 miles (~120 kilometers) from the water source (Harper, 2017). Unlike the irrigation practices discussed above, aqueducts more effectively altered the flow and level of the canalized water by allowing water to spill from steep drop-offs from higher to lower levels of the bridge. Roman aqueducts, in particular, evolved over time to address "supercritical flow" problems, that is, turbulent and torrential flows of water resulting from water spilling too rapidly from one level of the bridge to another. The Romans adopted several innovations to address supercritical flow problems including installing chutes flowing into stilling basins, stepped channels, and dropshafts (Chanson, 2000).

I've focused here on access to "fresh" water, but extensive networks of waterways in Mesopotamia, Rome, and elsewhere were also dug to canalize wastewater and stormwater away from villages and city centers (Tamburrino, 2010). The Roman sewer system, for example, took advantage of gravity to canalize waste downstream into the Tiber River. My particular emphasis on irrigation for purposes of drinking or crop fertilization should *not* be taken to mean that wastewater or stormwater or floodwater canalization are less important forms of infrastructure. The point is the collective innovation, construction, and utility of the structure, and the fact that if stormwater or wastewater sit for too long this can (and throughout history certainly did) cause mass death due to disease. Thus, wastewater, stormwater, or floodwater canalization, done well, are also forms of infrastructure critical to keeping people alive at scale.

And this brings us to an important point about irrigation and other water/waste-canalizing systems as infrastructure. Being collectively utilizable, they are also capable of causing great harm insofar as diseases and bacteria flow through the water supply. If each individual, family, or small community sought access to their own water sources, water-borne disease and infection might be localized and thus minimized. However, the more an irrigation system provides water to thousands, tens of thousands, and beyond, all from a shared set of water sources, the more vulnerable people (and thus society) will be to the quality of those few water sources. Irrigated water infested with pathogens can also contaminate crops, which can then lead to disease in the people who eat them (Steele and Odumeru,

2004). Also, water sources, especially if water is not kept flowing, can become breeding grounds for insects like mosquitos who carry disease (O'Sullivan et al., 2008). Thus, access to water from irrigation systems leads to a dependence that can also have a downside—the more people depend on collective water sources, the more vulnerable they are to viruses and bacteria facilitated by this water source.

The point is that any infrastructure that can be used as an, albeit unintended, mechanism for transporting bacteria or viruses can quickly become as deadly to a population as the proper functioning of the infrastructure was beneficial. And if, for whatever reason, canals were destroyed or rendered useless, the level of societal complexity would decline—the society existed *as a society* only insofar as the infrastructure enabled collective resource (in this case, water) extraction and distribution. For example, "in the canal-based agricultural systems of Mesopotamia, the destruction of a major canal might take years to repair, during which time the inhabitants might move elsewhere or revert to the more secure economic refuge of a nomadic lifestyle," (Kennedy, 2011, pg. 178). Successfully constructed and maintained infrastructure enables superordinate fusing; unsuccessful construction and maintenance of infrastructure drives fissioning and, potentially, the sort of widespread fissioning we might call societal collapse.

Up to this point, we've considered irrigation systems, *as systems*, providing water to many people from a single primary source (or a few of them). However, it is also worth considering the sense in which some components of irrigation systems were, themselves, infrastructural to some degree. In many regions, such as in river valleys where the water source did not sit above crop fields, or on flat plains or in deserts, sustained cultivation with gravity-fed or *qanat* irrigation was difficult or impossible. In these cases, proto-pumps (or "water-lifting devices") of various sorts were used. Most relied on human labor, but some later pumps began utilizing animal labor due to their greater strength. One, quite cruel, example is the practice of blindfolding horses or oxen, harnessing them to horizontal bars attached to a capstan pump, and forcing them to walk in circles until they die (Erickson, 2006). As the animals walked in circles, the movement caused a vertical drum to rotate above, lifting water from wells. Similarly constructed "horse whims" were also used to turn rotary grain mills in ancient Greece (~300 BCE).

Archeologists' earliest estimation is that, by around the 15th century BCE, people in Mesopotamia began lifting water out of streams with ropes attached to pulleys. By 3000 BCE, Mesopotamians were using "shadoofs," which are wooden poles laid atop a sturdy fulcrum with a counterweight on one end of the pole and a bucket for lifting water on the other end of the pole (Zhang and Yang, 2020). By 1100 BCE, the "windlass," a cylinder attached to a crank fastened to a stand that can be used to lower a bucket into a well, was being used in China. Then, between 200 and 300

BCE, the Greek mathematician Archimedes is credited with developing "Archimedes' screw" (Zhang and Yang, 2020). This device required carving out a huge helix shape from wood or bronze and placing the helix/screw inside of a tube with one end dipped into a water source and the other end attached to a crank, which, when cranked, would move the screw inside. As a person cranks the device, water snakes up the screw and can be deposited into a bucket or onto an elevated basin or canal. Some 600 years later, beginning around 300 CE, people in the Roman and Muslim world were using *norias*, or open-framed water wheels affixed with ceramic buckets that lifted water out of a moving stream as the wheel rotated. These *norias*, some of which reached 65 feet in diameter, were eventually re-engineered to extract and then pour water directly into canal systems (Zhang and Yang, 2020).

Many other innovations in water-lifting might be cited, and no doubt many have been lost to history. But, these examples of water-lifting devices hopefully help illustrate the sense in which tools and infrastructure differ along a continuum. Let's suppose a simple device used to lift water out of a stream takes two people to build, and the bucket used to lift water can provide water for three or four people. This is different from a simple garden hoe, which might be made by one person and is only usable by one person at one time (even if the crops ultimately cultivated with the hoe and other tools and infrastructure can feed many). Relatively speaking, the garden hoe is less of a piece of infrastructure than the water-lifting device described above, which requires more people to build and which can directly extract resources (water) usable by more than one person. However, both the garden hoe and the water-lifting device are less infrastructural than a canal irrigation system or aqueduct, which requires more people to construct and from which more people can benefit. As these examples show, devices can be more or less infrastructural, and thus more or less implicated in the system-wide growth of a society.

The capacity to extract, process/regulate (via dikes and dams), and distribute water at scale was crucial for the growth of societies. Symmetrically, the incapacity to do so spelled collapse. For example, droughts spanning several decades appear to have contributed to the decline of three of China's most durable dynasties: the Tang (618–907), the Yuan (1271–1368), and the Ming (1368–1644) (Webber, 2019). Droughts have felled countless other societies from the Mayans in 950 CE to perhaps an entire intersocietal system collapse in the Late Bronze Age (Drysdale et al., 2006; Cline, 2014; Douglas et al., 2015). Today, regions suffering from the highest levels of relative poverty and political instability are often those places—from Detroit, USA, to Aleppo, Syria—where water is either difficult to obtain, poorly processed, or inadequately distributed.

The collective relevance of infrastructure is further reflected in the development of legal codes and laws to protect its use. Tool usage is sometimes legally regulated, but infrastructure is almost always legally regulated. The difference lies in the relatively collective utilizabilty of the latter and the relatively individual utilizability of the former. Infrastructural systems are "commons" (Hardin, 1968) in a way that tools are not. Consider the following passage regarding the administration of water law in Mesopotamia:

> Based on the various codes it appears that water was a communal asset, especially as local authorities, acting in their own behalf or on behalf of regional governors, would grant rights to communal water supply and act quickly to alleviate any irrigation or other usage issues. Irrigation was only possible because of dams, sluices, canals and other water diversion structures. These and even the river itself were a communal rather than an individual asset. Some structures were so large that one individual would be incapable of taking care of them, "even if he had a proprietary right to them." In large areas of Mesopotamia, therefore, the practice was to appoint a local official, who was fully familiar with the area, the facts on the ground, and earlier precedents, and who would tend to irrigation and other water conflicts or affairs on an immediate basis. Consequently, in any given water dispute between two members of the community, this communal representative was responsible for arbitrating or mediating the individual claims.
>
> (Kornfeld, 2009, pg. 30)

My intent here is not, and could not be, to review the history of irrigation in society. I am only hoping to make some important conceptual points. Let's move on to another example, that of shipping waterways.

5.2.2 Shipping Waterways

As described above, irrigation systems extracted, processed/regulated, and distributed water to people, farm animals, and crop fields. Waterways were another very important form of infrastructure, which aided in the distribution (via ships) of food, and construction materials like wood, throughout agricultural city-states and kingdoms. Cities in Mesopotamia were strategically built to facilitate access to waterways, because these were critically important shipping routes transporting goods between regions (Leick, 2002). Kish, Nippur, Uruk, Lagash, Babylon, Nina, Larsa, Ur, and many other Sumerian city-states dotted the land where the Tigris and Euphrates Rivers empty out into the Persian Gulf. The flourishing coastal cities of agricultural ancient Greece similarly benefitted from their location along key harbors, and many other examples might be given, past and present (such as the present-day affluent harbor cities of New York and Los Angeles).

Waterways required substantial investments from elites (in terms of funding and planning) and from labor (in terms of construction and maintenance), and waterways also needed to be defended from unauthorized use and piracy (Leick, 2002). In many cases, existing rivers and streams could be used as a means of transport (though labor was nevertheless needed to maintain and defend these waterways), but in other cases artificial human-made canals were dug and maintained. In the earliest massive farming societies of ancient Mesopotamia, archeologists, in practice, have a difficult time discerning which waterways were dug by laborers and which were naturally occurring, because people of the time referred to both as *shatt* (Wilkinson et al., 2015). Still, we can consider some examples. Shatt el-Nil appears to have been an artificially dug waterway cutting across what is today southern Iraq (Leick, 2002). Several thousand years ago, the Shatt el-Nil constituted an important Mesopotamian shipping route linking the ancient Sumerian cities of Nippur, Abu Salabikh, and Uruk. Or, consider "the first navigable canal," Shatt-el-Hai, which was carved out in 2200 BCE to link the Tigris and Euphrates Rivers (Galil et al., 2008). Much later, between 300 and 400 BCE, Chinese laborers dug the Grand Canal in order to connect the bustling agricultural cities of Peking and Hangzhou (Galil et al., 2008).

As I mentioned above with irrigation systems, these canals were also transportation routes for disease, and their cleaning and maintenance was a project unto itself. Defense of waterways (artificially dug or otherwise) was also critically important. Many examples might be cited. The ancient agricultural city-states of Sumer, as one example, were continuously threatened by the Akkadian Empire to the north, which eventually conquered Sumer between the 23rd and 24th centuries BCE (Bertman, 2005). Before being conquered, however, Sumerian city-states like Babylon were under continual threat, and the Euphrates River, along which Babylon sat, could facilitate an invasion just as easily as it could facilitate the trading of goods. Insofar as waterway construction and maintenance was a royal project requiring the coordination of labor, and insofar as people with access to city-state markets benefitted from the resultant trade economy, we must consider waterways as aspects of the infrastructure of agricultural societies. Though perhaps not as significant as irrigation canals for drinking and (more often) crop-growing, waterways for transportation and trade were still an important early form of infrastructure; in both cases, humans were harnessing the energy enabled by the capturing and redirection of water, and societies were growing and changing as a result.

Waterways were infrastructural, but the cargo ships that traversed them offer us another opportunity to consider the tool–infrastructure continuum.

Rafts and boats were made in Mesopotamia using domesticated sheep or goat skin stretched across reeds, palm leaves, and palm fibers, which could be found along the Euphrates and Tigris (McIntosh, 2017). These watercraft were used for fishing and for transporting people and agricultural produce from place to place. Larger, sturdier ships were made using wooden planks tied with rope and tenons fit into mortices. The use of not only local pine but also teak from India and cedar from Lebanon attests to the importance of markets and trade for imported materials in the construction of ancient ships.

Technological innovations in mortice/tenon joint construction, sails, oars, and hulls of ships would, of course, accumulate over time, though long periods of stagnation and the occasional reversal of innovation after societal collapse are important caveats. The Phoenicians are perhaps the society best known for having the first fleet of ships around 3000 BCE (Smith, 2012). Phoenician ships came in many forms from large freighter-like merchant ships and warships to smaller utility ships, and each was constructed according to the established best practices of Egyptian shipbuilding, because the Egyptians had been perfecting travel up and down the Nile River for hundreds of years by that point (Aubet, 1993).

How should we conceptualize the import of ships to societal development over time? Clearly, a large, well-made Phoenician merchant ship will take more than one person to construct and will be of use to more than one person through the mass transportation of food and other resources. Ships, then, are a bit more infrastructural than they are tool-like. But, this is and must remain a distinction of degree, not kind. What of tools used to load and unload cargo onto ships, or to move cargo generally? I am talking about devices like wheels and axles, levers, pulley systems, inclined planes, or "endless" screws?

Certainly, depending on each tool's size, they would require more than one person to make and, depending on the size of their carriage, more than a few people could benefit from the resources they hauled. Again, we must think about this as a difference of degree, not kind: compared to devices used for lifting cargo, the ships used for mass transportation of cargo, such as cargo ships, were larger structures, often requiring more labor and ultimately capable of benefitting more people. Within such a continuum, there will be a fair amount of grey area as to what is more tool than infrastructure. But, the distinctions I hope to make here are only ones beyond dispute—an axle or lever is more of a tool than is a cargo ship, which is more of tool than the waterway itself. Yet, as we move from axle to cargo ship to waterway we are moving from the lefthand side of the tool–infrastructure continuum to the righthand side.

5.2.3 *Roads*

Waterways are infrastructural insofar as they require group coordination to build, maintain, and defend, while being usable as a means of distributing resources to large numbers of people sharing societal membership. Roads satisfy the same criteria. While we may think of roads as being simplistic and straightforward in the ancient world—just dirt paths, basically—the reality is that roads have always been an evolving form of infrastructure critically important to the distribution of goods within a societal territory.

It is nevertheless true to say that most roads in ancient farming societies were probably soft dirt paths that became muddy and pitted during rainy seasons, and dusty and cracked during the summer (Smil, 2017). Yet, the traversability of a road is critical in determining how useful it is for the distribution and transportation of essential materials (e.g., wood or copper) and sustenance (e.g., food). The more sunken pits or crumbling sides on a roadway, the longer goods can take to transport, and fewer of them, if they are transported at all. Draft animals being used to move goods might get injured on poorly maintained roads, or carriages and baskets might sway too violently left to right, causing goods to spill out, or wheels might break, causing the entire load to topple over. To ensure adequate transportation across poorly maintained or uneven roads, merchants and traders sometimes used more draft animals to carry fewer supplies each. The more resources were lost, or the slower and more difficult it was to transport them, the higher the overall cost of trade—put simply: "Low speeds and low capacities of land transport translated into excessive costs" (Smil, 2017, pg. 184). Smil (2017) points out:

> The differences in energy requirements between moving a load on a smooth, hard, dry road and on a loose, gravelly surface are enormous. In the first case a force of only about 30kg is needed to wheel a 1 ton load, the second instance would call for five times as much draft, and on sandy or muddy roads the multiple can be seven to ten times higher.
>
> (Smil, 2017, pg. 181)

People also innovated various tools to move resources along these roads—things like rolling logs, wheels attached to axles, and, eventually, sliding bearings and then rolling bearings along with various lubricants for these bearings (Sun and Li, 2016). For example, axle lubricants made from animal fat and plant oils have been in use since the second millennium BCE, and bronze bearings with wooden rollers have been in use since the first century BCE (Smil, 2017).

But, I must hasten to add that roads are themselves a product of cumulative modifications and innovations (Smil, 2017). The massive agricultural Incan Empire was networked by an extensive road system spanning nearly 25,000 miles, with roads cutting through the Andes surfaced with stone. In third-century BCE China, a road network spanning a similar length was surfaced with a layer of very tightly packed gravel and rubble which provided some elasticity and shock absorption. Or, consider the Via Appia, a long road connecting Rome to Capua built at the beginning of the 4th century BCE, that was surfaced with gravel concrete, cobblestones, and slabs of rock set in mortar.

The importance of innovations in road construction cannot be understated, however easy it might be for us to take them for granted. Up until very recently, at least in historical terms, roads in England, for example, were so poor that they were actively constraining economic growth. On this, Smil writes:

> Into the 18th century … it was cheaper to import many goods into England by sea from Europe rather than to carry them by pack animals from the country's interior. Travelers described the state of English roads as barbarous, execrable, abominable and infernal. Rain and snow made poorly laid-out soft dirt or gravel roads impassable; in many cases their limited width allowed only pack traffic. Roads in continental Europe were in similarly bad shape, and coach horses harnessed in teams of four to six animals lasted on average less than three years.
>
> (Smil 2017, pg. 185)

Roads in England, as with roads everywhere, were steadily improved to varying degrees by being widened, more effectively drained of rain or floodwater, and surfaced with complex mixtures of compacted rubble, stone slabs, asphalt, or concrete to make them smoother and more durable.

5.3 Does "Symbolic Infrastructure" Constitute a Counterexample?

The organized labor necessary to develop, fund, construct, and maintain infrastructure would have also stimulated, to varying degrees, awareness, surface contact, and mutuality amongst laborers and elites. Most important, however, is that the increasing energy capture from the environment enabled by (well-constructed and well-maintained) infrastructure would have reduced the intensity of peoples' immediate survival concerns, allowing them more time to be alone or to pursue idiosyncratic projects (fission) and/or more time to associate voluntarily with others.

When staring starvation or dehydration in the face, people will fuse with whoever is co-present in order to coordinate the search for food, or, if edible food is rare, people will simply go it alone. Subsistence stress, thus, encourages a less voluntary fusion, and less voluntary fission, than is available to people whose basic needs are met to some degree. If food or water procurement are not immediate concerns, or are becoming less of a concern, because the infrastructure in a society enables the extraction, processing, and/or distribution of surplus, people can spend more time alone on their own idiosyncratic pursuits or more time in voluntary collectives pursuing goals outside of mere survival.

Infrastructure therefore facilitates more flexible, more voluntary, fissioning and fusing. It does this by increasing the captured energy from the environment and facilitating its transfer to people throughout a social system. I mean energy in a *literal* sense here, not in a metaphorical sense. This might be obvious when I am talking about food as energy, but units of infrastructure can also generate energy. Horizontal waterwheels, for example, were capable of providing about 300 watts of energy around 300 BCE, but by 500 CE vertical waterwheels were capable producing well over 1,000 watts (Smil, 2017). In fact, Smil regards waterwheels as perhaps the most efficient form of energy in traditional societies:

> a small watermill, manned by fewer than 10 workers, would grind enough in a day (10 hours of milling) to feed some 3,500 people, a fair-sized medieval town, while hand milling would have required at least 250 laborers.
>
> (Smil, 2017, pg. 154)

When survival is paramount, fusion occurs out of strategic necessity, and/or time spent fissioned is oriented toward the project of finding food and fresh water. As the necessities of life become slowly met via infrastructure, fission–fusion oscillation can become incrementally more open and more flexible in terms of the goals people pursue. Some social intuitions (e.g., that outgroups are monolithic) might nevertheless reduce the openness of the fission—fusion oscillation that occurs within a society. But, as we will see in the coming chapters, the successful infrastructuralization of a society can produce secondary effects—the easier access is to food, fresh water, building materials, electricity, mass transportation, and so on, the easier it becomes to sustain institutions like education, media, medicine, and science, which can help feed back on and dispel some of the fatuous, errant intuitions that discourage people from fusing with those superficially different from themselves.

To sharpen our analysis, let's consider three cultural phenomena that might be difficult to cleanly categorize as either "tools" or "infrastructure": (1) pictograms, logograms, and alphabetic writing, (2) standardized currency, and (3) cultivation strategies like crop rotation and multicropping.

5.3.1 Pictograms, Logograms and Alphabetic Writing

It is sensible to say that pictograms are as old as human beings if we appreciate the communicative and potentially educational role of cave drawings. The earliest example known to archeologists of people attempting to tell stories or communicate mythology with drawn art can be found in a landscape scene drawn in a limestone cave in Indonesia (Aubert et al.,

2019). In the scene, which dates to about 44,000 years ago, human–animal hybrids appear to be stalking or hunting a large anoa (an animal that resembles a small water buffalo), amid a landscape of large frolicking pigs. The archeologists who documented the drawing speculate that the scene was used for religious storytelling, mythmaking, or some other important form of communication.

If we wanted to date the emergence of logographic writing, and its development into cuneiform, we would need to look back at least 5,000 years to ancient Sumerian tablets (Kramer, 2010). By at least 3,600 years ago, Canaanites had developed a "proto-alphabet," and had begun etching various messages onto clay jars in what is, today, Israel (Fischer, 2001). The Canaanites and, later, the Phoenicians, would diffuse this system of alphabetic writing through their trade relationships. From there, alphabetic writing systems were eventually adopted and modified by the Greeks, Romans, and others (Ostler, 2005).

It is often pointed out by archeologists that these early writings seem to have mostly been directed toward accounting and contractual purposes: keeping track of who owes what to whom and who is obligated to what (Kornfeld, 2009). Great written literature was apparently rare (or poorly preserved), but the jotting down of accounting issues was abundant. Some stone tablets from the second millennium BCE, for example, have been found bearing inscriptions denoting that the owner of the tablet was owed 300 units of barley by the indebted person, which were to be paid at the conclusion of the next harvest (Ferguson, 2008). But, frankly, the same is true today—how much more often do we write out a grocery list than compose fiction?

These early writings also seem to have been directed toward another purpose common today—stating and explaining rules and codes of conduct. New problems emerge as societies grow in size, the construction, regulation, and maintenance of infrastructure being one of them. Writing was used for this purpose, and also for purposes of specifying citizenship requirements and other challenges of administering and regulating the flow of resources to a massive society of people.

The key difference between logograms/cuneiform and alphabets is the degree of abstraction and, thus, flexibility (Ostler, 2005). Alphabets contain more decomposable parts, letters, than did pictographic or cuneiform writings, which rely more on small drawings or sketches meant to stand for entire words. Alphabets, therefore, had a greater potential for recombination of component parts (letters being recombined into new words) than did pictographic or cuneiform writing, and consequently, people were able to communicate a larger number of different meanings more easily.

So, there can be no doubt about the connection between the development of ever more abstract, flexible, forms of writing and the growth of large agricultural states. In fact, some form of writing emerged in every large agricultural region known to archeology. Though few people were literate in ancient agricultural societies—only the 1% to 5% of the population who worked as scribes were typically literate—it was nevertheless a skill useful for building and maintaining empires (Cline, 2017).

Having said all of this, I submit to you that literacy and writing systems are *less* infrastructural than are irrigation systems, waterways, and roads. At the same time, I would suggest that literacy and writing systems are *more* infrastructural than a hoe or a scythe or an axle. On what basis am I making these distinctions? After all, it would seem clear that many people are required to develop a common form of writing and that many people benefit from it. Why not, then, consider literacy and writing systems as consummately infrastructural?

The answer is that literacy and writing systems are less proximate to survival-relevant resource extraction, processing, and distribution. Canals, dikes, and dams direct and distribute water, which humans need to survive. Well-made roads directly facilitate (literally, in the sense of reduced friction) the distribution of food, which humans need to survive. The use of a common alphabet or cuneiform, by contrast, helps to extract, process, and distribute *information*. And, while this information may be useful in the planning, construction, or maintenance of more central forms of infrastructure, the transference of meaning through writing does not as proximately or directly deliver food or water to mouths the way a road system might, or the way an irrigation system might. The meaning of etched symbols or words is subjectively constructed and exists only in the minds of those who understand the language. A functioning irrigation system, on the other hand, is quite physical, quite material, and will continue on canalizing water regardless of an observer's cultural literacy.

Again, this is a distinction of degree: I would not argue with anyone calling writing systems a form of *symbolic* infrastructure. Yet, I would point out that writing systems are not *physical* infrastructure and, as such, writing systems are several steps removed from the actual extraction, processing, and distribution of survival-relevant resources. I do not discount writing's role in planning or constructing physical infrastructure; in fact, I intend to make the case that engineering principles, equations, and diagrams are the central forms of information driving cultural evolution. Engineering principles, equations, and diagrams, particularly to the extent that they are differentially stored in communication technologies, constitute the "unit of selection" in cultural evolution. But, they are not the "unit of evolution" (this distinction between units of selection and units of evolution is owed to John Maynard Smith); infrastructural systems and their constituent units are the units of evolution.

We are getting ahead of ourselves. There is plenty of room left to make this case. For now, it should do simply to reiterate the basic point:

alphabets and logograms, as such, certainly constitute a shared social system, but one that provides a means of communicating about infrastructure (and other cultural concerns); it is not the infrastructure itself.

5.3.2 Standardized Currency

What about money? Before the standardized currencies of large agricultural city-states, people exchanged domesticated animals, furs, shells, feathers, pottery, spices, and valuable metals or rocks like copper, bronze, gold, silver, and lapis lazuli as forms of barter currency. The value of a piece of lapis lazuli, spice, fur, and so on was typically determined by how hard that object was to obtain in the particular geographic region wherein the exchange occurred. Rarer items or animals could be used to barter for more goods. Rarity seems to matter as well for more standardized currency like paper money—the more of it, the higher the inflation rate. However, people exchanging standardized currency need to infer its value from others to a greater degree than in a barter system, where the rarity of this or that animal or this or that rock was more self-evident: either a particular style of pottery, a certain amount of copper, or a particular animal was common around where a person lived, or it wasn't.

Standardized coins used as currency were apparently first struck from gold and silver alloy in the Kingdom of Lydia, in modern-day Turkey, sometime between 500 and 1000 BCE (Howgego, 1995). However, even though coins were first issued in Lydia, it is nevertheless "valid to interpret coinage as a Greek phenomenon," due to how widespread coin usage became in Greek city-states (Howgego, 1995). Coinage, for example, was produced in the 5th century BCE Persian Empire, but only in Greek provinces within the Empire like Cyrene and Cyprus.

Paper money, which comes into widespread use beginning around 800–1000 CE in China (Horesh, 2014), contains less objective value than gold or silver coins, but, as a consequence, it is also cheaper to make. And, provided there is enough public trust of the economy and government, paper money can be just as effective as a means of exchange. While debt and indebtedness have always existed, the widespread use of financial credit is much more recent, beginning perhaps in the 15th century CE when explorers sought credit from the crown to fund their projects of colonization. Most recently, we've seen the emergence of what Randall Collins (1990) calls financial "metamarkets," where stocks, bonds, bundled debt, derivatives, and other abstract financial aggregations are traded on their own markets.

Regardless of the specific origin of formal coinage and paper money, there are several important theoretical considerations. The exchange of standardized currency, relative to the various items exchanged in a barter system, requires more trust in a centralized authority to set a particular value for the currency, because, after all, a central government structure is actually producing the currency. Economists refer to this as endowing currency with value by fiat, since people participating in the economy must take for granted that the value of a particular coin or piece of paper is stable enough to negotiate with (Dowd, 2001). The Roman Empire, for example, steadily reduced the amount of pure silver struck into their coinage as their economy began to collapse after about 200 CE, and this both contributed to inflation and marked a decline in people's trust of governing institutions (Tainter, 1988; Cline, 2014).

Currency is, then, an emergent, collectively constituted form of value that can benefit large numbers of people insofar as it helps them interpret, and thus take part in, a market. Markets for goods and services are as old as humanity; all that's changed is their scale and scope along with the means of exchange.

Consequently, it is fair to regard currency, especially formalized currency, as an emergent form of symbolic infrastructure. But, we should be aware of some important caveats. Currency certainly constitutes a shared social system but one that provides the means of constructing physical infrastructure and is not the infrastructure itself. Like alphabets and logograms, currency is a few steps removed from the infrastructure that directly canalizes energy into towns, villages, and cities.

On a continuum filled with fine-grained distinctions, currency is less infrastructural than, say, a well-surfaced road: it is not itself a physical path for resource extraction, processing, or distribution. Another way to put it is that much of the usefulness of money relies on subjective assessment—trust and legitimacy in the rareness or value of currency—as discussed above. By contrast, the usefulness of an irrigation system is quite a bit more straightforward—dug well and mediated by dikes and dams, water will be funneled regardless of a person's subjective opinion about canals, dikes, and dams.

5.3.3 Crop Cultivation Strategies

What about innovative ideas that improved crop yields? According to some scholars, crop rotation and multicropping practices were "revolutionary" (Chorley, 1981). The question is, are such practices a form of infrastructure?

Rotating crops reduces the depletion of nutrients in soil, because the roots of different plant species extract different amounts of nutrients from soil. Perhaps the most common example of this is the importance of nitrogen to soil fertility, and thus crop yields. Planting legumes reliably restores ammonium nitrogen to soil, and the incorporation of leguminous crops into the cultivation schedule of other nitrogen-depleting crops has been called the "core of all intensive agricultural systems," because of the aggregate increase in crop yields that result (Smil, 2017, pg. 85). Also, infestations of pests become less likely if the crop, and therefore the pest's food source, is changed regularly. Multicropping involves this identification of plants compatible in their nutrient profiles, and sequentially planting these crops in the same area of soil within the same harvesting season. Assuming the nutrient needs of various crops are balanced, multicropping using crop rotation massively increases yields threefold or more, all without having to endure the effects of soil erosion.

Successful crop rotation and multicropping required knowledge of the relationship between crop yield and soil fertility and knowledge of the various sorts of complementary crops that might be grown and/or the nitrogen-enriching effects of legumes. Farmers would also need the tools of digging, turning, seeding, and so on, as well as access to manure (another important source of fertilizing nitrogen). In short, the idea of crop rotation and multicropping requires that quite a few intermediary steps be met before being realizable in practice. For this reason, and because ideas are often not transmitted between people with any exactitude, the *ideas* of crop rotation and multicropping were not themselves sufficient for the successful *widespread adoption* of crop rotation and multicropping.

The strategies of crop rotation and multicropping did indeed become more common, at least in part because they were useful. But nothing about the idea or practice of multicropping necessarily implies group construction or group benefits. Moreover, innovations in farming practices are not themselves physical forms of infrastructure directly involved with the extraction, processing, or distribution of energy—this is plain to see when we consider the futility of having the ideas necessary to employ crop rotation, but lacking the irrigation system necessary to put this knowledge to good use in actually growing crops at scale. Might we still consider these farming innovations as critically important forms of symbolic infrastructure? Absolutely, but the ideational (as opposed to physical) and relatively less-collective aspects of these innovations in farming practice make them a different form of infrastructure than the "ideal types" of irrigation systems, waterways, roads, and so on.

To summarize broadly, alphabets, currencies, and cultivation strategies are not infrastructural to the same degree as the development, construction, and maintenance of waterways, roads, and irrigation canals. However, alphabets, currencies, and cultivation strategies are substantially more infrastructural than hoes or plows or seed drills. Alphabets, currencies, and cultivation strategies or, for that matter, standards of measurement, the Code of Hammurabi, and other various codes and laws are also unlike physical infrastructure in an important way. Alphabets, currencies, and the rest have meaning and effects insofar as they are understood subjectively as containing some value or interpretable information. Roads and irrigation systems, by contrast, have their effects regardless of the subject states of those observing them.

Perhaps a thought experiment will help clarify this point. Imagine an irrigation system, complete with an elevated water source and a network of dikes, dams, and branching canals. Next, suppose that all of the humans who constructed this system suddenly disappear from the face of the Earth. Indeed, let's suppose all human beings everywhere disappear from the face of the Earth. The meaning and important effects of money or of ideas about cultivation or of codes and laws will now be absent as well—without human brains to perceive value in money or in laws or in ideas, these coins, tablets, or thoughts cease their circulation in time and space. However, the irrigation system, once built, will nevertheless continue canalizing water until its component parts disintegrate with time.

Merely cultural artifacts like money or laws or ideas are "ontologically subjective" in that their existence depends on human subjectivity: money "works" or laws "exist" only insofar as various human brains understand the meaning these symbols convey (Searle, 2010). The physicality, the materiality, of the irrigation system is different. It is "ontologically objective" in that its literal structure, and its effects on the Earth in canalizing energy (in this case water) exist, once constructed, quite independently of human subjectivity.

Of course, irrigation construction is a profoundly cultural practice, requiring the mobilization of labor and resources, using various mythologies and claims to power. Yet, despite the fact that the development, construction, and maintenance of irrigation systems are cultural processes, the actual resultant physical structure, and its objective impact on the extraction, processing, or distribution of survival-relevant resources, is subjectivity-independent.

Chapter 6

The Tools and Infrastructure of Fossil Fuel Societies

Only recently have mass numbers of people abandoned rural life as agriculturalists in order to head for the cities and work with machines, first in factories, then in offices, then telecommuting from the comforts of home.

This shift occurred, and is occurring, on a massive scale. An entire book could be written (and many have been written) documenting the global transition from agricultural to industrial, hydrocarbon-fueled societies. I can't begin to do justice to the full scope of this transition. So, as with the prior chapters, I will be selective in my attention and emphasize the import of infrastructure and of the extraction, processing, and distribution of survival-relevant resources within and between societies.

For most of human history, people have relied on wood, straw, water, fire, and animals as sources of fuel. Fossil fuel use is comparatively more recent, though accounts of the intermittent use of coal date back several thousand years. Coal, for example, was used during the Han Dynasty in China to make iron, but it was not used in Europe until 1113 CE in Belgium (Smil, 2017). Widespread use of fossil fuels does not begin to occur in Europe until the 1500s but, rapidly, coal begins to predominate as a source of fuel due to regional wood shortages. Miners used various tools, from cutting picks to mallets, in order to extract the coal, and, initially, windmills and waterwheels helped pump groundwater out of coal mines. The more efficiently water could be pumped from mines, the more coal could be recovered. And, when regional shortages of wood drove up the cost of wood fuel in Europe, the incentives for intensified coal production were set in place. Seemingly everyone was employed in the mines, from adult men and women to children as young as six, and the labor was as brutally difficult as any seen in the ancient world (Smil, 2017). By the early seventeenth century, people in Europe were using coal to heat their households and forges and even to make soap.

Fossil fuel use then begins to grow cumulatively: use of coal as a source of fuel begins rising dramatically in the first half of the 1800s, use of crude oil rises in the latter half of the 1800s, use of natural gas takes off in the early 1900s and nuclear energy use starts to become more prominent

DOI: 10.4324/9781003266020-6

after 1950. These changes in fossil fuel use were motivated by various innovations. Natural gas, for example, was extracted from coal by following a carbonization process similar to the one used to make charcoal from wood—coal was heated in large, oxygen-deprived ovens, and the gas released was highly combustible and, therefore, useful as fuel. Shortly thereafter, in London circa 1812, a centralized supply of natural gas was chartered, and the commercial use of this gas to light homes soon followed (Smil, 2017).

Throughout this period, reliance on traditional forms of power—from wood to water to wind to human and farm animal labor—steadily and rapidly declined. France in the early 1800s gleaned over 90% of its energy from wood (or charcoal derived from carbonizing the wood), but this had dropped to less than 50% by 1875; or, consider that Japan's energy supply in 1880 was 85% wood-based, and that this had dropped to less than 50% by 1901 (Smil, 2017). In 1800, only one of the world's top ten largest cities was in a coal-dominated country (London), but by 1900 nine out of the ten largest cities were in countries dependent on coal (Smil, 2017). Only recently have water, wind, and solar energy made a resurgence due to their renewability as sources of energy. And some very recent forms of energy, like nuclear energy, are both renewable and totally historically novel. Yet, the important point is that the infrastructure powered by coal, natural gas, and, eventually, crude oil and nuclear energy substantially transformed people's opportunities and, subsequently, their worldviews. Infrastructure using these energy sources drove cultural change.

Human labor and animal labor have been the most common forms of labor power throughout human history. People provide less labor power (in terms of estimated watts of energy per task) than do cattle, which, in turn, are less powerful than horses. Well-made waterwheels are a better source of power than all three. However, the best-made waterwheels pale in comparison to the power provided by steam engines, then by steam or gas turbines and then by internal combustion engines. In fact, the largest modern turbines attached to electrical generators are capable of producing almost *two million times* (about six orders of magnitude) the power of the largest draft horses (Smil, 2017).

These new forms of machine labor power are also becoming lighter and, generally, more energy efficient. Considering the watts of power provided per gram of weight, jet engines are lighter than internal combustion engines, which are lighter than steam engines, which are lighter than draft animals. This relative increase in the efficiency of power generation over time has opened up the commercialization of this power:

> The mass/power ratio of internal combustion engines (first gasoline engines, then diesels) declined by two orders of magnitude in less than 50 years after the first commercial models, horizontal engines

> fueled by coal gas, were introduced during the 1860s. That precipitous drop opened the way to the affordable mechanization of road transport (cars, buses, trucks) and made aviation possible.
>
> (Smil, 2017, pg. 400)

The more the efficiency of a machine increases (i.e., the more power generated per unit mass), the cheaper it generally becomes to create. And, the cheaper machines become to create, the easier they are to sell to the public for profit. Though perhaps dry-sounding and mundane, the consequences of this are *profound*. Increased access to personal forms of transportation (cars, buses, airplanes) allows people to form friendships, business agreements, and cooperative groups with others increasingly geographically distant from themselves. The geographic distance between people becomes less important as a barrier to interaction and cooperation when the speed of transportation rises, as we've seen with the transition from walking (the original form of transportation!) to various forms of animal transport, to ships, to trains, to cars, and to airplanes.

Even more important, given the inevitable financial barriers to personal transportation, is this: to the degree that a tax-funded public transportation system exists in a city, we have an example of a secondary form of infrastructure (reliant on the more primary infrastructure of electricity and roads) capable of expanding the opportunities, and thus worldviews, of entire cities of people. Businesses also benefit from commercial forms of transportation (delivery trucks, container ships), which increase the rate and distributary scope of resources and, thus, of various commodities markets. The combined effect is an increasing rate and scope of circulating goods and people in space. Collaborations grow, markets expand, and new markets open.

This increased rate and scope of circulation (of both people and goods) facilitates, and is facilitated by, open-system fissioning and fusing, and this fissioning–fusing drives further innovation and further opportunity. Nicolas Baumard (2019), for example, notes that the equivalized per capita yearly income in early farming societies works out to about $400 dollars per year, about $2,000 in early modern Britain, and nearly $40,000 in contemporary North America, Western Europe, and parts of East Asia. Baumard further cites the economic historian Deirdre McCloskey (2016), who points out that this growth in per capita annual income from 1800 CE to the present amounts to the typical person in these regions enjoying a 2,900% to 10,000% increase in their access to goods and services.

This is an astonishing change that goes largely ignored by social scientists, who spend most of their days searching for critiques of modernity. Of course, all of my talk of technological efficiency and economic productivity is not to sidestep the issue of climate change and environmental pollution. Indeed, while car transport may be a more efficient form of transport than transport by horse, not all cars are equally efficient (relative to a well-maintained car engine, a non-maintained car engine loses nearly two-thirds of its efficiency), and cars come with environmental costs that horses do not.

But I need to save these issues for a bit later on. First, I need to try and establish the drastic changes in infrastructure that have occurred over the last 200 years, and how this increased the available power and, thus, opportunity afforded to people. No, this access to power and opportunity has not been, and is not now, equally distributed across the globe. Externalities and inequalities are important parts of the conversation about infrastructure, but they cannot be (and too often are) the only aspects that social scientists discuss. We must stay focused on the first theoretical point: access to infrastructure reliant on hydrocarbons, relative to that reliant only on traditional wind, water, or human, and animal labor, provides greater access to survival-relevant resources and thus greater opportunities for mental and physical self-actualization.

We have to keep in mind that human and draft animal labor, along with the conversion of wind or water into kinetic energy (in the form of waterwheels, windmills, sails, and so on), were the only forms of energy in historical societies. When fossil fuse use began to rise dramatically in the 1850s (see Ritchie, 2017), waterwheels and windmills did not simply disappear. In fact, the use of these devices increased in the short-run, as did the reliance on human labor for working in coal mines, metalwork industries, and manufacturing. For these reasons, the rise of fossil fuel use should not be seen as a sudden new stage of history but rather as a slowly shifting emphasis on new machines and new forms of infrastructure reliant on new forms of energy.

Steel, for example, emerged in Germany in the 1700s when people begin lacing heated wrought iron with charcoal, thus increasing the carbon content and making the iron alloy more bendable and shapable for use in building construction and commercial machines. Steel would not be mass produced, however, until Henry Bessemer developed the "Bessemer Process," which involved shooting a powerful stream of air through molten pig iron, removing its carbon and silicon, thus converting large amounts of pig iron into steel within minutes.

Further innovations followed. One strategy was to add molten spiegel (a combination of manganese, carbon, and iron) to the molten pig iron so that slightly less carbon was blown out of the pig iron by the blast of cold air, making the steel stronger (Spoerl, 2004). Open hearths, another innovation, used large shallow furnaces to convert a mix of wrought iron and pig iron into steel in much larger batches. These open hearths were also heated with burning gas, and this allowed them to reach a higher temperature than Bessemer furnaces. And, because the iron could be cooked for a longer period of time in open hearths, the process allowed for more inspection by workers, in real time, of the changing chemistry of the metal.

As we can see today, due to these innovations and others steel became the standard material for building important forms of infrastructure, like railways, which would increase the rate and scope of resource distribution to levels never before seen in history:

> Consider a brief and incomplete list of the products made possible (or better or more affordable) by cheap, abundant steel: railroads, oil and gas pipelines, refineries, power plants, power lines, assembly lines, skyscrapers, elevators, subways, bridges, reinforced concrete, automobiles, trucks, buses, trolleys, refrigerators, washing machines, clothes dryers, dishwashers, nails, screws, bolts, nuts, needles, wire, watches, clocks, canned food, battleships, aircraft carriers, oil tankers, ocean freighters, shipping containers, cranes, bulldozers, tractors, farm implements, fences, knives, forks, spoons, scissors, razors, surgical instruments, ball bearings, turbines, drill bits, saws, and tools of every sort.
>
> (Spoerl, 2004, pg. 4)

Important entrepreneurial groups existed at three points of this process of innovation: those that innovated the forms of energy used to operate the machines that make steel, those that innovated the machines themselves, and those that innovated modes of usage. Any given entrepreneur, from Bessemer to Carnegie, existed in entrepreneurial social niches and, thus, it is probably true to say that if Bessemer or Carnegie, for example, hadn't done what they'd done, someone else in their social milieu would have.

Recall that I've defined a tool as something that, relatively speaking, requires less collective development or construction and is less accessible to, and thus utilizable by, collectives. Infrastructure, on the other end of the continuum, consists of technologies that require a relatively larger coordinated effort for construction, and that are capable of being accessed and utilized by larger numbers of people. While, for example, blast furnaces (especially very large ones) are certainly more infrastructure-like than a garden hoe or plow, relative to systems of electricity or undersea cables used to spread internet access, they are more of a tool. In the next sections of this chapter, I will suggest that industrial forms of infrastructure, such as electrical grids, are more akin to the irrigation systems of ancient agricultural societies—something which must be collectively built and/or funded, and something that tends to provide benefits to massive numbers of people.

What follows is a discussion of some of the core infrastructures of industrial societies, using the case studies of electricity and advancements in irrigation. *These case studies are not exhaustive of relevant forms of core infrastructure in industrial societies.* However, they should serve to make the broader point.

6.1 Electrical Systems

In the introduction to her "biography" of the electrical grid, Julie Cohn reflects on the fact that,

> each moment of the day [people] turn on lights, computers, coffee-makers, vacuum cleaners, cars, conveyor belts, and other devices using electricity. Without having to know what electricity is, where it is generated, or how it gets from the power plant to the switch, [we] rely utterly on the everyday miracle of electrification. Most … may not realize [the complex system of] generators, transformers, transmission lines, distribution lines, motors, chargers, plugs, and bulbs that comprise our interconnected world.
>
> (Cohn, 2018, pg. 1)

Let's step back to consider the beginning of this winding road to electricity. Shallow stone cups filled with animal fat appear to be the earliest form of "lamps," and date to about 40,000 years ago (De Beaune and White, 1993). Carved handle lamps, which were being used about 17,500 years ago, contained a small groove on one end of a long handle made of ground-down red sandstone. The length of the handle ensured that the side being held was far enough away from the flame that it would be cool to the touch (De Beaune and White, 1993).

Wax or fat candles do not facilitate a very efficient transfer of energy into light. In fact, wax and fat-based candles convert only about 0.01% of their chemical energy into light (Smil, 2017). Candles and oil lamps also give off a smoky, weak light, and their component parts could be expensive for subsistence farmers. By the late nineteenth century, Thomas Edison's light bulbs were about *10 times* more efficient. Today, natural gas turbines and fluorescent lights are about *90 times* more efficient than wax or tallow candles.

A story I long thought was apocryphal, but isn't, is that of Benjamin Franklin setting out to show that lightning is composed of a certain energy, namely, electricity (Franklin, 1752; Gupton, 2017). So, in June 1752 Franklin took a standard kite, attached some metal wire to the top of it, and to the bottom of the kite he attached a hemp string and a metal key. He then let the kite go, during a storm, hoping to capture some of the ambient electrical charge from the storm clouds. Thought it apparently took a while, eventually Franklin could feel a sharp spark when he touched his knuckle to the key.

Sensing the significance of what he'd found, Franklin declared the phenomenon "electric fire" as though fire had been discovered in new form. Franklin would go on to store as much of this electricity as he could in so-called "Leyden jars." These jars had been invented just seven years before

Franklin's classic experiment by a German physicist named Ewald Jürgen von Kleist (Scholz, 2011). These jars were glass containers of alcohol or water, with the top of the jar stuffed with cork and a nail, or wire shoved down through the cork into the fluid. Next, Kleist attached this nail to an electrostatic generator. These generators go as far back as the 15th century, but did not become widely experimented with until the 18th century. One version of these generators, for example, included two circular sheets of glass or plastic, covered with bits of tin, attached to a crank. When cranked, the sheets of tin rubbed against metal brushes, producing an electrical charge. Kleist discovered that when the jar's nail was touched to an electrostatic generator, painful electrical charges could be felt in the body upon touching the jar.

Over the course of many small innovations developed by different inventors (such as Pieter van Musschenbroek, Jean Antoine Nollet, and Andreas Cunaeus), the Leyden jar developed into a device that allowed electrical charges to be stored in water, which could then be transported and used for electricity when the circuit of the jar was closed with some wire or other metal object (Scholz, 2011).

Fast-forward about 40 years to the Italian anatomist Luigi Galvani, who, in 1791, released his descriptions of ten years of experimentation showing that the tissue of dead frogs could be animated by electrostatic generators (Piccolino, 1998). Galvani generated a static electrical charge, connected it to a copper wire, and touched the copper wire and another metal wire to exposed nerves in dead frog legs. This produced a closed circuit of electrons, jolted the frog's muscle tissue, and the legs of the decapitated frog began to move as though they were alive (Galvani's experiments served as the inspiration for Mary Shelley's *Frankenstein*). Surprised by this apparent reanimating (albeit not reviving) of the dead, experimentalists the world over rushed to duplicate Galvani's work with whatever dead animals they could find.

However, Galvani had also discovered something else, just as important as the role of electricity in biological functioning: he intimated the structure of the first batteries. Galvani discovered that biological tissue, in particular the acids in the tissue, could conduct the transfer of electrons between metals like copper and iron, and that it was this transfer of electrons that was animating the frog. He further found that some metals, like gold and silver, were highly efficient conductors of this "animal electricity," while materials like glass were useless (Piccolino, 1998). Some liquids, like water, were also better conductors of electricity than oil or alcohol.

For Galvani, this only provided evidence that electricity had a biological origin. His public debate with physicist Alessandro Volta, who insisted that it was the *metals* that were producing the electrical charge and not the *bodies* of the dead frogs, pushed our understanding of electricity further.

Motivated to show that electricity could be generated without the bodies of organisms serving as conductors, Volta developed the first electric battery in 1800, which came to be known as the "Voltaic Pile" (Piccolino, 1998; for the original, see Volta, 1800). The Voltaic Pile was literally a vertically stacked pile of alternating circular disks of zinc and copper, with each disk separated by a circular piece of cardboard that had been previously soaked in saltwater. The saltwater-soaked paper served as an electrolyte capable of transferring the positively-charged ions in copper and negatively-charged ions in zinc. When a metal wire was then snaked through this stack of copper and zinc, a weak electrical charge was produced. Just like that, Volta had proven that electricity could be generated without relying on biological tissue.

Volta (1800) published many configurations of his Voltaic Pile, some of which involved placing a strip of metal connected to the bottom of the pile directly into a cup of water, which could then store the electrical charge. Interestingly, even though Volta was becoming convinced of the metallic drivers of electricity, he nevertheless referred to his Voltaic Pile battery as an "artificial electrical organ," a sign of the massive impact of Galvani's earlier experiments on frogs (Piccolino, 1998, pg. 389). The contemporary unit of measurement describing the force of an electric current, "voltage" or "volt," commemorates Volta's successful experiments. Today, middle school kids in science fairs know they can construct a "lemon battery" by jabbing a copper wire (or a penny) and a sharp piece of zinc (typically, a zinc-coated nail or paperclip) into a lemon, which naturally contains copious electrolytes in its juice. The copper and zinc can then transfer electrons through the lemon juice, creating a weak electrical charge. Though the concept of electricity is more accessible to us now, Volta's discovery of how to produce electricity without the need for biological organisms was a truly groundbreaking innovation. Lemons and dead frog legs aren't necessary, after all: any chemical medium facilitating the flow of electrons can be used to create a battery.

Many innovations followed those discussed above. Among the most important, perhaps, was the discovery of the exact connection between electricity and magnetism. In 1819, Hans Ørsted discovered that a stable electric current could produce a magnetic field. By 1831, Michael Faraday had provided evidence that, conversely, a changing magnetic field was capable of producing an electrical current. For example, simply moving a strong magnet back-and-forth toward and then away from a roll of copper wire (thus altering the magnetic field the copper is in) is sufficient to begin circulating electrons in the wire, producing electricity. If the magnet stops moving, the electrons stop circulating, and no electricity is produced.

In 1834, Emil Lenz formulated "Lenz's Law," which began to conceptualize formally (if not yet mathematically) what Faraday had discerned: pushing a magnet toward the copper produces a magnetic *resistance* in the copper, whereas pulling the magnet away produces an opposite magnetic *pull* from the copper. The insight was that the strength of an electric current could be modified by the rate of change in a magnetic field. This induction-opposition effect of a moving magnetic field, and the movement of electrons and thus electricity that results from this effect, became the foundation for the commercialization of electricity. No longer were messy Voltaic Piles or Leyden Jars or, worse, dead frogs, needed for the production of electricity.

The commercialization of electricity began with the light bulb. An especially important early milestone occurred in 1879, when Thomas Edison began adorning nearby railroad stations, streets, and his own workshop with his new light bulbs. Edison's bulbs contained a carbonized cotton thread filament inside of blown glass; the filament slowed down the circulating electrical current, and the result was a hot glow. Even if light bulbs were incredibly inefficient (the light given off lasted only 14.5 hours), they were nevertheless an important improvement—Edison's bulbs were *100 times* brighter than a candle and around *10 times* brighter than gas lanterns (Matulka and Wood, 2013; Smil, 2017).

Edison's laboratory in Menlo Park, New Jersey, drew interested and talented nascent electricians from all over the world in a semi-open system of innovation (Hounshell, 2002). I regard Edison's laboratory compound as "semi-open" in the sense that most employees or collaborators appear to have been reasonably well-to-do young men and (for a variety of reasons quite independent of Edison) not truly a sampling of all intelligent people. My point is only that, though we tend to identify individuals (like Edison and the others discussed here) as the sources of innovation, we cannot forget that the actual *source* is open-system fission–fusion.

Part of this open system was the urban (and, thus, relatively population-dense and intellectually diverse) location of Edison's laboratory compound, and, part of the open system involved his team's intermittent contact with others all around the world, including competitors from other countries like Joseph Swan and Nikola Tesla. Edison and his various teams around the world would continue to innovate, and over the subsequent years Edison—as the figurehead and leader—would file over 180 patents for new filaments, lamps, and machines generating and distributing electricity.

In January of 1882, an Edison-owned company in London completed construction of the first electrical power plant. Shortly thereafter, Edison opened a power plant on Pearl Street in New York City. This "Pearl Street Station" was coal-powered and, using a direct current generator, provided consumer electricity for 11,000 light bulbs within just a year of opening (Smil, 2017). Not too long thereafter, power stations like these began sweeping across the United States and around the world. Massive amounts of electricity were generated and stored in these stations, where it could then be commercially metered out to people living within a given radius.

Edison's protégé Samuel Insull (who was the figurehead of his own oscillating teams) raised the funding for an electrical power plant on Harris Street in Chicago, which opened in 1894 (Hughes, 1979). The direct current electricity generators in the plant were powered with steam engines. Shortly thereafter, however, these stations would become obsolete because of the innovations of Tesla and his own teams.

Nikola Tesla was, himself, a former Edison protégé and would, with partners like Samuel Westinghouse and others, introduce a new strategy for transmitting currents much further than Edison could with his direct current. Tesla reasoned that if electrical currents could travel further across geographic space when voltage was higher, but that high voltage would also cause fire or injury, all that was needed were convertors that could effectively reduce the voltage across space so that the current was usable (and safe) by the time it reached residential or commercial establishments. Edison, not wanting to lose important contracts with cities, doubled down on his safer, lower voltage, direct current system. The resultant competition between Edison's direct current system and Tesla's alternating current system, became known as the "war of the currents" (see Jonnes, 2004; Cole and Chandler, 2019).

Alternating current electrical systems won out, once Tesla adequately demonstrated their safety to the public. Edison and his company, however, became consolidated with General Electric, and for this and other reasons Edison's legacy often shines brighter. But, this is all of little relevance, given that we know not to attribute too much innovativeness to individuals as opposed to the open-system fission–fusion stimulated by their ecologies.

But, by this point, city leaders in places like New York and London had already heavily invested in Edison's direct current system. Though safer on account of being lower voltage, direct current power stations were also more expensive because of the many low-voltage underground cables necessary for distribution of the electricity (Hughes, 1979). The compromise was to turn Edison's stations into substations that could serve as convertors (i.e., transformers) that reduced the extremely high voltage of the power station source down to an acceptable voltage for residential and commercial use.

Technologies like rotary convertors were used at these substations to change high-voltage alternating currents sent from the station to low-voltage direct currents for consumers. In 1895, Tesla, Westinghouse, and their teams oversaw the establishment of the largest hydroelectric alternating current power station in the world. This station, built in Niagara Falls, New York, utilized 6,000,000 horsepower converted from the 210,00 cubic feet of water flowing over the falls each second (Sharlin, 1961). By 1899,

> the Niagara Falls powerplant was well established. The plan to produce large quantities of power and distribute it [over long distances] was a proved success. The engineering world hailed the achievement as representing the coming of age of electrical engineering and a final demonstration of the superiority of the alternating current system over the direct current system. Niagara had pioneered the way in the development of large centralized electric utilities which supplied the power for the twentieth-century expansion of the US economy.
>
> (Sharlin, 1961, pg. 74)

The extraction (via generators), processing (via substations), and distribution (via lines, pylons, and towers) of electricity would, of course, become essential for consumer electronics like televisions, computers, or smartphones. Much more importantly, though, electricity also keeps people alive, whether by powering medical tools during surgeries or electrical heaters that keep people warm enough to sleep during blizzards. Electricity also powers the means of self-actualization, from the cars, buses, or railways carrying people to arts and science programs to new computers in schools used to teach children how to code. On these points, I should quote Harold Sharlin a bit further:

> [What Edison and others had not foreseen] was that electricity would have many more uses than lighting. One of the largest and growing uses of electricity … was for motors on street railway cars. Electric motors were also being used for driving sewing machines and elevators. [Niagara power station engineering consultant George Forbes] reported to the Institution of Electrical Engineers, "The officers of the company and myself … looking at the purposes for which our machinery is being set up, felt sure that the proportion of electricity which would be used for lighting purposes would not be large, and that we must look upon our whole plant as a *power* producing and distributing plant, and that our object must be to distribute *power* in the most efficient and economical manner."
>
> (Sharlin, 1961, pgs. 72–73, italics in original)

In the ensuing years, people could more cheaply and safely light and heat their homes and they could rely on a host of secondary commercial benefits ranging from consistently refrigerated perishables kept at grocery stores to schools with computers to hospitals with electrical tools.

To bring us up to the present day, I must say a bit about the development of electrical grid systems. "Electrical grid" is a term used to describe the interlinked modern system of electrical production, transmission, and distribution. Substantively, electrical grids are linked networks of computer-monitored generators, substations, transformers, pylons, distribution lines, sensors, and meters. Grids are the veins by which electricity is distributed from generators to residential and commercial consumers.

This happens across three broad steps: (1) electricity is generated in one of several ways, such as by burning fossil fuels in power plants, using hydroelectric dams, by using photovoltaic panels to absorb energy from the sun's rays, by using wind turbines, or by nuclear fission; (2) electricity is then distributed by wire to a substation, where the current's voltage is increased to enable further travel across long distances via transmission towers/pylons, where, eventually; (3) the voltage is stepped down at various substations along the route before traveling to distribution lines (i.e., wires attached to electrical poles that contain their own smaller sensors and transformers to regulate voltage) which, finally, deliver electricity to vehicles, homes, businesses, and other institutions via outlets (Gerrity and Lantero, 2014). Electricity in a grid is stored in various ways such that if too much is produced, or less becomes needed, two-way "smart" meters can communicate information about usage between consumers and utility companies, facilitating efficient responses to power outages or sudden declines in use.

This infrastructural system requires a variety of directly and indirectly cooperating groups—line workers, residential and commercial electricians, generator/plant operations staff, construction and design engineers, city, county, and state employees, and, of course, tax-paying consumers. The planning, designing, building, and maintaining of a society's electrical infrastructure never ends and is never perfect—the US Department of Energy, for example, admits that "70 percent of the grid's transmission lines and power transformers are over 25 years old, and the average age of power plants is over 30 years old … Parts of this network are more than a century old" (Gerrity and Lantero, 2014). This aging of electrical infrastructure is separate from climate or weather damage or defects of materials. Setting aside the United States's particular struggles with infrastructure, it should go without saying that no infrastructural system survives long unmaintained, and, as we've discussed above, the breakdown of infrastructure can be deadly.

For example, a recent blackout in South America's grid system—affecting Argentina, Uruguay, and Paraguay—had devastating, if short-lived, consequences. An NPR reporter on the ground had this to say:

> People … woke up for, you know, what they hoped would be a nice, peaceful Sunday to discover that the power was out across almost all of Argentina, which is the second largest country in this region, and also in parts of neighboring Uruguay and Paraguay, which get electricity … from the Argentine grid … So trains stopped running. Water supplies were disrupted. Gas stations couldn't pump gas …

> Phones and the Internet were disrupted. It happened on a day in Argentina—in parts of Argentina, where there were gubernatorial elections. These actually still went ahead, but people had to use their [cellphone lights] … to give themselves enough light to vote by. And it also happened on Father's Day, when people were hoping to go out for Sunday lunch but had to cancel because, you know, restaurants and businesses were shut. It took all day to get the lights completely back on; they are now back on. But people have a lot of questions about what precisely happened and what's going on in the region … Now, officials are saying that this was a failure in the grid's interconnection system, which happened in the northeast, between two big installations there, and then triggered this unprecedented chain reaction.
>
> (Reeves, 2019)

For now, electrical grids are not global, but regional systems. The North American grid is composed of two interconnected, alternating current grids composed of numerous regional and neighborhood-level "microgrids." According to the US Energy Information Administration, the Eastern grid covers areas to the east of the Rocky Mountains including the northern tip ("panhandle") of Texas. The Western grid covers the area west of the Rocky Mountains. The rest of Texas receives electricity from the Electric Reliability Council of Texas, a nonprofit corporation. The Eastern and Western grids are also interconnected with the Canadian power grid. In Europe, the grid is broken into five interconnected systems (the largest of which is the Continental European Synchronous system) covering over 30 countries, and including nearly 200,000 miles of transmission lines that, "if laid out … would circle the earth's circumference more than seven times" (Hagem and Andraesen, 2015, pg. 9). Russia is covered under the Unified Power System, China receives power from two grids (with a large proportion of electricity coming from the Three Gorges Dam), and Africa generates electricity across four grid systems (Medinilla et al., 2019.)

For farmers and small-scale artisans living in agricultural societies, the burning of wood, charcoal, animal dung, collected twigs, grasses, and crop detritus provided "all the energy needed for household heating, cooking and lighting" (Smil, 2017, pg. 163). Clearly, the accessibility/utilizability of electricity has expanded the accoutrements and opportunities available to people in modern life. Our perceived "needs," along with our dependencies, have grown with the expansion of this infrastructure.

6.2 Advances in Water Management and Irrigation

For all of human history, up until about 1800, the global population was below 1 billion people. By 1950, the global population had more than doubled to 2.5 billion people and by 2015 there were 7.3 billion people on Earth (see West, 2017, pg. 210). Projections suggest that 9.3 billion people will be on Earth by 2050 (though the number will soon level off, as access to literacy, education, birth control and higher per capita GDP generally reduces the number of children couples choose to have). All of these people require a lot of water for drinking, yes, but also for growing crops and for hydrating animals used for food, labor or companionship.

Let's consider, first, waste management. Waste management refers to both human and industrial waste management, but I'll arbitrarily focus here on human material and biological waste (exciting, I know). In foraging societies, waste is buried and, if it builds up, no problem, because people can just pick up their camp and move. However, as we've seen, this nomadism becomes more difficult the more people rely on growing their food, because populations become denser and people accumulate more goods.

The construction of street drains for wastewater dates to the existence of the Mesopotamian empires around 4,000 BCE though, even by the time of the Roman Empire thousands of years later, sewage systems and aqueducts were prevalent but not linked to people's homes (so feces and urine still had to be kept in buckets and dumped outside) (Abellán, 2017). Ancient sewage systems, to the degree they were built at all, were typically composed of aboveground canals (or easily cracked earthen pipes), which exposed people to disease even as the waste shuffled along out to sea (Burian and Edwards, 2002; for a great review, see De Feo et al., 2014). Indeed, in large agrarian societies—both historical and contemporary—waste is dumped along the sides of country roads, city streets, or into landfills, funneled via canals into streams and rivers, or simply swept out of sight by laborers. However, dumping, funneling, or sweeping away waste, especially in dense areas, can expose people to deadly diseases like typhoid, cholera, hepatitis A, and polio (World Health Organization, 2019). And, in more modern agrarian societies, technologies like batteries, computers, rubber tires, and healthcare-related waste increase the potential toxicity of dumpsites (Ferronato and Torretta, 2019).

According to the World Bank, over 90% of human waste in developing countries today is dumped or burned and, in addition to exposure to disease and toxins, landslides of piled waste destroy homes and kill people with surprising frequency (Kaza and Yao, 2018). The 50 largest dumpsites in the world are actively putting more than 64 million people at risk today all over the world, and research indicates that the hazards of open dumpsites reduce a population's life expectancy to a greater degree than does malaria (Chatham-Stephens et al., 2013). The World Health Organization (2019) reports that just under half of the global population has access to well-maintained and well-managed sanitation systems. And consider the statistics that "673 million [people] still defecate in the open, for example in street gutters, behind bushes or into open bodies of water," and that about 10% of the global population subsists on crops irrigated with sewage-laden water. Even in rich countries like the United States, over one-third of people lacked access to indoor plumbing as recently as 1950 (Fishman, 2014).

Effective sanitation systems only began emerging in the nineteenth century in response to the unprecedented growth of cities. Not only does infectious disease spread faster the denser a population is, but urban residents are typically more geographically removed from water sources and more proximate to waste dumping sites compared to their rural counterparts (Abellán, 2017). For these reasons, in countries where urbanization initially grew the fastest, such as the United Kingdom, life expectancy for urban residents temporarily fell below that of rural residents. At the time, most cities (~85%) across Europe did not have piped water systems and relied entirely on (frequently clogged) sewers emptying out into distant rivers and streams (Hassan, 1985). From Paris to Madrid, waste would be collected in indoor cesspools, and dumped into the streets and sewers at night. Despite these conditions, people nevertheless migrated from the countryside to the city in search of more stable factory employment (compared to the seasonal uncertainty of subsistence farming) and new economic markets.

Then, in the early 1830s, an epidemic of cholera, with a 50% fatality rate, hit Europe's rapidly growing cities (Abellán, 2017). Governments across Europe responded much as they would today and attempted to enforce quarantines. These quarantines, of course, swiftly decimated economies because food deliveries and market transactions slowed, leading to inflationary food pricing, bankruptcy of small businesses and a spike in unemployment. Consequently, populist revolts broke out in London and Paris in 1832, Seville in 1833, Madrid in 1834, and elsewhere (Abellán, 2017). However, the fact that the disease was spreading, despite people quarantining, convinced city officials that the disease was stemming from something being used inside peoples' homes. The combination of high death rates from disease and their effect on stymying the growth of urban economies motivated government authorities to begin constructing more effective forms of sanitation infrastructure.

For the most part, only the wealthiest elites of the 1800s had private plumbing; everyone else collected their waste in cesspools and dumped it out the window into the street at night. However, this and much else changed shortly after the cholera outbreak (Abellán, 2017). For one, sewage channels were built underground instead of above-ground near streets. The next step was to directly connect all residences to this underground sewer system, so that people did not need to collect and dump their own waste. This sewer system still emptied out into rivers (like the Thames) which contaminated the drinking water. The solution was to create separate channels for wastewater (which was used as fertilizer, though this has its own downsides) and stormwater (which could safely empty out into rivers).

In 1893, another solution was to add bacteria to reservoirs of wastewater, allow the organisms to eat any organic matter, and simply scoop out the heavy, sludgy, bacteria which eventually sunk to the bottom of the water. This system, known as the "activated sludge system," is arguably the first attempt at water treatment, and thus the first sludge system facilities might also be regarded as the first water treatment plants (De Feo et al., 2014). Later, electrical pumps were introduced, which helped direct the flow of wastewater across the uneven terrain of a city or town.

Today, the most sophisticated treatment plants are automated and machine-operated. Wastewater is pumped through various levels of filtration, which remove garbage, sediment, and other solids, before bacteria, protozoans, and other reagents are added to consume or dissolve any remaining organic materials. So-called "Fenton's reagent," for example, is a solution composed of ferrous iron, sulfate, and hydrogen peroxide, and will dissolve organic material (Bidga, 1995). To increase the effectiveness of this reagent, the surface of the water can also be pretreated with electricity (Panizza and Cerisola, 2001). After this process, chlorine or ultraviolet light is used to kill off any residual harmful bacteria, though if chlorine is used it must be removed before water is reintroduced to rivers or streams.

There are, however, other problems outside of contamination. Providing water to people living in dry areas is another logistical issue. Let's consider, arbitrarily, the southwestern United States, specifically Los Angeles, and how a city (and county) of such massive size could exist in an otherwise dry region prone to drought. The Los Angeles River can only provide drinking water to around 150,000 people, and while this would be plenty for an ancient city, the population of Los Angeles county, today, is about 10 million people (not counting the large populations of surrounding counties) (Smith, 2019). Clearly, the natural landscape of Los Angeles is insufficient for providing sustenance for this many people. The answer was to commission a massive engineering project in 1907 known as the Los Angeles Aqueduct.

The LA aqueduct is a massive system of canals shuffling water from the Owens River near the Sierra Nevada, hundreds of miles away, into a huge reservoir in the San Fernando Valley. Along the way, several smaller dammed storage reservoirs collect the canalized water. Construction of the aqueduct took place over five years, required the labor of about 5,000 workers (supplemented by teams of mules), and cost 23 million dollars (Sahagun, 2013). Canals were dug out with shovels, while tunnels and dams were excavated using 6 million pounds of dynamite. When finished in 1913, 280 miles of pipe had been laid and 142 tunnels had been excavated.

Construction of the Los Angeles Aqueduct also took advantage of many new technologies. Caterpillar tractors, for example, were first used as tools for aqueduct construction in 1909 and were immensely helpful for backfilling excavated areas, moving steel, and serving as dollies for other heavy materials (Hurlbut et al., 1942). Though at least 5,000 people labored to construct the aqueduct, many more would have been needed were it not for these tractors. The difference in time and energy between backfilling a hole with a tractor and doing so using a team of human shovelers is not small. Some of the heavier steel pipes (much more durable than the stone-cut pipes used in ancient Greek and Roman aqueducts) weighed around 26 tons and would need to be transported on specially designed wagons propelled by tires wrapped around 24-inch steel wheels (Hurlbut et al., 1942). Teams of over 50 mules pulled these wagons; even given technological advances in metallurgy and construction machinery, without the labor of draft animals, the aqueduct never would have been completed so quickly (Hurlbut et al., 1942).

Other new technologies like hydroelectric plants, telephone lines, and railroads, themselves more infrastructural in nature than tractors or blast furnaces, contributed to the building of the aqueduct. This, in essence, represented a synergy of infrastructures supporting infrastructural extension. To the extent that infrastructure facilitates the extraction, processing, and distribution of energy and resources, *infrastructure begets infrastructure*—more power is available for construction and more laborers can be fed, making new infrastructures easier to build.

As much of an engineering feat as the Los Angeles Aqueduct is, much tragedy came with it. For one, 43 men died during the construction of the aqueduct (Sahagun, 2013). The aqueduct also choked the Owens River it drew water from, and Owens Lake essentially dried up, killing off the wildlife that called the lake home. Tragedy also resulted from the completed aqueduct itself; because the aqueduct was intended to be usable by many people, it was, of course, unusually large, and when it broke, devastation followed. The most famous example is the collapse of the St. Francis gravity dam, a critical substructure of the aqueduct, regulating the flow of water down the Sierra Pelona Mountains 35–40 miles northwest of the city of Los Angeles. This dam rapidly filled to capacity, and in March of 1928 water pressure broke the dam, releasing an immense torrent of 12 billion gallons of water (Smith, 2019). The disaster destroyed farms and homes over a 50-mile stretch, killing over 400 people. As I've said above, the very collective accessibility/utilizability of large-scale infrastructure—perhaps especially infrastructure built at the scale of industrial societies—makes its malfunction as devastating as its proper functioning is life-giving.

Nevertheless, the aqueduct served its purpose of hydrating hundreds of thousands of people, and today it provides water and energy for millions of people. In fact, just within seven years of the completion of the aqueduct, the square mileage of the city of Los Angeles more than tripled, from 107 square miles to 364 square miles (Sahagun, 2013). The proud chief water engineer for the city, William Mulholland, is recorded as having said: "Whoever brings the water will bring the people." And he, like all of the ancient irrigation planners of societies past, was quite correct (Sahagun, 2013). However, unlike societies past, this aqueduct was substantially larger and more securely engineered, even down to the two steel wheels that Mulholland turned to open the first gates of the aqueduct.

The Los Angeles Aqueduct, given its extensiveness, required an open-system fission (when the workday ended)–fusion (when the workday began) of laborers—whoever was available and could do the work was let on the project. In practice, this required the concerted attentional allocation of people from a diverse pool of ethnic groups—"Greeks, Italians, Bulgarians, Serbs, Swiss, Mexicans and Native Americans" (Sahagun, 2013). These people, together, managed the risks associated with the use of explosives, cave-ins during excavations, avalanches, and vehicular accidents. For their part, planners, architects, funders, politicians, and others fused in a slightly less open system in order to coordinate labor. The result was that the dam was built ahead of schedule, and the final expense was less than what had been initially budgeted.

This coordinated, collaborative, and ongoing maintenance continued in the ensuing decades. Around 20 years after it was first built, the aqueduct was extended 150 miles in order to capture water from five different streams running out of the basin of Mono Lake near Yosemite National Park (Sahagun, 2013). A second aqueduct was opened in 1970, and this added 50% greater capacity, bringing the total to about 430 million gallons of water delivered per day to the city of Los Angeles alone. Countless ongoing maintenance projects filled the gaps of these milestone achievements. Indeed, just in 2013 cracked concrete (which was used to reinforce pipes) was replaced, and all 12 of the aqueduct's hydroelectric generators were rewired and rebuilt (Sagahun, 2013). Today, much longer aqueducts feed water into Los Angeles from the Colorado River, and so the Los Angeles Aqueduct is less intensively relied on. But, it is still used, and provides an added "safety net" for a region so prone to draught.

Today, complex water treatment and delivery systems exist in countries throughout much of the world. Aquifer systems, pumping wells, pipes, and water treatment stations keep us alive, and provide us the luxury of not having to find water, know much about how it is extracted, or understand much about how it is distributed to our faucet or garden. We just wake up, turn on the faucet, and take the whole thing for granted.

Equally important, however, is that "climate change, basin-scale water balance changes, river flow regulation, sediment fluxes, chemical pollution, microbial pollution, and changes in biodiversity" threaten to reduce the adequate supply of water to people and land (Linton, 2014, pg. 114). Furthermore, infrastructural maintenance and constructional re-engineering—to, for example, avoid lead-poisoned water as we've seen in Flint, Michigan, and elsewhere —are critically important for the effective distribution of water. Secondary causes of infrastructural damage, for example, droughts leading to brushfires that destroy infrastructure, require a competent governmental vigilance to plan ahead with protective measures. Given how dependent people become on their society's infrastructure for survival, infrastructural quality is essential to any increases in societal complexity. Infrastructure is an extended human phenotype that increases survival, but just the same it can cause massive reductions in survival or in opportunities insofar as this phenotype erodes, breaks down, or is destroyed.

Let's take a specific example to help underscore this point: deadly arsenic leeching into the water supply of San Joaquin Valley in California. Levels of arsenic in drinking water have been correlated with increased regional rates of several forms of cancer, including lung, kidney, bladder, and skin cancer. In a study of over 400 community water systems—mostly groundwater systems supplying water to the same small number of residential customers year-round—Carolina Balazs and her colleagues (2012) found that almost 14% of residents in the valley had been exposed to water containing levels of arsenic deemed unsafe by the US Environmental Protection Agency. This buildup of arsenic in groundwater resulted from a disruption of naturally occurring arsenic-laden sediment from water-pumping and irrigation construction. Balasz and her colleagues also show that arsenic levels are higher in areas with lower home-ownership rates, indicating a disproportionate impact on people of lower socioeconomic status.

We might also speculate that residents who are renting, and do not own, their houses may be less invested in advocating local governance to address infrastructural problems. That is, people with fewer resources might both be the most harmed and, on account of feeling as though they have no property stake in the area, least invested in local infrastructural maintenance. Were people able to afford buying these homes, their financial and social stake in the local community would be higher, and might, in turn, motivate political support for city leaders who pay closer attention to the management and funding of constructional engineering. As with any critical infrastructure, the collective utilizability of the resource itself (in this case, water) is mediated by infrastructural quality and maintenance as well as by the legitimacy and transparency of the governmental apparatus charged with this construction and maintenance.

Today, the United States alone has 1.6 million miles of water supply mains connected to residences (Fishman, 2014). This works out to about 26 miles of water piping for each mile of interstate highway, a core infrastructural system in its own right. Despite this, in the United States each mile of water piping breaks about every six years on average (causing losses to water utility companies and to consumers), and large cities often schedule repairs to water pipes only every couple of centuries! For example, Philadelphia and Los Angeles have a formal schedule to replace piping every *300 years*, and Washington, DC has a replacement cycle every *200 years* (Fishman, 2014). As of 2020, the average age of water and sewage pipes in the United States is 45 years, around 600 counties have iron pipes over 100 years old, and, though lead water pipes were formally banned in the United States 30 years ago, many remain buried underneath the soil (Tabuchi, 2017). In fact, some 8,000 children in Flint, Michigan, alone have recently been exposed to toxic levels of lead in their drinking water. Currently, plastic and iron manufacturers are in a bidding war to win the 300 billion dollars that are estimated to be spent on pipe replacements and repairs nationwide in the U.S. over the next ten years.

What's at stake? Quite a bit. Safe drinking water and efficient sewage treatment reduce disease, increase life expectancy, and contribute to the core infrastructure of schools, grocery stores, fire departments, hospitals, and other vital community organizations. I can be even more specific about these benefits: the World Health Organization (2019) estimates that for *every dollar* in the United States spent on sanitation (to say nothing of the drinking water system), $5.50 is saved in healthcare costs, occupational productivity, and reduced mortality.

6.3 Infrastructural Layering

Core infrastructure—for example, electrical systems, irrigation systems, undersea electrical cables, roadways—provides the preconditions for the emergence of secondary forms of infrastructure such as gas stations, subway stations, schools, parks, hospitals, community centers, social services departments (post offices, welfare offices), fire departments, and so on, all of which rely on efficient roadways, electrical systems and water systems. Distinctions between core and secondary forms of infrastructure are distinctions of embeddedness or of relative aggregation (e.g., a modern waste management system requires electrical and irrigation systems; a modern hospital requires electricity, irrigation, and sanitation systems, and so on).

Gas stations, subway stations, schools, parks, hospitals, community centers, social services departments, libraries, museums, movie theatres, arts and crafts stores, coffee shops, and so on are all secondary, emergent products of core infrastructure. They are, in effect, layered on top of more core infrastructure and dependent upon it.

Let's take a brief look at three examples of infrastructural layering: (1) railways and public transportation; (2) fuel stations; and (3) electronically mediated communication.

6.3.1 Railways and public transportation

Electricity was used as a means to power public trolleys beginning in the late nineteenth century in order to transport people (and their goods) around urban centers. To get a sense of the massive importance of these railways, and their rapid growth, consider that in 1890 1,261 miles of electrified railway had been constructed in the United States and that this would grow to 21,920 miles by 1902 (Sharlin, 1961). Today, in addition to trolleys, people around the world make use of public buses, aboveground commuter rail (powered by diesel or electric engines) or light rail (powered by overhead electrical wires), and below-ground subways. To take the United States as an example, the Bureau of Transportation Statistics reports that, in total, transit busses transported people an overall total of *20 billion* revenue passenger miles in 2011 alone, while railways (mostly metro subways) transported people nearly *another* 20 billion revenue passenger miles (Bureau of Transportation Statistics, 2014).[1] These are astonishing figures that underscore the necessity of electricity in mass transportation (to say nothing of the importance of electricity for personal vehicles).

An important caveat is that these various types of public transit are not uniformly funded, constructed, or maintained across different cities, states, and countries. Lack of funding or maintenance of public transportation might especially reduce the mobility of frequent transit users, who are often young people, racial minorities, or immigrants (Karner et al., 2016). The types of transit discussed above are also not exhaustive—many cities around the world have, for example, public bicycles available for rent that rely on electronic storage facilities, tracking systems, and even electrical motors built into the bike to ease peddling (Guidon et al., 2019; Eren and Uz, 2020). However, though these are all important points, the most important takeaways should be that (1) the degree of funding and the quality of construction and maintenance all take for granted a core electrical and roadway infrastructure; and (2) the ability for people and goods to be transported in space facilitates opportunities for economic exchange (i.e., market growth) and self-actualization (i.e., educational or recreational opportunities).

6.3.2 Fuel Stations

Natural gas can be found trapped underground all around the world. Like crude oil, natural gas is a byproduct of the compression and heating of dead plants and animals as they sunk deeper and deeper under sediment over hundreds of millions of years. Natural gas tends to flow through tiny cracks in between rocks or in rocky sediment, so tools for reading seismic waves (which help surveyors determine rock formations underground) are used to find locations that may have natural gas reservoirs (Energy Information Administration, 2019b).

If a possible site is detected, exploratory wells are drilled to verify the presence of natural gas and, if gas is present, the rock formation is broken open with a high-pressure solution of water, sand, and toxic chemicals in a process known as "fracking" (Elliott et al., 2017). When the rock formations containing pockets of natural gas are broken apart, the gas flows up the well to the surface, and then through pressurized steel pipes into processing facilities. At these facilities, machines extract water vapor along with nonhydrocarbons like carbon dioxide and hydrogen sulfide and hydrocarbons like ethane, propane, and butane (Energy Information Administration, 2019b).

Once processed, the gas is distributed—using automated (electrical) compression stations that vary pipe pressure in order to keep the gas flowing—to underground storage facilities, where it can be accessed by commercial gas companies. Gas companies then meter this energy out to residences, businesses, or other manufacturing plants. However, before it is ready for commercial use, odorant chemicals (typically sulfur) are injected back into the gas so that any leaks can be detected by scent, making the naturally odorless gas safe for consumers. The United States alone contains 3 million miles of natural gas pipeline linking production sites and processing facilities to consumers (Energy Information Administration, 2019b). In 2018, this system provided 75 million customers with almost 28 trillion cubic feet of natural gas (Energy Information Administration, 2019b).

Unlike (dry) natural gas, which is mostly methane, the crude oil we use for automobile fuel contains far more carbon. The oil is extracted from the ground using drilling rigs of various sizes and levels of technological complexity, and then transported (via pipeline, railroad, waterway/ship, or road using oil tank trucks) to a refinery. At the refinery, the oil is heated to a boil in order to produce a vapor that can then be distilled into a variety of chemical forms, including naphtha (which can be transformed into commercial gasoline after passing through a series of reforming reactors), diesel, and kerosene. From the refineries, oil is transported via pipe systems to large storage containers where it can then be shipped by tanker trucks to commercial gasoline stations (Energy Information Administration, 2019a).

Technologically sophisticated oil refineries are not, per se, necessary for refining crude oil into diesel and other valuable products. In Nigeria, for example, impoverished people (suffering from other infrastructural deficits) illegally break into existing oil pipelines in order to extract crude oil which is then heated using a makeshift refinery: large oil-filled drums sitting over open fires (Taylor, 2013). This process is both inefficient and very dangerous, but, given the value of crude oil products, an economic incentive is there if people are desperate enough. Safety, by the way, is also a continual concern for natural gas extraction and processing—explosions from leaking pipes kill about 17 people in the United States annually and cause an estimated 133 million dollars of property damage (Jackson et al., 2014). Natural gas leaks are also the primary source of human-caused greenhouse gas pollution in the United States, and the second-largest source worldwide (Jackson et al., 2014). Insofar as gas extraction, refining, and distribution processes are safe and efficient—and this is best accomplished with complex electronically monitored machinery—it will be more accessible/utilizable.

Today, for example, there are about 115,000 gas stations throughout the United States, about 93,000 across the European Union, Norway, Switzerland, and Turkey; 12,551 in Mexico; and 4,600 in South Africa (Cooper, 2019; Petrol Plaza, 2020; South African Petroleum Industry Association, 2020; U.S. Census Bureau, 2020). These numbers have all been declining over the last several decades as people have begun carpooling more, driving less, and purchasing more fuel-efficient (i.e., electric) cars (Ferris, 2020).

I fully expect fuel sources and fuel types to change over time with advances in technologies, so my point here should not be taken as a defense of the importance of gas stations and systems *per se*. The point I am trying to make is that something as simple as a "gas station," is in fact an emergent property of core infrastructural systems: electricity, oil, and natural gas extraction, processing, and distribution. Yet, all we notice is the station where we pump our fuel. The immensely complex network of pipes and sensors and refineries goes mostly unnoticed, that is, until we cannot fill our car with gas and we miss an exam at the local college (itself emergent from core infrastructural systems), setting us back in our pursuit of our dream job.

6.3.3 Electronically Mediated Communication

I smiled when writing the header of this section because, of course, *all* animal communication is electronically mediated, given that neurons and nervous systems are electrical-chemical structures. But this isn't exactly what I mean here. In this section, I will describe how the entire globe is becoming something akin to a neural network, albeit at a higher-order, emergent, level.

Telegraph machines were a revolutionary form of communication, allowing for near-instantaneous discussions between people across thousands of miles for the first time in history. The so-called "Morse Code" (named for Samuel Morse, who helped invent the telegraph) that users used to communicate with one another was composed of short vs. long pulses of electricity, which were created by turning an electrical circuit switch on or off at each communicator's machine. Up until about 1848, communication between people within countries, or between countries, could only occur as fast as people (or letters) could travel by ship, train, or horseback (Solymar, 2000).

This was an astonishingly slow pace of communication compared to the rapidity offered by the telegraph, telephone and now, the internet. Because communication between individuals is a form of fusion, we can and should understand the pace of fusion across geographic space prior to 1800 as fundamentally slower than it is today.

It is revealing to reflect back on just how slow the pace of communication was throughout much of human history. Lewis Coe (2003) reports that in 1825, prior to the widespread use of the telegraph, Samuel Morse himself wrote a letter to his wife, but had no way of knowing that she had been dead for several days! To put some numbers to the issue, consider this:

> In the pre-railroad United States of the 1840s, it took 10 ½ days to send a one-page letter the 850 miles from New York to Chicago at a cost of 25 cents for postage. By the 1850s, railroads had reduced that to two days at a cost of 3 cents. But in the same decade, the telegraph made the transfer of one page of information possible in a matter of minutes, though at a much higher cost—about $7.50 on average between New York and Chicago.
>
> (Phillips, 2000, pg. 270)

But the telegraph would quickly come down in cost and become widely used. In 1867, one year after huge electrical cables were successfully placed under the Atlantic Ocean in 1866 (which enabled electronic communication across the great body of water), the Western Union Telegraph company recorded almost 6 million telegrams sent. This number grew steadily; about 60 million telegrams were sent in 1892 and 90 million were sent in 1913 (Phillips, 2000). With more users, costs could be lowered—by 1899 Western Union was charging only 30 cents to send a telegram. By the early 1900s, telegraphs had become essential to mainstream businesses, and large companies made sure to have their own personal telegraph operators directly connected to local relay offices (Coe, 2003).

Marshall McLuhan (1964) was onto something when he speculated that media technology was an externalization and extension of humans' central nervous system. I would say that it is *core infrastructure*, not per se media technology, that is the extension, but no doubt the media technologies built upon core infrastructure are consequential for how we relate to one another and, thus, the degree of organismality of societies and intersocietal systems. The Austro–Prussian War, for example, was influenced significantly (both for better and for worse) by telegraphic communication. Abraham Lincoln, apparently, slept on a cot in his telegraph office during Civil War battles, and was apparently always keeping abreast of what he called his "lightning messages" (Wheeler, 2009).

The proximate core infrastructures undergirding telegraphs, telephones, and the internet are undersea and underground electrical cables (along with the fuel networks that powered the machines that manufactured them). These cables were both time-consuming and expensive to lay (especially the undersea cables), but they provided unprecedented opportunities for open-system fission–fusion oscillation.

Consider the colossal undertaking of laying undersea cables. The first successful laying of 2,000 miles of massive undersea cables across the Atlantic Ocean happened in 1866. Several failed attempts preceded it; the first cable laid from Eastern Canada to Ireland in 1859 had failed in less than a month, at a loss of about 1.2 million dollars at the time (Nonnenmacher, 2001). The second, ultimately successful, undertaking involved weeks of loading cable onto huge steamships on either side of the Atlantic Ocean, along with the inventions of new cable-laying equipment and signal enhancers/detectors (such as galvanometers). While 1866 is the typical milestone for gauging the beginning of the telegraph era, many prior milestones are worth noting: Morse's telegraph machine patent was granted in 1838, the first telegraph message was sent between Washington, DC, and Baltimore in 1843, the Associated Press formed in order to aggregate and report on telegraph traffic in 1848, and train schedules were being coordinated via telegraph by 1851 (Nonnenmacher, 2001).

The telephone was patented in 1876 by Alexander Graham Bell, who referred to the device quite accurately as a "talking telegraph" (Nonnenmacher, 2001). Western Union, the predominant company transmitting telegraphs, had the opportunity to buy Bell's patent but decided against expanding their technological portfolio in favor of pursuing existing revenue from telegraphs. This was a mistake, but the consequences were delayed. Telegraphs were still the preferred form of distance communication into the 1920s, but by the end of World War II, AT&T, with their proto-telephone lines, had surpassed Western Union in revenue (Nonnenmacher, 2001).

Innovations in electrical communication only picked up pace from there.

Consider this: it took 38 years for telephones to be used by at least 30% of the US population, 17 years for televisions to be used by 30% of the public, 13 years for personal computers (PCs), and only 7 years for the internet (Phillips, 2000). The diffusion of technology throughout a population tends to happen from the top down, that is, political, media, and scientific elites begin using these technologies first, followed by high-income and more educated members of the general populace. This has nothing to do with some sort of innate technological literacy, and everything to do with the initially high cost of this technology, in addition to the initial educational barriers for using it (Rogers, 1962). Nevertheless, we can quantitatively assess the rapidity of diffusion of electronic communication technology. For example, among Americans with an income of $75,000 or more, about 10% had access to electronic mail (e-mail) in 1994, compared to almost 45% just four years later in 1998 (Phillips, 2000). Even among lower-income groups, the increased access to e-mail over a short period is astonishing: only about 2.5% of Americans with an income between $25,000 and $34,900 per year had access to e-mail in 1994, but this would already climb to about 15% just four years later in 1998.

This growth in electronic communication access was (and is) uneven, but it is worldwide. There were already 61 million internet users worldwide by 1996, and this number grew more than fivefold to 320 million by the year 2000 (Phillips, 2000). Today, the internet is accessible to over 3 billion people around the globe (Tranos and Stich, 2020). The present scale of fission-fusion oscillation is unmatched in human history; ideas are shared and jettisoned, groups are formed and dissolved, and goods are produced and purchased online at a rate so fast as to be unimaginable by any prior generation.

6.4 Significant Closing Points

Because of the relative material complexity and coordinated engineering necessary for making modern tools (e.g., a personal computer, cell phone, or personal power generator), many tools in contemporary societies would appear more *infrastructural* by the standard of a traditional farming society. In other words, the common tools and machines of modern society become relatively more collectively/internationally designed and assembled and are, thus, relatively more infrastructural than the tools of agrarian societies (and especially of foraging societies), which tended to be built locally by fewer people with more regionally sourced materials.

Yet, if we stopped here, we'd miss a crucial theoretical point. Notice, with regard to Figure 5.1, that one dimension remains diagnostic: collective accessibility/utilizability. No matter how collectively designed a cell phone, computer or electric car is, and no matter how many laborers in however many countries are involved with assembling it, cell phones and computers and electric cars are still only utilizable by one (or a few) people at a time. What the evolution of infrastructure does for us is clarify which characteristic of infrastructure is most central to organismality: *collective utilizability.* This hardly means the other elements are unimportant. Designing, constructing, and maintaining undersea cables or refinery piping networks or electrical grids still takes a substantial number of skilled experts.

I must make three more broad points. First, the larger societies grow, the more niche economic opportunities open up, and thus the more specialized people's educational/apprenticeship experiences become and, consequently, their skillsets and interests (Durkheim [1893] 2014). This means that the growth of societies will tend to make infrastructure relatively less collectively produced in two important senses: (1) absolute population growth reduces the total *proportion* of the public needed to serve as laborers in order to build or maintain infrastructural systems; and (2) occupational specialization obscures the constructional engineering and technological nuance of infrastructural systems from the average non-specialist (i.e., nonengineer, nonchemist, nonphysicist, non–plant worker). Put succinctly, there is an emerging asymmetry between the proportion of people necessary for construction, along with their specialized knowledge, and the number of people who can utilize the resource. How many civil or constructional engineers do you know personally? And yet, your life, minute to minute, second to second, depends on their work.

Second, though utterly dependent on core infrastructural systems such as electricity or drinking/sanitation systems for the housing, heating, lighting, and internet they enjoy, the typical pizzeria employee, journalist, celebrity, or sociology graduate student has no idea whatsoever how these systems were constructed. My claim, then, is that occupational specialization will enhance the tendency for nonengineers/nonspecialists to (1) take infrastructural systems for granted (people tend to presume that what exists today has long existed; see Eidelman et al., 2009); (2) falsely presume the engineering simplicity of infrastructure (people think they understand far more than they actually do; see Rozenblit and Keil, 2002); and (3) fail to connect present well-being or opportunities to the core infrastructural systems that, in fact, sustain both. Each of (1)–(3) is a palpable risk to social cohesion in its own right.

Third, the more complex infrastructure becomes, the more component tool-like parts will comprise it. Along a tool-infrastructure continuum, a steam engine is much more a tool (for generating power), and an industrial spot-welding gun is much more a tool (for connecting metals), than each is an infrastructural system. However, both steam engines and industrial spot welders are *also* important components of larger infrastructural systems, and both are certainly more complex and expensive tools than digging sticks or garden hoes or wrenches.

We can, then, distinguish (1) tools that are used to manufacture components of infrastructure (i.e., components like electromagnetic coils, semiconductor rectifiers, electrical transformers) from (2) tools used to extract the energy (i.e., solar panels, oil rigs) that fuels infrastructure. *Crucially*, however, the production of these tools is predicated on core infrastructure; a company that manufactures semiconductor chips powers its machine tools, warehouses, and offices with electricity, flushes its toilets and removes its industrial waste on account of existing processing systems, and accepts deliveries of materials from trucks driving on roads. This is the sense, again, in which infrastructural systems become layered or embedded.

Note

1 "Revenue passenger miles" are calculated by multiplying the number of paying passengers by the total distance traveled.

Chapter 7

Cities Drive the Metabolism of Societies

> Many find it alarming that ... cities ... are now enormously larger and more numerous. Yet ... cities use radically less carbon fuel per person than suburban or rural housing, and the alarmed [critics] are often themselves perched in high-rise buildings downtown ... We can look with nostalgia back on the rose-covered cottages and Maypole dancing of the countryside, but people vote with their feet worldwide in favor of cities. Villages sound swell until you live in one and find that everyone knows your business and often enough wants to interfere with it. At $3 a day or less the villages are intolerable. The left's old claim that people are pushed from the countryside into the cities has been shown repeatedly by economic historians to be a myth. The people are not pushed but pulled.
>
> (McCloskey, 2016, pg. 619)

It is hard to date the rise of cities. Part of this difficulty is due to how hard it can be to define a city. Ancient cities, by our modern standards, would have been very small. Even a small-to medium-sized modern city of 200,000 people would have been unheard of 5,000 years ago. In fact, 5,000 years ago, the city of Uruk, the largest city in the world at that point, might only have contained 50,000 people.

It is also difficult to pin down the rise of cities because cities are as much a behavioral and ideological phenomenon—composed of labor markets, commodities markets, diverse circulating populations, cosmopolitan philosophies, and so on—as they are a physical, archeologically discernable phenomenon. It is easier to unearth the rubble of ancient buildings than it is to discern the degree of population diversity or market goods that circulated throughout that particular territory.

Nevertheless, we can try to date the origin of the first city. One candidate is Tell Maghzaliyah, a walled-off settlement of seminomadic agricultural hobbyists in northeastern Mesopotamia dating to about 8,500 years ago. Another candidate would be Tell es-Sawwan, dating to about 7,300 years ago and located just north of modern-day Baghdad. This protocity contained irrigated fields organized behind walls that were defended by guards armed with slings and stones. Tell Brak in northern

DOI: 10.4324/9781003266020-7

Mesopotamia around 4,300 BCE is another possibility—here, archeologists have unearthed houses, temples, specialized crafting/building areas, and roadways presumably used by farmers and herders who had migrated from surrounding villages (Ur, 2010; Smith, 2019).

One clue to the rise in prevalence of urban centers comes from between 3,500 BCE and 2,500 BCE, when the sea level and water volume of the Tigris and Euphrates Rivers dropped dramatically (Scott, 2017). As the extended veins of these rivers dried up, the main channels became centralized zones (we might call them "fusion hotspots") where people could still irrigate crops. Thus, the threat posed by increasing aridity could have motivated populations to fuse to a greater extent so as to successfully coordinate water-pumping and irrigation. The accomplishment of such tasks—not only in Mesopotamia, of course, but along the Yellow River in China, the Ganges River in India, and elsewhere—appears to have given rise to the very earliest large cities of people.

We can say for certain that by at least 5,000 years ago, in ancient Mesopotamia during the Uruk period, the formation of cities appears to be commonplace. And, not only commonplace, but also quite recognizable to our modern sensibilities: distinct areas of commerce, central planning, specialized forms of employment, and neighborhoods (Flannery and Marcus, 2012).

The formation of cities seems to be driven by a set of intersecting interests. The origin of cities lies (1) in the desire of elites to amass labor for infrastructural, religious, and military projects; (2) in landowning individuals seeking to coordinate their crop planting and harvesting; (3) in people from surrounding urban and rural areas seeking vibrant markets within which to trade their wares; and (4) in refugees from nearby societies and/or migrants from the surrounding countryside seeking greater political stability or protection from local warlords (Flannery and Marcus, 2012; Scott, 2018). Each is a motive to congregate in a central area, and each is a motive to insist that this central area be defended from outside, conquest-seeking warlords.

Most all cities, whether ancient Mesopotamian cities or industrial cities, start off as slums, and develop unevenly from there (Smith, 2019). Part of this is because cities did not exist before there were people there; thus, aggregated little communities of people preceded the urban infrastructure necessary to sustain them and grow their numbers. Cities then develop unevenly, because residents with more money or political influence will generally advocate more successfully for infrastructure and accommodations to be built into the part of the city where they reside.

Cities were not, then, initially very well planned, but rather emerged from the (at times competing) interests of different parties to occupy a single, defensible space for market activity, coordinated planning, and laborious pursuits. Yes, leaders set tax policies and bureaucrats apportioned taxes for labor, land, and goods in pursuit of various state projects. But, cities are in the end emergent products of the actions and reactions of the buzzing masses, all drawn to various degrees by the attractants of bustling markets, relative protection from raids, the energy of crowds, social fads, and the neurological stimulation wrought by different people and ideas.

As such, cities and their concentrated fission–fusion oscillations have effects beyond city limits. Extensive road networks connected cities to surrounding territories and markets, which helped render cities resilient to perturbations associated with intermittent famines, disease, or poor city management. Monica Smith aptly describes how roads into and out of ancient city centers fanned out

> like the spokes of a wheel, with each spoke connecting outlying communities. As a result, a city could also get food from elsewhere. If any particular link was broken because of a supply disruption brought about by localized crop failure or warfare or stubborn noncompliance, there were plenty of other links that could still supply the city from some other direction. Urban expansion thus not only changed ... [the economic circumstances of] specific local ecologies but leveraged changes in entire regions.
>
> (Smith, 2019, pg. 86)

The more people traveled to cities to specialize occupationally or to sell specialized wares, the less time there was to spend growing food to feed themselves or their families, and for this reason agricultural surplus was a precondition for the economic growth of cities. To wit, archeologists have found evidence of sidewalk vendors likely hawking "take-out" food for urban dwellers (Smith, 2019). And if this description of peoples' motivations to move to cities feels overly instrumental/economic, let's not forget the "permanent festival atmosphere" of cities both ancient and modern (Smith, 2019, pg. 77). The concentration of busy markets, creative expression, and diverse people and cultures were no doubt exhilarating and motivating to ancient city dwellers, just as they are to us today.

For their part, rulers appear to have been happy to allow people into their cities; early city boundaries were maintained, but they were porous (Scott, 2018). In fact, this porousness of city boundaries was an important reason why early cities were apparently quite vulnerable to raids and attacks from smaller surrounding societies, especially from bandit groups that lived in mountainous areas and could therefore easily retreat while being hard to follow.

The porousness of city boundaries also constituted an open fission–fusion system, with markets and job opportunities drawing people together in conversation and exchange, but binding no one. After a job was complete, people could leave, so long as they weren't indentured workers or captured slaves. Merchants traveled into and out of city bazaars as they pleased. The more a society's infrastructure could support a large, circulating city population, the more rulers benefited from a large pool of laborers, architects, and designers who might be employed (in the case of laborers, fed or perhaps given alcohol) to build temples and palaces, or as warriors in growing militaries (Flannery and Marcus, 2012).

Ancient societies grew relatively large in terms of geographic area and population size, but they also hit significant limits to growth. First, wars of conquest became more expensive the more successful they were (each new stretch of conquered land had to be defended from nearby aspiring warlords and encroaching foreign empires) and came with increasing risks to rulers' legitimacy (more wars on more fronts meant a greater possibility of losing any one war, or having to retreat, both of which made kings look potentially incompetent or vulnerable). Second, resources were finite: lumber wasn't a rapidly renewable resource, and yet it was often a central building material as well as a central source of energy alongside human and animal labor. Wood was used constantly for everything from heating, to gardening tools, to scaffolding for landmarks, to carts used at the market to hold goods; ancient cities were in many ways wood-fueled cities.

The total caloric consumption of preindustrial cities—including not only food calories, but the overall averaged amount of energy used from burning wood for cooking, heating, and manufacturing—ranged from between 5 and 30 watts per square meter of land. However, wood from surrounding forests reliably yielded only 0.1–1 watts per square meter, meaning that the typical ancient city depended on forests 50 to 150 times larger than the size of the city itself (Smil, 2015; 2017). Wood can always be imported, but this importation is predicated on the health of existing trade relations, road quality, and mechanisms of transport (i.e., large wooden carts). And, the harder lumber was to come by, the fewer buildings could be erected and the less food could be harvested and imported.

7.1 Rise of the Urban Middle Class

Cities, with their dense populations and concentrated market activities, gave rise to a bureaucratic "middle class" (Smith, 2018). I put "middle class" in quotes because this is not the sort of middle class we would recognize today. No, this was a middle class in only the most nascent form, less a full class of people than flashes of opportunities for those without royal blood.

Temples in the ancient Mesopotamian city of Nippur housed an estimated 350,000 sheep and goats, for example, and someone other than farmers, rulers, and the military needed to keep records regarding this collective resource (Smith, 2019). Bureaucrats were needed to issue and monitor the contracts given to the herders that managed these animals, and other bureaucrats were needed to make sure the animals were adequately being taken care of and not being illegally sold or embezzled. Additional bureaucrats were needed to plan, clear, and maintain grazing land for these animals. Still more bureaucrats were needed to record and monitor the relationship between the supply of animals (or their products, such as milk, cheese, wool, or leather) brought to market relative to the day-to-day consumer demand. A managerial class was not *only* needed to monitor the production, consumption, and storage of domesticated animals, but also, and equally, of flour ground from barley, sesame seed oil, beer, dried herbs, cosmetics, musical instruments, jewelry, baskets, bronze tools or weapons, and any other commodity necessary for, or desired by, an increasingly large, concentrated, populace (Sterba, 1976).

So, who were these bureaucrats? Many were probably the children or associates of elites, but others were likely appointed commoners who'd developed a name for themselves as smart, reliable, or particularly skilled in accounting or writing (Flannery and Marcus, 2012).That both elites and (less so) commoners were now pursuing careers which required specialized knowledge and skills is a sign of the ancient emergence of "knowledge workers" who enjoyed relatively high salaries working with their minds instead of with their hands (Smith, 2019). These people were scribes, controllers, accountants, and managers working in hierarchical organizations and paid standardized wages decreed by rulers. Their tasks were to create plans for resource extraction and allocation, budgets for resource extraction and maintenance, and labor assignments for accomplishing these needs (Sterba, 1976). Rigid production schedules, product categories, and prices were recorded to ensure enough "data" were available for the coercive central planning of ruling elites.

In the cities of ancient Mesopotamia, bureaucracies were assumed to be guided by local temple gods (Sterba, 1976). Of course, since gods weren't actually involved, ultimate bureaucratic authority for any local temple was typically given to a "high priest" who managed two lower-ranked priests: "ceremonial priests" and "administrative priests." Local monks, diviners/seers, and prostitutes, who were employed to work at the temple, were regulated and managed by the ceremonial priest. Local scribes, accountants, and architects, on the other hand, were managed by the administrative priest. Project foremen and superintendents worked underneath these scribes, accountants, and architects while permanent paid laborers (often landless peasants) and slaves worked underneath the foremen and superintendents (Sterba, 1976). It is less clear how many support staff/assistants each priest, scribe, accountant, architect, foreman, or superintendent had, but they probably had as many as the city-state could support. Modern bureaucratic bloat isn't likely to be a new phenomenon in *kind*, only in *extent* (contrary to Weber's insistence).

While it is easy to roll one's eyes at the rigidity and incompetence of bureaucrats and their hierarchies (to say nothing of the often absurd levels of incompetence of ruling religious and political elite hierarchies), we cannot forget that this nascent middle class provided the administrative scaffolding for infrastructural construction/maintenance which, collectively, raised the standard of living for increasing numbers of people. Large agrarian city-states—from Babylon and Sumer in Mesopotamia to Athens and Alexandria in Ancient Greece and Rome—were places where forms of status and occupational prestige began to really proliferate for the first time in human history. Smith (2019) describes that

> [there were] many ways that people exhibited their middle-class status to others. There was a range of housing styles and sizes and a tremendous variety of consumer goods that people bought, used, and discarded to show their sense of style and urban savvy. There were fancy pottery drinking cups and vases decorated with popular scenes of mythology, sporting events, and sex. There were personal-care goods and furniture that made for a cozy home life, as well as ornaments and clothing for going out that sparkled in the bright [sunlight].
>
> (Smith, 2019, pgs. 195–196)

I definitely do *not* want to overstate the size of this emerging middle class in ancient agrarian societies. The proportion of literate full-time bureaucrats living and working in these cities was probably only around 5% (or less) of the population (Lenski, 2005). However, the bustling, open-air markets (i.e., "bazaars") for tools, materials, food, jewelry, and so on, which relied in some cases distally (as when migrants moved into the city and set up shop) and in some cases quite proximately (as when city-commissioned goods were brought to market) on local temple bureaucracies, were nevertheless available to anyone who might wander inside the city walls (Scott, 2018).

Urbanization is thousands of years old, yet, the size and political influence of the urban middle class appears to have reached an inflection point by the late 1700s CE.[1] Geoffrey West (2017) considers Manchester, England, to be the first "industrial city" because it was both the hub of a lucrative and fast-growing textile industry and, consequently, a substantial contributor to British culture and politics. Manchester's population grew from 20,000 people in 1771, to 120,000 in 1831, to 2 million by the early twentieth century. The composition of the middle class during this period shifted from mostly nepotistic bureaucratic appointments to an entire class of people capable of leveraging various skillsets and credentials in order to live outside the confines of subsistence farming. By this period, semiautomated machines in factories were also mass producing goods that, due to the scale of production, were increasingly affordable to this middle class of merchants, bureaucrats, lawyers, doctors, writers, and scientists. Innovations in chemical manufacturing, iron production, waterpower, sanitation, electricity, transportation, the use of coal fossil fuel, and so on opened up new industries and new jobs, and people flocked to, and prospered from, the cities like never before in history.

The term "middle class" was first used in the *Oxford English Dictionary* in 1745. Strictly speaking, the middle class did not emerge in the 1700s, as I described above, but this dictionary entry was a sign that the term was becoming mainstream, a useful descriptor for an unprecedentedly large (and growing) segment of the population. The concept of a large-scale middle class, distinct in taste and political influence from lower-class peasants and commoners becomes clearly distinguished around the period of the Napoleonic Wars (~1803–1815) (McCloskey, 2016). Even leaders of the Third Estate, so pivotal in the French Revolution preceding the Wars, had not *overtly* distinguished the middle class from upper-middle-class capitalists or from peasants the way we might today. Nevertheless, in the late eighteenth and nineteenth centuries, rulers increasingly spoke well of this burgeoning group. In the early nineteenth century, for example, King George III publicly regarded the "middling sort" as pious, dignified, honest, and proper (McCloskey, 2016).

To ever greater degrees, ruling elites pursued economic collaborations with middle-class professionals and business owners in pursuit of national profits while concerning themselves less and less with economically wasteful and distracting aristocratic rivalries (McCloskey, 2016). Elites were coming to understand that economic prosperity produced, and required, a robust middle class. Today, an economic and cultural middle class exist in just about every society on Earth, and cities as engines of economic growth and innovation were the backbone of this growth.

7.2 Modern Industrial Cities

Cities today are in many ways much as they always were—geographically concentrated markets growing amid dense populations. What *is* new is the rate and scope of circulation of people in space. Subways, cars, busses, trolleys, trucks, electric scooters, bicycles (a surprisingly recent invention dating only to the 1800s), and internet messaging move people and ideas rapidly around urban ecologies to an unprecedented degree. Cities today are also quite a bit larger and quite a bit more population-dense, owing to innovations in technology. For example, the energy capacity of electrical motors (which revolutionized transportation by replacing steam engines) grew 60-fold from 1899 to 1929 and constituted 82% of all generated power by 1929 (Smil, 2017).

And, cities have changed over time regarding their predominant occupations—from artisanal and agricultural produce markets in ancient societies, to factory work, to service work and technological design work more recently in so-called "postindustrial" societies. In 1871, about a quarter of all workers (24%) in the West worked with their hands to make a living in jobs in agriculture and construction and factories; only 1% of workers worked in care/service professions such as healthcare, teaching, or childcare (Smil, 2017). By comparison, in the United States today over 80% of employed people work in the service sector in jobs like retail, education, healthcare, social work, leisure/hospitality, state and local government, and various nonretail consumer-oriented businesses (Bureau of Labor Statistics, 2020). It is worth noting that just under 12% of employed people in the United States work in construction and manufacturing, and only about 1% work in agriculture!

This (broad, nonlinear) shift from agricultural production, to manufacturing, to service has occurred to some degree in all societies. After all, the more peoples' incomes rise with economic growth, the more services they demand and can afford. Deprivation, if any, becomes relative to the prosperity of others.

Globalized cities are also rapidly becoming the norm, crowding out the relevance of nation-states as political entities. As recently as the year 1800, only two cities had populations greater than 1 million people: Beijing and London. By 1900, 13 cities had populations greater than 1 million people, but today over 550 cities have a population this size (Smil, 2017). Urban populations make up almost two-thirds of many Western nations, and about 90% of Brazil and 80% of Mexico (Smil, 2017). China is rapidly urbanizing, with just over half (~55%) of its massive population living in cities; about 47% of the people in Nigeria live in cities, and 35% of people living in India live in cities. Almost everywhere, though, these numbers are growing at a pace almost too rapid to track.

The year 2008 marked the first time in history that over half of humanity lived in urban areas (McCloskey, 2016). The United Nations projects that, by 2050, nearly the entire world will live in urban areas, and most of these gains will be in countries like China, India, and Africa (Bettencourt and West, 2010). All of the brilliant individuals in these countries will soon join the rhythmic open system of fission–fusion characteristic of cities. As Deirdre McCloskey (2016) points out, the next Jane Austen or Albert Einstein may be living on two dollars a day in an agricultural village in China or India right now, with no access to core infrastructure or its secondary manifestations (i.e., hospitals, schools, museums). This is a loss for the world. But it won't be a loss for much longer.

Infrastructural innovations made cities of large scale possible, and as I will describe further below, population density increases the efficiency of electricity and fossil fuels because each unit of energy can serve more people at once. A bus in a rural area wastes gas because fewer people use it than in an urban area, and the same is true of a rural gas station, school, or hospital. Economic productivity increases as well because open-system fission–fusion generates rapid innovations and rapid diffusion of innovations, and provides equally rapid feedback about the marketability of such innovations. Each time a city doubles in size, economic productivity grows on average 115%–130%; bigger cities require more energy and resources, yes, but each unit of expended energy tends to benefit larger numbers of people and, thus, institutional and cultural complexity can increase (Bettencourt and West, 2010).

Infrastructure, as I've described it, is obviously different in modern cities than it was in ancient cities. More and more people today can live in urban areas because buildings can be built higher and higher on account of being reinforced with steel "skeleton" frames (i.e., criss-crossed I-beams and columns) instead of being reinforced only with stone (Webber, 2019). Once a high-rise or skyscraper is built, and people move into them as residences or as business offices, water, people, and materials must be lifted vertically into the air to sustain them. We take for granted that this problem has been solved, but the regular processing of waste, the availability of water, and the movement of people vertically into the air is no small feat. Electricity is today used to accomplish these tasks: water is pumped up to tanks on rooftops, where it can flow by gravity into sinks and toilets (Webber, 2019). Electricity also made indoor climate control (air conditioning and heating) possible, meaning that cities could grow to unprecedented sizes in areas that would otherwise have been too hot or too cold to occupy for extended periods.

Indoor lighting, plumbing, and climate control undergirded the proliferation of homes and businesses, as well as schools, police departments, fire departments, hospitals, grocery stores, social services offices, and other essential secondary infrastructure. Street lighting allowed people to exit their residences and roam about without having to bring their own personal torch or lamp. Traffic lights helped regulate the movement of heavy, potentially dangerous vehicles throughout cities at all hours of the night. With streetlamps and safe indoor lighting, businesses like bars and restaurants and offices can now continue making money and providing services during all hours of the night (in the case of product businesses, literally 24 hours a day because of the internet) and people can be located and aided in emergencies at any time (especially now with GPS location technology). Michael Webber describes the cutting edge of integrated urban electrical lighting and sensing systems when he writes,

> Smart lighting—that is, equipping [street] lights with data collection capabilities—presents an opportunity to get a lot more information about a city, improving public health and safety. Placing air quality sensors on streetlights helps give real-time and finely resolved information about air pollution that can be used for mitigation programs like ozone-action days and incentives for people to use mass transit or carpool. Acoustic sensors are [another new possibility that] can pick up sudden noises such as gunshots to help first responders dispatch more quickly while identifying the right place to go.
>
> (Webber, 2019, pgs. 176–177)

Cities the world over consistently reveal three broad characteristics: (1) decreasing space per capita due to high-rise living and increased infrastructural energy efficiency; (2) increasing pace of innovation and economic productivity; and (3) proliferation of crime, pollution, and disease (Bettencourt and West, 2010). West (2017) summarizes these characteristics of cities in a small set of mathematical laws (verified against real-world data on cities around the world) that reveal *sublinear* scaling of infrastructure and *superlinear* scaling of creative ideas, economic products, and social disorder.

Infrastructure scales *sublinearly* in that, for example, fewer electrical lines, roads, water pipes, or gas stations tend to be present than one would expect if these tracked population growth linearly. Specifically, on average worldwide, the prevalence of such infrastructure increases only about 85% for every 100% increase in a city's population (Bettencourt et al., 2007). So, as West (2017) notes, a city of 20 million people will generally require about 15% fewer infrastructural units as compared to two cities containing 10 million people each. Analyses of the prevalence of things like gasoline stations or post offices in cities in France, Columbia, Germany, Brazil, the Netherlands, Japan, Spain, China, and elsewhere clearly show a general sublinear scaling with increasing population size (Kühnert et al., 2006; West, 2017). Or, consider that the length of electrical voltage cables increased only about 8%–92% for every 100% increase in population (Kühnert et al., 2006).

As cities grow, primary infrastructure like electrical lines, gas lines, water pipelines, and roads serve more people more cheaply, as does secondary infrastructure. Infrastructure, then, reveals an economy of scale each time population growth doubles; the larger and denser the city, the less infrastructure is needed. This increase in efficiency can directly be measured in terms of a reduced per capita carbon footprint in cities: relative to suburban or rural living, modern cities tend to have lower per capita carbon emissions relative to their nation's average (though this may be less true in the very early stages of modern urbanization due to factory pollution) (Bettencourt and West, 2010; Pumain, 2012).

We can go a step further and postulate that a *necessary*, but not sufficient, condition for urban population growth is the sublinear scaling of infrastructure. If core infrastructure does not become more efficient and thus less resource-intensive, the city will not be able to serve and provide opportunity to increasingly large numbers of people. In turn, the more people can rely on heating, water, food, and transportation, the more they can focus their energies on creative collaborations and entrepreneurial projects. Paradoxically, the result is that you can expect to find shorter underground electrical cables, fewer energy stations, fewer gas stations, and so on, per capita, in growing urban areas compared to suburban areas or rural areas (West, 2017).

This sublinear scaling of infrastructure does *not mean* that infrastructure is becoming less important as societies grow in population—quite the opposite, infrastructure is becoming *more* essential and thus selection pressures for innovation and efficiency grow more intensive over time. The sublinear scaling of infrastructure also does not mean innovations, renovations, or maintenance of infrastructure *always* constitute improvements in efficiency or productivity, or that infrastructure *necessarily* exists for the "function" of continuously improving energy efficiency or productivity.

Clearly, this is not the case—roads in modern cities crater and crack, water and gas lines break, and electrical substations can be poorly built or maintained. The argument I am making is not for *inevitable, linear* improvements in infrastructural efficiency or productivity. Rather, the argument is that over time, if a city is to grow in size (and thus innovation, creativity, and per capita income are to increase), there will need to be net gains in infrastructural efficiency and productivity. If these gains do not occur (and they may not), the city's size and productivity will stagnate or, potentially, decline. The thriving cities we see today are feats of evolved efficiency.

The infrastructural components of both plant and animal vascular and respiratory systems also scale sublinearly as a function of the size of the plant or the body of the animal (West et al., 1997). These "scaling laws," in other words, are natural phenomena, not only social constructs. The tunnels, trash/waste rooms, and nursery rooms of anthills (i.e., ant cities) and tunnels, storage cells, and brood cells of beehives (i.e., bee cities) also appear to scale sublinearly with population increases (Bettencourt and West, 2010). If the primary infrastructure of cities, beehives, or anthills was not built (consciously or otherwise) so as to be better utilized by larger numbers of creatures, it would be impossible for the overall population to grow in complexity.

On the other hand, in human societies, rates of innovation, productivity, and social disorganization/disorder (pollution, crime) scale *superlinearly* with population. This means that with each doubling of a city's population (i.e., with each 100% increase), the number of patents issued per year,

GDP, wages per capita, business assets, and a variety of other economic indicators grow about 115%; just the same, violent crime, pollution, and the incidence of socially transmitted diseases (e.g., flu, HIV) increase about 115% (West, 2017). Businesses where experimental innovation poses few risks to infrastructural functioning—like chef's schools, art schools, law schools, or museums—also scale superlinearly approximately to a similar degree. These findings hold across cities in different countries around the world (see West, 2017). It seems that modern cities everywhere are culturally distinct but are also roughly equally scaled versions of one another. Once new innovations are rendered mundane in the city center (roughly about the time these innovations become diffused to outlying suburbs and rural areas), economic and social incentives arise for yet another wave of innovation, along with all of the pollution and social disorder wrought by rapid oscillations of people in space. (Pumain, 2012).

Geoffrey West explains his findings and those of his colleagues thusly:

> If you are given the size of a city … you can predict with 80 to 90 percent accuracy what the average wage is, how many patents it's produced, how long all of its roads are, how many AIDS cases it's had, how much violent crime was committed, how many restaurants there are, how many lawyers and doctors it has, et cetera … There are, of course, outliers and variations around such estimates … [but] … The good, the bad and the ugly come as an integrated, predictable, package.
>
> (West, 2017, pg. 278; Bettencourt and West, 2010, pg. 913)

But why should this be so? Why should rates of creativity, economic productivity, and social disorganization all outpace the rate of population growth? The short answer is that innovations in infrastructural efficiency produce a context where people can spend more time interacting and collaborating with others. When each of us has to grow our own food (as opposed to shopping at a grocery store), find our own water (as opposed to turning on a faucet), wash our own clothes (by hand!), take care of our own illnesses (as opposed to doctors doing so), defend our own property (as opposed to police/firefighters doing so), take care of our own children (as opposed to childcare workers doing so), and so on, there is less time for casual interaction and non-survival related goal pursuits with those we might not know well. Simply put, the less we interact with one another, especially with dissimilar or unfamiliar others, the less creative we are and the less productive we become. At the same time, on the downside, the more we interact with those defined as dissimilar or unfamiliar, the greater the potential for conflict or transmission of disease.

Interestingly, the number of interactions with others in a city scales in opposition to increases in infrastructural efficiency. In other words, infrastructural units tend on average to become about 15% smaller or less prevalent for every doubling of the population, while at the same time the volume of social interactions increases about 15% (West, 2017). I don't mean in-depth, emotional social interactions necessarily. Rather, I mean the total number of social interactions with different people, even if these interactions are often fleeting and short-term (e.g., chatting with someone in line at a coffee shop, on the bus, or in the office).

In the existing research, contacts between people are often measured as the number of reciprocated mobile phone or landline calls. For example, across 15 months the typical resident of Lisbon (the capital city of Portugal, with a population around 560,000) made twice as many reciprocated phone calls as did the typical resident of the small rural town of Lixa (with a population OF around 4,200) (West, 2017). Non-reciprocated calls were especially prevalent in the city relative to the countryside. Also, the diversity of people called was higher in the urban center, spanning calls to friends or family, colleagues, and various local businesses.

However, the raw number of people who appeared to know one another *didn't* differ between rural Lixa and urban Lisbon, and in fact tends not to differ across various cities. Why might this be? Perhaps it is because peoples' social networks have limitations to how diffuse they can become; if so, this may be attributable to some stable physiological limitation in how many different social relationships people can keep track of. Hiroko Kudo and Robin Dunbar (2001), for example, find that social network size is strongly constrained by the volume of neocortical tissue within species. Thus, it is not that urbanites have some greater neurological capacity for friendship or network formation, but rather that urbanites interact with a more diverse range of people more frequently and more fleetingly.

On the increasing volume of social interactions in cities, West writes:

> The approximate 15% increase in social interactions and therefore in socioeconomic metrics such as income, patents and crime generated with every doubling of city size can be interpreted as a bonus, or payoff, arising from the 15% savings in physical infrastructure and energy use. The systematic increase in social interaction is the essential driver of socioeconomic activity in cities: wealth creation, innovation, violent crime, and a greater sense of buzz and opportunity are all propagated and enhanced through social networks and greater interpersonal interaction.
>
> (West, 2017, pg. 322)

In my terms: the very increase in survival, sustenance, and self-actualization offered by electrical grids, water lines, sewage systems, and underground cables, along with the social services offices, schools, county hospitals, and businesses that they scaffold, produces an emergent, often quite disordered, dynamic: increasingly open-system fission–fusion oscillation. Aggregations are sometimes ephemeral (as when people aggregate on a subway train to get to work and then disperse, with the occasional conversation here and there) and sometimes more stable (as when people aggregate to pursue a shared occupational or recreational goal), but these oscillations, occurring across contexts, generate continual recombinations of language and of ideas, of opinions and assertions, of cultural or economic products and buyers.

There is, of course, much disorder that comes as a consequence and not *just* pollution, crime, or disease (which are troubling enough). Many products that are wanted are not made, many that are made are not bought, many new ideas are not shared, many (good) shared ideas are not remembered, many groups do not persist, many persistent groups interact only rarely, and so on. Most tragic of all, those in need of strong, stable, social (or financial) support may not find it, and those who have it might find it suffocating. The relative increase in the rate of circulating emotions, ideas, and goods across contexts in cities produces an emergent property—a form of group information-processing that is innovative, energizing, and productive as well fleeting and chaotic.

I must underscore another important point about the superlinear scaling of rates of innovation in particular. If infrastructural efficiency doesn't increase at an accelerating pace, fewer people will be able to draw benefits from infrastructure; at the same time, if pollution or toxicity or crime becomes too extreme, people will choose not to live in the city, or to not spend much time there (e.g., as tourists). The bigger cities get, the more capable of innovation people in those cities become, and this is quite convenient because the bigger a city gets, the more rapid rates of innovation *must* become to sustain the population (West, 2017). Ever-accelerating rates of innovation in infrastructural efficiency are therefore essential to the growth of cities, so it should not surprise us that rates of innovation (for example, the number of utility patents issued) scale superlinearly with population. Innovativeness must outpace population growth *even as* the actual infrastructural units become smaller or less prevalent on account of their becoming more efficient.

The superlinear scaling of wealth, innovation, and disorder is embodied. That is, life in cities feels fast because it *is* fast. People living in cities walk faster, talk faster, and, probably, think faster compared to people living in rural areas (Simmel [1902] 1964; West, 2017). As much as 80% of the variation in walking speed, for example, can be explained by population density (Bettencourt et al., 2007). Obviously, people have limits to how fast they are willing to walk, but, still, walking speed increases about 200% when comparing people living in small towns with populations of a couple of thousand to people living in cities with populations in excess of 1 million (West, 2017). This pace of movement and thought is classically expressed in the city as art, theater, music, and other creative endeavors.

Even nonhuman urban dwellers like birds, racoons, or rodents are riskier, more curious, more behaviorally flexible, and better at solving novel problems compared to their rural counterparts (Ducatez et al., 2017; Daniels et al., 2019; Audet, 2020; Mazza et al., 2020). This is not to say that there aren't brilliant artists in the countryside; indeed, this isn't a commentary on individuals much at all, but rather an observation about how existing in an open-system fission–fusion ecology can produce emotional and physical energy that may, in some people some of the time, be expressed as innovative creativity. *It is the social structure of the city that produces creativity less than the particular individuals who end up expressing it.*

These findings on the role of urban environments in activity and creativity are consistent with research on "social facilitation" in psychology (Triplett, 1898; Zajonc, 1965) and on "collective effervescence" in sociology (Durkheim [1912] 2008; Collins, 2004). Animals from rats to humans are more active when in the presence of conspecifics relative to when they are alone, and this appears to be due to an increased level of physiological arousal, that is, of electrical-chemical energy in the body. Think of yourself resting, alone, at home as opposed to taking a break at work with co-workers. Even if there are no particular differences in stressors or pressures (suppose that your job is secure, all of these co-workers are familiar to you, and none have managerial authority over you), the degree of energy and low-level (i.e., nondysphoric) anxiety is typically going to be higher with your colleagues and lower when alone at home.

The mere fact of social co-presence increases the readiness of the body to respond to incoming stimuli. Put another way, the body must recruit metabolic energy to allocate attention to other people, and this is most simply captured in rising heart rate, a direct sign of increases in electrical activity in the body (Belletier et al., 2019). There may even be a functional difference in the neurons activated in the brain when thinking about tasks in social encounters compared to thinking in isolation. A study of Rhesus monkeys, for example, found that the monkeys performed better on a simple task when in the presence of another monkey, and that some neurons in the prefrontal cortex were consistently more active in the social context than in the isolation context (Demolliens et al., 2017).

This relative rise in internal electrical-chemical activity among people in social settings often aids performance on familiar or very easy tasks, especially when others in the encounter have a higher status (Zajonc, 1965). But improved performance only occurs for simple tasks, like identifying which light among 20 lights (arranged in a circle) has gone out. Another, more relevant, simple task is that of eating food, and people in groups eat more food than those eating alone (Herman, 2015). More complex tasks, however, require greater cortical control along with greater recruitment of semantic and, possibly, episodic memory (Belletier et al., 2019). Thus, for complex tasks like technological and infrastructural innovation, co-presence isn't going to be sufficient for innovation. Typically, neither will individual cognition in isolation. Complex innovations will tend, therefore, to result only from sustained periods of open-system fission–fusion. In such a system, ideas are (1) stimulated by co-presence during fusion periods, (2) critically reflected on in relative isolation or during periods of reduced group size during fission periods, and (3) combined or recombined during oscillations. This will guarantee not that *any one individual or small group* will innovate, but that *some individuals or groups* will increasingly innovate over others, with the outcome being potentially beneficial to system growth or change.

However, and this is important, the relatively higher degree of dissimilarity or unfamiliarity characteristic of (combinatory) exchanges in open-system fission–fusion oscillation may produce levels of anxiety and/or anticipatory failure that are so high that they reduce co-presence (Geen and Gange, 1977). The capacity for open-system fission–fusion oscillation at scale, then, rests on people being to some degree habituated to this fluid form of interaction and, also, sufficiently materially and mentally stable to cope with emotional problems during periods devoid of strong-tie support. If people enter into transient/instrumental or cooperative encounters with others fearing failure or filled with anxiety, this will not only limit the flow of ideas (i.e., information) between people, but it will also increase cognitive load, thus reducing peoples' capacity to reflect creatively on their experiences or ideas. This tells us that a precondition for optimal open system fission–fusion oscillation at the scale of a modern city is some form of urban socialization/acclimation, and sufficient monetary and mental stability to go potentially prolonged periods without the benefit of easily accessible in-person strong-tie support.

7.2.1 How Cities Differ from One Another

Obviously, not all cities are constructed in the same way using the same infrastructure or proximate (politically or geographically) to the same resources. Some parts of the world began urbanizing at different paces than others at different points in history: for example, 7,000 years ago, cities were nascent if they existed at all in Europe while they were growing and flourishing in the Middle East. Developing cities are also more variable in their scaling rate than are more established cities (Bettencourt and West, 2010). This is due to a path dependence that results from the narrowing of future construction and organization possibilities once prior problems of infrastructure or social organization have been addressed.

Even still, some established modern cities have more physicians (New York), while others have more computer programmers (San Jose) or chefs (Chicago) (West, 2017). So, while cities scale their creativity and production to approximately similar degrees, the nature of those products and that creativity vary considerably depending on the particular developmental history and demography of a given city. Specifically, West (2017) estimates that at least 10%–20% of the measurable characteristics of cities vary independently of population size; this means that at least 10%–20% of a city's characteristics are attributable to a unique "character," or path of historical/cultural development.

The data shows that within-city occupational scaling can vary widely even if between-city occupational scaling is fairly predictable and regular (Pumain, 2012). In other words, even if indicators of economic innovation tend to grow stably somewhere between 110% and 120% faster than population growth regardless of the city, just *which* particular industries or sectors are *most* innovative will vary depending on the idiosyncratic path dependencies associated with the unique development of given city (as well as the path dependencies associated with the larger national milieu within which the city exists).

Overall, it seems that the degree to which the growth trajectory of a city's industries or sectors is unique (i.e., unattributable to population size or scaling laws), this uniqueness may be due to "founders effects" (i.e., unique habits or attitudes among those who most influenced the early stages of city development), the particular geopolitical influence (or lack thereof) of the city, or it may be due to differences in historical threats experienced (i.e., pathogens, natural disasters, civil wars). So, while general superlinear/sublinear scaling laws are useful for discerning course-grained similarities in city growth regardless of the city in question, this does not mean that there isn't important variation among cities.

7.2.2 Cities and Social Isolation

Moving to, and living in, cities can also lead to significant changes to network composition and, potentially, network disruption. People may gain friends and lose friends in cities more often than they do elsewhere: social relations are more transient and more chronically in flux. That cities should be places of isolation and social mercuriality has been suggested by sociologists at least since George Simmel and Robert Park in the nineteenth and early twentieth centuries. Contemporary sociologists studying social networks find, indeed, that urbanites have fewer, weaker (i.e., lower interactional frequency with any one tie), local social ties than people living in rural areas (Wang et al., 2021). This is consistent with what I would call a "distributed effervescence" form of social interaction. Among urbanites, any one person is less likely to be interacted with, but the volume of total interactions with different people increases.

Independent of this relative increase in weak ties among urbanites, the migration process to cities is itself potentially disruptive. This disruptiveness is, theoretically, the disruption that occurs when people leave relatively more closed-system, fused, social ecologies (e.g., a lower-population-density rural town, where the average—often kin-based—tie is stronger) and migrate to relatively more open-system, fission–fusion social ecologies (e.g., a higher-population-density urban center, where ties—less often kin-based—are weaker). Though migrants to cities may integrate themselves into ethnic enclaves containing ethnically or religiously strong ties, another possibility is that migrants will become "triple withouts" (Cheng et al., 2017). This term emerged among Chinese analysts who noticed that rural migrants to bustling Chinese cities often found themselves without three important forms of social integration: without stable employment, without close emotional bonds to others, and without a permanent residence.

"Triple withouts" are drawn to the city by economic aspirations, but once they've arrived, they may find themselves confronted by expensive housing (a consequence of the concentration of housing markets in space), intense loneliness (having left family and childhood friends behind in the countryside), and unemployment (due to heavy competition for the most desirable jobs). The result is a certain listlessness and alienation that can, under certain conditions, lead to crime, drug abuse, and homelessness (Cheng et al. 2017; McCaffree, 2018). According to the Chinese Administration of Public Security, anywhere between 50%–80% of the people arrested for street crimes in cities like Beijing and Shanghai are "triple withouts" (Bakken, 2018).

Let me be clear that this phenomenon of social disruption among urban dwellers is not unique to China, not unique to migrants, and not unique to contemporary cities. Traveling businesspeople or salespeople or tourists also rely on short-term housing and potentially loosely known associates. Yes, migrants from the countryside might feel displaced and alone in the city, but just about *everyone* in a city has felt something similar. More abstractly, this social disruption represents important challenges of integration for any urban center, that is, for any social system predicated on truly open, large-scale, fission–fusion oscillation.

7.3 The Important Difference between Cities and Organizations

Organizations are aggregates of people who are, to various degrees, mutually oriented toward a shared goal. The most obvious example of an organization is a business. Not all employees or owners are equally committed or motivated, but in their capacity as employees and owners all are working toward the goal of building the business. Another example of an organization might be a basketball team. Here, the goal wouldn't be to make money per se, but to win games. Yet another example is that of a social movement / activist group. In this example, the shared goal may be to fundraise, but it may also be to build prestige or awareness for the group's cause.

The point I want to make here is that organizations are different from cities. The goal of an organization is to formalize relationships and streamline interactions. Cities, by contrast, do not have a delimited set of goals per se, but are rather the messy emergent property of numerous goals, interactions and exchanges. City governments have a of goals, certainly, but city governments are organizations, whereas the *city itself* is a diffuse mass of interactions occurring within a defined territory.

Organizations tend to winnow down new ideas and new behaviors in favor of formally (i.e., bureaucratically) and informally (i.e., normatively) regulated ideas and behaviors. This winnowing is a by-product of the leadership's focus on a delimited set of goals, and thus the closing of the fission–fusion system (those not professing to pursue those goals are not admitted into organizational fused states). As a business grows in size, the emphasis on innovation shifts to a emphasis on regularity, predictability, stability, and, therefore, bureaucratic structure. By contrast, cities contain many different groups with many different goals (some of which are opposed), and do not have membership/employee boundary requirements in the way businesses, or sports teams, or political organizations tend to.

Let's take the example of businesses as paradigmatic organizations. Worldwide, it seems that the scaling exponent for businesses both small and large is about 0.9 (West, 2017). This means that we would expect branches and offices to increase about 90% for every 100% increase (doubling) of employees. This would seem to indicate that the larger a business, the more organizationally efficient it tends to become. However, if innovative ideas and behaviors *decrease* as a function of business size, we would expect eventual bankruptcy or merger on account of an inability to adapt to changing conditions. As it turns out, this is exactly what researchers have found: about 50% of all publicly traded companies are defunct (i.e., split, merged, or liquidated) within ten years, less than 5% are still in business within 30 years, and almost none are in business 50 years hence (West, 2017). Granted, some businesses consistently last longer than others, in particular very small, highly niche businesses serving a stable clientele such as high-end wineries, boutique hotels, or restaurants.

Cities, by contrast, may live on much longer, even if they are renamed when new groups come into national political power. The ancient cities of Mesopotamia or Asia or the Mediterranean, for example, were actually early stages of cities that continue (albeit with new names and new infrastructure) today. Unlike businesses and other organizations, cities are open systems and become more complex, multidimensional, and diverse over time.

It is worth pointing out that our modern notion of businesses (and other organizations like schools, hospitals, and so on) is very new—corporate businesses are only a few hundred years old compared to the many thousands of years that cities have been developing. In order for businesses to have developed into mainstream economic organizations, people have had to develop particular clerical or sectorial skillsets, and only recently in history have most people in a society been freed from subsistence agriculture. Still, the substantive difference between businesses (and other organizations) and cities is the emphasis on particular superordinate group goals that require some degree of conformity in behavior or belief. Cities, by contrast, do not contain centralized, imposed, goals for particular forms of belief or behavior; organizations have dress codes and weekly expectations, cities don't. Cities are open systems to a degree that corporate groups are not.

Making these points, West notes:

> Companies typically operate as highly constrained top-down organizations that strive to increase efficiency of production and minimize operational costs so as to maximize profits. In contrast, cities embody the triumph of innovation … Cities aren't … driven by a profit motive and have the luxury of being able to balance their books by raising taxes. They operate in a much more distributed fashion, with power spread across multiple organizational structures from mayors and councils to businesses and citizen action groups. No single group has absolute control. As such, they exude an almost laissez-faire, free-wheeling ambience relative to companies.
>
> (West, 2017, pg. 408)

Businesses, regardless of product or sector, scale about linearly with a city's population size—double the size of a city, and you can expect about twice as many businesses (West, 2017). Typically, this works out to about one business for every 22 people regardless of city size. However, for every doubling of businesses, only about 5% represent new sectors or products (West, 2017). That is, only around 5% of each doubling in the number of businesses is attributable to new occupational specializations. A large increase in the volume of businesses, then, is needed to produce a small rise in innovative products or services.

A final point: cities can flourish as nations decay and decline (Tainter, 1988; Smith, 2019). Cities are less dominated by particular people with particular national affiliations. This is because cities contain the universal attractants I mentioned above. Go to the French or American or Chinese or Egyptian or Indian countryside, and you will find ethnic and ideological homogeneity along with a nationalist orientation; but, then, go to Paris or Los Angeles or Beijing or Cairo or Mumbai, and you will find ethnic and ideological differentiation, along with a global orientation. A nation can suffer as its cities flourish; perhaps the nation suffers *because* its cities flourish: city dwellers tend to develop different political outlooks than do rural dwellers, potentially leading to levels of cultural and political polarization that can be damaging to national political discourse. But, the relationship between cities and their nation needn't be so zero-sum. Cities come with their pathologies, of course, both new and old. Yet, what they offer is, itself, a crown jewel of humanity—creativity and innovation.

Note

1 A plausible prior inflection point was that of the middle class in the ancient Greek city-state of Athens.

Chapter 8

An "Oscillation-Infrastructural" Theory of Cultural Evolution

> The history of life is a history of transitions between different units of selection. Novel selective scenarios dominate at times of transition between units of selection. Whereas the lower self-replicating unit was previously selected by the external environment alone, following the transition it became selected by traits expressed by the higher unit.
>
> (Buss, 1987, viii).

I'd like to propose an integrative theory of cultural evolution predicated on group information-processing, differential retention of engineering information, and the accumulation of modifications to infrastructure.

There are five important concepts that constitute this theory, none of which are specific to me except for their combination: (1) organismality; (2) "alloliving"; (3) intuitive cognition; (4) fission–fusion group-learning; and (5) infrastructure.

These components are important for theories of cultural evolution because they ground such theories in the observations that (1a) human societies vary in their degree of cohesion and connectedness, (2a) societies are all reliant on a geographically distributed division of labor (amongst potentially anonymous others) oriented toward child-rearing, defense, and energy procurement, (3a) humans process information at both the individual intuitive, and (4a) group oscillatory levels, and (5a) cultural shifts are predicated on increasingly efficient means of energy extraction, processing, and distribution via infrastructure.

Components (1)–(5) are also interrelated, as I've tried to describe in the preceding pages. Our perceived needs for childcare, community defense, and ever-growing amounts of energy in order to flourish constitute a motivation for establishing increasingly infrastructurally interconnected societies that allow for varying rhythms of progressively more open fission–fusion oscillation which, in turn, erodes peoples' social and physical intuitions and thus accelerates technological and infrastructural complexity.

What follows is an explication of each of these theoretical components.

DOI: 10.4324/9781003266020-8

8.1 Organismality

Major evolutionary transitions have occurred *at least* five separate times (Maynard Smith and Szathmáry, [1995] 2010). The eukaryotic cell transition, perhaps the first major transition, increased the oxygen- and energy-processing capacities of formerly prokaryotic cells. Other, later, transitions include human language, which allows the transmission of information in new symbolic forms. This capacity of the human brain to create, store, and transmit ideas is, typically, regarded as the most recent evolutionary transition. The extent to which human society might have undergone yet another major evolutionary transition—some form of group selection—remains debated.

In a recent article, Eörs Szathmáry discusses what all evolutionary transitions seem to have in common. He writes:

> We see key elements [in] transitions: cooperation (including reproductive leveling and food sharing), a form of eusociality, a powerful novel inheritance system, and living in groups ... transition theory strongly suggests that, if we see, even in rudimentary form, that originally independently reproducing units join, somehow use functional synergies among the units, and that there is some novelty in the inheritance system as well, then the population is definitely on its way to a "major transition."
>
> Szathmáry (2015, pgs. 10106, 10110)

My argument in this book is that we can identify the emergence of a new unit of evolution, one that is wholly dependent on organic hosts (us). It is just not just our bodies that are holobiomes, but our social environments as well. Infrastructural innovations have augmented our phylogenetic abilities—we can see at night and communicate across oceans—but these capacities primarily rely on classes of people dedicating their lives to the development, funding, implementation, and maintenance of infrastructural systems. What makes cultural evolution interesting is that it has emerged from relationships between two units of evolution (human beings + configurations of terminal units of infrastructure) and two units of selection (genes stored in human individuals + engineering principles and equations stored in communication technologies).

Societies do not phase-shift from nonorganismic to organismic. Rather, as I've discussed, societies are more or less organismic to the degree that they contain (1) mechanisms facilitative of co-operation between unfamiliar individuals and groups and (2) mechanisms that reduce enough conflict between individuals and groups that emergent "infrastructural" systems of energy extraction, processing, and distribution can be implemented, sustained, and transmitted intergenerationally. Infrastructural systems, that is, systems of energy extraction, processing, and distribution that are (relatively) collectively held and (relatively) collectively utilized are important in human societies because they provide the energy to sustain "alloliving" at a scale far beyond the small foraging bands humans biologically evolved in.

From an organismic perspective, social systems are temporary, porous, aggregations of people with sufficiently shared traits or symbols to be able to interact co-operatively, even with unfamiliar others. Social systems are, in turn, composed of institutions, organizations, political territories (like state lines), neighborhoods, communities, and families. Just as the human body differentiates internal structures (like the organs of the brain, lungs, kidneys, etc.) as it develops, so too do societies differentiate internal structures (like the institutions of politics, medicine, education, or religion).

And, just as bodies develop circulatory systems and limbs to extend the reach of nutrients within the body and between the body and the environment, so too do cities (the energy hub of societies) contain branching, space-filling, networks of pipes, wires, roads, bridges, waterways, and cables.

These branching networks are hierarchically organized, meaning that they are denser at the source of energy production compared to where the energy is being distributed (West, 2017). So, for example, the pulmonary arteries carrying just-oxygenated blood cells out of your lungs are larger in diameter than the veins that end up finally providing this oxygenated blood via capillaries to the tissues, say, in your foot, hand, or nose. Similarly, the bundles of fibers in heavy electrical cables are larger and denser when leaving the generating station or substation, or when traveling along the road as suspended wires, compared to the wires that end up being connected to the few electrical outlets in your bedroom. Or consider the size of the water pipes connected to your local filtration facility or water tower compared to the size of the pipes that end up being installed in your household. This hierarchical branching is the means by which "macroscopic reservoirs" of energy are transported to "microscopic sites" whether the system is an organic body or a city (West, 2017, pg. 103).

Hierarchical branching networks in organisms and in cities are also space-filling, meaning that they tend to expand, not necessarily optimally, until energy is distributed to "all local ... active subunits of the system" (West, 2017, pg. 113). Circulatory systems in multicellular eukaryotic organisms provide oxygen and essential nutrients to subunits of the organism, while branching infrastructural distribution networks in societies provide heat, water, light, and so on to the structures housing families and organizations. The flow of energy in these infrastructural networks is continuous, until it isn't, and this continuousness coupled with the energy dependency of system subunits (people, groups and organizations) produce "continuous multiple feedback and fine-tuning mechanisms" (West, 2017, pg. 115). The consequences of an impeded flow of energy in a social system (or nutrients and oxygen in the case of biological individuals) is that subunits reduce their capacity to operate or cease operating at all. Societal (mini-)collapse can result when energy flow is impeded to entire communities or institutions. In short, the stakes are high for these branching infrastructural networks to be efficient and accessible, leading, over time, to a differential retention of infrastructural designs perceived to be maximally efficient and accessible.

Though perhaps paradoxical, robust and healthy systems can maintain their productivity and energy flows despite substantial, potentially damaging, perturbations and fluctuations. Indeed, the sign of a healthy system is its capacity to fluctuate significantly without losing (too much) productivity or capacity. For example, if a major hydroelectric dam breaks and destroys the surrounding communities and homes, this will produce a substantial decline in (electrical) energy output. However, resources from elsewhere in the system will be recruited to reconstruct the dam, now with the additional insight accrued from what went wrong in its original construction. Social systems, like biological systems, are thus antifragile, and can gain in complexity from disorder (Taleb, 2012). Societies are systems composed of (varying degrees of) open-system fission–fusion oscillations that can result, over time, in an adaptive flexibility to potentially severe threats regardless of where they occur in the system.

8.2 Alloliving

Social systems, to the extent that they reveal "organismality," facilitate an extension of human beings' "alloliving" capacities, in particular alloparenting, allodefense, and alloforaging.

Keep in mind, as you read through this, that we are dealing with a considerable degree of jargon here. The prefix "allo" literally means "other," but I cannot just use the terms "other-defense," "other-hunting," or "other-parenting." I cannot use these terms because "alloparenting" is a technical term denoting an animal behavior, found outside humans, that implicates important aspects of the social context within which humans evolved. Though instances of alloparenting, allodefense, and alloforaging are not necessarily entirely unique to humans, humans are unusually dependent on them for survival. So, what I mean by the prefix "allo" is, of course, "other." But what I intend to communicate with terms like "alloparenting" is the long process of gene-culture coevolution occurring in humans with regard to these three social practices.

In forager bands, anyone with the time and aptitude to do so will be expected to help with others' childcare and child socialization. The weathered phrase "it takes a village to raise a child" is applicable to a time long before there were villages—child socialization in our ancestral environment was shared amongst many people, not just the child's parents.

However, beginning around 12,000 years ago, groups settling in stationary locations to tend plots of land began, more and more, relying on childcare help within just the home, or within just the local village/family network. The number of children born to each family also began rising. This posed mobility problems: if a family, for whatever reason, traveled long distances to a foreign land, there was no guarantee of any childcare being available (outside, of course, of the family itself). Indeed, until we reached our very modern volume of captured and distributed energy enabled by fossil fuels and various infrastructural innovations, there were no childcare organizations open for general business. You either relied on your own family, extended family, or some network contacts. Today, childcare centers exist in countries all around the world, where a person can pay a fee to have someone they do not know watch and mentor their children while these children slowly build the social and technical skillsets necessary to make money in emerging markets. This dynamic is unique to modernity, and it is as much an extension of alloliving as it is a mechanism of economic growth.

Roughly the same could be said for another form of alloliving: alloforaging. In the forager bands within which human beings evolved, the procurement of food was shared—those who went out hunting were often unsuccessful (perhaps outside of small game), and so they relied for their dinner on those who had stayed back at camp and foraged for the more reliable berries, roots, or nuts. If someone gets sick, or becomes frail with age, or has a child they cannot feed, others in the band typically come through, or try to come through, with aid. The assumption is one of reciprocal altruism—if I have enough to share with you today, while you are in need, perhaps another day when I am in need, you will feel motivated to share with me. This reciprocal altruism, and the cohesion it can foster in small groups, underlies both alloparenting and alloforaging. Hunting, perhaps not quite to the same extent as childcare, is challenging and demands a great deal of patience and skill. Independent of food-sharing, the actual act of hunting was itself also collaborative; one forager with a spear stands little chance against a bison, but a team of foragers stands a substantially better chance. This teamwork would have had reciprocal payoffs, too, as I've described: alloparenting enhances the socialization environment's flexibility and complexity, and allohunting increases the available dietary fat and protein for brain development.

Yet, as with alloparenting, those people who began settling for longer and longer periods into sedentary villages began relying on fewer and fewer people for food procurement. Small-plot farmers are most concerned about the yield of their own land because their neighbors' generosity is harder to rely on the larger and more dense communities become (and, thus, the less familiar in lineage one's neighbors become). Sure, there have always been markets—first barter markets, then markets predicated on the exchange of various valuable coins. In this sense, people living in ancient cities always had access to a source of alloforaging; when a person walks into a city bazaar and buys fruit to eat that they did not collect themselves, this should be understood as sort of pecuniarily mediated alloforaging. Still, nothing like grocery stores or soup kitchens existed in any formal way for most of human history. Individual people (most specifically village chiefs) were no doubt generous on occasion, and grain storage was certainly a ubiquitous practice, but the changes societies have undergone from ancient Mesopotamia to today are, critically, changes involving the extent to which organizations and institutions facilitate various forms of alloparenting and alloforaging.

Allodefense is implied in both alloparenting and alloforaging. Without relying on unrelated, potentially unfamiliar, others for some degree of protection and defense, no collective foraging or child-rearing would have been possible. Any social structure that developed to facilitate communal childcare or communal foraging, which was immediately and swiftly dissolved at the slightest hint of a threat or danger, wouldn't have been a structure worth maintaining in the first place. Tribal loyalty and ingroup preference provided the motivations for people to protect the emerging alloparenting and alloforaging systems they depended on for survival.

But, as societies grew in size and interconnectedness, these tribal loyalties and ingroup preferences would've limited the scale at which alloliving could be achieved.

Perhaps, the "principle reason for maintaining cohesion is predation risk" (Dunbar and Shultz, 2020, pg. 9). A fair amount of prior work does show that the size of an animal's group is a primary factor in reducing the risk of predation, either because an animal has a better chance of escape when the group scatters (compared to if it were alone), or because group defense responses are more substantial than individual defense responses. Yet, for humans, perhaps moreso than any other mammal, cohesion is not merely defensive, but *actively productive*. Cohesion provides not just protection, but also the intensive level of childcare, eldercare, social stimulation / social learning, and nutrition that human societies, since their earliest forms, have relied on.

My approach does not need to assume that humans are adapted at the group level in any genetic sense. Here, I am disagreeing with those, like E. O. Wilson, who have suspected that the human capacity for altruism and normativity constitute genetic adaptations enabling human groups—as groups—to survive. I am not very convinced of this. Sure, humans have incredible empathic abilities; in effect, humans can extend their ingroup to include any person on the globe, so long as symbolic identifiers and group affiliations are understood broadly enough. This is no doubt a spectacular ability. But it is just as easily leveraged to produce incredible enmity and hatred; indeed, the more we can be made to love "our" ingroup, the more we can be motivated to commit atrocities against those defined as "other." Humans can generate impassioned empathic responses, yes, and these can be extended to unfamiliar or dissimilar others, yes, but there is nothing in the human genome that mandates this. The most brutal dictators known to humanity have, often, been very passionate people quite convinced of the moral perfection and righteousness of their particular group/nation/religion. As Paul Bloom (2017) has argued, the more emotionally impassioned we become regarding some righteous cause, the harder it can be to reflect, analyze, and think critically about who we are helping and why. Very easily, people can be led by their passions to disenfranchise, stigmatize, or abuse an outgroup that, in our predictable flurry of righteous anger, couldn't seem more obviously evil. The road to hell is, in almost every case, paved with good intentions.

I do not find adequate evidence to suggest that humans are genetically hardwired to display some sort of unique group-level altruism. They don't need to be. Human infants are so dependent, and primates live so long, that some degree of alloliving would just have been common sense for our early ancestors. Living alone, with dependent elders and children, amid any number of vicious savannah predators, would have been certain death for ancestral humans. And, of course, many early species of *homo* did indeed go extinct. *Homo sapiens* could have too. But we didn't. And, not because we developed a hardwired genetic propensity to display altruism and empathy for nonrelated others, but rather because alloliving was obviously practical, especially for a highly-genetically related primate able to easily construe connectedness using emotionally-infused symbols and language. Adopting this practice of alloliving (behaviorally, not in a hardwired genetic sense) came with immediate subsequent benefits—better diet, more protection, healthier babies, longer lifespan, more free time, less stress. In some cases, as in Henrich's (2017) gene-cultural coevolution framework, improved diet (i.e., increased carnivory from allohunting) did improve genetic capacities to some extent (i.e., increased tissue volume in the prefrontal cortex), but, again, this genetic capacity would still need to be molded during an extended period of socialization so that children of each new generation understood the burdens on them to help the collective.

Eusociality in humans, then, is *not* genetically determined in the ways it is in bees or in ants. The capacity for eusociality in humans is better conceptualized as a *eusocialness*, enabled by our abilities for symbolism and abstraction. We can more easily define unfamiliar or dissimilar individuals as symbolic, honorary, family members than can other mammals, and this enables us to expand our various child-related, elder-related, food-related, and defense-related safety nets. In doing so, we develop superordinate symbolic abstractions—abstractions related to "meaning," "purpose," or "duty"—which drive us to sacrifice for others, work for others, and care for others. This is not genetically hardwired, but is rather a reliably socialized expression of our species-specific neurological capacity for symbolism and abstraction. Thus, *eusocialness* in humans emerges as an indirect effect of other cognitive repertoires (we might, even, call it a "cognitive gadget"; see Heyes, 2018).

Eusocialness in humans, because it is not strictly genetically determined (though humans are unusually highly genetically related to one another, as discussed in Chapter 1), expresses itself in widely varying ways. If a person today is raised in a very cloistered community, or exposed to very homogeneous social networks, they may develop prejudices and biases toward those dissimilar or unfamiliar, thus reducing, in principle, this person's capacity to benefit from possible childcare, eldercare, food, defense, or other resources provided by outgroup others. Even still, this person, within their parochial community, will likely interact with unfamiliar others frequently over their life-course. And, when doing so, they will rely on symbolic abstractions defining group membership. Even the most close-minded ideologue occasionally goes to places where they meet others whom they do not know, and so as long as there is a tiny bit of wiggle room in how the ideologue defines their group membership, these unfamiliar others might still be related to as "fictive kin." Potential informal network benefits—from help with childcare to help with a legal defense—can then follow suit.

Few people, thankfully, are close-minded ideologues. Most are quite open to altering the definition or content of their symbolic abstractions to include larger numbers of different kinds of people. Today, few if any lawyers crusade only for their personal religious, race, or gender group. Rather, they defend anyone with a case (and money). The same might be said for schoolteachers, medical doctors, therapists, or any business owner; the content defining basic social categories like "citizen," "customer," "partner," "client," "patient," "student," and so on is now sufficiently broad in most countries to include, in principle, *any* adult. In more and more countries around the world, some degree of civil legal protection exists to ensure the broad applicability of these categories. This constitutes a formal bureaucratic "institutionalization" of a particularly high level (historically speaking) of *eusocialness* in human society.

The extent of alloparenting, alloforaging, and allodefense in the massive societies of modernity is staggering. But it is often subtle and, undoubtedly, less efficient and productive than it could or will be.

Consider an example of how subtle, yet crucial, alloliving is today. As the division of labor has become more and more specialized, the amount of education required to step into newly developing professions is substantial. This is important for the following reasons. First, there is the time spent competing for positions and learning the niche jargon and skillset required to become, for example, a well-paid physicist, orthodontist, developmental psychologist, computer programmer, or heart surgeon. Second, consider how much more prevalent this sort of occupational specialization is today in rich democracies relative to ancient societies; never before in history have more people spent more time specializing in highly technical careers in pursuit of the opportunity to make a middle-class (or greater) living. However, third, consider that all of this time spent learning specialized knowledge and skills and competing for coveted positions is time spent away from family, and potentially time spent away from dating, courting, and having children.

The subtlety and profundity of *eusocialness* is to be found here. While people might be spending more time and more money pursuing education and careers, they are not necessarily spending less time (and money) on kin, given humans' existing high levels of genetic relatedness (see Chapter 1) as well their ability to construe connectedness with emotionally-infused symbols and ideologies. There is a real sense in which kin-based mechanisms motivate many lawyers, doctors, professors, dancers, architects, painters, engineers, actors, astronomers, musicians, and firefighters as they hope to "contribute" to human knowledge, health, engineering, beauty, or justice "in general."

The 38-year-old spinal surgeon chasing occupational prestige is, yes, of course, pursuing their own personal wealth and status. No doubt. But we tend to focus on this only. In reality, this person is *also* spending their time and their effort, and certainly in graduate school their money, to, quite plainly, help repair peoples' spines. And this applies not just to their friends' spines or family members' spines or those of people with whom they share politics or religion. But, *anyone's* spine, or at least, anyone with good enough health insurance! This relative indiscriminateness in care can be found in the time, effort and attention provided by attorneys to their clients or that daycare workers provide for others' children brought to their center or that nurses provide for their patients or that professors provide to their graduate students. Time which could be spent mate bonding, reproducing, and raising children is, increasingly, spent developing a specialized skillset so as to better tend to anonymous others.

This is not only alloparenting, but *allocare* more generally, and, pointedly, it is care given relatively indiscriminately and care that requires a large personal investment of time, money, and effort on the part of the caregiver. The time, money, and effort spent becoming a civil engineer is hard to distinguish from the time, money, and effort these individuals will spend "taking care" of others in their society through the carrying out of meticulously planned construction projects. Just the same, the time, money, and effort spent becoming a professor or a nurse or a theater teacher should be considered relative to the time, money, and effort these individuals will spend "taking care" of others in their society through the provisioning of services, guidance, or mentorship.

Some analysts have been puzzled by the so-called "second demographic transition" occurring as countries grow wealthier around the world, whereby couples begin having fewer children later in life (Lesthaeghe, 2010; Zaidi and Morgan, 2017). This is typically considered to represent an overall, perhaps irreversible, "decline in fertility." But the issue is more complicated than this. If two people, a man and a woman, spend their 20s, into their 30s, developing careers in medicine and engineering, respectively, how many lives will they contribute to saving before they are both dead, even if neither of them ever have children of their own? How many other people will be able to have families and raise children because they were kept alive by the medical practices of the doctor or because of the innovations in water treatment constructed by the engineer?

Even if the "reproductive fitness" of individuals has declined with greater economic opportunity, birth control, or education, the time and energy spent contributing to the well-being and, potentially, genetic fitness of totally unknown unfamiliar others, simply in the due course of performing one's occupational duties, has never before been greater in human history. And, when couples in rich democracies do have kids (as they still often do), they invest more time and money into each child, representing an increase in parental investment per child. This high investment is partly due to the lower overall number of children being born to each couple in recent centuries—it would be hard to purchase college educations and summer camps for six or ten kids! But we should look at this another way, also. Parents are having fewer children and investing more time and resources into ensuring those children can acquire the skills and connections necessary to flourish in elite occupations, occupations that, inevitably, at their best, are oriented toward helping, serving, or informing the "public." This represents an increasing degree of behavioral *eusocialness* across human history.

8.3 Fission–Fusion Oscillation

Fission–fusion oscillation is a form of group information-processing found in humans and in other mammals. Zoologists find that animal groups fission for a variety of reasons, perhaps because the group is getting too big and conflict is increasing, or perhaps because the age or sex distributions of animals in the group are leading to different behavioral patterns or roaming ranges (Seebacher and Krause, 2017). Conversely, in more uncertain circumstances (i.e., introduction of a new predator), or when a large collective resource can be plundered (i.e., a large lake), individuals and small groups will reliably coalesce back into larger collectives.

Fission represents a different, temporary, state compared to fusion. Though each state is interesting and rife with implications for the individuals (or subgroups) involved, it is the oscillation between the states, occurring day in and day out, that generates cultural change, development, and evolution. Another critically important insight, which we must keep in mind, is that individual subjectivities—values, attitudes, beliefs, desired behaviors—are not stable characteristics of individuals that we come to only upon personal reflection and hold to only out of conviction. No, the contents of our mind are always a probability distribution, even if it seems as though our subjectivities are stable because our oscillations between and among groups stays relatively stable over time. Yet, if a highly socially integrated individual finds themselves alone for long stretches, or perhaps, increasingly embedded in a new group, they will also find that their attitudes, values, beliefs, or behaviors shift or become more malleable.

When social scientists measure a given person's subjective state, the probability distribution associated with their likelihood of expressing any given attitude, value, or belief collapses into a single measured state. We say "this person expressed an intention to vote for candidate X," or "this person endorses policy Y," or "this person has ideological commitment Z," and so on. Yet, what we are doing in these surveys is forcing the person's brain to express a given subjective state, which is drawn (subconsciously or not) from a number of possible states associated with varying probabilities linked to their (often unmeasured) integration into various groups. Depending on (1) how fused a person is to this or that group, (2) how fissioned a person is, or (3) whether their trajectory is moving from a more fused state to a more fissioned state, or from a (4) more fissioned state to a more fused state, the probability distribution of expressed attitudes, values, or behaviors will change and, thus, so too might their expressed response to our questions.

We social scientists are so enamored with "individuals" and their "thoughts." Yes, people subjectively express attitudes. We must not lose sight of the underlying reality, though: individual subjectivities are temporary, probabilistic, aggregations reflecting particular levels of integration (or disintegration) across groups over time. Our minds house a wave of probabilities, and we capture just one emanation of such probabilities on surveys or in interviews. Do not take this to mean that peoples' thoughts are constantly in flux; it is quite the opposite. To the degree that humans seek stability in their group commitments and obligations, we can expect fairly consistent attitudinal responses. The point to remember is that this stability is a consequence of particular, perhaps stable, rhythms of fission–fusion oscillation and, less so, a consequence of an individual's (or subgroup's) demographic characteristics or life experiences.

Fission and fusion states are inextricably linked. In closing this book, and with the above in mind, I should make a few final summary points.

8.3.1 Fissioned States and Fused States

Fusing concentrates opportunities for social learning, can facilitate consensus/agreement, and can facilitate the storing of information in collective documents/repositories (or, in brains, the first repositories).

Broadly speaking, we can think about fusion as occurring at three levels of intersubjectivity: awareness, surface contact, and mutuality. At the lowest level of intersubjectivity, fusion can take the form of awareness—here, think about people on mass public transit, or bustling along a city street or co-present in a huge seminar. Though people might be aware of others and may actively navigate around them (as when passing people on the street or negotiating where to sit in a crowded room), the level of interaction is minimal. Surface contact occurs when individuals begin interacting with one another by substantively engaging in conversation and in the exchange of gestures. Mutualism involves collaboration of some sort, toward some shared goal. Clearly, mutualism is a rarer form of fusion than awareness, and surface contact is fairly commonplace if often insubstantial.

The great benefit of fusion—social facilitation and altercentric cognition (Kampis and Southgate, 2020)—is also its great hindrance. Compared to when they are alone, when people are co-present with others and thinking about their role and social identities, they experience greater motivation and energy, measurable quite practically in something like heart rate. But co-presence can also in some cases make people feel anxious, stifled, or overly controlled. We are, in a literal sense, moved by others as much by their expectations as by their indiscretions. Nevertheless, existing data shows that, from 14 months (and probably earlier), human infants take others' actions into account when deciding how to act themselves, for example, whether to look in a box for objects (Kampis and Kovács, 2020). This attentiveness to others is detectable at an early age in humans, apparently, because we are uniquely normative in our behavior; humans are believed to have a unique capacity, refined through individual development, for "collective intentionality" (Tomasello, 2019). This inclination among humans to attend to others, and specifically, to attend to what others are attending to, is the foundation of our sense of an unseen normative structure but, also, sometimes equally, of the suffocating weight of that normative structure.

Groups, in particular large groups, rely on hierarchies in order to coordinate individual members. These hierarchies can be prestige hierarchies predicated on skill, merit, or ability, they can be power hierarchies predicated on coercion, or, typically, some mix of the two. In smaller groups, more temporary "heterarchies" tend to emerge; in larger groups, more permanent (i.e., longer-term) positions within hierarchies are more likely. In "heterarchies," people move fluidly and dynamically into and out of positions of influence within the group (Aime et al., 2014), but this requires a level of trust and sense of familiarity with others; otherwise, the high turnover in positions may seem threatening or anxiety-inducing.

Now, there is nothing *necessarily* preventing larger groups from relying on more open "heterarchies," as opposed to more closed, stable hierarchies. Indeed, the extent to which a group fuses around a "heterarchical" form of social coordination is the sense in which a fusion context might be considered relatively more open or porous. Fused groups, then, are not only open/porous with regard to ingroup/outgroup boundaries, but also with regard to the porousness of hierarchies within the group.

Fusion can be highly formal in the Weberian ([1922] 1978) sense (e.g., bureaucratically or legally regulated and organized) or informal (e.g., a recreational hobby group or, even, a cult or extremist group). In either case, the liabilities of overintegration are always present for groups fused too strongly or for too long: conformity, rigidity, repressiveness, and/or hierarchies divorced from merit. Pluralistic ignorance, for example, is a form of peer pressure and conformity whereby people endorse norms they privately do not agree with because they assume everyone else endorses them (and others, making the same calculation, act as though they endorse the idea or behavior as well) (Taylor, 1982; Willer et al., 2009). Pluralistic ignorance is a particularly dangerous (to accuracy and adaptability), but incredibly common, form of groupthink in fused groups.

As distinct from highly fused states, fissioned states can provide relatively more opportunities for reflection or critical thinking, and they can also help reduce conflict/tension within groups. Without states of relative fissioning, group norms, attitudes, behaviors, hierarchies, and so on would be difficult to think about critically or envision changing. This doesn't mean there aren't hazards associated with being fissioned to a high degree or for a prolonged period. People can be too mobile (moving so often, they fail to form stable friendships), live extremely distinct or eccentric lifestyles that make it difficult to find commonalities with others, or become socially isolated and lonely. These aren't minor concerns—some research has shown that perceiving oneself as having no social contacts has equivalent effects on mortality to smoking up to 15 cigarettes a day (Holt-Lunstad, 2017). Social isolation can reduce life expectancy through a variety of mechanisms—a reduced ability to cope, less positive social control to deter drug use or other self-harming behaviors, less access to people who might give advice or help with medical referrals, and so on.

Fissioning can have other, perhaps more subtle, downsides. For example, social expectations and norms can become more unrealistic or unclear when they are less often, or less consistently, discussed or enacted. In other words, the less time people spend with one another, the greater the opportunity for absent-mindedness or self-focus to produce conflicting expectations when (or if) individuals reconvene. On account of having some distance from the collective, fissioned individuals may appear more malleable behaviorally or ideologically compared to the more rigid, resistant, dogmatism characteristic of individuals in highly integrated groups. But this does not necessarily mean the fissioned individual is impressionable or stupid; rather, it is an indication that their beliefs and behaviors are not being canalized or dictated by perceived group expectations or group supervision.

Fission, then, is a different state, by degree, than is the state of fusion. But, when individuals are "fissioned" from one group, they are not necessarily alone. They might be in a different group, or in a subset of the superordinate group. Generally, to fission means to interact at a relatively lower rate and for shorter durations; to fuse means to interact at relatively higher rates and for longer durations. Yet, this is perhaps only the most potent, physical, face-to-face form of fission–fusion. People can fission and fuse symbolically and virtually, as well, not only physically.

Consider symbolic fission–fusion. When you are relaxing on your couch after work, you are fissioned in that no one else (let's presume you live alone) is co-present with you. But you are only superficially "alone." The memes, worldview, role, and social identities in your mind continue to constitute a large portion of your subjectivity, even sitting alone on the couch. This combination of symbolic information along with semantic and episodic autobiographic memories of social experiences and interactions ensures that you remain, even if in a more generic and low-intensity way, fused to the group symbols, roles, social attitudes, and worldviews with which you identify. This is symbolic fusion, but the same could be said of symbolic fission—just because people are co-present or interacting does not mean they are coming to the same conclusions about the meaning of this or that idea, behavior, policy, or group boundary. If people become symbolically fused enough, motivation for face-to-face interaction becomes greater; in a mirrored way, if people become symbolically fissioned within a group, a decline in the rate and duration of shared attention or intention is similarly likely. These are two, opposite, sides of a similar coin.

And then there is virtual fission–fusion. Shortly, realistic facsimiles in virtual reality will depict the entirety of our personality and mannerisms. The realism of the computer mediation itself determines the extent to which such communication operates akin to (or even more effectively than) physical, face-to-face interaction. The more accurately our virtual avatars depict who we are (or who we aspire to be), and the more multisensory computer communication becomes, the more such interaction will approximate physical, face-to-face interaction. Virtual fissioning is also possible—consider the possibility of two or more people, "friends" online, deciding to ignore/block one another's messages on social media because of the ostensibly intolerable offensiveness of their political opinions.

Fission–fusion is thus a fractal phenomenon. We might be fissioned from one group while fused in another, or we might be fissioned from a larger collective only to more freely associate with a subset group of that larger collective. Or, we might be sitting alone in our cars, but still preoccupied with this or that song, idea, or identity that was gleaned, of course, socially. Or, perhaps we are hundreds of miles away from those we are talking to, but a virtual representation of their face on a computer screen allows for a stable rate and duration of attention or intention over time (as with working groups using videoconferencing, or families talking to loved ones overseas). My personal favorite example is that of the division of labor in growing economies—specialized occupational niches embedded within the larger economy represent pockets of relative fissioning (i.e., occupational niches with their specialized cultural capital and particular group boundaries) that help increase coordination and productivity within a larger superordinate group (i.e., the American, Brazilian, etc., or global economy).

Perhaps the only *absolute* state of fission—in the sense of complete social isolation—occurs in so-called "feral" children (though such children no doubt attempt to fuse with the animals or environment around them), while the only *absolute* state of fusion—in the sense of complete social merging—occurs when individuals are still in the womb of their mothers (though even *in utero*, children develop independent nervous systems and subjectivities). Outside of these extreme cases, even when fissioned to some extent, we are still fused with others in various ways, and even when fused strongly, we retain (even if only slightly) our individual subjectivities.

I should make a few more technical, but summative, points here about the sorts of variation and competition that can prolong (or shorten) the length of fission states and fused states. I'll discuss four here, two forms of variation and two forms of competition: (1a) between-group cultural variation; (1b) within-group cultural variation; (2a) between-group competition; and (2b) within-group competition.

Between-group cultural variation refers to differences between groups regarding symbolic information, exhibited in things like values, worldviews, ideas and behaviors. This sort of variation can distinguish one group from another, by degrees. Measuring this between-group cultural variation is at the heart of cultural sociology, anthropology, psychology, and of the sort of political science work I've reviewed (e.g., Inglehart, 1990; Welzel, 2013). Between-group cultural variance can be fission-promoting because it can lead to intergroup anxiety or difficulty communicating on account of a lack of shared values, ideas, or behaviors. Critically, however, a high degree of genetic relatedness among human beings tends to mitigate the degree to which cultures vary from one another; even in the most distinct cultures on Earth, more will be shared in common than will differ, from food (proteins, starches) to various diverse instantiations of similar concerns ranging from music to poetry to art to coming-of-age rituals to parenthood to infrastructure (Brown, 2000; 2004). Indeed, the overwhelming *sameness* of humans from country to country is criminally underdiscussed and underestimated because, of course, we are most interested in what is rarest and most bizarre: our differences (Hanel et al., 2019).

But between-group cultural variation can also be fusion-promoting. Under conditions of low general threat and relative material security, cultural variation begins to seem more novel, interesting, and curiosity-piquing. Individuals perceived to be from culturally different groups may also be preferred as interaction partners because they are perceived to harbor new, possibly helpful or insightful, ways of thinking and behaving. Between group cultural variation can signal that each group, precisely on account of their differences, is a viable partner for innovative collaborations.

Within-group cultural variation refers to differences in symbolic information amongst those identifying (or co-present) as members of the same group. This sort of variation distinguishes one individual (or one group) from other individuals (or groups) within the group (or superordinate group). Within-group cultural variation can be fission-promoting for the same reasons just described above: people can find one another so different, so unrelatable, so intolerant that they cease attending to, or intending with, one another at the same average rate or for the same average duration (if they interact at all). This has been termed the "narcissism of small differences" (Werman, 1998): when individuals share our group membership, we can become *more* frustrated with disagreement (because we expect conformity) than when individuals are members of a group different from ours. This appears to be due to a motivation to see ingroup members (moreso than outgroup members) as similar to ourselves (and vice versa).

Within-group cultural variation can also be fusion-promoting, and again, for precisely the same reasons as discussed above. Differences between people can increase anxiety and avoidance but under conditions of relatively greater material security and lower threat, cultural variance can be attractive/exciting/intriguing, thus increasing the rate and duration of interaction within the group. The more individual group members (or individual groups) perceive one another as exciting sources for potentially collaborative innovation, the more productive exchanges will develop among group members, potentially increasing group cohesion (Lawler et al., 2009).

Between-group competition involves two or more groups that perceive competing interests with regard to some valued symbolic or material resource. As with the above forms of variation, between-group competition also has fission-promoting and fusion-promoting aspects. It can be fission-promoting in that perceived competition with an outgroup can trigger the emotionally motivating construal of individual outgroup members as bad, evil, or dangerous. The perception that others we are competing with are fundamentally bad or corrupt appears to be pretty intuitive to people of all cultures; it is regarded as a component of our evolved "tribal psychology" (Clark et al., 2019). Of course, perceiving the members of competing outgroups as bad, untrustworthy, immoral, and so on will tend to raise anxiety and motivate behavioral avoidance (or, if conditions are severe and competition is perceived to be significantly zero-sum, aggression and violence).

Enmity toward outgroups can facilitate cohesion in the ingroup (the so-called "Simmel-Coser" principle in sociology; see Hanneman et al., 1995), but other work has suggested that group cohesion varies independently from outgroup conflict (Allport, 1954; Brewer, 1999). Perceiving a competitive outgroup as bad or dangerous *can* increase the tie strength of ingroup members (as people tighten their norms and hierarchies to mobilize for defense), but probably at the significant cost of anxiety, fear, impulsiveness, and general allostatic load. And, besides, ingroup cohesion can be bolstered by mechanisms other than outgroup fear, for example through innovative or productive collaboration (Lawler et al., 2000; Thye et al., 2019).

Between-group competition can also be fusion-promoting. Social science is in a great theoretical debt to people like Lewis Coser (1956) and Randall Collins (2016) who have, in different ways, so elegantly shown how competition can be a source of intergroup cohesion. When two groups compete with one another, several rather subtle consequences emerge that get ignored due to the intensity and flamboyance of the frustration, resentment, focus, drive, and potential indignity and cruelty of competition.

Outside of the thrill of feeling like one's group is gaining ground, and outside of the depression or anger of feeling like one's group is being walked on, competition often produces, among other things, (1) some degree of between group consensus about the terms of competition, such as shared rules or shared guidelines determining who should or should not be "rewarded" or "advantaged" or "punished"; (2) non-zero-sum outcomes, such that even "winners" of a competition appreciate the act of competing and "losers" of a competition appreciate the benefits accrued from being challenged; (3) opportunities to define and redefine group boundaries to determine which individuals or groups are on which sides of the competition (group boundary redefinitions produce group porousness); (4) some degree of collective catharsis, recreation, or enjoyment (particularly when competition is low–medium stakes); and (5) avenues for apportioning status and influence between groups.

Finally, *within-group competition* involves individuals within a group (or groups embedded within a superordinate group) perceiving competing interests with regard to some valued resource. As with the others above, within-group competition has fission-promoting aspects and fusion-promoting aspects. Within-group competition can be fission-promoting to the extent that (1) individuals perceive the competition to be zero-sum, (2) to the extent that status in the group hierarchy is linked to competition outcomes, or (3) to the extent that competition isn't perceived to be voluntary and/or the terms of competition are seen as unfair. But, within-group competition can also be fusion-promoting, for precisely the same four reasons mentioned above for between-group competition. When individuals within a group (or groups within a superordinate group) compete with one another, (1) collaborations over the terms of competition/exchange, (2) benefits to self-esteem or group commitment, (3) social catharsis/recreation/fun, and (4) opportunities to change within-group role definitions to demonstrate skill or ability can all facilitate intra-group attention or intention.

8.3.2 Fission–Fusion and Innovation

Periods of relative fissioning can help produce innovative ideas because individuals (or subgroups of superordinate groups) may have unique experiences and/or may think more critically, abstractly, or openly about group ideas and behaviors when not acutely under group surveillance or involved in group activities. Then, if/when individuals reconvene in their embedded groupings, there is a nonzero probability that some of these novel ideas will be brought up, or actively created in conversation.

However, even absent fissioned states, fused states are capable, especially under certain conditions, of generating innovations. In case I've left this point underemphasized in prior pages, let's consider a bit more the role of fused states in generating innovation.

Fused states vary with regard to the depth of their within-group cultural variance. Jie Wang and her colleagues (2019), for example, distinguish between "surface-level" and "deep" diversity within groups. Surface-level diversity refers to superficial physical differences between people—things like skin color, age, and sex. In prior studies, surface-level diversity is most often measured as nationality or race (Stahl et al., 2010). Deep-level diversity refers to "unobservable attributes" of people such as reasoning styles, personalities, worldviews, and values (Wang et al., 2019). Deep-level diversity results, in significant part, from differences in peoples' lifestyle and/or life experiences, akin to the "habitus" of tastes and preferences that people glean subtly from their social milieu as they grow up (Bourdieu [1980] 1990).

It appears that deep-level diversity in working groups, much more than surface-level diversity, increases groups' innovativeness (Wang et al., 2019). Do not take this to mean that deep-level diversity cannot pose coordination and integration problems for groups; it certainly can. But, if we set aside group cohesion/coordination for a moment and just consider innovative and creative potential, deep-level diversity is more important. In fact, this research suggests that the benefits to creativity typically outweigh any costs to cohesion/coordination.

Surface-level diversity is a bad proxy for experiential differences or habitus differences. It is a bad proxy for these things because, in fact, demographic differences between people are not usually reliable markers of ideological, attitudinal, or value differences. Knowing a person is 23 years old, Hispanic, or male tells me absolutely nothing, practically speaking, about what this person is likely to believe, what values they hold, or what behaviors they find routine. Sure, social scientists can statistically calculate average sample attitudes for 23-year-old Hispanic men on this or that issue. But this is a statistical abstraction, an average drawn from a sample that deviates from the actual population in, inevitably, a variety of ways. Worse, it would be a survey of people's *self-reported* attitudes, and this may or may not be the same as what they privately think or believe. The practical reality is that knowing a person's demographic characteristics tells us little if anything about their internal subjective states. We can try to generalize, but that is what we're doing, generalizing.

This is why surface-level diversity is not reliably related to group creativity in meta-analyses (Wang et al., 2019). *Sometimes* individuals of different ages, races, sexes, or nationalities harbor the sort of variation in worldview, values, attitudes, or behaviors that might stimulate the conversations, questions, debates, refinements, and clarifications that produce innovation. But such surface-level differences are no guarantee of underlying differences in subjectivity. On the other hand, groups composed of individuals with deep differences are groups with the variation in perspective necessary for synergy and innovation.

Here's an example. If the group I'm embedded in (or the collective of groups my group is embedded in) is pursuing a goal I regard as important and that I, on my own, could never achieve, then I will tend to be motivated to interact with other ingroup members in furtherance of this pursuit. Now, within this group, the more individuals (or subgroups) differ in their worldviews or values, the more they will need to clarify, try to speak precisely, explain, refine, question, and re-explain. Notice that this sort of collective "thinking" wouldn't occur so intensively where individuals within a group (or a group within a larger group) share more of their worldviews, values, and so on. This negotiated sharing of our variance in subjectivity, within in the context of larger, *superordinately shared* goals (even if those goals are proximately selfish, as when individuals want to contribute to the group in order to elevate their own status), constitutes a mechanism driving not only interaction, cohesion, and excitement, but also ideational complexity.

Within groups, individuals with high status or power can act in ways that either facilitate or impede the production of this ideational complexity (Wang et al., 2019). To increase the probability of facilitating innovative, creative outputs, those with situational influence (status or power) within groups can (1) attempt to recruit and/or attract individuals with deep-level differences, or provide opportunities for people to discover deep-level differences amongst one another, (2) avoid prioritizing or overfocusing on surface-level differences (as these may not be reliable proxies for substantive differences in subjectivity), (3) organize subteams and task designs to facilitate conversation, debate, and an open exchange of ideas, and (4) provide or encourage "complex and interdependent tasks," which require people to think beyond their initial intuitions or assumptions and seek others' input.

Then, there is the very real "paradox of creativity" (Bonetto et al., 2021). Expressing an idea that seems new, or an idea that seems unpopular, often comes with social costs. Ostracism, criticism, stigma, distrust, disgust—throughout history, these have all been common responses to those individuals or groups who buck the dominant trend of thought or discourse on a topic. Once a group of people comes to a consensus, perceived or actual, the force of that consensus feels objective, external, constraining; this is the social force of a norm, and to "break" or "violate" this consensus is to risk appearing insubordinate. I cannot be sure how emotionally equivalent it would be for an individual to attempt to insist on the merits of a new idea, as compared to a group of people attempting to insist, as a collective to other collectives, on the merits of a new idea. But, in either case, to the extent that a perceived consensus is challenged, people—particularly those people most financially or socially invested in that consensus—may resist and stigmatize the challengers, even when the idea is sensible, helpful, and practical.

But we mustn't think of resistance to innovation and novelty as, in every case, mere irrational stupidity. It isn't, always. There is real value in group consensus and stability, just as there is real value in group debate and innovation. After all,

> evolving organisms must balance their need to change in response to the variations in the environment against their need to maintain a proper functioning … The paradox of creativity can be considered as an expression of this broader necessity to balance between conservatism and novelty. If the former is [a] synonym of security, the latter is [a] synonym of uncertainty, since the innovation can be beneficial and/or detrimental.
>
> (Bonetto et al., 2021, pg. 4)

In other words, constant, continuous innovation (and the debate/discussion/refinement that fuels it) may eventually destroy the cohesion, stability, and continuity of the collective generating it. Conversely, stability (and the disinterest/passivity/vacuity that fuels it) may utterly destroy the potential for novelty, creativity, or innovation that might aid in the survival or flourishing of the group. As ideal-typical states, neither consistent stability nor constant flux are helpful in dynamic, changing environments.

Let's take a step back to consider the big picture.

It is a very revealing fact that utility patents (which represent innovations in machine or product functionalities) are today more likely to be granted to teams instead of individuals (Singh and Fleming, 2010). The same isn't true for design patents (which represent innovations in aesthetics or appearance of a machine or product), which are just as likely to be granted to individuals. This fact reveals something very important—the more complex machines and products in a society become, the harder it is to develop further innovations that are actually more useful, not merely different or better-looking.

The sheer difficulty of developing new technological innovations regarding devices that have been the target of centuries (in some cases) of cumulative innovation is, increasingly, surpassing the particular social learning and creative capacities of any one individual. The future of innovation is team-based, deep-level diversity-based, and predicated on porous fission–fusion oscillation. The notion of a lone genius—at least with regard to major innovations in infrastructure, and in the technologies we all rely on every day—is soon to become an artifact of history, an artifact of simpler times when we didn't need one another as much in order to make life better for everyone.

The number of major inventions and discoveries has been growing exponentially since about 1600 CE, though a slower process of accumulating innovations probably stretches back to the first hominins and, certainly, to the first humans. By Gerhard Lenski's (1970, see also Wilson, 1975) estimate, for example, there were about 150 major innovations in each of the 15th and 16th centuries CE. There were just over 200 major innovations between 1600 and 1699. Then, this number jumps to 600 between 1700 and 1799, then over 2,000 from 1800 to 1899, and it begins to climb exponentially from there. This exponential growth rate will need to *increase*, not merely hold stable, in order to meet energy demands for an expanding global population.

Interestingly, and despite the fact that teams dedicated to developing innovations of all kinds have never been larger, more diverse, or more active, the rate of productive innovation is declining in the United States, China, Germany, and probably elsewhere (Bloom, 2017; Bloom et al., 2020; Böing and Hünermund, 2020). Why might this be?

Well, consider that the size, diversity, and effort required of research teams to develop innovative computer chips in the year 2021 is many multiples greater than what was required in 1970. Nicholas Bloom and colleagues estimate that over *eighteen times* as many researchers are needed today to generate the innovations necessary to double computer chip density compared to the number of researchers required to do so in 1970. Considering the situation in the United States, they conclude:

> Our robust finding is that research productivity is falling sharply everywhere we look. Taking the US aggregate number as representative, research productivity falls in half every 13 years: ideas are getting harder and harder to find. Put differently, just to sustain constant growth in GDP per person, the United States must double the amount of research effort every 13 years to offset the increased difficulty of finding new ideas. Future work in the growth literature should determine how best to understand this fact. One possibility is the … "Red Queen" prediction in which we have to run faster and faster to maintain constant exponential growth.
>
> (Bloom et al., 2020, pg. 1138)

Rest assured, there are many mitigating factors here. We should not assume a necessary decline in innovation. The spread of broadband internet and literacy and tertiary education access and transportation around the world is still an ongoing project that is sure to accelerate innovation. Immigrants to new countries are far overrepresented as patent-holders and Nobel laureates (Shambaugh et al., 2017), indicating that the solution to stagnant rates of innovation is to provide opportunities to more and more people around the world to get involved in the research process. The point is that we can't simply take exponential increases in innovation for granted. The more complex society becomes, the more difficult further innovation will be, but, so too, the better groups become at thinking in complicated ways (e.g., oscillating at hard to sustain but productive tempos).

8.3.3 Fission–Fusion Rhythms

My concern is not centrally about states of fission or states of fusion (and their correlates). I am more interested in the social rhythm represented by oscillating states of fusion and fission. The habit of coming apart provides the opportunities for reflection, critical thinking, and abstraction unhindered by social norms and surveillance that can, when we come back together, lead to the sharing of new ideas and, potentially, after a long line of conjecture and institutional negotiating, the differential storing of some good ideas over others.

As you may have discerned, the ideas that I feel are most direct and central to cultural evolution are ideas about energy extraction, processing, and distribution, or, infrastructure. Changes in the energy available for individuals (literally, the calories of energy that they can consume or utilize in technologies) causes changes in their worldviews and values over time. Such changes in worldviews and values are not society-specific or really even era-specific (the "Axial Age" is proving quite silly to try and date with any exactitude). Rather, these changes in worldview and values are ongoing changes to human subjectivity, across the expanse of history, enabled by the extension of human capacities through infrastructural innovations.

Energy access, then, is not just access to food or water, but also, for example, access to gas to put in your car, heating for your home, refrigeration for food, electricity powering the computers your child uses at school, even the electricity animating the large magnetic coils circulating in the MRI machine right now at the city hospital, which you might need at a moment's notice should tragedy strike. A world with this degree of access to energy is very different than a world without. As Ronald Inglehart (2018) and others have shown, a safer more abundant world does seem to alter peoples' outlook on life and their attitudes toward others.

Recall that fission–fusion oscillation has two main structural components, which are characteristic of any wave-like phenomenon: wavelength and amplitude. The *wavelength* of fission–fusion oscillation represents the length of time between the most fused states in a given period (the crests or peaks of an oscillation wave) or the length of time between the least fused states (the troughs of an oscillation wave).

The *amplitude* of fission–fusion oscillation will also vary depending on the society, and the time frame, analyzed. But amplitude is distinct from wavelength; amplitude represents the magnitude of increase (or decrease) in how fused or fissioned groups become relative to a baseline point. If, for example, a region of a country has been continuously hard hit by natural disasters, disease, or civil war over the last 150 years, the baseline degree of fusion is likely going to be higher (as defensive responses to threats become enculturated and institutionalized) compared to a region that has experienced relatively less upheaval. Obviously, there is no perfect "starting point" at which to begin calculating such a baseline—some degree of measurement error is inevitable when studying such a complex system. And societies contain millions of these "baselines" for each different organization, institution, or city that comprises them.

Fission–fusion oscillation does not just vary in wavelength and amplitude, but also in the degree of group boundary porousness. Fission–fusion oscillation, in other words, can be more or less "open" or "closed" in its operation. It is easier to enter and exit some groups over others, and this is true for the groups we form as individuals and for the groups that form partnerships to create organizations and institutions. Many groups—such as prestigious occupational groups—have credential barriers or are associated with gatekeeping organizations that, by design, enforce and maintain group boundaries.

Not just anyone can waltz in and take on the role of brain surgeon in a hospital setting, and for good reason. Modern hospitals, occupationally, are relatively more closed systems of fission–fusion oscillation due to the credentialing and hiring process. And, where people go untreated for lack of money or health insurance, hospitals are clearly closed systems to some. But hospitals are also fairly open systems in that anyone with the means can, in principle, take advantage of their resources, anyone at all can roam the grounds and eat at the cafeteria, and increasingly larger swaths of the public are perceiving the educational opportunities available to become medical doctors themselves. Fission–fusion oscillation in organizations and institutions is not either open *or* closed but rather both in different ways.

Lastly, to underscore: the oscillating structure is not incidental. *After groups fission, they more effectively fuse; after groups fuse, they more effectively fission.* The unrestricted search for information, the freedom to blow off steam, and the opportunities to reflect provided by more fissioned periods improve groups' ability to integrate information, build emotional energy, and reach consensus when in more fused states. The interesting and adventurous weak social ties characteristic of a fissioned state help maximize the information and experience brought to strong-tie relationships characteristic of more fused states. If groups do not fuse, to some extent some of the time, fissioning will lead to isolation, depression, suicide, and aimlessness; if groups do not fission to some extent some of the time, fusion will lead to dogmatism, pluralistic ignorance, hierarchies divorced from prestige/skill, and inflexibility.

8.4 Infrastructure

Units of infrastructure and associated infrastructural systems are the "units of evolution" in cultural evolution; they are the relatively discrete, material, entities that acquire modifications and adaptations. The stored information (plans, equations, charts, diagrams, verbal models, descriptions) that help describe how to create infrastructural units (and infrastructural systems) are the "units of selection" in cultural evolution; it is the information most central to a society's capacity to extract, process, and distribute energy, and its differential retention over time influences what form secondary infrastructure (e.g., grocery stores, schools, museums), and thus the rest of the society, can take. Core infrastructure is the energetic basis for the rest of the extended phenotype of society; core infrastructure enables humans to build niches of specialized resource-providing containers—homes, schools, businesses, community centers, and everything in between.

For any unit of selection, there will be sources of variation and "forces" of selection and retention. The sources of variation in infrastructure-related information are numerous; here are four: (1) variation in the extent to which people and groups rely on their intuitions about physics or chemistry, (2) the particular dynamics of fission–fusion oscillation in a given society and the impact of this on the recombination and synthesis, or lack thereof, of ideas, (3) misunderstandings, misrememberings, or misrecordings of information (some of which may prove to be accidental improvements), and (4) various outcomes of market competition for public interest and safety.

There are also numerous forces of retention, not just selection, influencing which infrastructure-related information—from sketched plans to complex charts and diagrams to mathematical principles and equations—is likely to be retained.

Some are obvious. We can presume that the infrastructure-related information that seemed better able to enhance the probability of survival would be selectively retained. This doesn't mean, at all, that *actually* survival-enhancing information is *always* retained. On the contrary, throughout history up to the present minute, many unhelpful or inefficient design plans are selectively stored or retained in memory or on paper or in electronic databases. This nonoptimal information then becomes, once constructed materially, part of the (temporary) modification of infrastructural units. So, the claim is not that people always selectively retain adaptive engineering information; rather, the claim is that information that *appears to be* capable of informing the construction of efficient, productive, reliable, safe, accessible, and sustainable infrastructure will *tend to be* selectively retained over information that appears to be less capable of generating infrastructure with those qualities.

This means, for example, that the degree to which infrastructural units are perceived to (1) easily corrode, erode, or degrade given climate conditions, (2) be expensive or associated with undesired externalities, (3) adequately satisfy public/consumer demand and usage, (4) be easy as opposed to difficult to construct (in terms of safety, time, or labor), (5) have originated with creators who are symbolically similar or familiar to oneself, and, of course, (6) the degree to which the new engineering idea is considered attractive or elegant (aesthetic concerns are always in the background) will all be forces of selection and retention altering the potential infrastructural information that is likely to be stored in each generation.

It might need to be said as regards (3) above that, especially before modern physics or computer simulation models existed, the trial and error of engineering experience was the only guide as to which forms of infrastructure were most useful. This could be hazardous to say the least. Obviously, core infrastructural breakdowns can be lethal to social coordination and collective living, but so too can unnecessary or inefficient modifications. We should not overestimate peoples' ability to accurately perceive the efficiency, productivity, reliability, safety, or sustainability of the infrastructure they rely on.

How an innovation is discussed or presented is also an important factor determining the likelihood of adoption and retention. The more ideas are visualized in diagrams or charts (as opposed to only expressed verbally), the easier the ideas will be for others to conceptualize. Good (that is to say, easily understood) engineers use diagrams, make mechanistic inferences, frequently update their sketches and models, and, critically, take into account the current knowledge, perceived problems, and likely intuitions of those they are communicating with. In short, good engineers are skilled at taking the perspective of others (Tversky, 2019).

There is another point I should reiterate: infrastructure is layered. Primary infrastructure, like electrical systems, waste treatment systems, and roadways are composed of terminal units, things like power lines, water pipes, steam turbines, transformers, electric motors, or, in the case of roads, specifically sized sheets of bitumen or macadam. Primary infrastructure provides the energy for the potential emergence of secondary forms of infrastructure that are more removed from survival but also more oriented toward self-actualization, self-expression, and self-exploration—things like schools, community centers, museums, national parks, and research centers.

Distinctions between primary and secondary infrastructure are, in many cases, distinctions between survival and self-actualization. Survival and self-actualization are not a dichotomy, just a relative difference in emphasis. Irrigation systems are more proximate to survival than are grocery stores, fire departments, or hospitals (which rely on irrigation systems), but fire departments, grocery stores, and hospitals are more proximate to survival than are research centers, schools, or museums (which rely on the comfort and survival-security granted by fire departments, grocery stores, hospitals, and so on). Primary infrastructure contributes to secondary infrastructure and vice versa: without primary infrastructure, people would have trouble surviving together, but without secondary infrastructure, adaptation and innovation would slow, leading to failed—or less optimal—responses to social and natural crises.

What distinguishes infrastructure from tools, in my conceptualization, is the sharedness in construction and usage. I can buy a rake, use a rake and lend it to my neighbor who has too many leaves on their own lawn. A rake is a tool, not because *only one* person can ever use it, but rather, because *sharedness* is limited by virtue of the goal of the construction of the tool: the point of creating the rake was for one person to use it at a time while cleaning up leaves.

Infrastructure might be regarded as a tool, at least in how most people use it. After all, having a functioning toilet sure is better than not having one, and only one person at a time can use any given toilet (as far as I know!). But unlike the rake example, a toilet, sink, electrical outlet, and heater are all connected to a more widely accessible infrastructural system—composed of generators linked to gas lines or electrical lines and treatment plants linked to water lines—which serve, in principle, entire communities of people simultaneously. And recall that the important sense of "sharedness" regarding infrastructure derives from the centralized coordination necessary for financing, building, maintenance, and usage.

I'd like to share a revealing anecdote from the anthropologist Robert Kelly regarding the rapid pace of innovation that emerged sometime between 1500 and 1600 CE:

> A future archaeologist could … calculate that the speed of change in material culture vastly increased after [about 1500 CE]. Think, for example, of how much change occurred in the lives of Paleolithic hunter-gatherers between 25,500 and 25,000 [BCE]—comparatively speaking, none. But think of the difference between 1500 [CE] and today. In fact, think of the difference between just the early twentieth and the early twenty-first centuries.
>
> When my father was born in 1925 in Pawtucket, Rhode Island, the cool technology was the zipper (invented in 1913). Television and talking movies appeared when he was two years old, penicillin when he was three. His father ferried mail between Pawtucket and Boston in a biplane. My father's childhood icebox was, in fact, kept cold by ice, brought to his house by horse and wagon. He remembers hand-cranking a Model A. And yet he flew on the Concorde and saw men walk on the moon.
>
> Computers didn't exist when my father was born; in fact, vacuum tubes (1910) were the latest technology, later replaced by transistors (1947), my generation's cool technology, which was in turn replaced by microchips. In graduate school I wrote computer programs using punch cards, and I thought an IBM Selectric typewriter was all the technology I would ever need. I remember life before the internet and cell phones and Apple and the "Cloud"—and I'm not that old! We take for granted that technology changes every six months, yet such rapid change is a characteristic of only this era in history.
>
> Kelly (2016, pg. 105)

Without describing it explicitly, each of these innovations described by Kelly had its origins determined, first, by innovations in infrastructure. The infrastructure underneath our feet and above our heads is so utterly influential to our capacities as human beings; infrastructure extends the capacities of our nervous system. This historically unprecedented pace of innovation is only recognizable to us, or capable of being appreciated by us, when we are not utterly taking it for granted and complaining about the vicissitudes of our own imperfect existence.

Once we account for the taken-for-granted cumulative infrastructural modifications that have made our modern world, we ought to regard cities as the next unsung hero of this precarious and incomplete advancement. When the population of a city doubles, the productivity of its economy grows by 115% to 130%—far more than would be expected presuming linear increases in productivity (Pan et al., 2013). Cities, for all of their disorder and disease (which, I should say, is not a given, and has lessened over time), are also the freest, most porous containers for open-system fission–fusion oscillation. Cities are more than just the people in them—the creativity of cities emerges from the relationships *between* people, and this is why linear increases in population produce superlinear increases in innovation and cultural complexity. Cities are becoming more commonplace, and larger, with time. With this growth of cities will come an increased pace of a society's metabolism and, thus, its oscillatory complexity.

8.5 Intuition and Wisdom

The human brain produces rapid intuitions in order to appraise people, groups, objects, environments, and relationships (see Evans, 2008; Lizardo et al., 2016; Pennycook, 2017; Leschziner, 2019). Animals, groups, objects, environments, and relationships are all things brains (and their precursors, nerve nets) have been adapting to for at least hundreds of millions of years. As a result, we can now make rapid, if sometimes flawed, snap judgments about all sorts of things.

The intuitions humans have about the world around them are, in total, complex and often contradictory (Shtulman, 2017; Boyer, 2018). Intuitions are not simply errors of reasoning or inference; certainly, they can be wrong or misleading, but they are not necessarily so. Some people's intuitions will be more accurate than others; those intuitions, for example, which are generated after extensive experience or training are often more accurate than the intuitions of novices. Research shows, for example, that individuals in professions where performance feedback is more common develop more accurate intuitions about their work compared to professions where performance feedback is less common (e.g., Shanteau, 1992).

Our intuitions about the social world are a heuristic, a scaffolding, to frame our initial responses to our experiences. When we see someone displaying lavish wealth, we're liable to conclude that such wealth was, somehow someway, stolen from others (*power/wealth is like a substance that is gained by some and thus lost by other in zero-sum fashion*). When we meet someone who wears something we've never seen, our intuition is that they must be wearing something representative of their "group" (*groups are like big people: if a person dresses this way, their group must dress this way*), despite the fact that only some fraction of people wearing that garment share other important similarities.

These are what we might call "sociological intuitions." There is almost no research on the contours of these intuitions or their degree of variation across people and across groups. As a result, much of my sketch in this book is speculative, though I'm relying on the work that does exist. I'm happy to be shown to be wrong in my sketches; I'd just like to see more work on the topic.

There are, however, other intuitions people seem to have that are very important for our discussion of infrastructure, in particular, peoples' intuitions about physics. The Accademia Del Cimento, or the Academy of Trials/Experiments, was founded in Florence, Italy, in 1657 for the purpose of, among other things, exploring how and why liquids expand upon freezing, why solids seem to expand when heated, and how heat and cold impacted pressure (Shtulman, 2017). These were topics that were little understood, at least in Europe at the time. Experimenters at this academy dumped containers of different liquids (from vinegar to water to wine) into freezing water to measure their expansion and, also, heated different materials to measure their expansion.

But these, and other, experimenters were fighting against stubborn intuitions about how the natural world operated. One intuition they had when putting various liquids into freezing water was that "coldness" was being transferred to the contents of the containers through the medium of the water. For this reason, they measured the temperature of the liquid in the container by inserting a thermometer into the ice bath next to the container (to capture the rushing "coldness"), instead of in the container itself (where the actual temperature change was occurring). These early physicists did not realize that, if anything, the room temperature of the liquid in the container would *raise* the temperature of the surrounding water (once any ice had melted). They did not realize that "coldness" was not a separate entity from heat but, rather, simply the lack of heat.

How many other examples might be given? It was not terribly obvious to anyone that matter was composed of particles (excepting, to some extent, ancient Greek atomists) or that, for example, metals of all kinds could be heated into liquids and combined with one another, increasing their strength and resistance. It was also not obvious to anyone that something like copper and saline could conduct electricity, or, indeed, what electricity was!

Regardless, progress in understanding has been made, and this progress, in almost every instance, represented an updating and refining of our intuitions about each other, what the world is, and how the world works. Open-system fission–fusion oscillation is a universal acid that dissolves our inaccurate intuitions about each other, and about the physical world, enabling and accelerating infrastructural innovation and, thus, cultural evolution. While our intuitions about the social and physical world are not always wrong, they very, very often are, and false beliefs about people limit our willingness to interact with one another (i.e., the porousness of our group boundaries), while false beliefs about the physical world limit our ability to understand how best to extract, process, and distribute energy. Put simply: our social intuitions can limit our ability to learn from one another, while our physical intuitions can limit our ability to understand how best to extract, process, and distribute energy; combined, our intuitions can lock us into a solipsistic, socially homogeneous, cage of deprivation and confusion.

The intuitions I've discussed in this book are only some of our intuitions. And though I say "our," these intuitions are going to vary person to person, occupation to occupation, society to society. But I still say "our" because I hope to emphasize our general proneness to such intuitions, even if this proneness varies. Our intuitions, sociological and physical, become more of a burden on us especially as our societies grow in size and density and as we must interact with more, different, people with more needs.

The cultural evolution of infrastructure—something all societies have taken part in—affords opportunities to moderate, or adjust, our intuitions about both the physical and social world. Innovations in the efficiency, productivity, or accessibility of primary infrastructure increases life expectancy and decreases absolute deprivation and threat. This provides people more opportunities to reflect critically on their intuitions, if for no other reason than they are (even if only slightly) less panicked about their own survival. Secondary infrastructure does much the same; secondary infrastructure leverages the energy provided by core infrastructure to create survival-enhancing entities like hospitals (for illness), social services offices (for employment), grocery stores (for food), and public transit.

And then there are the "cultural assemblages" most distant from absolute deprivation or immediate survival, things like schools, universities, coffee shops, malls, museums, think tanks, theaters, and gyms. Though these entities cater to concerns rather distant from those suffering absolute deprivation, this does not mean they are unrelated to it. Quite the opposite.

Secondary infrastructure might take the form of a heated, electrically wired building with fresh water for formal education focused on understanding our intuitions about physics (as it does in the contemporary K–12 system used in many countries). Or perhaps it takes the form of a similar building for recreation and self-actualization (as with museums, theaters, and gyms). Secondary infrastructures, again, are not just sites for concerted social learning, but are, rather more broadly, sites for potentially open-system fission–fusion oscillation oriented toward goals of self-discovery, self-actualization, creativity, or innovation.

I'll end with the simplest way to make my case. I think open-system fission–fusion oscillation produces what we might call "wisdom" at the group level, if we define "wisdom" as the careful, reflective, application of reason and experience.

What are the components of "wisdom" at the individual level? According to Igor Grossman's (2017) review of the research, wisdom involves a tendency toward (1) intellectual humility, (2) recognition of uncertainty/change, (3) integration of others' perspectives, (4) consideration of the broader context outside of the immediate issue at hand, and (5) a willingness to compromise. Grossman also finds that experiencing adversity in life can lead to greater wisdom, as defined above.

I suggest that the same is true of a relatively porous oscillating fission–fusion system. For example, imagine a working group that meets (fuses to some extent) three days a week and fissions into subgroups or into independent individuals going their own way all other times. Now, suppose that the rules determining who can join this group are flexible, arranged around a core interest or expertise, but open with regard to the class background, race/ethnicity, sex, and political or religious beliefs of members. Imagine, also, that rates of upward mobility in the larger society are sufficient to enable the circulation of a wide variety of individuals into and out of group membership. Assuming competent leadership (as discussed above), this is a group equipped to generate wisdom. Depending on the composition of the group, and their goals, perhaps meeting three days a week is too much, and leads to conflict or rising tensions; perhaps it is too little, and people forget the nuances of their shared goals. But, surely, some optimal range of (potentially implicit) meeting schedules exists, albeit calibrated to the goals at hand and to the on-average needs of members.

To be wise is to be helpful under conditions of uncertainty. I think open-system fission–fusion oscillation, calibrated in amplitude and wavelength according to group composition, external circumstances, and group goals, is a key mechanism for the aggregation of ideas and the curation of innovations from this aggregation. It is not only individuals who can be wise, then, but groups too. Our intuitions can influence our initial frame of reference, but our discussions and conversations with others, whose experiences are slightly (or significantly) different from our own, is our collective means of seeing more clearly beyond these intuitions.

References

Abbink, K., and G. Doğan. "How to Choose Your Victim." *Games and Economic Behavior* 113 (2019): 482–496.

Abellán, J. "*Water Supply and Sanitation Services in Modern Europe: Developments in 19th–20th Centuries.*" Paper presented at the Twelfth International Congress of the Spanish Association of Economic History, University of Salamanca, Spain, September 6–9, 2017.

Aime, F., S. Humphrey, D. S. DeRue, and J. B. Paul. "The Riddle of Heterarchy: Power Transitions in Cross-Functional Teams." *Academy of Management Journal* 57, no. 2 (2014): 327–352.

Aktas, M., M. J. Gelfand, and P. J. Hanges. "Cultural Tightness-Looseness and Perceptions of Effective Leadership." *Journal of Cross-Cultural Psychology* 47, no. 2 (2016): 294–309.

Allport, G. W. *The Nature of Prejudice.* Cambridge, MA: Addison-Wesley, 1954.

Amos, W., and J. I. Hoffman. "Evidence that Two Main Bottleneck Events Shaped Modern Human Genetic Diversity." *Proceedings of the Royal Society B: Biological Sciences* 277, no. 1678 (2010): 131–137.

Andersson, C., and P. Törnberg. "Toward a Macroevolutionary Theory of Human Evolution: The Social Protocell." *Biological Theory* 14, no. 2 (2019): 86–102.

Antón, S. C., H. G. Taboada, E. R. Middleton, C. W. Rainwater, A. B. Taylor, T. R. Turner, J. E. Turnquist, K. J. Weinstein, and S. A. Williams. "Morphological Variation in Homo Erectus and the Origins of Development Plasticity." *Philosophical Transactions of the Royal Society B: Biological Sciences* 371, no. 1698 (2016): 20150236.

Apicella, C. L. "Upper-Body Strength Predicts Hunting Reputation and Reproductive Success in Hadza Hunter-Gatherers." *Evolution and Human Behavior* 35, no. 6 (2014): 508–518.

Apicella, C. L., F. W. Marlowe, J. H. Fowler, and N. A. Christakis. "Social Networks and Cooperation in Hunter-Gatherers." *Nature* 481, no. 7382 (2012): 497–501.

Aral, S., and M. Van Alstyne. "The Diversity-Bandwidth Trade-Off." *American Journal of Sociology* 117, no. 1 (2011): 90–171.

Aubert, M., R. Lebe, A. A. Oktaviana, M. Tang, B. Burhan, A. Jusdi, B. Hakim, J. X. Zhao, I. M. Geria, P. H. Sulistyarto, and R. Sardi. "Earliest Hunting Scene in Prehistoric Art." *Nature* 576, no. 7787 (2019): 442–445.

Aubet, M. E. *The Phoenician and the West: Politics, Colonies and Trade.* Cambridge: Cambridge University Press, 1993.

Audet, J. N. "Neurobiological and Ecological Correlates of Avian Innovation." *Integrative and Comparative Biology* 60, no. 4 (2020): 955–966.

Aureli, F., C. M. Schaffner, C. Boesch, S. K. Bearder, J. Call, C. A. Chapman, R. C. Connor, A. Di Fiore, R. I. M. Dunbar, S. P. Henzi, K. Holekamp, A. H. Korstjens, R. Layton, P. Lee, J. Lehmann, J. H. Manson, G. Ramos-Fernandez, K. B. Strier, and C. P. van Schaik. "Fission-Fusion Dynamics: New Research Frameworks." *Current Anthropology* 49, no. 4 (2008): 627–654.

Babich, A., and D. Senk. "Coke in the Iron and Steel Industry." In *New Trends in Coal Conversion Combustion, Gasification, Emissions, and Coking*, edited by I. Suárez-Ruiz, M. A. Diez, and F. Rubiera, 367–404. Duxford, UK: Woodhead Publishing, 2019.

Bader, O. "'Being in a Group': The Emotional Scaffolding of the Evolution of Collective Intentionality." In *Landscapes of Collectivity in the Life Sciences*, edited by B. Snait, E. L. Gissis, and S. Ayelet, 155–168. Cambridge, MA: MIT Press, 2017.

Bagci, S. C., Z. E. Piyale, E. Sen, and O. Yildirim. "Beyond Shifting Intergroup Attitudes: Intergroup Contact's Association with Socio-Cognitive Skills and Group-Based Ideologies." *Journal of Theoretical Social Psychology* 3, no. 3 (2019): 176–188.

Bain, N., and D. Bartolo. "Dynamic Response and Hydrodynamics of Polarized Crowds." *Science* 363, no. 6422 (2019): 46–49.

Bakken, B. *Crime and the Chinese Dream.* Hong Kong: Hong Kong University Press, 2018.

Balaresque, P., N. Poulet, S. Cussat-Blanc, P. Gerard, L. Quintana-Murci, E. Heyer, and M. A. Jobling. "Y-Chromosome Descent Clusters and Male Differential Reproductive Success: Young Lineage Expansions Dominate Asian Pastoral Nomadic Populations." *European Journal of Human Genetics* 3, no. 10 (2015): 1413–1422.

Balazs, C. L., R. Morello-Frosch, A. E. Hubbard, and I. Ray. "Environmental Justice Implications of Arsenic Contamination in California's San Joaquin Valley: A Cross-Sectional Cluster Design Examining Exposure and Compliance in Community Drinking Water Systems." *Environmental Health* 11, no. 1 (2012): 84–96.

Barbujani, G., S. Ghirotto, and F. Tassi. "Nine Things to Remember about Human Genome Diversity." *Tissue Antigens* 82, no. 3 (2013): 155–164.

Barcus, C. U. "What Elephant Calls Mean: A User's Guide." *NationalGeographic.org.* Retrieved from 'https://www.nationalgeographic.com/news/2014/5/what-elephant-calls-mean/', 2014.

Bastardoz, N., and M. Van Vugt. "The Nature of Followership: Evolutionary Analysis and Review." *The Leadership Quarterly* 30, no. 1 (2019): 81–95.

Baumard, N. "Psychological Origins of the Industrial Revolution." *Behavioral and Brain Sciences* 42, e189 (2019): 1–63.

Baumeister, R. F., E. Bratslavsky, C. Finkenauer, and K. D. Vohs. "Bad Is Stronger than Good." *Review of General Psychology* 5, no. 4 (2001): 323–370.

Bechara, A., H. Damasio, and A. R. Damasio. "Emotion, Decision Making and the Orbitofrontal Cortex." *Cerebral Cortex* 10, no. 3 (2000): 295–307.

Bellah, R. N., R. Madsen, W. Sullivan, A. Swidler, and S. M. Tipton. *Habits of the Heart: Middle America Observed*. London: Hutchinson, 1985.

Belletier, C., A. Normand, and P. Huguet. "Social-Facilitation-and-Impairment Effects: From Motivation to Cognition and the Social Brain." *Current Directions in Psychological Science* 28, no. 3 (2019): 260–265.

Ben-Dor, M. "How Carnivorous Are We? The Implications for Protein Consumption." *Journal of Evolution and Health: An Ancestral Health Society Publication* 3, no. 1 (2018): 1–9.

Bentley, G., and R. Mace, (eds.). *Substitute Parents: Biological and Social Perspectives on Alloparenting in Human Societies*. New York: Berghahn Books, 2012.

Berger, P. L., B. Berger, and H. Kellner. *The Homeless Mind*. London: Pelican Books, 1974.

Berger, J., and D. G. Wagner. "Expectation States Theory." In *The Blackwell Encyclopedia of Sociology*, edited by G. Ritzer, 1–5. Malden, MA: Blackwell, 2016.

Bertman, S. *Handbook to Life in Ancient Mesopotamia*. New York: Oxford University Press, 2005.

Bettencourt, L. M., J. Lobo, D. Helbing, C. Kühnert, and G. B. West. "Growth, Innovation, Scaling, and the Pace of Life in Cities." *Proceedings of the National Academy of Sciences* 104, no. 17 (2007): 7301–7306.

Bettencourt, L. M., and G. West. "A Unified Theory of Urban Living." *Nature* 467, no. 7318 (2010): 912–913.

Betzig, L. "Eurosociality: From the First Foragers to the First States." *Human Nature* 25, no. 1 (2014): 1–5.

Bian, L., S. Sloane, and R. Baillargeon. "Infants Expect Ingroup Support to Override Fairness When Resources Are Limited." *Proceedings of the National Academy of Sciences* 115, no. 11 (2018): 2705–2710.

Bidga, R. J. "Consider Fenton Chemistry for Wastewater Treatment. " *Chemical Engineering Progress* 91, no. 12 (1995): 62066.

Blanco, F. "Cognitive Bias." In *Encyclopedia of Animal Cognition and Behavior*, edited by J. Vonk and T. Shackelford, Vol. 1–6. New York: Springer, 2017.

Blau, P. M. *Exchange and Power in Social Life*. Piscataway, NJ: Transaction Publishers, 1986.

Blau, P. M. *Structural Contexts of Opportunities*. Chicago: University of Chicago Press, 1994.

Blau, P. M., and J. E. Schwartz. *Crosscutting Social Circles: Testing a Macrostructural Theory of Intergroup Relations*. Piscataway, NJ: Transaction Publishers, 1997.

Bloom, N., C. I. Jones, J. Van Reenen, and M. Webb. "Are Ideas Getting Harder to Find?" *American Economic Review* 110, no. 4 (2020): 1104–1144.

Bloom, P. *Against Empathy: The Case for Rational Compassion*. New York: Random House, 2017.

Bloom, P. *Just Babies: The Origins of Good and Evil*. New York: Broadway Books, 2013.

Bloom, P., and D. S. Weisberg. "Childhood Origins of Adult Resistance to Science." *Science* 16, no. 5827 (2007): 996–997.

Boehm, C. "Ancestral Hierarchy and Conflict." *Science* 336, no. 6083 (2012): 844–847.

Boehm, C. *Hierarchy in the Forest: The Evolution of Egalitarian Behavior*. Cambridge, MA: Harvard University Press, 1999.

Boehm, C. *Moral Origins: The Evolution of Virtue, Altruism, and Shame*. New York: Basic Books, 2012.

Bogin, B., J. Bragg, and C. Kuzawa. "Humans Are Not Cooperative Breeders but Practice Biocultural Reproduction." *Annals of Human Biology* 41, no. 4 (2014): 368–380.

Böing, P., and O. Hünermaud. "A Global Decline in Research Productivity? Evidence from China and Germany." *Economics Letters* 197, no. 109646 (2020).

Bonetto, E., N. Pichot, J. B. Pavani, and J. Adam-Troïan. "The Paradox of Creativity." *New Ideas in Psychology* 60, no. 100820 (2021): 1–7.

Borges, J. L. *Other Inquisitions 1937–1952*. New York: Washington Square Press, 1966.

Bourdieu, P. *Distinction: A Social Critique of the Judgement of Taste*. London: Sage, 1984.

Bourdieu, P. *Reproduction in Education, Society and Culture*. London: Sage, 1977.

Bourdieu, P. "Structures, Habitus, Practices." In *The Logic of Practice*, translated by R. Nice, 52–65. Stanford, CA: Stanford University Press, [1980] 1990.

Boyd, R., and P. J. Richerson. *The Origin and Evolution of Cultures*. New York: Oxford University Press, 2005.

Boyer, P. *Minds Make Societies: How Cognition Explains the World Humans Create*. New Haven, CT: Yale University Press, 2018.

Boyer, P., R. Firat, and F. van Leeuwen. "Safety, Threat, and Stress in Intergroup Relations: A Coalitional Index Model." *Perspectives on Psychological Science* 10, no. 4 (2015): 434–450.

Boyer, P., and M. B. Petersen. "Folk-Economic Beliefs: An Evolutionary Cognitive Model." *Behavioral and Brain Sciences* 41 (2018): e158.

Boyette, A. H., and B. S. Hewlett. "Teaching in Hunter-Gatherers." *Review of Philosophy and Psychology* 9, no. 4 (2018): 771–797.

Brent, L. J., D. W. Franks, E. A. Foster, K. C. Balcomb, M. A. Cant, and D. P. Croft. "Ecological Knowledge, Leadership, and the Evolution of Menopause in Killer Whales." *Current Biology* 25, no. 6 (2015): 746–750.

Brewer, M. B. "The Psychology of Prejudice: Ingroup Love and Outgroup Hate?" *Journal of Social Issues* 55, no. 3 (1999): 429–444.

Briffa, M., and S. M. Lane. "The Role of Skill in Animal Contests: A Neglected Component of Fighting Ability." *Proceedings of the Royal Society B: Biological Sciences* 284, no. 1863 (2017): 20171596.

Bronowski, J. *Science and Human Values*. New York: Faber & Faber, [1958] 2011.

Brooks, A. S., J. E. Yellen, R. Potts, A. K. Behrensmeyer, A. L. Deino, D. E. Leslie, S. H. Ambrose, J. R. Ferguson, F. d'Errico, A. M. Zipkin, S. Whittaker, J. Post, E. G. Veatch, K. Foecke, and J. B. Clark. "Long-Distance Stone Transport and Pigment Use in the Earliest Middle Stone Age." *Science* 360, no. 6384 (2018): 90–94.

Brown, D. E. *Human Universals*. New York: McGraw-Hill, 1991.

Brown, D. E. "Human Universals and their Implications." In *Being Humans: Anthropological Universality and Particularly in Transdisciplinary Perspectives*, edited by N. Roughley, 156–174. Berlin: De Gruyter, 2020.

Brown, D. E. "Human Universals, Human Nature Human Culture." *Daedalus* 133, no. 4 (2004): 47–54.

Brown, S. "Are Music and Language Homologues?" *Annals of the New York Academy of Sciences* 930, no. 1 (2001): 372–374.

Bruce, S. *Secularization: In Defence of an Unfashionable Theory*. Oxford: Oxford University Press, 2011.

Buckels, E. E., and P. D. Trapnell. "Disgust Facilitates Outgroup Dehumanization." *Group Processes & Intergroup Relations* 16, no. 6 (2013): 771–780.

Bureau of Labor Statistics. "Table 2.1 Employment by Major Industry Sectors." *U. S. Department of Labor*. Retrieved from https://www.bls.gov/emp/tables/employment-by-major-industry-sector.htm, 2020.

Bureau of Transportation Statistics. "Table 3–1 An Overview of the Passenger Transportation System, 2005 v. 2011." *US Department of Transportation*. Retrieved from https://www.bts.gov/archive/publications/passenger_travel/chapter3/table3-1, 2014.

Burian, S., and F. Edwards. "Historical Perspectives of Urban Drainage." In *Global Solutions for Urban Drainage*, edited by E. W. Strecker and W. C. Huber, 1–16. Reston, VA: Society of Civil Engineers, 2002.

Burt, R. "Structural Holes and Good Ideas." *American Journal of Sociology* 110, no. 2 (2004): 349–399.

Burt, R. *Structural Holes: The Social Structure of Competition*. Cambridge, MA: Harvard University Press, 1992.

Buss, L. W. *The Evolution of Individuality*. Princeton, NJ: Princeton University Press, 1987.

Calcott, B., and K. Sterelny. *The Major Transitions in Evolution Revisited*. Cambridge, MA: MIT Press, 2011.

Campbell, M. C., and S. A. Tishkoff. "African Genetic Diversity: Implications for Human Demographic History, Modern Human Origins, and Complex Disease Mapping." *Annual Review of Genomics and Human Genetics* 9 (2008): 403–433.

Carey, S. "Where Our Number Concepts Come From." *Journal of Philosophy* 106, no. 4 (2009): 220–254.

Carr, E. W., P. Winkielman, and C. Oveis. "Transforming the Mirror: Power Fundamentally Changes Facial Responding to Emotional Expressions." *Journal of Experimental Psychology: General* 143, no. 3 (2014): 997–1003.

Casari, M, and C. Tagliapietra. "Group Size in Social-Ecological Systems." *Proceedings of the National Academy of Sciences* 115, no. 11 (2018): 2728–2733.

Castellanos, C. B. "World-Systems Theory." In *The International Encyclopedia of Anthropology*, edited by H. Callan, 1–9. Hoboken, NJ: John Wiley & Sons, 2018.

Chanson, H. "Hydraulics of Roman Aqueducts: Steep Chites, Cascades, and Dropshafts." *American Journal of Archaeology* 104, no. 1 (2000): 47–72.

Charbonnier, J. "The Ethnoarchaeology of Ganāt Systems: A Comparative Study of Water-Sharing Practices in the Old World." *Water History* 10, no. 1 (2018): 53–71.

Charbonnier, J., and K. Hopper. "The Qanāt: A Multidisciplinary and Diachronic Approach to the Study of Groundwater Catchment Systems in Archaeology." *Water History* 10, no. 1 (2018): 3–11.

Chatham-Stephens, K., J. Caravanos, B. Ericson, J. Sunga-Amparo, B. Susilorini, P. Sharma, P. J. Landrigan, and R. Fuller. "Burden of Disease from Toxic Waste

Site in India, Indonesia, and the Phillippines in 2010." *Environmental Health Perspectives* 121, no. 7 (2013): 791–796.

Cheng, J., J. Liu, and J. Wang. "Domestic Migration. Home Rentals, and Crime Rates in China." *Journal of Chinese Sociology* 4, no. 1 (2017): 1–21.

Chi, M. T. "Commonsense Conceptions of Emergent Processes: Why Some Misconceptions Are Robust." *Journal of the Learning Sciences* 14, no. 2 (2005): 161–199.

Chi, M. T., R. D. Roscoe, J. D. Slotta, M. Roy, and C. C. Chase. "Misconceived Casual Explanations for Emergent Processes." *Cognitive Sciences* 36, no. 1 (2012): 1–61.

Chiu, L., and S. F. Gilbert. "The Birth of the Holobiont: Multi-Species Birthing through Mutual Scaffolding and Niche Construction." *Biosemiotics* 8, no. 2 (2015): 191–210.

Chopra, S., M. H. Tessler, and N. D. Goodman. "*The First Crank of the Cultural Ratchet: Learning and Transmitting Concepts Through Language.*" Paper presented at the Proceedings of the 41st Annual Meeting of the Cognitive Science Society, Montreal, CA, July 24–27, 2019.

Chorley, G. P. H. "The Agricultural Revolution in Northern Europe, 1750–1880: Nitrogen, Legumes, and Crop Productivity." *Economic History Review* 34, no. 1 (1981): 71–93.

Chudek, M., R. McNamara, S. Burch, P. Bloom, and J. Henrich. "Developmental and Cross-Cultural Evidence for Intuitive Dualism." *Psychological Science* 20 (2013): 1–19.

Churchland, P. S. *Braintrust: What Neuroscience Tells Us about Morality*. Princeton, NJ: Princeton University Press, 2011.

Clare, D. D., and T. R. Levine. "Documenting the Truth-Default: The Low Frequency of Spontaneous Unprompted Veracity Assessments in Deception Detection." *Human Communication Research* 45, no. 3 (2019): 286–308.

Clark, C. J., B. S. Liu, B. M. Winegard, and P. H. Ditto. "Tribalism Is Human Nature." *Current Directions in Psychological Science* 28, no. 6 (2019): 587–592.

Clark, C. J., and B. M. Winegard. "Tribalism in War and Peace: The Nature and Evolution of Ideological Epistemology and Its Significance for Modern Social Science." *Psychological Inquiry* 31, no. 1 (2020): 1–22.

Clarke, E. "Origins of Evolutionary Transitions." *Journal of Biosciences* 39, no. 2 (2014): 303–317.

Cline, E. H. *1177 BC: The Year Civilization Collapsed*. Princeton, NJ: Princeton University Press, 2014.

Cline, E. H. *Three Stones Make a Wall: The Story of Archaeology*. Princeton, NJ: Princeton University Press, 2017.

Crespi, B. J., and D. Yanega. "The Definition of Eusociality." *Behavioral Ecology* 6, no. 1 (1995): 109–115.

Crespi, B. J. "The Insectan Apes." *Human Nature* 25, no. 1 (2014): 6–27.

Coe, L. *Telegraph—A History of Morse's Invention and Its Predecessors in the United States*. Jefferson, NC: McFarland & Company, 2003.

Cohn, J. A. *The Grid: A Biography of an American Technology*. Cambridge, MA: MIT Press, 2018.

Cole, B. M., and D. Chandler. "A Model of Competitive Impression Management: Edison versus Westinghouse in the War of the Currents." *Administrative Science Quarterly* 64, no. 4 (2019): 1020–1063.

Collins, R. *Conflict Sociology: A Sociological Classic Updated.* Abridged and edited by S. K. Sanderson. New York: Routledge, 2016.

Collins, R. *Interaction Ritual Chains.* Princeton, NJ: Princeton University Press, 2004.

Collins, R. "Market Dynamics as the Engine of Historical Change." *Sociological Theory* 8, no. 2 (1990): 111–135.

Comte, A. "The Social Aspect of Positivism as Shown by Its Connection with the General Revolutionary Movement of Western Europe." In *Auguste Comte and Positivism: The Essential Writings*, edited by G. Lenzer, 334–347. New York: Harper & Row ([1851–1854] 1975a).

Comte, A. "Conclusion: The Religion of Humanity." In *Auguste Comte and Positivism: The Essential Writings*, edited by G. Lenzer, 381–389. New York: Harper & Row ([1851–1854] 1975b).

Comte, A. "The Positive Theory of the Family." In *Auguste Comte and Positivism: The Essential Writings*, edited by G. Lenzer, 413–415. New York: Harper & Row ([1851–1854] 1975c).

Comte, A. "Theory of Social Organization." In *Auguste Comte and Positivism: The Essential Writings*, edited by G. Lenzer, 429–436. New York: Harper & Row ([1851–1854] 1975d).

Conway, G. L., A. Zubrod, and L. Chan. "The Paradox of the Tribal Equalitarian." *Psychological Inquiry* 31, no. 1 (2020): 48–52.

Cooper, J. "Statistical Report 2019." *FuelsEurope.* Retrieved from https://www.fueIseurope.eu/wp-content/uploads/FuelsEurope-Statistical-Report-2019-2.pdf, 2019.

Correll, S. J., and C. L. Ridgeway. "Expectation States Theory." In *Handbook of Social Psychology*, edited by J. Delamater, 29–51. Boston, MA: Springer, 2006.

Coser, L. *The Functions of Social Conflict.* Glencoe, IL: The Free Press, 1956.

Curry, O. S., M. J. Chesters, and C. J. Van Lissa. "Mapping Morality with a Compass: Testing the Theory of 'Morality-as-Cooperation' with a New Questionnaire." *Journal of Research in Personality* 78 (2019): 106–124.

Curry, O. S., D. Hare, C. Hepburn, D. D. Johnson, M. D. Buhrmester, H. Whitehouse, and D. W. McDonald. "Cooperative Conservation: Seven Ways to Save the World." *Conservation Science and Practice* 2, no. 1 (2020): e123.

Crawford, L. E., L. E. Knouse, M. Kent, D. Vavra, O. Harding, D. LeServe, N. Fox, X. Hu, P . Li, C. Glory, and K. G. Lambert. "Enriched Environment Exposure Accelerates Rodent Driving Skills." *Behavioural Brain Research* 378 (2020): 112309.

Damasio, A. R. "Emotion and the Human Brain." *Annals of the New York Academy of Sciences* 935, no. 1 (2001): 101–106.

Daniels, S. E., R. E. Fanelli, A. Gilbert, and S. Benson-Amram. "Behavioral Flexibility of a Generalist Carnivore." *Animal Cognition* 22, no. 3 (2019): 387–396.

David, A. R. *The Pyramid Builders of Ancient Egypt: A Modern Investigation of Pharaoh's Workforce.* New York: Routledge, 1997.

Davis, M. *Planet of Slums.* London: Verso, 2006.

Dawkins, R. "The Descent of Edward Wilson." *Prospect Magazine*, June 2012, 1–59.

Dean, L. G., R. L. Kendal, S. J. Schapiro, B. Thierry, and K. N. Laland. "Identification of the Social and Cognitive Processes Underlying Human Cumulative Culture." *Science* 335, no. 6072 (2012): 1114–1118.

De Beaune, S. A., and R. White. "Ice Age Lamps." *Scientific American* 268, no. 3 (1993): 108–113.

De Feo, G., G. Antoniou, H. F. Fardin, F. El-Gohary, X. Y. Zheng, I. Reklaityte, D. Butler, S. Yannopoulos, and A. N. Angelakis. "The Historical Development of Sewers Worldwide." *Sustainability* 6, no. 6 (2014): 3936–3974.

Delagnes, A., P. Schmidt, K. Douze, S. Wurz, L. Bellot-Gurlet, N. J. Conrad, K. G. Nickel, K. L. Van Niekerk, and C. S. Henshilwood. "Early Evidence for the Extensive Heat Treatment of Silcrete in the Howiesons Poort at Klipdrift Shelter (Layer PBD, 65 KA), South Africa." *PLoS ONE* 11, no. 10 (2016): e0163874.

Demolliens, M., F. Isbaine, S. Takerkart, P. Huguet, and D. Boussaoud. "Social and Asocial Prefrontal Cortex Neurons: A New Look at Social Facilitation and the Social Brain." *Social Cognitive and Affective Neuroscience* 12, no. 8 (2017): 1241–1248.

De Oliveira, S., and R. E. Nisbett. "Culture Changes How We Think about Thinking: From 'Human Inference' to 'Geography of Thought'." *Perspectives on Psychological Science* 12, no. 5 (2017): 782–790.

DeSilva, J. M., and J.J. Lesnik. 2008. "Brain Size at Birth Throughout Human Evolution: A New Method for Estimating Neonatal Brain Size in Hominins." *Journal of Human Evolution* 55 no. 6 (2008): 1064–1074.

De Silva, S., V. Schmid, and G. Wittemyer. "Fission-Fusion Processes Weaken Dominance Networks of Female Asian Elephants in a Productive Habitat." *Behavioral Ecology* 28, no. 1 (2017): 243–252.

Deutsch, D. *The Beginning of Infinity: Explanations That Transform the World.* London: Penguin, 2011.

De Waal, F. *Mama's Last Hug: Animal Emotions and What They Tell Us about Ourselves.* New York: W. W. Norton & Company, 2019.

Dewhirst, F. E., T. Chen, J. Izard, B. J. Paster, A. C. R. Tanner, W. H. Yu, A. Lakshmanan, and W. G. Wade. "The Human Oral Microbiome." *Journal of Bacteriology* 192, no. 19 (2010): 5002–5017. Diamond, J. M. *The World Until Yesterday: What Can We Learn from Traditional Societies?*New York: Penguin, 2012.

Díaz-Muñoz, S. L., A. M. Boddy, G. Dantas, C. M. Waters, and J. L. Bronstein. "Contextual Organismality: Beyond Pattern to Process in the Emergence of Organisms." *Evolution* 70, no. 12 (2016): 2669–2677.

Dishaw, L. J., and G. W. Litman. "Invertebrate Allorecognition: The Origins of Histocompatibility." *Current Biology* 19, no. 7 (2009): 286–288.

Domínguez-Rodrigo, M., and L. Alcalá. "3.3-Million-Year-Old Stone Tools and Butchery Traces? More Evidence Needed."*PaleoAnthropology* (2016): 46–53.

Dong, A., E. Collier-Baker, and T. Suddendorf. "Building Blocks of Human Design Thinking in Animals." *International Journal of Design Creativity and Innovation* 5, no. 1–2 (2017): 1–15.

Dor, D. "From Experience to Imagination: Language and Its Evolution as a Social Communication Technology." *Journal of Neurolinguistics* 43 (2017): 107–119.

Dor, D. *The Instruction of Imagination: Language as a Social Communication Technology.* New York: Oxford University Press, 2015.

Douglas, P. M., M. Pagani, M. A. Canuto, M. Brenner, D. A. Hodell, T. I. Eglinton, and J. H. Curtis. "Drought, Agricultural Adaptation, and Sociopolitical Collapse in the Maya Lowlands." *Proceedings of the National Academy of Sciences* 112, no. 18 (2015): 5607–5612.

Dowd, K. "The Emergence of Fiat Money: A Reconsideration." *Cato Journal* 20, no. 3 (2001): 467–476.

Drysdale, R., G. Zanchetta, J. Hellstrom, R. Maas, A. Fallick, M. Pickett, I. Cartwright, and L. Piccini. "Late Holocene Drought Responsible for the Collapse of Old World Civilizations Is Recorded in an Italian Cave Flowstone." *Geology* 34, no. 2 (2006): 101–104.

Du, P., and H. Chen. "Water Supply of the Cities in Ancient China." *Water Science and Technology* 7, no. 1 (2007): 173–181.

Ducatez, S., J. N. Audet, J. R. Rodrigues, L. Kayello, and L. Lefebvre. "Innovativeness and the Effects of Urbanization on Risk-Taking Behaviors in Wild Barbados Birds." *Animal Cognition* 20, no. 1 (2017): 33–42.

Dunbar, R. I. "Coevolution of Neocortical Size, Group Size and Language in Humans." *Behavioral and Brain Sciences* 16, no. 4 (1993): 681–694.

Dunbar, R. I. *Human Evolution: Our Brains and Behavior*. New York: Oxford University Press, 2016.

Dunbar, R. I. "The Social Brain: Psychological Underpinnings and Implications for the Structure of Organizations." *Current Directions in Psychological Science* 23, no. 2 (2014): 109–114.

Dunbar, R., and S. Shultz. "The Evolution of Self-Control." *BioRxiv* (2020): 1–20.

Duncan, B. L. "Differential Social Perception and Attribution of Intergroup Violence: Testing the Lower Limits of Stereotyping of Blacks." *Journal of Personality and Social Psychology* 34, no. 4 (1976): 590–598.

Dunham, Y., A. S. Baron, and S. Carey. "Consequences of 'Minimal' Group Affiliations in Children." *Child Development* 82, no. 3 (2011): 793–811.

Dunham, Y., E. E. Chen, and M. R. Banaji. "Two Signatures of Implicit Intergroup Attitudes: Developmental Invariance and Early Enculturation." *Psychological Science* 24, no. 6 (2013): 860–868.

Dunn, M. "*Reviving the Organismic Analogy in Sociology: Human Society as an Organism*." PhD Dissertation, University of California, Riverside, 2016.

Durkheim, É. *Rules of Sociological Method*. New York: Simon and Schuster, [1895] 1982.

Durkheim, É. *The Division of Labor in Society*. Translated by W. D. Halls. New York: Simon and Schuster, [1893] 2014.

Durkheim, É. *The Elementary Forms of Religious Life*. Translated by C. Cosman. Edited by M. S. Cladis. New York: Oxford University Press, [1912] 2008.

Durkheim, É., and M. Mauss. *Primitive Classification*. New York: Routledge, [1903] 2009.

Eidelman, S., C. S. Crandall, and J. Pattershall. "The Existence Bias." *Journal of Personality and Social Psychology* 97, no. 5 (2009): 765–775.

Eidelman, S., J. Pattershall, and C. S. Crandall "Longer Is Better." *Journal of Experimental Social Psychology* 46, no. 6 (2010): 993–998.

Einstein, A. "On the Electrodynamics of Moving Bodies." *Annalen der Physik* 17, no. 10 (1905): 891–921.

Elliott, E. G., A. S. Ettinger, B. P. Leaderer, M. B. Bracken, and N. C. Deziel. "A Systematic Evaluation of Chemicals in Hydraulic-Fracturing Fluids and

Wastewater for Reproductive and Developmental Toxicity." *Journal of Exposure Science & Environmental Epidemiology* 27, no. 1 (2017): 90–99.

Ellis, L. "A Discipline in Peril: Sociology's Future Hinges on Curing Its Biophobia." *The American Sociologist* 27, no. 2 (1996): 21–41.

Emerson, R. M. "Power-Dependence Relations." *American Sociological Review* 27, no. 1 (1962): 31–41.

Emerson, R. M. "Social Exchange Theory." In *Social Psychology: Sociological Perspectives*, edited by M. Rosenberg and R. H. Turner, 30–65. New York: Basic Books, 1981.

Engelmann, J. M., and E. Herrmann. "Chimpanzees Trust Their Friends." *Current Biology* 26, no. 2 (2016): 252–256.

Energy Information Administration. "Natural Gas Explained." *US Department of Energy*. Retrieved from https://www.eia.gov/energyexplained/natural-gas/, 2019a.

Energy Information Administration. "Gasoline Explained." *US Department of Energy*. Retrieved from https://www.eia.gov/energyexplained/gasoline/where-our-gasoline-comes-from.php#:~:text=Most%20gasoline%20moves%20from%20refineries, truck%20to%20gasoline%20fueling%20stations, 2019b.

Eren, E., and V. E. Uz. "A Review on Bike-Sharing: The Factors Affecting Bike-Sharing Demand." *Sustainable Cities and Society* 54 (2020): 101882.

Erickson, H. H. "History of Horse Whims, Teamboats, Treadwheels, and Treadmills." *Equine Veterinary Journal* 38, suppl. 36 (2006): 83–87.

Estes, J. A., J. Terborgh, J. S. Brashares, M. E. Power, J. Berger, W. J. Bond, S. R. Carpenter, T. E. Essington, R. D. Holt, J. B. Jackson, and R. J. Marquis. "Trophic Downgrading of Planet Earth." *Science* 333, no. 6040 (2011): 301–306.

Evans, J. S. B. T. "Dual-Processing Accounts of Reasoning, Judgment, and Social Cognition." *Annual Review of Psychology* 59 (2008): 255–278.

Evans, J. S. B., and K. E. Stanovich. "Dual Process Theories of Higher Cognition: Advancing the Debate." *Perspectives on Psychological Science* 8, no. 3 (2013): 223–241.

Facchini, G., E. Patacchini, and M. F. Steinhardt. "Migration, Friendship Ties, and Cultural Assimilation." *The Scandinavian Journal of Economics* 117, no. 2 (2015): 619–649.

Fahy, G. E., C. Boesch, J. J. Hublin, and M. P. Richards. "The Effectiveness of Using Carbonate Isotope Measurements of Body Tissues to Infer Diet in Human Evolution: Evidence from Wild Western Chimpanzees (Pan Troglodytes Verus)." *Journal of Human Evolution* 88 (2015): 70–78.

Falcón-Cortés, A., D. Boyer, and G. Ramos-Fernández. "Collective Learning from Individual Experiences and Information Transfer during Group Foraging." *Journal of the Royal Society Interface* 16, no. 151 (2019): 20180803.

Feldblum, J. T., S. Manfredi, I. C. Gilby, A. E. Pusey. "The Timing and Causes of a Unique Chimpanzee Community Fission Preceding Gombe's 'Four Years War'." *American Journal of Physical Anthropology* 166, no. 3 (2018): 730–744.

Ferguson, N. *The Ascent of Money: A Financial History of the World*. New York: Penguin, 2008.

Ferris, R. "America's Gas Stations and Convenience Stores Grapple with an Uncertain Future." *Consumer News and Business Channel*. Retrieved from https://www.cnbc.com/2020/03/18/americas-gas-stations-and-convenience-stores-grapple-with-an-uncertain-future.html, 2020.

Ferronato, N., and V. Torretta. "Waste Mismanagement in Developing Countries: A Review of Global Issues." *International Journal of Environmental Research and Public Health* 16, no. 6 (2019): 1060–1088.

Finkel, E. J., M. I. Norton, H. T. Reis, D. Ariely, P. A. Caprariello, P. W. Eastwick, J. H. Frost, and M. R. Maniaci. "When Does Familiarity Promote Versus Undermine Interpersonal Attraction? A Proposed Integrative Model from Erstwhile Adversaries." *Perspectives on Psychological Science* 10, no. 1 (2015): 3–19.

Fischer, S. R. *History of Language*. London: Reaktion Books, 2001.

Fischer, R., R. Callander, P. Reddish, and J. Bulbulia. "How Do Rituals Affect Cooperation?" *Human Nature* 24, no. 2 (2013): 115–125.

Fishman, C. "13 Things You Probably Don't Know About the U.S. Water System (But Should)." *National Geographic*. Retrieved from https://blog.nationalgeographic.org/2014/08/12/13-things-you-probably-dont-know-about-the-u-s-water-system-but-should/, 2014.

Flannery, K. and J. Marcus. *The Creation of Inequality: How Our Prehistoric Ancestors Set the Stage for Monarchy, Slavery, and Empire*. Cambridge, MA: Harvard University Press, 2012.

Fligstein, N., and D. McAdam. *A Theory of Fields*. Oxford: Oxford University Press, 2012.

Fligstein, N., and D. McAdam. "Toward a Theory of Strategic Action Fields." *Sociological Theory* 29, no. 1 (2011): 1–26.

Forstmann, M., and P. Burgmer. "The Mind of the Market: Lay Beliefs about the Economy as a Willful, Goal-Oriented Agent." *Behavioral and Brain Sciences* 41 (2018): 1–7.

Franklin, B. "A Letter from Benjamin Franklin, Esq. to Mr. Peter Collinson, F. R. S. Concerning an Electrical Kite." *Philosophical Transactions of the Royal Society* 47 (1752): 301.

Fröhlich, M., C. Sievers, S. W. Townsend, T. Gruber, and C. P. van Schaik. "Multimodal Communication and Language Origins: Integrating Gestures and Vocalizations." *Biological Reviews* 94, no. 5 (2019): 1809–1829.

Galil, B. S., S. Nehring, and V. Panov. "Waterways as Invasion Highways–Impact of Climate Change and Globalization." In *Biological Invasions*, edited by W. Nentwig, 59–74. Berlin, Germany: Springer, 2008.

Geen, R. G., and J. J. Gange. "Drive Theory of Social Facilitation: Twelve Years of Theory and Research." *Psychological Bulletin* 84, no. 6 (1977): 1267–1288.

Gelfand, M. J. *Rule Makers, Rule Breakers: Tight and Loose Cultures and the Secret Signals That Direct Our Lives*. New York: Scribner, 2019.

Gelfand, M. J., J. R. Harrington, and J. C. Jackson. "The Strength of Social Norms across Human Groups." *Perspectives on Psychological Science* 12, no. 5 (2017): 800–809.

Gelfand, M. J., J. L. Raver, L. Nishii, L. M. Leslie, J. Lun, B. C. Lim, L. Duan, A. Almaliach, S. Ang, J. Arnadottir, and Z. Aycan. "Differences between Tight and Loose Cultures: A 33-Nation Study." *Science* 332, no. 6033 (2011): 1100–1104.

Gelman, S. A. "Psychological Essentialism in Children." *Trends in Cognitive Sciences* 8, no. 9 (2004): 404–409.

Gelman, S. A. *The Essential Child: Origins of Essentialism in Everyday Thought*. Oxford: Oxford University Press, 2003.

Gerrity, S., and A. Lantero. "Understanding the Grid." *US Department of Energy*. Retrieved from https://www.energy.gov/articles/infographic-understanding-grid, 2014.

Ghazanfar, A. A., and D. Rendell. "Evolution of Human Vocal Production." *Current Biology* 18, no. 11 (2008): R457–R460.

Gibbons, A. "Pleistocene Population Explosions." *Science* 262, no. 5130 (1993): 27–29.

Gilbert, S. F. "A Holobiont Birth Narrative: The Epigenetic Transmission of the Human Microbiome." *Frontiers in Genetics* 5, no. 282 (2014): 1–7.

Gilbert, S. F., E. Rosenberg, and I. Zilber-Rosenberg. "The Holobiont with Its Hologenome Is a Level of Selection in Evolution." In *Landscapes of Collectivity in the Life Sciences*, edited by S. N. Gissis, E. Lamm, and A. Shavity, 305–324. Cambridge, MA: MIT Press, 2017.

Goffman, E. *Encounters: Two Studies in the Sociology of Interaction*. Indianapolis: Bobbs-Merrill, 1961.

Goffman, E. *The Presentation of Self in Everyday Life*. New York: Doubleday. 1959.

Gowlett, J. A. "The Discovery of Fire by Humans: A Long and Convoluted Process." *Philosophical Transactions of the Royal Society B: Biological Sciences* 371, no. 1696 (2016): 20150164.

Granovetter, M. "The Strength of Weak Ties: A Network Theory Revisited." *Sociological Theory* 1 (1983): 201–233.

Grant. F., and M. A. Hogg. "Self-Uncertainty, Social Identity, Prominence and Group Identification." *Journal of Experimental Social Psychology* 48, no. 2 (2012): 538–542.

Gray, P. "The Play Theory of Hunter-Gatherer Egalitarianism." In *Ancestral Landscapes in Human Evolution: Culture, Childrearing and Social Wellbeing*, edited by D. Narvaez, K. Valentino, A. Fuentes, J. J. McKenna, and P. Gray, 192–215. New York: Oxford University Press, 2014.

Grice, E. A., and J. A. Segre. "The Skin Microbiome." *Nature Reviews Microbiology* 9, no. 4 (2011): 244–253.

Grosberg, R. K., and R. R. Strathmann. "The Evolution of Multicellularity: A Minor Major Transition?" *Annual Review of Ecology, Evolution, and Systematics* 38 (2007): 621–654.

Grossmann, I. "Wisdom in Context." *Perspectives on Psychological Science* 12, no. 2 (2017): 233–257.

Guidon, S., H. Becker, H. Dediu, and K. W. Axhausen, "Electric Bicycle-Sharing: A New Competitor in the Urban Transportation Market? An Empirical Analysis of Transaction Data." *Transportation Research Record* 2673, no. 4 (2019): 15–26.

Gupton, N. "Benjamin Franklin and the Kite Experiment." *The Franklin Institute*. Retrieved from https://www.fi.edu/benjamin-franklin/kite-key-experiment, 2017.

Gurven, M., and Hill, K. "Why Do Men Hunt? A Reevaluation of 'Man the Hunter' and the Sexual Division of Labor." *Current Anthropology* 50 (2009): 51–74.

Habermas, J. *The Theory of Communicative Action*, Vol. 1. London: Heinemann, 1984.

Habermas, J. *The Theory of Communicative Action*, Vol. 2. Cambridge: Polity Press, 1987.

Hagem, B., and P. Andreasen. "ENTSO-E at a Glance." *The European Network of Transmission System Operators for Electricity*. Retrieved from https://eepublicdown

loads.entsoe.eu/clean-documents/Publications/Statistics/Factsheet/entsoe_sfs2015_web.pdf, 2015.

Haidt, J. *The Righteous Mind: Why Good People Are Divided by Politics and Religion.* New York: Vintage, 2012.

Hamilton, W. D. "The Genetical Evolution of Social Behavior, II." *Journal of Theoretical Biology* 7, no. 1 (1964): 17–52.

Hanneman, R. A., R. Collins, and G. Mordt. "Discovering Theory Dynamics by Computer Simulation: Experiments on State Legitimacy and Imperialist Capitalism." *Sociological Methodology* 25 (1995): 1–46.

Hanschen, E. R., D. E. Shelton, and R. E. Michod. "Evolutionary Transitions in Individuality and Recent Models of Multicellularity." In *Evolutionary Transitions to Multicellular Life* edited by I. Ruiz-Trillo and A. M. Nedelcu, 165–188. Dordrecht, Netherlands: Springer, 2015.

Hanschen, E. R., D. R. Davison, Z. Grochau-Wright, and R. E. Michod. "Individuality and the Major Evolutionary Transitions." In *Landscapes of Collectivity in the Life Sciences*, edited by S. N. Gissis, E. Lamm, and A. Shavity, 255–267. Cambridge, MA: MIT Press, 2017.

Hanel, P. H., G. R. Maio, and A. S. Manstead. "A New Way to Look at the Data: Similarities between Groups of People Are Large and Important." *Journal of Personality and Social Psychology* 116, no. 4 (2019): 541–562.

Hardecker, S., M. F. Schmidt, and M. Tomasello. "Children's Developing Understanding of the Conventionality of Rules." *Journal of Cognition and Development* 18, no. 2 (2017): 163–188.

Hardin, G. "The Tragedy of the Commons." *Science* 162, no. 3859 (1968): 1243–1248.

Hargis, M. B., M. C. Whatley, and A. D. Castel. "Remembering Proper Names as a Potential Exception to the Better-Than-Average Effect in Younger and Older Adults." *Psychology and Aging* 35, no. 4 (2020): 497–507.

Harpending, H., and A. Rogers. "Genetic Perspectives on Human Origins and Differentiation." *Annual Review of Genomics and Human Genetics* 1, no. 1 (2000): 361–385.

Harper, K. *The Fate of Rome: Climate, Disease, and the End of an Empire.* Princeton, NJ: Princeton University Press, 2017.

Harmand, S., J. E. Lewis, C. S. Feibel, C. J. Lepre, S. Prat, A. Lenoble, X. Boës, R. L. Quinn, M. Brenet, A. Arroyo, and N. Taylor. "3.3-Million-Year-Old Stone Tools from Lomekwi 3, West Turkana, Kenya." *Nature* 521, no. 7552 (2015): 310–315.

Hassan, J. A. "The Growth and Impact of the British Water Industry in the Nineteenth Century." *Economic History Review* 38, no. 4 (1985): 531–547.

Hawkes, K. "Grandmothers and the Evolution of Human Longevity." *American Journal of Human Biology* 15, no. 3 (2003): 380–400.

Hawkes, K. "Primate Sociality to Human Cooperation: Why Us and Not Them?" *Human Nature* 25, no. 1 (2014): 38–48.

Hayden, B. S. "Ecological Adaptations of Modern Hunter/Gatherers." In *Omnivorous Primates: Gathering and Hunting in Human Evolution*, edited by R. Harding and G. Teleki, 344–421. New York: Columbia University Press, 1981.

Heijkoop, M., J. Semon Dubas, and M. A. van Aken. "Parent-Child Resemblance and Kin Investment: Physical Resemblance or Personality Similarity?" *European Journal of Developmental Psychology* 6, no. 1 (2009): 64–69.

Henrich, J. *The Secret of Our Success: How Culture Is Driving Human Evolution, Domesticating Our Species, and Making Us Smarter*. Princeton, NJ: Princeton University Press, 2017.

Herman, C. P. "The Social Facilitation of Eating A Review." *Appetite* 86, (2015): 61–73.

Hermann, C. F. "Some Consequences of Crisis which Limit the Viability of Organizations." *Administrative Science Quarterly* 8 (1963): 343–358.

Hespos, S. J., and K. van Marle. "Physics for Infants: Characterizing the Origins of Knowledge about Objects, Substances, and Number." *Wiley Interdisciplinary Reviews: Cognitive Science* 3, no. 1 (2012): 19–27.

Heyes, C. *Cognitive Gadgets: The Cultural Evolution of Thinking*. Cambridge, MA: Harvard University Press, 2018.

Hewstone, M. "The 'Ultimate Attribution Error'? A Review of the Literature on Intergroup Causal Attribution." *European Journal of Social Psychology* 20, no. 4 (1990): 311–335.

Hill, K. R., R. S. Walker, M. Božičević, J. Eder, T. Headland, B. Hewlett, A. Magdalena Hurtado, F. Marlowe, P. Wiessner, and B. Wood. "Co-Residence Patterns in Hunter-Gatherer Societies Show Unique Human Social Structure." *Science* 331, no. 6022 (2011): 1286–1289.

Hirschfeld, L. A. "The Child's Representation of Human Groups." In *The Psychology of Learning and Motivation: Advances in Research and Theory*, edited by D. L. Medin, 133–185. San Diego: Academic Press, 1994.

Hochschild, A. R. *Strangers in Their Own Land: Anger and Mourning on the American Right*. New York: The New Press, 2016.

Hodson, G., R. J. Crisp, R. Meleady, and M. Earle. "Intergroup Contact as an Agent of Cognitive Liberalization." *Perspectives on Psychological Science* 13, no. 5 (2018): 523–548.

Hogg, M. A., and J. Adelman. "Uncertainty-Identity Theory: Extreme Groups, Radical Behavior, and Authoritarian Leadership." *Journal of Social Issues* 69, no. 3 (2013): 436–454.

Holt-Lunstad, J. "The Potential Public Health Relevance of Social Isolation and Loneliness: Prevalence, Epidemiology, and Risk Factors." *Public Policy & Aging Report* 27, no. 4 (2017): 127–130.

Horesh, N. *Chinese Money in Global Context: Historic Junctures between 600 BCE and 2012*. Stanford, CA: Stanford University Press, 2014.

Hounshell, D. "The Modernity of Menlo Park." In *Working at Inventing: Thomas A. Edison and the Menlo Park Experience*, edited by W. Pretzer, 116–133. Baltimore: Johns Hopkins University Press, 2002.

Howgego, C. *Ancient History from Coins*. New York: Routledge, 1995.

Hrdy, S. B. *Mothers and Others: The Evolutionary Origins of Mutual Understanding*. Cambridge, MA: Harvard University Press, 2011.

Huang, X., W. Qian, W. Wei, J. Guo, and N. Liu. "3D Numerical Simulation on the Flow Field of Single Tuyere Blast Furnaces: A Case Study of the Shuiquangou Iron Smelting Site Dated From the 9th to 13th Century in China." *Journal of Archaeological Science* 63 (2015): 44–58.

Hublin, J. J., and M. P. Richards. *The Evolution of Hominin Diets: Integrating Approaches to the Study of Palaeolithic Subsistence*. Dordrecht, Netherlands: Springer Science & Business Media, 2009.

Hughes, T. P. "The Electrification of America: The System Builders." *Technology and Culture* 20, no. 1 (1979): 124–161.

Hurlbut, W. W., B. S. Grant, and H. S. Price. "Steel Siphon Rehabilitation on the Los Angeles Aqueduct." *American Water Works Association* 34, no. 11 (1942): 1635–1666.

Iannaccone, L. R. "Why Strict Churches Are Strong." *American Journal of Sociology* 99, no. 5 (1994): 1180–1211.

Inglehart, R. *Cultural Evolution: People's Motivations Are Changing, and Reshaping the World*. Cambridge: Cambridge University Press, 2018.

Inglehart, R. *Culture Shift in Advanced Industrial Society*. Princeton, NJ: Princeton University Press, 1990.

Jackson, R. B., A. Down, N. G. Phillips, R. C. Ackley, C. W. Cook, D. L. Plata, and K. Zhao. "Natural Gas Pipeline Leaks across Washington, DC." *Environmental Science & Technology* 48, no. 3 (2014): 2051–2058.

Jaeggi, A. V., J. M. Stevens, and C. P. Van Schaik. "Tolerant Food Sharing and Reciprocity Is Precluded by Despotism among Bonobos but Not Chimpanzees." *American Journal of Physical Anthropology* 143, no. 1 (2010): 41–51.

Johnson, S. G. B., J. Zhang, and F. Keil. "*Win-Win Denial: The Psychological Underpinnings of Zero-Sum Thinking*."*PsyArXiv* (2020): 1–55.

Johnstone, R. A., and M. A. Cant. "The Evolution of Menopause in Cetaceans and Humans: The Role of Demography." *Proceedings of the Royal Society B: Biological Sciences* 277, no. 1701 (2010): 3765–3771.

Joiner, T. E., M. A. Ham, C. R. Hagan, and C. Silva. "Suicide as a Derangement of the Self-Sacrificial Aspect of Eusociality." *Psychological Review* 123, no. 3 (2016): 235–254.

Jong, J., H. Whitehouse, C. Kavanagh, and J. Lane. "Shared Negative Experiences Lead to Identity Fusion Via Personal Reflection." *PLoS ONE* 10, no. 12 (2015): e0145611.

Jonnes, J. *Empires of Light: Edison, Tesla, Westinghouse, and the Race to Electrify the World*. New York: Random House, 2004.

Jost, J. T. "Working Class Conservatism: A System Justification Perspective." *Current Opinion in Psychology* 18 (2017): 73–78.

Jost, J. T., M. R. Banaji, and B. A. Nosek. "A Decade of System Justification Theory: Accumulated Evidence of Conscious and Unconscious Bolstering of the Status Quo." *Political Psychology* 25, no. 6 (2004): 881–919.

Jost, J. T., and O. Hunyady. "The Psychology of System Justification and the Palliative Function of Ideology." *European Review of Social Psychology* 13 (2002): 111–153.

Jost, J. T., A. Ledgerwood, and C. D. Hardin. "Shared Reality, System Justification, and the Relational Basis of Ideological Beliefs." *Social and Personality Psychology Compass* 2, no. 1 (2008): 171–186.

Judd, M. "Jebel Sahaba Revisited." In *Archaeology of Early Northeastern Africa*, edited by M. K. Kroeper, 153–166. Poznań, Poland: Poznań Archaeological Museum, 2006.

Kahneman, D. *Thinking, Fast and Slow*. New York: Farrar, Straus and Giroux, 2011.

Kaminski, G., E. Gentaz, and K. Mazens. "Development of Children's Ability to Detect Kinship through Facial Resemblance." *Animal Cognition* 15, no. 3 (2012): 421–427.

Kampis, D., and Á. M. Kovács. "Seeing the World From Others' Perspective: 14-Month-Olds Show Altercentric Modulation Effects by Others' Beliefs." *PsyArXiv*, (2020): 1–29.

Kampis, D., and V. Southgate. "Altercentric Cognition; How Others Influence Our Cognitive Processing." *Trends in Cognitive Sciences* 24, no. 11 (2020): 945–959.

Kappelman, J., R. A. Ketcham, S. Pearce, L. Todd, W. Atkins, M. W. Colbert, M. Feseha, J. A. Maisano, and A. Witzel. "Perimortem Fractures in Lucy Suggest Mortality From Fall Out of Tall Tree." *Nature* 537, no. 7621 (2016): 503–507.

Karner, A., D. Rowangould, and J. London. *We Can Get There Here: New Perspectives on Transportation Equity*. Davis: University of California Press, 2016.

Kavanagh, C. M., J. Jong, R. McKay, and H. Whitehouse. "Positive Experiences of High Arousal Martial Arts Rituals Are Linked to Identify Fusion and Costly Pro-Group Actions." *European Journal of Social Psychology* 49, no. 3 (2019): 461–481.

Kay, A. C., D. Gaucher, J. L. Napier, M. J. Callan, and K. Laurin. "God and the Government: Testing a Compensatory Control Mechanism for the Support of External Systems." *Journal of Personality and Social Psychology* 95, no. 1 (2008): 18–35.

Kaza, S., and Yao, L. "At a Glance: A Global Picture of Solid Waste Management." In *What a Waste 2.0: A Global Snapshot of Solid Waste Management to 2050*, edited by S. Kaza, L. Yao, P. Bhada-Tata, and F. V. Woerden. Washington, DC: World Bank, 2018. doi:10.1596/978-1-4648-1329-0.

Keil, F. C. *Concepts, Kinds, and Cognitive Development*. Cambridge, MA: MIT Press, 1992.

Kelly, R. L. *The Fifth Beginning: What Six Million Years of Human History Can Tell Us about Our Future*. Oakland: University of California Press, 2016.

Kelly, R. L. *The Lifeways of Hunter-Gatherers: The Foraging Spectrum*. Cambridge: Cambridge University Press, 2013.

Kennedy, H. "The Feeding of the Five Hundred Thousand: Cities and Agriculture in Early Islamic Mesopotamia." *IRAQ* 73 (2011): 177–199.

Kilduff, M., and D. Krackhardt. *Interpersonal Networks in Organizations: Cognition, Personality, Dynamics, and Culture*. Cambridge: Cambridge University Press, 2008.

Kim, S., and E. S. Spelke. "Learning from Multiple Informants: Children's Response to Epistemic Bases for Consensus Judgments." *Journal of Experimental Child Psychology* 192 (2020): 104759.

Kitayama, S., B. Mesquita, and M. Karasawa. "Cultural Affordances and Emotional Experience: Socially Engaging and Disengaging Emotions in Japan and the United States." *Journal of Personality and Social Psychology* 91, no. 5 (2006): 890–903.

Kitayama, S., M. Karasawa, I. Grossmann, J. Na, M. E. W. Varnum, and R. E. Nisbett. "East-West Differences in Cognitive Style and Social Orientation." *PsyArXiv.com*. Retrieved from https://psyarxiv.com/c57ep, 2019.

Kite, M. E., and B. E. Whitley Jr. *Psychology of Prejudice and Discrimination*. Hove, UK: Psychology Press, 2016.

Kluttz, D. N., and N. Fligstein. "Varieties of Sociological Field Theory." In *Handbook of Contemporary Sociological Theory*, edited by S. Abrutyn, 185–204. New York: Springer International Publishing, 2016.

Kornfeld, I. E. "Mesopotamia: A History of Water and Law." In *The Evolution of the Law and Politics of Water*, edited by J. W. Dellapenna and J. Gupta, 15–28. Dordrecht, Netherlands: Springer Verlag, 2009.

Knobloch-Westerwick, S., C. Mothes, and N. Polavin. "Confirmation Bias, Ingroup Bias, and Negativity Bias in Selective Exposure to Political Information." *Communication Research* 47, no. 1 (2020): 104–124.

Korsgaard, C. M. *Self-Construction: Agency, Identity, and Integrity*. Oxford: Oxford University Press, 2009.

Korsgaard, C. M. *The Sources of Normativity*. Cambridge: Cambridge University Press, 1996.

Kossinets, G., and D. J. Watts. "Origins of Homophily in an Evolving Social Network." *American Journal of Sociology* 115, no. 2 (2009): 405–450.

Kramer, S. N. *The Sumerians: Their History, Culture, and Character*. Chicago: University of Chicago Press, 2010.

Krasnow, M. M., A. W. Delton, J. Tooby, and L. Cosmides. "Meeting Now Suggests We Will Meet Again: Implications for Debates on the Evolution of Cooperation." *Scientific Reports* 3, no. 1747 (2013): 1–8.

Krause, J., and G. D. Ruxton. *Living in Groups*. New York: Oxford University Press, 2002.

Krummer, H. *Primate Societies: Group Techniques of Ecological Adaptation*. Chicago: Aldine Press, 1971.

Kteily, N. S., J. Sidanius, and S. Levin. "Social Dominance Orientation: Cause or 'Mere Effect'? Evidence for SDO as a Casual Predictor of Prejudice and Discrimination against Ethnic and Racial Outgroups." *Journal of Experimental Social Psychology* 47, no. 1 (2011): 208–214.

Kudo, H., and R. I. Dunbar. "Neocortex Size and Social Network Size in Primates." *Animal Behaviour* 6, no. 4 (2001): 711–722.

Kühnert, C., D. Helbing, and G. B. West. "Scaling Laws in Urban Supply Networks." *Physica A: Statistical Mechanics and Its Applications* 363, no. 1 (2006): 96–103.

Landau, M. J., A. C. Kay, and J. A. Whitson "Compensatory Control and the Appeal of a Structured World." *Psychological Bulletin* 141, no. 3 (2015): 694–722.

Lane, J. E. "The Emergence of Social Schemas and Lossy Conceptual Information Networks: How Information Transmission Can Lead to the Apparent 'Emergence' of Culture." In *Emergent Behavior in Complex Systems Engineering: A Modeling and Simulation Approach*, edited by S. Mittal, S. Diallo, and A. Tolk, 321–348. Chichester, UK: Wiley Blackwell, 2018.

Lansing, J. S., and K. M. Fox. "Niche Construction on Bali: The Gods of the Countryside." *Philosophical Transactions of the Royal Society B: Biological Sciences* 366, no. 1566 (2011): 927–934.

Larson, J. M. "The Weakness of Weak Ties for Novel Information Diffusion." *Applied Network Science* 2, no. 14 (2017): 1–15.

Laughlin, W. S. "Hunting: An Integrating Behavior System and Its Evolutionary Importance." In *Man the Hunter*, edited by R. B. Lee and I. DeVore, 304–320. Chicago: Aldine Press, 1968.

Lawler, E. J., S. R. Thye, and J. Yoon. "Emotion and Group Cohesion in Productive Exchange." *American Journal of Sociology* 106, no. 3 (2000): 616–657.

Lawler, E. J., S. Thye, and J. Yoon. *Social Commitments in a Depersonalized World*. Thousand Oaks, CA: Sage, 2009.

Lawler, E. J., S. R. Thye, and J. Yoon. "Social Exchange and Micro Social Order." *American Sociological Review* 73, no. 4 (2008): 519–542.

Leakey, R. E., and A. C. Walker. "Australopithecus, Homo Erectus and the Single Species Hypothesis." *Nature* 261, no. 5561 (1976): 572–574.

Lee, R. B. "Eating Christmas in the Kalahari." *American Museum of Natural History*, December 1969, 60–63.

Lee, G. Y., and B. S. Kisilevsky. "Fetuses Respond to Father's Voice but Prefer Mother's Voice after Birth." *Developmental Psychology* 56, no. 1 (2014): 1–11.

Leick, G. *Mesopotamia: The Invention of the City*. New York: Penguin, 2002.

Leiser, D., and Y. Shemesh. "Economic Complexities and Cognitive Hurdles: Accounting for Specific Economic Misconceptions without an Ultimate Cause." *Behavioral and Brain Sciences* 41 (2018): e176.

Lenski, G. *Ecological-Evolutionary Theory: Principles and Applications*. Boulder, CO: Paradigm Press, 2005.

Lenski, G. *Human Societies: A Macrolevel Introduction to Sociology*. New York: McGraw-Hill, 1970.

Leschziner, V. "Dual-Process Models in Sociology." In *The Oxford Handbook of Cognitive Sociology*, edited by W. H. Brekhus and G. Ignatow, 170–191. New York: Oxford University Press, 2019.

Leslie, S. J. "The Original Sin of Cognition: Fear, Prejudice, and Generalization." *Journal of Philosophy* 114, no. 8 (2017): 393–421.

Lesthaeghe, R. "The Unfolding Story of the Second Demographic Transition." *Population and Development Review* 36, no. 2 (2010): 211–251.

Levine, T. R. "Truth-Default Theory (TDT): A Theory of Human Deception and Deception Detection." *Journal of Language and Social Psychology* 33, no. 4 (2014): 378–392.

Lewis, J. E., and S. Harmand. "An Earlier Origin for Stone Tool Making: Implications for Cognitive Evolution and the Transition to Homo." *Philosophical Transactions of the Royal Society B: Biological Sciences* 371, no. 1698 (2016): 20150233.

Lew-Levy, S., R. Reckin, N. Lavi, J. Cristóbal-Azkarate, and K. Ellis-Davies. "How Do Hunter-Gatherer Children Learn Subsistence Skills?" *Human Nature* 28, no. 4 (2017): 367–394.

Li, Y., C. Ma, Y. Murakami, Z. Zhou, Y. Yang, and Y. Li. "Cast Iron Smelting and Fining: An Iron Smelting Site of the Eastern Han Dynasty in Xuxiebian, Sichuan Province, China." *Sungkyun Journal of East Asian Studies* 19, no. 1 (2019): 91–111.

Linton, J. "Modern Water and Its Discontents: A History of Hydrosocial Networks." *WIREs Water* 1, no. 1 (2014): 111–120.

Linton, R. "Totemism and the AEF." *American Anthropologist* 26, no. 2 (1924): 296–300.

Lizardo, O. R. Mowry, B. Sepulvado, D. S. Stoltz, M. A. Taylor, J. Van Ness, and M. Wood. "What Are Dual Process Models? Implications for Cultural Analysis in Sociology." *Sociological Theory* 34, no. 4 (2016): 287–310.

Lloyd, E. A. "Holobionts as Units of Selection: Holobionts as Interactors, Reproducers, and Manifestors of Adaptation." In *Landscapes of Collectivity in the Life*

Science, edited by S. B. Gissis, E. Lamm, and A. Shavit, 351–365. Cambridge, MA: MIT Press, 2017.

Luef, E. M., and S. Pika. "The Evolution of Cooperative Communication: Analogies and Homologies." In *Landscapes of Collectivity in the Life Science*, edited by S. B. Gissis, E. Lamm, and A. Shavit, 133–144. Cambridge, MA: MIT Press, 2017.

Lye, T. P. *Changing Pathways: Forest Degradation and the Batek of Pahang, Malaysia*. Lanham, MD: Lexington Books, 2004.

Machalek, R. "The Evolutionary of Macrosociety: Why Are Large Societies Rare?" *Advances in Human Ecology* 1 (1992): 33–64.

Machalek, R., and M. W. Martin. "Sociology and the Second Darwinian Revolution: A Metatheoretical Analysis." *Sociological Theory* 22, no. 3 (2004): 455–476.

Mack, A. *In Time of Plague: The History and Social Consequences of Lethal Epidemic Disease*. New York: NYU Press, 1991.

Macrae, C. N., and G. V. Bodenhausen. "Social Cognition: Thinking Categorically about Others." *Annual Review of Psychology* 51 (2000): 93–120.

Manin, B. "On Legitimacy and Political Deliberation." *Political Theory* 15, no. 3 (1987): 338–368.

Marineau, J., and S. Krishnakumar. *Gender and Ethnic Homophily in Organizational Culture Perception: A Social Network View*. Briarcliff, NY: Academy of Management, 2014.

Marshall, D. "Sociology's Contentious Courtship with Biology." In *The Oxford Handbook of Evolution*, edited by R. Hopcroft, 33–62. Kettering, UK: Oxford University Press, 2018.

Martin, J. L. "What Is Field Theory?" *American Journal of Sociology* 109, no. 1 (2003): 1–49.

Maryanski, A. "African Ape Social Networks: A Blueprint for Reconstructing Early Hominid Social Structure." In *Archaeology of Human Ancestry*, edited by S. Shennan and J. Steele, 67–90. London: Routledge, 1995.

Maryanski, A. "*African Ape Social Structure: A Comparative Analysis*." PhD Dissertation, University of California, Riverside, 1986.

Maryanski, A. *Émile Durkheim and the Birth of the Gods: Clans, Incest, Totems, Phratries, Hordes, Mana, Taboos, Corroborees, Sodalities, Menstrual Blood, Apes, Churingas, Cairns, and Other Mysterious Things*. New York: Routledge, 2018.

Maryanski, A. "The Pursuit of Human Nature in Sociobiology and Evolutionary Sociology." *Sociological Perspectives* 37, no. 3 (1994): 375–389.

Maryanski, A., and J. H. Turner. *The Social Cage: Human Nature and the Evolution of Society*. Stanford, CA: Stanford University Press, 1992.

Massen, J. J., and S. E. Koski. "Chimps of a Feather Sit Together: Chimpanzee Friendships Are Based on Homophily in Personality." *Evolution and Human Behavior* 35, no. 1 (2014): 1–8.

Matulka, R., and D. Wood. "The History of the Lightbulb." *US Department of Energy*. Retrieved from https://www.energy.gov/articles/history-light-bulb, 2013.

Maynard Smith, J. "How to Model Evolution." In *The Latest on the Best: Essays on Evolution and Optimality*, edited by J. Dupré, 119–131. Cambridge, MA: MIT Press, 1987.

Maynard Smith, J., and E. Szathmáry. *The Major Transitions in Evolution*. Oxford: Oxford University Press, [1995] 2010.

Maynard Smith, J., and E. Szathmáry. *The Origins of Life: From the Birth of Life to the Origin of Language*. New York: Oxford University Press, 1999.

Mazza, V., M. Dammhanh, E. Lösche, and J. A. Eccard. "Small Mammals in the Big City: Behavioural Adjustments of Non-Commensal Rodents to Urban Environments." *Global Change Biology* 26, no. 11 (2020): 6326–6337.

McCaffree, K. "The Growth of Chinese Think Tanks and the Question of Crime." *East Asia* 35, no. 1 (2018): 43–58.

McCauley, R. N. *Why Religion Is Natural and Science Is Not*. New York: Oxford University Press, 2011.

McCloskey, D. N. *Bourgeois Equality: How Ideas, Not Capital or Institutions, Enriched the World*. Chicago: University of Chicago Press, 2016.

McGuigan, N., J. Makinson, and A. Whiten. "From Over-Imitation to Super-Copying: Adults Imitate Casually Irrelevant Aspects of Tool Use with Higher Fidelity than Young Children." *British Journal of Psychology* 102, no. 1 (2011): 1–18.

McIntosh, J. R. *Mesopotamia and the Rise of Civilization: History, Documents, and Key Questions*. Santa Barbara, CA: ABC-Clio, 2017.

McLuhan, M. *Understanding Media*. New York: McGraw Hill, 1964.

McMullan, J. B., and M. J. Brown. "A Qualitative Model of Mortality in Honey Bee (Apis Mellifera) Colonies Infested with Tracheal Mites (Acarapis Woodi)." *Experimental and Applied Acarology* 47, no. 3 (2009): 225–234.

McPherson, M., K. Smith-Lovin, and J. M. Cook. "Birds of a Feather: Homophily in Social Networks." *Annual Review of Sociology* 27, no. 1 (2001): 415–444.

Mead, G. H. *Mind, Self and Society*. Chicago: University of Chicago Press, [1934] 1962.

Medinilla, A., B. Byiers, and K. Karaki. "African Power Tools." *The European Center for Development Policy Management*. https://docs.google.com/viewerng/viewer?url=https://ecdpm.org/wp-content/uploads/DP-244-African-Power-Pools-1.pdf&hl=en_US, 2019.

Meleady, R., R. J. Crisp, G. Hodson, and M. Earle. "On the Generalization of Intergroup Contact: A Taxonomy of Transfer Effects." *Current Directions in Psychological Science* 28, no. 5 (2019): 430–435.

Mercier, H. "How Gullible Are We? A Review of the Evidence from Psychology and Social Science." *Review of General Psychology* 21, no. 2 (2017): 103–122.

Mercier, H. *Not Born Yesterday: The Science of Who We Trust and What We Believe In*. Princeton, NJ: Princeton University Press, 2020.

Mercier, H., Y. Majima, N. Claidière, and J. Léone. "Obstacles of the Spread of Unintuitive Beliefs." *Evolutionary Human Sciences* 1, e10 (2019): 1–15.

Merkle, J. A., M. Sigaud, and D. Fortin. "To Follow or Not? How Animals in Fusion-Fission Societies Handle Conflicting Information during Group Decision-Making." *Ecology Letters* 18, no. 8 (2015): 799–806.

Michod, R. E. "Evolution of Individuality during the Transition from Unicellular to Multicellular Life." *Proceedings of the National Academy of Sciences* 104, suppl. 1 (2007): 8613–8618.

Mikolajczak, M., J. J. Gross, A. Lane, O. Corneille, P. de Timary, and O. Luminet. "Oxytocin Makes People Trusting, Not Gullible." *Psychological Science* 21, no. 8 (2010): 1072–1074.

Milton, K. A. "A Hypothesis to Explain the Role of Meat-Eating in Human Evolution." *Evolutionary Anthropology* 8, no. 1 (1999): 11–21.

Minkowski, H. "Space and Time." *Annual Report of the German Association of Mathematicians* 18 (1909): 75–88.

Miramontes, O., D. Boyer, and G. Ramos-Fernández. "Understanding Fission-Fusion Dynamics in Social Animals through Agent-Based Modelling." *Proceedings of the European Conference on Artificial Life* 13 (2016): 338–339.

Mitani, J. C., D. P. Watts, and M. N. Muller. "Recent Developments in the Study of Wild Chimpanzee Behavior." *Evolutionary Anthropology: Issues, News, and Reviews* 11, no. 1 (2002): 9–25.

Mithen, S. *The Singing Neanderthals: The Origins of Music, Language, Mind, and Body*. Cambridge, MA: Harvard University Press, 2006.

Moffett, M. W. "Human Identity and the Evolution of Societies." *Human Nature* 24, no. 3 (2013): 219–267.

Moffett, M. W. *The Human Swarm: How Our Societies Arise, Thrive, and Fall*. New York: Basic Books, 2019.

Molm, L. D. "Theoretical Comparisons of Forms of Exchange." *Sociological Theory* 21, no. 1 (2003): 1–17.

Mora-Bermúdez, F., F. Badsha, S. Kanton, J. G. Camp, B. Vernot, K. Köhler, B. Voigt, K. Okita, T. Maricic, Z. He, and R. Lachmann. 2016. "Differences and Similarities between Human and Chimpanzee Neural Progenitors during Cerebral Cortex Development." *eLife* 5, no. 18683.

Morris, I. *Foragers, Farmers, and Fossil Fuels: How Human Values Evolve*, Vol. 41. Princeton, NJ: Princeton University Press, 2015.

Muthukrishna, M, and J. Henrich. "Innovation in the Collective Brain." *Philosophical Transactions of the Royal Society B* 371, no. 1690 (2016): 20150192.

Nagel, K., R. S. Olguin, and M. Tomasello. "Processes of Social Learning in the Tool Use of Chimpanzees (Pan Troglodytes) and Human Children (Homo Sapiens)." *Journal of Comparative Psychology* 107, no. 2 (1993): 174–186.

Naveh, D. "Social and Epistemological Dimensions of Learning among Nayaka Hunter-Gatherers." In *Social Learning and Innovation in Contemporary Hunter-Gatherers*, edited by H. Terashima and B. S. Hewlett, 125–133. Tokyo: Springer, 2016.

Needham, J. *Science and Civilization in China*, Vol. 6: *Biology and Biological Technology*. Cambridge: Cambridge University Press, 1984.

Nickerson, R. S. "Confirmation Bias: A Ubiquitous Phenomenon in Many Guises." *Review of General Psychology* 2, no. 2 (1998): 175–220.

Nisbett, R. *The Geography of Thought: How Asians and Westerners Think Differently… And Why*. London: Simon and Schuster, 2004.

Nonnenmacher, T. "History of the U.S. Telegraph Industry." *Economic History Encyclopedia*. Retrieved from http://eh.net/encyclopedia/history-of-the-u-s-telegraph-industry/, 2001.

Oc, B., and M. R. Bashshur. "Followership, Leadership and Social Influence." *The Leadership Quarterly* 24, no. 6 (2013): 919–934.

O'Connell-Rodwell, C. E., J. D. Wood, C. Kinzley, T. C. Rodwell, J. H. Poole, and S. Puria. "Wild African Elephants (Loxodonta Africana) Discriminate between Familiar and Unfamiliar Conspecific Seismic Alarm Calls." *Journal of the Acoustical Society of America* 122, no. 2 (2007): 823–830.

Okasha, S. "Multilevel Selection and the Major Transitions in Evolution." *Philosophy of Science* 72, no. 5 (2005): 1013–1025.

Olmstead, A. L., and P. W. Rhode. "Beyond the Threshold: An Analysis of the Characteristics and Behavior of Early Reaper Adopters." *Journal of Economic History* 55, no. 1 (1995): 27–57.

Olson, M. *The Logic of Collective Action: Public Goods and the Theory of Groups*. Cambridge, MA: Harvard University Press, 1965.

Ostler, N. *Empires of the World: A Language History of the World*. New York: Harper Collins, 2005.

Ostrom, E., T. Dietz, N. Dolsak, P. Stern, S. Stonich, and E. U. Weber. *The Drama of the Commons*. Washington, DC:National Academy Press, 2002.

O'Sullivan, L., A. Jardine, A. Cook, and P. Weinstein. "Deforestation, Mosquitoes, and Ancient Rome: Lessons for Today." *BioScience* 58, no. 8 (2008): 756–760.

Otten, S. "The Minimal Group Paradigm and Its Maximal Impact in Research on Social Categorization." *Current Opinion in Psychology* 11 (2016): 85–89.

Paladino, M. P., M. Mazzurega, F. Pavani, and T. W. Schubert. "Synchronous Multisensory Stimulation Blurs Self-Other Boundaries." *Psychological Science* 21, no. 9 (2010): 1202–1207.

Pan, W., G. Ghoshal, C. Krumme, M. Cebrian, and A. Pentland. "Urban Characteristics Attributable to Density-Driven Tie Formation." *Nature Communications* 4, no. 1 (2013): 1–7.

Pancer, Z. and M. D. Cooper. "The Evolution of Adaptive Immunity." *Annual Review of Immunology* 24 (2006): 497–518.

Panizza, M., and G. Cerisola. "Removal of Organic Pollutants from Industrial Wastewater by Electrogenerated Fenton's Reagent." *Water Research* 35, no. 16 (2001): 3987–3992.

Paoli, T., E. Palagi, and S. B. Tarli. "Reevaluation of Dominance Hierarchy in Bonobos (Pan Paniscus)." *American Journal of Physical Anthropology: The Official Publication of the American Association of Physical Anthropologists* 130, no. 1 (2006): 116–122.

Pardo, M. A., J. H. Poole, A. S. Stoeger, P. H. Wrege, C. E. O'Connell-Rodwell, U. K. Padmalal, and S. de Silva. "Differences in Combinatorial Calls among the 3 Elephant Species Cannot Be Explained by Phylogeny." *Behavioral Ecology* 20, no. 3 (2019): 809–820.

Pauker, K., N. Ambady, and E. P. Apfelbaum. "Race Salience and Essentialist Thinking in Racial Stereotype Development." *Child Development* 81, no. 6 (2010): 1799–1813.

Pennisi, E. "The Momentous Transition to Multicellular Life May Not Have Been so Hard After All.' *Science* 28 (2018).

Pennycook, G. "A Perspective on the Theoretical Foundation of Dual Process Models." In *Dual Process Theory 2.0*, edited by W. De Nays, 5–27. New York: Routledge, 2017.

Pepperberg, I. M. "Symbolic Communication in Nonhuman Animals." In *APA Handbook of Comparative Psychology: Basic Concepts, Methods, Neural Substrate, and Behavior*, edited by J. Call, G. M. Burghardt, I. M. Pepperburg, C. T. Snowdon, and T. Zentall, 663–679. Washington, DC: American Psychological Association, 2017.

Pescosolido, B. A. "Migration, Medical Care Preferences and the Lay Referral System: A Network Theory of Role Assimilation." *American Sociological Review* 51, no. 4 (1986): 523–540.

Petrol Plaza. "Mexico: Over 50% of Fuel Retail Market to be Run by Private Companies." *Petrol Plaza*. Retrieved from https://www.petrolplaza.com/news/24162, 2020.

Pettigrew, T. F., and L. R. Tropp. "A Meta-Analytic Test of Intergroup Contact Theory." *Journal of Personality and Social Psychology* 90, no. 5 (2006): 751–783.

Phillips, R. J. "Digital Technology and Institutional Change from the Gilded Age to Modern Times: The Impact of the Telegraph and the Internet." *Journal of Economic Issues* 34, no. 2 (2000): 267–289.

Piccolino, M. "Animal Electricity and the Birth of Electrophysiology: The Legacy of Luigi Galvani." *Brain Research Bulletin* 46, no. 5 (1998): 381–407.

Pinker, S. *Enlightenment Now: The Case for Reason, Science, Humanism, and Progress*. London: Penguin, 2018.

Pinker, S. *The Better Angels of Our Nature: Why Violence Has Declined*. New York: Penguin, 2011.

Pinker, S. "The Cognitive Niche: Coevolution of Intelligence, Sociality, and Language." *Proceedings of the National Academy of Sciences* 107, suppl. 2 (2010): 8993–8999.

Pinker, S. *The Village Effect: How Face-to-Face Contact Can Make Us Healthier and Happier*. Toronto: Vintage Canada, 2015.

Poole, J. H., P. L. Tyack, A. S. Stoeger-Horwath, and S. Watwood. "Elephants are Capable of Vocal Learning." *Nature* 434, no. 7032 (2005): 455–456.

Proffitt, T., L. V. Luncz, T. Falótico, E. B. Ottoni, I. de la Torre, and M. Haslam. "Wild Monkeys Flake Stone Tools." *Nature* 539, no. 7627 (2016): 85–88.

Pumain, D. "Urban Systems Dynamics, Urban Growth and Scaling Laws: The Question of Ergodicity." In *Complexity Theories of Cities Have Come of Age*, edited by Y. Portugali, H. Meyer, and E. Stolk, 91–103. Heidelberg, Germany: Springer, 2012.

Queller, D. C., and J. E. Strassmann. "Beyond Society: The Evolution of Organismality." *Philosophical Transactions of the Royal Society B: Biological Sciences* 364, no. 1533 (2009): 3143–3155.

Quinlan, R. J., and M. B. Quinlan. "Human Lactation, Pair-Bonds, and Alloparents." *Human Nature* 19, no. 1 (2008): 87–102.

Quiroga, R. Q. "Neural Representations across Species." *Culture and Evolutionary Process* 363, no. 6434 (2019): 1388–1389.

Quoidbach, J., D. T. Gilbert, and T. D. Wilson. "The End of History Illusion." *Science* 339, no. 6115 (2013): 96–98.

Ramos-Fernandez, G., A. J. King, J. C. Beehner, T. J. Bergman, M. C. Crofoot, A. Di Fiore, J. Lehmann, C. M. Schaffner, N. Snyder-Mackler, K. Zuberbühler, F. Aureli, and D. Boyer. "Quantifying Uncertainty Due to Fission-Fusion Dynamics as a Component of Social Complexity." *Proceedings of the Royal Society B: Biological Sciences* 285, no. 1879 (2018): 20180532.

Rayne, L., and D. Donoghue. "A Remote Sensing Approach for Mapping the Development of Ancient Water Management in the Near East." *Remote Sensing* 10, no. 12 (2018): 2042.

Reeves, P. "After Grid Failure, Millions In 3 Latin American Countries Lack Electricity." *National Public Radio*. Retrieved from https://www.npr.org/2019/06/17/733317659/after-grid-failure-millions-in-3-latin-american-countries-lack-electricity, 2019.

Reicher, S. D., A. Templeton, F. Neville, L. Ferrari, and J. Drury. "Core Disgust Is Attenuated by Ingroup Relations." *Proceedings of the National Academy of Sciences* 113, no. 10 (2016): 2631–2635.

Rhodes, M., and L. Chalik. "Social Categories as Markers of Intrinsic Interpersonal Obligations." *Psychological Science* 24, no. 6 (2013): 999–1006.

Rhodes, M., and L. Chalik. "The Interplay between Intuitive Psychology and Intuitive Sociology." *British Journal of Developmental Psychology* 32, no. 3 (2014): 248–251.

Ridgeway, C. L. *Framed by Gender: How Gender Inequality Persists in the Modern World*. Oxford: Oxford University Press, 2011.

Rinkevich, B. "Allorecognition and Xenorecognition in Reef Corals: A Decade of Interactions." *Hydrobiologia* 530, no. 1 (2004): 443–450.

Ritchie, H. "Fossil Fuels." *OurWorldInData.org*. Retrieved from https://ourworldindata.org/fossil-fuels, 2017.

Ritchie, H. "Does the News Reflect What We Die From?" *OurWorldInData*. Retrieved from https://ourworldindata.org/does-the-news-reflect-what-we-die-from#licence, 2019.

Ritzer, G. *The McDonaldization of Society*. Thousand Oaks, CA: Sage, 1964.

Rizzolatti, G., and M. A. Arbib. "Language within Our Grasp." *Trends in Neurosciences* 21, no. 5 (1998): 188–194.

Robinson, G. E., Heuser, L. M., LeConte, Y., Lenquette, F., and R. M. Hollingworth. "Neurochemicals Aid Bee Nestmate Recognition." *Nature* 399, no. 6736 (1999): 534–535.

Roff, D. A. *Life History Evolution*. Sutherland, MA: Sinauer Associates Inc., 2002.

Rogers, E. M. *Diffusions of Innovations*. New York: The Free Press, 1962.

Roser, M., and E. Ortiz-Ospina. "Global Extreme Poverty." *OurWorldInData*. Retrieved from https://ourworldindata.org/extreme-poverty, 2020.

Rosling H, O. Rosling, A. Rosling Rönnlund. *Factfulness: Ten Reasons We're Wrong about the World – and Why Things Are Better than You Think*. New York: Flatiron Books, 2018.

Rossano, M. J. "How Ritual Made Us Human." In *Handbook of Cognitive Archaeology*, edited by T. Henley, M. J. Rossano, and E. P. Kardas, 333–353. Milton, UK: Routledge, 2019.

Rost, S. "Water Management in Mesopotamia from the Sixth Till the First Millennium." *Wiley Interdisciplinary Reviews: Water* 4, no. 5 (2017): e1230.

Rozenblit, L., and F. Keil. "The Misunderstood Limits of Folk Science: An Illusion of Explanatory Depth." *Cognitive Science* 26, no. 5 (2002): 521–562.

Ruef, M. "Strong Ties, Weak Ties and Islands: Structural and Cultural Predictors of Organizational Innovation." *Industrial and Corporate Change* 11, no. 3 (2002): 427–449.

Ryan, C. "Stereotype Accuracy." *European Review of Social Psychology* 13, no. 1 (2003): 75–109.

Sahagun, L. "The LA Aqueduct at 100." *Los Angeles Times*. Retrieved from https://graphics.latimes.com/me-aqueduct/, 2013.

Sahlins, M. "Notes on the Original Amuent Society." In *Man the Hunter*, edited by R. B. Lee and I. DeVore, 85–89. Chicago: Aldine Press, 1968.

Sahlins, M. *Stone Age Economics*. Chicago: Aldine Press, 1972.

Salvucci, E. "Microbiome, Holobiont and the Net of Life." *Critical Reviews in Microbiology* 42, no. 3 (2016): 485–494.

Samson, K., and P. Kostyszyn. "Effects of Cognitive Load on Trusting Behavior: An Experiment Using the Trust Game." *PLoS ONE* 10, no. 5 (2015): e0127680.

Sánchez, J. S., and J. L. M. Fenollós. "Restudying the Beveled Rim Bowls: New Preliminary Data from Two Uruk Systems in the Syrian Middle Euphrates 1." *Res Antiquitatis: Journal of Ancient History* 3 (2012): 263–277.

Sapolsky, R. M. "The Influence of Social Hierarchy on Primate Health." *Science* 308, no. 5722 (2005): 648–652.

Schaller, M. "The Parental Care Motivational System and Why It Matters (For Everyone)." *Current Directions in Psychological Science*, 27, no. 5 (2018): 295–301.

Schlebecker, J. T. "The Changing American Farm, 1831–1981." *Material Culture* 38, no. 2 (2006): 19–38.

Schlebusch, C. M., H. Malmström, T. Günther, P. Sjödin, A. Coutinho, H. Edlund, A. R. Munters, M. Vicente, M. Steyn, H. Soodyall, M. Lombard, and M. Jakobsson. "Southern African Ancient Genomes Estimate Modern Human Divergence to 350,000 to 260,000 Years Ago." *Science* 358, no. 6363 (2017): 652–655.

Schoeninger, M. "Diet, Evolution of." In *The International Encyclopedia of Biological Anthropology*, edited by W. Trevathan. Hoboken, NJ: Wiley-Blackwell, 2018.

Scholz, F. "From the Leiden Jar to the Discovery of the Glass Electrode by Max Cremer." *Journal of Solid State Electrochemistry* 15, no. 1 (2011): 5–14.

Schutz, A., and T. Luckmann. *The Structures of the Life-World*, Vol. 1. London: Heinemann, 1973.

Schutz, A., and T. Luckmann. *The Structures of the Life-World*, Vol. 2. Evanston, IL: Northwestern University Press, 1989.

Scott, J. C. *Against the Grain: A Deep History of the Earliest States*. New Haven, CT: Yale University Press, 2017.

Searle, J. *Making the Social World: The Structure of Human Civilization*. Oxford: Oxford University Press, 2010.

Searle, J. *The Construction of Social Reality*. New York:Simon and Schuster, 1995.

Seebacher, F., and J. Krause. "Physiological Mechanisms Underlying Animal Social Behaviour." *Philosophical Transactions of the Royal Society B*. 373, no. 1727 (2017): 20160231.

Shambaugh, J., R. Nunn, and B. Portman. "Eleven Facts About Innovation and Patents." *The Brookings Institute*. Retrieved from https://www.brookings.edu/wp-content/uploads/2017/12/thp_20171213_eleven_facts_innovation_patents.pdf, 2017.

Shanteau, J. "Competence in Experts: The Role of Task Characteristics." *Organizational Behavioral and Human Decision Processes* 53 (1992): 252–266.

Sharlin, H. I. "The First Niagara Falls Power Project." *Business History Review* 35, no. 1 (1961): 59–74.

Shavit, A., A. Kolumbus, and Y. Silver. "Epistemic Collectives, Heterogeneity, and Injustice: The Case for Town Square Academia." In *Landscapes of Collectivity in the Life Science*, edited by S. B. Gissis, E. Lamm, and A. Shavit, 199–209. Cambridge, MA: MIT Press, 2017.

Sheehan, M. J., and E. A. Tibbetts. "Specialized Face Learning Is Associated with Individual Recognition in Paper Wasps." *Science* 334, no. 6060 (2011): 1272–1275.

Sherman, J. W., S. J. Stroessner, F. R. Conrey, and O. A. Azam. "Prejudice and Stereotype Maintenance Processes: Attention, Attribution, and Individuation." *Journal of Personality and Social Psychology* 89, no. 4 (2005): 607–622.

Sherman, P. W., E. A. Lacey, H. K. Reeve, and L. Keller. "The Eusociality Continuum." *Behavioral Ecology* 6, no. 1 (1995): 102–108.

Shtulman, A. *Scienceblind: Why Our Intuitive Theories about the World Are So Often Wrong*. Hachette, UK: Basic Books, 2017.

Shtulman, A., and K. Harrington. "Tensions between Science and Intuition across the Lifespan." *Topics in Cognitive Science* 8, no. 1 (2016): 118–137.

Shtulman, A., and J. Valcarcel. "Scientific Knowledge Suppresses but Does Not Supplant Earlier Intuitions." *Cognition* 124, no. 2 (2012): 209–215.

Simmel, G. "The Metropolis and Mental Life." In *The Sociology of Georg Simmel*, edited by K. Wolf, 409–424. New York: The Free Press, [1902] 1964.

Simpson, B., and R. Willer. "Beyond Altruism: Sociological Foundations of Cooperation and Prosocial Behavior." *Annual Review of Sociology* 41 (2015): 43–63.

Singh, J., and L. Fleming. "Lone Investors as Sources of Breakthroughs: Myth or Reality?" *Management Science* 56, no. 1 (2010): 41–56.

Smil, V. *Energy and Civilization: A History*. Cambridge, MA: MIT Press, 2017.

Smil, V. *Power Density: A Key to Understanding Energy Sources and Uses*. New York: MIT Press, 2015.

Smith, A. M. "*Phoenician Ships: Types, Trends, Trade and Treacherous Trade Routes*." PhD Dissertation. University of South Africa, 2012.

Smith, M. L. *Cities: The First 6,000 Years*. New York, NY: Penguin Books, 2019.

Smith, M. L. "Urbanism and the Middle Class: Co-Emergent Phenomena in the World's First Cities." *Journal of Anthropological Research* 74, no. 3 (2018): 299–326.

Smith, P. E. "Family Burials at Hayonim." *Paleorient* 1, no. 1 (1973): 69–71.

Smith, P. E. "Why Do Good Hunters Have Higher Reproductive Success?" *Human Nature* 15, no. 4 (2004): 343–364.

Smith, P. K., and J. C. Magee. "The Interpersonal Nature of Power and Status." *Current Opinion in Behavioral Sciences* 3 (2015): 152–156.

Solymar, L. "The Effect of the Telegraph on Law and Order, War, Diplomacy, and Power Politics." *Interdisciplinary Science Reviews* 25, no. 3 (2000): 203–210.

South African Petroleum Industry Association. "South African Fuel Industry." *Sapia.org*. Retrieved from https://www.sapia.org.za/Overview/South-African-fuel-industry, 2020.

Spencer, H. *The Principles of Ethics*, Vol. 2. New York: D. Appleton & Company, 1897.

Sperber, D. "Instincts or Gadgets? Not the Debate We Should Be Having?" *Behavioral and Brain Sciences* 42 (2019): e183.

Spoerl, Joseph S. "A Brief History of Iron and Steel Production." Retrieved from https://pergelator.blogspot.com/p/a-brief-history-of-iron-and-steel.html, 2004.

Stahl, G. K., M. L. Maznevski, A. Voigt, and K. Jonsen. "Unraveling the Effects of Cultural Diversity in Teams: A Meta-Analysis of Research on Multicultural Work Groups." *Journal of International Business Studies* 41, no. 4 (2010): 690–709.

Stark, R. *The Rise of Christianity: A Sociologist Reconsiders History*. Princeton, NJ: Princeton University Press, 1996.

Staw, B. M., L. E. Sandelands, and J. E. Dutton. "Threat Rigidity Effects in Organizational Behavior: A Multilevel Analysis." *Administrative Science Quarterly* 26, no. 4 (1981): 501–524.

Steele, M., and J. Odumeru. "Irrigation Water as Source of Foodborne Pathogens on Fruit and Vegetables." *Journal of Food Protection* 67, no. 12 (2004): 756–760.

Stephan, C. W., and W. G. Stephan. "Intergroup Anxiety." *The International Encyclopedia of Intercultural Communication*, edited by Y. Y. Kim, 1–15. Hoboken, NJ: John Wiley & Sons, 2017.

Sterba, R. L. "The Organization and Management of the Temple Corporations in Ancient Mesopotamia." *Academy of Management Review* 1, no. 3 (1976): 16–26.

Stoeger, A. S., and P. Manger. "Vocal Learning in Elephants: neural Bases and Adaptive Context." *Current Opinion in Neurobiology* 28 (2014): 101–107.

Stroeymeyt, N., M. Giurfa, and N. R. Franks. "Improving Decision Speed, Accuracy and Group Cohesion through Early Information Gathering in House-Hunting Ants." *PLoS ONE* 5, no. 9 (2010): e13059.

Sueur, C., A. J. King, L. Conradt, G Kerth, D. Lusseau, C. Mettke-Hofmann, C. M. Schaffner, L. Williams, D. Zinner, and F. Aureli. "Collective Decision Making and Fission-Fusion Dynamics: A Conceptual Framework." *Oikos* 120, no. 11 (2011): 1608–1617.

Sun, L., and A. Li. "Rolling-Element Bearings in China: From Ancient Times to the 20th Century." *Frontiers of Mechanical Engineering* 11, no. 1 (2016): 33–43.

Sunstein, C. "The Law of Group Polarization." *Journal of Political Philosophy* 10, no. 2 (2002): 175–195.

Surowiecki, J. *The Wisdom of Crowds*. New York: Anchor Books, 2005.

Swedell, L., and T. Plummer. "A Papionin Multilevel Society as a Model for Hominin Social Evolution." *International Journal of Primatology* 33, no. 5 (2012): 1165–1193.

Szathmáry, E., and J. Maynard Smith. "The Major Evolutionary Transitions." *Nature* 374, no. 6519 (1995): 227–232.

Szathmáry, E. "Toward Major Evolutionary Transitions Theory 2.0." *Proceedings of the National Academy of Sciences* 112, no. 33 (2015): 10104–10111.

Tabuchi, H. "$300 Billion War Beneath the Street: Fighting to Replace America's Water Pipes." *The New York Times*. Retrieved from https://www.nytimes.com/2017/11/10/climate/water-pipes-plastic-lead.html, 2017.

Taga, M. E., and B. L. Bassler. "Chemical Communication among Bacteria." *Proceedings of the National Academy of Sciences* 100, suppl. 2 (2003): 14549–14554.

Tainter, J. *The Collapse of Complex Societies*. Cambridge: Cambridge University Press, 1988.

Tajfel, H., M. G. Billig, R. P. Bundy, and C. Flament. "Social Categorization and Intergroup Behaviour." *European Journal of Social Psychology* 1, no. 2 (1971): 149–178.

Takács, K. "Discounting of Evolutionary Explanations in Sociology Textbooks and Curricula." *Frontiers in Sociology* 3, no. 24 (2018): 1–14.

Taleb, N. N. *Antifragile: Things that Gain from Disorder*, Vol. 3. New York: Fandom House Incorporated, 2012.

Tamburrino, A. "Water Technology in Ancient Mesopotamia." In *Ancient Water Technologies*, edited by L. W. Mays, 29–51. Dordrecht, Netherlands: Springer, 2010.

Taylor, A. "Nigeria's Illegal Oil Refineries." *The Atlantic*. Retrieved from https://www.theatlantic.com/photo/2013/01/nigerias-illegal-oil-refineries/100439/, 2013.

Taylor, D. G. "Pluralistic Ignorance and the Spiral of Silence: A Formal Analysis." *Public Opinion Quarterly* 46, no. 3 (1982): 311–335.

Thye, S., E. J. Lawler, and J. Yoon. "The Formation of Group Ties in Open Interaction Groups." *Social Psychology Quarterly* 82, no. 2 (2019): 158–181.

Tianduowa, Z., K. C. Woodson, and M. W. Ersten. "Reconstructing Ancient Hohokam Irrigation Systems in the Middle Gila River Valley, Arizona, United States of America." *Human Ecology* 46, no. 5 (2018): 735–746.

Todorov, A. *Face Value: The Irresistible Influence of First Impressions*. Princeton, NJ: Princeton University Press, 2017.

Tognotti, E. "Lessons from the History of Quarantine: From Plague to Influenza A." *Emerging Infectious Disease* 19, no. 2 (2013): 254–259.

Tomasello, M. *Becoming Human: A Theory of Ontogeny*. Cambridge, MA: Belknap Press, 2019.

Tooby, J., and L. Cosmides. "On the Universality of Human Nature and the Uniqueness of the Individual: The Role of Genetics and Adaptation." *Journal of Personality* 58, no. 1 (1990): 17–67.

Tranos, E., and C. Stitch. "Individual Internet Usage and the Availability of Online Content of Local Interest: A Multilevel Approach." *Computers, Environment and Urban Systems* 79, no. 101371 (2020).

Triandis, H. C. *Individualism and Collectivism*. New York: Routledge, 1995.

Triplett, N. "The Dynamogenic Factors in Pacemaking and Competition." *The American Journal of Psychology* 9, no. 4 (1898): 507–533.

Trivers, R. L. "The Evolution of Reciprocal Altruism." *The Quarterly Review of Biology* 46, no. 1 (1971): 35–57.

Trivers, R. "*The Momentous Transition to Multicellular Life May Not Have Been So Hard After All.*" Unpublished manuscript, 2017.

Turchin, P. *Ultrasociety: How 10,000 Years of War Made Humans the Greatest Cooperators on Earth*. Chaplin, CT: Beresta Books, 2016.

Turnbaugh, P. J., R. E. Ley, M. Hamady, C. M. Fraser-Liggett, R. Knight, and J. I. Gordon. "The Human Microbiome Project." *Nature* 449, no. 7164 (2007): 804–810.

Turner, J. H. "Discovering Human Nature through Cross-Species Analysis." In *The Oxford Handbook of Evolution, Biology, and Society*, edited by R. Hopcroft, 89–112. Oxford: Oxford University Press, 2018.

Turner, J. H. *Human Emotions: A Sociological Analysis*. Hoboken, NJ: Taylor & Francis, 2007.

Turner, J. H. "Integrating and Disintegrating Dynamics in Human Societies." In *Handbook of Contemporary Sociological Theory*, edited by S. Abrutyn, 19–41. New York: Springer, 2016.

Turner, J. H. *Macrodynamics*, Vol. 3: *Microdynamics*. Secaucus, NJ: Springer Science & Business Media, 2010b.

Turner, J. H. *On Human Nature*. New York: Routledge, 2020.

Turner, J. H. *On the Origins of Human Emotions: A Sociobiological Inquiry into the Evolution of Human Affect*. Stanford, CA: Stanford University Press, 2000.

Turner, J. H. *Theoretical Principles of Sociology*, Vol. 1: *Macrodynamics*. Secaucus, NJ: Springer Science & Business Media, 2010a.

Turner, J. H. "The Stratification of Emotions: Some Preliminary Generalizations." *Sociological Inquiry* 80, no. 2 (2010): 168–199.

Turner, J. H., and A. Maryanski. *On the Origin of Societies by Natural Selection*. New York: Routledge, 2015.

Turner, J. H., and R. S. Machalek. *The New Evolutionary Sociology: Recent and Revitalized Theoretical and Methodological Approaches*. New York: Routledge, 2018.

Tversky, B. *Mind in Motion: How Action Shapes Thought*. New York: Basic Books, 2019.

Tversky, A., and D. Kahneman. "Loss Aversion in Riskless Choice: A Reference-Dependent Model." *Quarterly Journal of Economics* 106, no. 4 (1991): 1039–1061.

Ur, J. A. "Cycles of Civilization in Northern Mesopotamia, 4400–2000 BC." *Journal of Archaeological Research* 18, no. 4 (2010): 387–431.

U.S. Census Bureau. "The State of Gas Taxes." *Census.gov*. Retrieved from https://www.census.gov/library/audio/profile-america/profileeven/profile-even-08.html, 2020.

Vacca, R., G. Solano, M. J. Lubbers, J. L. Molina, and C. McCarty. "A Personal Network Approach to the Study of Immigrant Structural Assimilation and Transnationalism." *Social Networks* 53 (2018): 72–89.

Van den Berghe, P. "Why Most Sociologists Don't (and Won't) Think Evolutionarily." *Sociological Forum* 5 (1990): 173–185.

Vander Meer, R. K., M. D. Breed, M. Winston, and K. E. Espelie. *Pheromone Communication in Social Insects: Ants, Wasps, Bees, and Termites*. Boca Raton, FL: CRC Press, 2019.

Van Leeuwen, F., and M. B. Peterson. "The Behavioral Immune System Is Designed to Avoid Infected Individuals, Not Outgroups." *Evolution and Human Behavior* 39, no. 2 (2018): 226–234.

Varnum, M. E. W., I. Grossmann, D. Katunar, S. Kitayama, and R. E. Nisbett. "Holism in a European Cultural Context: Differences in Cognitive Style between Central and East Europeans and Westerners." *Journal of Cognition and Culture* 8, no. 3 (2008): 321–333.

Varnum, M. E., I. Grossmann, S. Kitayama, and R. E. Nisbett. "The Origin of Cultural Differences in Cognition: The Social Orientation Hypothesis." *Current Directions in Psychological Science* 19, no. 1 (2010): 9–13.

Verschuere, B., and S. Shalvi. "The Truth Comes Naturally! Does It?" *Journal of Language and Social Psychology* 33, no. 4 (2014): 417–423.

Villanea, F. A., and J. G. Schraiber. "Multiple Episodes of Interbreeding between Neanderthal and Modern Humans." *Nature Ecology & Evolution* 3, no. 1 (2019): 39–44.

Volta, A. "On the Electricity Excited by Mere Contact of Conducting Substances of Different Kinds." *Royal Society of Philosophical Transactions* 90 (1800): 403–431.

Von Rueden, C. R. and A. V. Jaeggi. "Men's Status and Reproductive Success in 33 Nonindustrial Societies: Effects of Subsistence, Marriage System, and

Reproductive Strategy." *Proceedings of the National Academy of Sciences* 113, no. 39 (2016): 10824–10829.

Wallis, J. L. "Church Ministry and the Free Rider Problem: Religious Liberty and Disestablishment." *American Journal of Economics and Sociology* 50, no. 2 (1991): 183–196.

Wang, J., G. H. L. Cheng, T. Chen, and K. Leung. "Team Creativity/Innovation in Culturally Diverse Teams: A Meta-Analysis." *Journal of Organizational Behavior* 40, no. 6 (2019): 693–708.

Wang, C., O. Lizardo, and D. Hachen. "Using Big Data to Examine the Effect of Urbanism on Social Networks." *Journal of Urban Affairs* 43, no. 1 (2021): 40–56.

Weber, M. *Economy and Society*. Edited by G. Roth and C. Wittich. Berkeley: University of California Press, [1922] 1978.

Weber, H., M. Schwenzer, and S. Hilmert. "Homophily in the Formation and Development of Learning Networks among University Students." *Network Science* 8, no. 4 (2020): 1–23.

Weber, M. "Politics as a Vacation." In *Essays in Sociology*, translated by H. H. Gerth and C. Wright Mills. Oxford: Oxford University Press, 1946.

Webber, M. E. *Power Trip: The Story of Energy*. New York: Basic Books, 2019.

Welzel, C. *Freedom Rising: Human Empowerment and the Quest for Emancipation*. New York: Cambridge University Press, 2013.

Wendorf, F. "Site 117: A Nubian Final Paleolithic Graveyard Near Jebel Sahaba, Sudan." In *The Prehistory of Nubia*, edited by F. Wendorf, 954–995. Dallas: Southern Methodist University Press, 1968.

Werman, D. S. "Freud's 'Narcissism of Minor Differences' A Review and Reassessment." *Journal of American Academy of Psychoanalysis* 16 (1988): 451–459.

West, G. B. *Scale: The Universal Laws of Growth, Innovation, Sustainability, and the Pace of Life in Organisms, Cities, Economies, and Companies*. New York: Penguin, 2017.

West, G. B., J. H. Brown, and B. J. Enquist. "A General Model for the Origin of Allometric Scaling Laws in Biology." *Science* 276, no. 5309 (1997): 122–126.

West, S. A., R. M. Fisher, A. Gardner, and E. T. Kiers. "Major Evolutionary Transitions in Individuality." *Proceedings of the National Academy of Sciences* 112, no. 33 (2015): 10112–10119.

Wheeler, T. *Mr. Lincoln's T-Mails: How Abraham Lincoln Used the Telegraph to Win the Civil War*. New York: HarperCollins, 2009.

Whitehouse, H., J. Jong, M. D. Buhrmester, Á. Gomez, B. Bastian, C. M. Kavanagh, M. Newson, M. Matthews, J. Lanman, R. McKay, and S. Gavrilets. "The Evolution of Extreme Cooperation via Shared Dysphoric Experiences." *Scientific Reports* 7, no. 44292 (2017): 1–10.

Whitehouse, H. and J. A. Lanman. "The Ties that Bind Us: Ritual, Fusion, and Identification." *Current Anthropology* 55, no. 6 (2014): 674–695.

Whiten, A., N. McGuigan, S. Marshall-Pescini, and L. M. Hopper. "Emulation, Imitation, Over-Imitation and the Scope of Culture for Child and Chimpanzee." *Philosophical Transactions of the Royal Society B: Biological Sciences* 364, no. 1528 (2009): 2417–2428.

Wilkins, J., B. J. Schoville, K. S. Brown, and M. Chazan. "Evidence for Early Hafted Hunting Technology." *Science* 338, no. 6109 (2012): 942–946.

Wilkinson, T. J., L. Rayne, and J. Jotheri. "Hydraulic Landscapes in Mesopotamia: The Role of Human Niche Construction." *Water History* 7, no. 4 (2015): 397–418.

Willer, R., K. Kuwabara, and M. W. Macy. "The False Enforcement of Unpopular Norms." *American Journal of Sociology* 115, no. 2 (2009): 451–490.

Wilson, D. S., E. Ostrom, and M. E. Cox. "Generalizing the Core Design Principles for the Efficacy of Groups." *Journal of Economic Behavior & Organization* 90 (2013): S21–S32.

Wilson, E. O. *The Insect Societies*. Cambridge, MA: Belknap, 1971.

Wilson, E. O. *Sociobiology*. Cambridge, MA: Belknap, 1975.

Wilson, E. O. *The Social Conquest of Earth*. New York: W. W. Norton & Company, 2012.

Wittfogel, K. *Oriental Despotism: A Comparative Study of Total Power*. New Haven, CT: Yale University Press, 1957.

Wobst, H. M. "Boundary Conditions for Paleolithic Social Systems: A Simulation Approach." *American Antiquity* 39 (1974): 147–178.

Wolpert, L., and E. Szathmáry. "Multicellularity: Evolution and the Egg." *Nature* 420, no. 745 (2002).

World Health Organization. "Sanitation: Key Facts." *World Health Organization*. Retrieved from https://www.who.int/news-room/fact-sheets/detail/sanitation, 2019.

Wrangham, R. *Catching Fire: How Cooking Made Us Human*. London: Basic Books, 2009.

Wrangham, R. "Control of Fire in the Paleolithic: Evaluating the Cooking Hypothesis." *Current Anthropology* 58, suppl. 16 (2017): S303–S313.

Wrangham, R. W., and M. L. Wilson. "Collective Violence; Comparisons between Youths and Chimpanzees." *Annals of the New York Academy of Sciences* 1036, no. 1 (2004): 233–256.

Wright, R. *Nonzero: The Logic of Human Destiny*. New York: Vintage, 2001.

Wright, E., J. Galbany, S. C. McFarlin, E. Ndayishimiye, T. S. Stoinski, and M. M. Robbins. "Male Body Size, Dominance Rank and Strategic Use of Aggression in a Group-Living Mammal." *Animal Behaviour* 151 (2019): 87–102.

Wu, J., D. Balliet, and P. A. Van Lange. "Reputation, Gossip, and Human Cooperation." *Social and Personality Psychology Compass* 10, no. 6 (2016a): 350–364.

Wu, J., D. Balliet, and P. A. Van Lange. "Reputation Management: Why and How Gossip Enhances Generosity." *Evolution and Human Behavior* 37, no. 3 (2016b): 193–201.

Wulff, H. E. "The Qanats of Iran." *Scientific American* (April 1968): 94–105.

Wynn, T. "Hafted Spears and the Archaeology of Mind." *Proceedings of the National Academy of Sciences* 106, no. 24 (2009): 9544–9545.

Yachi, S., and M. Loreau. "Biodiversity and Ecosystem Productivity in a Fluctuating Environment: The Insurance Hypothesis." *Proceedings of the National Academy of Sciences of the United States of America* 96, no. 4 (1999): 1463–1468.

Young, A., J. Laca, G. Dieffenbach, E. Hossain, D. Mann, and A. Shtulman. "Can Science Beat Out Intuition? Increasing the Accessibility of Counterintuitive Scientific Ideas." In *Proceedings of the 40th Annual Conference of the Cognitive Science Society*, edited by T. T. Rogers, M. Rau, X. Zhu, and C. W. Kalish, 1238–1243. Austin, TX: Cognitive Science Society, 2018.

Yudkin, D., S. Hawkins, and T. Dixon. *The Perception Gap: How False Impressions are Pulling Americans Apart*. New York: More in Common, 2019.

Zaidi, B., and S. P. Morgan. "The Second Demographic Transition Theory: A Review and Appraisal." *Annual Review of Sociology* 43 (2017): 473–492.
Zajonc, R. B. "Social Facilitation." *Science* 149, no. 3681 (1965): 269–274.
Žampachová, B., E. Landová, and D. Frynta. "Methods for Measuring Mammalian Personalities: In Which Animals and How Accurately Can We Quantify it?" *Lynx, New Series* 48, no. 1 (2017): 183–198.
Zerjal, T., Y. Xue, G. Bertorelle, R. S. Wells, W. Bao, S. Zhu, R. Qamar, Q. Ayub, A. Mohyuddin, S. Fu, and P. Li. "The Genetic Legacy of the Mongols." *The American Journal of Human Genetics* 72, no. 3 (2003): 717–721.
Zhang, C., and J. Yang. *A History of Mechanical Engineering*. Singapore: Springer Singapore, 2020.

Index

Page numbers in **bold** refer to figures.

abstract reasoning 28
abstraction 7, 117
Accademia Del Cimento, Florence 246
aggregates, collaboration of 66
allocare 226
allodefense 223
alloforaging 222–223
alloliving ix, 220, 221–227
alloparenting 14–16, 31, 221–222
alphabets 163
altercentric cognition 229
altruism 223–224; biological 3–10; evolutionary logic 3–4; kin selection 3–4; reciprocal 10–11, 105, 222
analogical reasoning 58
Andersson, C. 49–51
animal societies, fission–fusion in 55–59, 60–61
annual income, per capita growth 171
ants 4
aqueducts 153–154
Aral, S. 70
Arbib, M. 24
Archimedes 156
Archimedes' screw, the 156
AT&T 193
attachment 46
attentional allocation 79–80, 89–91; and intuition 128; shared 91
attentional bias 124
attitudes 52–53, 98–99, 228, 236
attribution bias 122
attribution styles 129
Australopithecus afarensis 32
Austro–Prussian War 192
authoritarianism 36
autonomy 76
aversive emotions 57
awareness 78–80, 229

Balazs, C. 187
Bastardoz, N. 36, 39
Baumard, N. 171
behavioral eusociality 6–7
behavioral synchronization 90
beliefs 52
Bell, A. G. 193
benevolence 46
Bessemer, H. 172–173
between-group competition 233–234
between-group cultural variation 232–233
Big Men 37–38
biological altruism 3–10
biology, sociology and 49
biophobia 49
birth control 28–29, 227
Black, J. 137
Blanco, F. 87
blast furnaces 172–173
Bloom, N. 238–239
Bloom, P. 224
Boehm, C. 27, 32–33
Bonetto, E. 237–238
Borges, J. L. 121
Bourdieu, P. 74–75
Boyer, P. 20, 108–110, 117
brain 6, 7, 77, 245; and diet 18, 51; genetic selection 23; information-processing 127; information-processing burden 82,

110; plasticity 117; size 14, 15, 23–24, 28
Brown, D. 105
Bureau of Transportation Statistics 189
bureaucracies 73, 151, 200–203
Burt, R. 69–70
businesses 215, 216

caloric consumption, cities 200
canals 158
cargo ships 158–159
cars 171–172
categorical essentialism 121–122
centralized authority 165–166
Charbonnier, J. 152
Chen, H. 153
child development 102–103
child-rearing, cooperative 14–16, 36–37, 221–222
childhood 27
children 114, 126, 132, 222; essentialism 120, 122; feral 232; socialization 28–32
chimpanzees 2–3, 21, 25–26, 26–27, 30, 39, 50, 55–56, 76–77, 102–103
China 146, 152–153, 155, 156, 160, 165, 204, 214
Chiu, L. 42
cholera 183
Chorley, G. P. H. 166
cities: boundaries 199–200; caloric consumption 200; characteristics 206; circulation of people 203; comparison with organizations 214–217; definition 197; disorder 210; diversity 212–213; energy use 205; first 197–198; fission–fusion oscillation 210, 212; flourishing 216–217; founders effects 213; goals 215; growth trajectory 213; hierarchical branching networks 220–221; industrial 198, 202, 203–212; infrastructure 198, 199, 205–207; limits to growth 200; occupational scaling 213; as open systems 215, 216; origins and development 197–200; path dependence 212–213; population growth 207, 207–208, 245; populations 204; predominant occupations 204; relationship with their nation 216–217; and rise of the urban middle class 200–203; road networks 199, 207; scaling 206–209, 210; size 197, 203–204; social interactions 208–211; and social isolation 213–214
civil engineering ix
cladistic analysis 21
class consciousness 122
climate change 22, 171, 186
climatological shift, Miocene 7–8
closed contexts 83–84
co-presence 211–212, 229; need for 89–91
coal 169, 170
Coe, L. 191
coercion 76
cognitive burdens, reducing 59
cognitive capacity 28
cognitive circuits 101–102
cognitive functioning 7
cognitive inference systems 126
cognitive mechanisms 9–10
cognitive resources 81–82
cohesion 218
Cohn, J. 174
coinage 165
collaborative circumstances 41–42
collapsed societies 66
collective agreements 115–116
collective development 142
collective effervescence 90, 211
collective intentionality 142, 229
collective potential x
collective relevance 157
collective utilizability 194
collectivist cultures 130
Collins, R. 13, 90, 165, 234
colony identities 5
combination, and recombination 71–78
commons, infrastructure 149, 157
communication 54, 59, 61, 64; canalized 75; electronically mediated 191–194; pace of 192; pictograms, logograms, and alphabetic writing 162–165; technologies 89–90
communities, scaling 2–3
community-embeddedness 130
competition 233–235
computer mediation 231–232
computer simulation models 242
Comte, A. 46–47
conceptual ties 77

confirmation bias 53–54, 124
conflict resolution 73
conflict theory 48–49
conflicts 32–33, 43–44, 62; decision-making 63–65; interpersonal 68
conformity 62, 216
connectedness 218
constructional engineering ix
contact, levels of 78–83, 79
continuums 133
cooking 17–18
cooperation 219; ingroup 107–108; modes of 105–106; morality as 105–106; with strangers 4–5
cooperative resource extraction **20**
Coser, L. 234
creative insight 70
creativity 212–213; paradox of 237–238; rate of 207–208, 210–211
crime 210
criminal justice system 33–34
crisis 87
crop cultivation strategies 166–167
cultural artifacts 168
cultural assemblages 247
cultural calibration 118–119
cultural intuitions 75
cultural shifts 218
cultural variation: between-group 232–233; within-group 233
culture, study of viii
cultures 20
cuneiform 163
currency 165–166
Curry, O. S. 105–106

daily life, habitus of 29
dangers and threats 32–34
Darwin, C. 121
decision-making 35, 57, 63–65, 73, 83–84, 126
deep-level diversity 235–236
defense 55, 56, 62, 89, 106, 223
demographic characteristics, and economic outcomes 74
deprivation 204
despotism 36
developmental psychology 102–103
dictators 224
diet 16–19, 51n2, 224
difference 82
disaggregating processes 82–83
disagreement 63–65, 68, 75
disease 154–155, 182, 183, 188, 210
distributed effervescence 213
diversity 235–237
diversity-bandwidth tradeoff 70
DNA 1–2
dominance hierarchy 28
Dor, D. 24–25
droughts 156
Du, P. 153
Dunbar, R. I. 223
Dunn, M. 19–20, 46–51
Durkheim, E. 46, 75, 78, 90, 104, 114–115, 119

e-mail 193–194
ecology 51
economic exchange 111–113
economic identity 78
economic opportunity 227
economic outcomes, and demographic characteristics 74
Edison, T. 174, 177–178, 179
education 225–226, 227
egalitarian hierarchies 27
egalitarianism 27, 106
Egyptians, Ancient 144, 145, 159
Einstein, A. 139
electric light bulb 177
electrical grids 179–181
electricity 139, 141–142, 174–181, 205
electronically mediated communication 191–194
elephants 59
embeddedness 99, 130
emergence 118
emotions and emotionality 7, 24, 56–57, 59, 130–131
empathic responses 223–224
energy 135, 137–138
energy capture 161–162
energy flow 220–221
energy sources and access 67, 170, 172, 239–240
energy use, cities 205
engineering infrastructure 135
engineers ix
entitativity 11–14, 22, 40
entrepreneurs 173
environment 44

equality 106
equivalence classes 58
essentialism 120–125
eukaryotic cells 41–43
eusocial insects 4
eusociality ix, 3, 219, 224–225
eusocialness 5–7, 14, 224–225, 226–227
evolution, units of viii, 135, 164, 219, 241–242
evolutionary biology 3
evolutionary logic 4
evolutionary processes 125–126
evolutionary psychology 6
evolutionary transitions 40–45, 219
exchanges 111–113
executive cognitive functioning 14, 24–25
eyesight 138–139

face-to-face contact, need for 89–91
fairness 106
Faraday, M. 176–177
farming societies: infrastructure in 149–161; tools and tool use in 144, 144–149
feedback loop 54
feral children 232
fertility, decline in 227
fictive kin 5, 26, 225
fields 88–89
fire 17–18, 143–144
fission–fusion 66–67; in animal societies 55–59, 60–61; between-group competition 233–235; between-group cultural variation 232–233; calibration 59–63; cities 210, 212; closing 215; cognitive demands 58; combination and recombination 71–78; and decision-making 63–65; dimensions 56–57; feedback loop 54; as fractal phenomenon 232; information-processing 53–54; and innovation 68–71; and Innovation 235–239; and intuition 127–132; levels of contact 78–83, **79**; longitudinal analysis 91–92; oscillation ix, x, 52–54, 58–59, 59–63, 83–84, 91–100, **92, 93, 94, 96, 97**, 227–241, 239–241, 247–248; Oscillation-Infrastructural Theory 227–241; process 53–54; rate of oscillation 59, 62–63; rhythms 239–241; stuck 62; symbolic 231; symmetry 84; and threat perception 84–89, **86**; tools 142; virtual 231–232; visualizations 92–100, **92, 93, 94, 96, 97**; within-group competition 234–235; within-group cultural variation 233
fission states 59–61, 62, 63–64, 66, 68, 84, 227–228, 230–231, 232; between-group competition 233–235; and intuition 127–132
fissioning 53, 58, 67
Flannery, K. 28, 103–108, 114
flexible contextualization 117
Flint, Michigan 187
fluidly ix
focused awareness 78–79
food supplies 161–162
foraging societies 8–9, 28, 221–222; dangers and threats 32–34; first principles 103–108; hierarchies 36–38; socialization 28–32
fossil fuel societies: annual income per capita growth 171; electrical systems 174–181; environmental costs 171–172; infrastructural layering 188–194; infrastructure 169–195; machine labor power 170–171; shift to 169–173; water management and irrigation 181–188
fossil fuel use 169–170
Fox, K. M. 149
France, energy supply 170
Franklin, B. 174–175
freedom 30, 31, 241
friendships 11, 25
fuel stations 189–191
Furuichi, T. 50
fusion hotspots 198
fusion states 53, 58, 61–62, 64, 66–67, 68, 80–81, 84, 228–229; between-group cultural variation 232–233; combination and recombination 71–78; and fission–fusion 127–132; and intuition 127–132; levels of contact 78–83, **79**; within-group cultural variation 233

Galvani, L. 175
gas stations 189–191

gene-cultural coevolution framework 224
genes, competition 43
genetic capacity 224
genetic conflict 43–44
genetic determinism 7
genetic eusociality 6
genetic fitness 227
genetic selection 23
genetic similarity 1, 3, 7–10, 14
Genghis Khan 9
geographic distance, shrinkage 171
Germany 172
Gilbert, S. F. 42
globalization 111–113
goal-oriented groupings 81
goals 236
gods 201
Goodall, J. 50
gossip 11
governments, as singular entities 109–110
grandmother hypothesis 5–6
Greece, Ancient 157
greenhouse gas pollution 191
Grossman, I. 248
group achievement 131
group boundaries ix, 107; porous 53, 83, 247
group cohesion 11–14
group composition 59
group consensus 65
group deliberation 83–84
group diversity 235–237
group formation 60
group identity 12, 25
group loyalty 29
group organization 54
groups, as singular entities 108–110
groupthink 64

Habermas, J. 89
habituation 87, 97
habitus 74–75, 123
Haidt, J. 105
Hamilton, W. D. 3–4, 10, 11
Hanel, P. 9–10
harvesting 147–148
HaYonim Cave, human skeletal remains 9
heat 137–138
Henrich, J. 224
Hermann, C. 87, 88
heroism/courage 106
heuristics 101
Heyes, C. 6
hierarchical branching networks 220–221
hierarchies 3, 26–28, 34–40, 110, 229–230; Big Men 37–38; closedness 35–36, **36**; definition 35; generic features 38–40; influences on **36**; and leadership 36–37; legitimacy 63–64; openness 35–36, **36**; rigid 40; social 125; spontaneous formation of 124
Hirschfeld, L. 101
hominins 1–2
Homo erectus 2, 12, 15, 23–24
Homo neanderthalensis 2, 23
Homo sapiens 2, 224
honesty 119–120
human evolution 1–2, 21–25; bottlenecks 7–10; dangers and threats 32–34; hierarchy and leadership 34–40, **36**; socialization 28–32
human nature ix, 102
humor 37
hunter-gatherers 8–9, 27; dangers and threats 32–34; hierarchies 36–38; socialization 28–32
hunting/foraging and defense 16–20, **20**, 28
Hussey, O. 147–148
hydroelectric power 178–179

identity 4–5, 61, 77–78; economic 78; ingroup 106–108; national 77–78; signifiers 77–78, 104–105
immigrants 112
Incan Empire 160
India 204
individual subjectivities 228
individuals: innovative potential 70–71; levels of contact 78–83, **79**
Indonesia 162–163
industrial societies: *see* fossil fuel societies
inequality 35, 112–113
infant and juvenile mortality 31
inferential reasoning 58
information: distribution 164; infrastructure-related 242–243; integration 68; search for 241;

sources of variation 242; storage 242–243; symbolic 233; transmittable 43
information brokers 69
information-containing structures 144
information-processing 101, 127, 218; fission–fusion 53–54; group ix–x; individual ix; recency bias 87; *see also* intuitive information-processing
information-sharing 68
information transfer 70
informational niches 20–21
infrastructural evolution x
infrastructural innovation x
infrastructural layering 188, 188–194, 195, 243
infrastructural networks 220–221
infrastructural shifts, centrality of ix
infrastructural systems 219–220
infrastructure: begets infrastructure 185; cities 198, 199, 205–207; collective relevance 156–157; as collective tool 142; collective utilizability 142; commons 149, 157; complexity 195–196; definition 141–142, 173; distinction from tools 141–144, **143**; electricity 174–181; electronically mediated communication 191–194; in farming societies 149–161; fossil fuel societies 169–195; fuel stations 189–191; importance viii–ix; information storage 242–243; innovation 149, 219; and intuition 247; irrigation systems 150–157, 164, 168; layering 188, 188–194, 195, 243; Oscillation-Infrastructural Theory 241–245; railways and public transportation 189; roads 159–161, 199, 207; scaling 206–207, 208–209; sharedness 152; shipping waterways 157–159; sources of variation in related information 242; symbolic 161–168; units of 241–242; water management 150–157, 164, 168, 181–188
Inglehart, R. 240
ingroups 57, 106–108; cohesion 234; superiority beliefs 122
innovation x; and combination 72; cumulative 238; drivers 68–70; and fission–fusion 68–71, 235–239; growth rate 238; individuals and 70–71; infrastructure 149–161, 219; network dimensions 68–71; openness to 51; pace of 244–245; rate of 207–208, 210–211; and recombination 72; resistance to 237–238; tools and tool use 144–149
insects 4
institutional fields 88–89
institutions 88–89, 115
Insull, S. 178
intentionality 67
inter-group violence 33
Interaction Ritual Theory 13
interaction rituals 13
interconnectedness 223
internal combustion engines 170–171
internet, the 43, 89, 91
interspecies comparisons 2–3
intersubjectivity 229
intolerance 106–108
intuitions 101; about the physical world 125–126, 134–140, 246–247; accuracy 245; cultural calibration 118–119; dispelling 134; education and 133; expression 102–108; and fission–fusion 127–132; flexibility 117; incomplete 110–111; and infrastructure 247; Oscillation-Infrastructural Theory 245–248; reflection on 134; reliance on 116–119; sets 127–128; sociological 245–246; sources 101–102; stubbornness 137; suppression 132–134
intuitive information-processing
intuitive information processing: 101–108, and intuitions about the physical world 125–126; psychological foundations 119–125; sociology 108–119, **108**
intuitive physics 125–126, 134–140
intuitive sociology 108–119, **108**; and intuitions about the physical world 125–126
invisible hierarchy 28
irrigation systems 150–157, 164, 168

Japan, energy supply 170
Jebel Sahaba cemetery site 34

joint productive exchanges 80
Jost, J. T. 125
Judd, M. 34

Kelly, R. 9, 18, 24–25, 27, 244–245
Kelly, R. L. 14
Kennedy, H. 155
Kenya 12
kin selection 3–4, 10, 105, 226
Kitayama, S. 131
Kleist, E. J. von 175
knowledge transmission 106
knowledge workers 201
Kostyszyn, P. 82
Krummer, Hans 55

labor: division of 35, 218, 225–226; proto–division of 19–20, **20**
labor power 170–171, 172
Lane, J. 77
language 7, 20–25, 43, 116
Lansing, J. S. 149
Larson, J. M. 70
Lawler, E. 13, 13–14, 80, 81
leadership 35, 36–38, 76, 110, 115–116, 248
learning 30
Lee, R. 34
legitimacy 166
Leiser, D. 113
Lenski, G. 238
Lenz, E. 176–177
Leslie, S.-J. 127
Leyden jars 174–175
life expectancy 183, 188, 230
life-worlds 89
lighting 174, 177, 205–206
Lincoln, A. 192
Linton, R. 104–105
Lisbon 209
literacy 162–165
longitudinal research 52
Los Angeles Aqueduct 184–186
Loughlin, W. 8
Luckman, T. 89
Lucy 32
Lye, T. P. 29
lying 119–120

McCloskey, D. 171, 204
McCormick, C. 147–148
McDonald's 40
Machalek, R. 3, 26, 49
machine labor power 170–171
McLuhan, M. 192
major evolutionary transitions 40–45, 49–51, 219
Manchester 202–203
Marcus, J. 28, 103–108, 114
markets 166, 223
marriage rules 8–9
Martin, J. 89
Martin, M. 49
Marx, K. 48–49
Maryanski, A. 7, 21, 22–23, 30
matter, conservation of 135–147
Mauss, M. 119
Maynard Smith, J. 41, 43, 44
meat-eating 18–19
mechanical reapers 147–148
media technology 192
membership obligations 64
menopause 15
Mercier, H. 134
Mesopotamia 145, 146–147, 150–151, 155, 157, 158–159, 197–198, 200–202
metamarkets 165
methodological individualism 47–48
middle class, rise of 200–203
migration 8, 214
minimal fusion 67
Minkowski, H. 139
mobs 63–64
modernity 171, 225
Moffett, M. 4, 26, 61, 76–77
money 165–166
moral attitudes 105–106
morality, as cooperation 105–106
Morse Code 191
Morse, S. 192
motion 140
motivation 131
Mulholland, W. 186
multicropping 166–167
musilanguage 24
mutualism 80–81, 229
mutualistic coordination 105
myths 119

Napoleonic Wars 203
national identity 77–78
natural gas 169, 170, 189–191
natural selection 41–42

negativity bias 124
network gaps 69
networks, branching 220
niche economic opportunities 194
Nigeria 190
Nisbett. R. 130
norms 114–116, 127, 128, 134, 230; internalization 29–30, 31
novelty 68–69, 72
nuclear energy 169–170, 170

occupational specialization 195
oil 170, 190
oneness, sense of 57
open contexts 83–84
organismality 19–20, 45–46, 45, 219–221; study of 46–51
organismic analogy, the 46
organizational complexity 40–41
organizational fields 88–89
organizations: comparison with cities 214–217; goals 215; and innovation 215
Ørsted, H. 176
Oscillation-Infrastructural Theory 218–248; alloliving 221–227; concepts 218; fission–fusion oscillation 227–241; fission states 230–231; fusion states 228–229; infrastructure 241–245; intuition and wisdom 245–248; organismality 219–221; symbolic fission–fusion 231; virtual fission–fusion 231–232
Ötzi 32
outgroup homogeneity effect 123
outgroups 224; competition with 233–234; essentialism 122–123; stigmatized 54

paper money 165
paper wasps 6
parental care motivation system 15–16
Park, R. 213
perceptual novelty 72
Persia 151–152
personal computers 193
Phoenicians 159, 163
physical world, intuitions about 125–126, 134–140, 246–247
Piaget, J. 135–136
Piccolino, M. 176
pictograms, logograms, and alphabetic writing 162–165
Pinker, Susan 90
planning 151
play 28–32
plows 144, 145–146
pluralistic deliberation 83–84
pluralistic ignorance 230
polarization 65
police and policing 33–34, 128
pollution 171, 187, 191, 210
polygynous sexuality 8–9
population growth 195
population numbers 3, 150, 181–182, 245
power 110–111
pregnancy 16
printing technology 43
prokaryotic cells 41–43
public transportation 189

qanats 151–153, 155
qualitative research 52
quantitative research 52

railways 189
rationality, irrationality of 40
reasoning 58–59, 128
recency bias 87, 97
reciprocal altruism 10–11, 105, 222
reciprocal exchange 105
recombination: and combination 71–78; and innovation 72
Reeves, P. 180–181
reflection 247
relational ties 77
reproductive castes 5–6, 15
reproductive fitness 227
reputation 11, 14, 31
resource acquisition 57
resource commons, the 78
resource extraction, cooperative 16–20, 28
resource flow 35
resource management 72–73, 76
respect/humility 106
rituals 12–14
Ritzer, G. 39–40
Rizzolatti, G. 24
roads 159–161, 199, 207
Rome, Ancient 153–154, 160–161, 166
Rost, S. 150

rules 114
Russia 181

Sahlins, M. 26
Samson, K. 82
sanitation systems 182–184, 188
scaling laws 207–208
Schutz, A. 89
scientific experimentation, institutionalization of 134
scientists 133
Searle, J. 115–116
second demographic transition 227
seed drills 146–147
self-actualization 172, 179, 243
self-control 59
self-orientation 130
self–other boundaries 90
self-understanding 129–130
serendipitous encounters 67
sewers 154, 182–184
shared attentional allocation 91
shared understandings 88–89
sharing 31
Sharlin, H. 178–179
Shavit, A. 64, 83
Shemesh, Y. 113
shipping waterways 157–159
Shtulman, A. 119, 132, 136, 138
Shultz, S. 223
Simmel-Coser principle 234
Simmel, G. 213
single-celled organisms 40–41
slaves and slavery 151
Smil, V. 148, 160, 161, 162, 181
Smith, J. M. 164
Smith, M. 199, 202
social categories 102–103, 121–122
social categorization 101
social collapse 66
social conflict 62
social cues 58
social disruption 214
social dominance orientation 108
social environments 219
social expectations 230
social facilitation 211, 229
social facts 114–116
social hierarchies 125
social information, processing 82
social integration 214
social interactions, cities 208–209, 213–214
social isolation 213–214, 230
social learning 6, 120
social networks 72, 110
social obligations 77
social organization 127–128; fission–fusion ix
social-psychological heuristics 101
social rapport 54
social reality 116
social regulation 89
social similarity 10
social status 31
social systems 220–221; and alloliving 221–227
social tension 54
social ties 21–22
social worlds 102
socialization 7, 13, 27, 28–32, 222
societal orientation 26
society: as major evolutionary transitions 49–51; as organisms 45–46, **45**, 46–51
sociological intuitions 108–119, **108**, 245–246; and intuitions about the physical world 125–126; psychological foundations 119–125; sociology 108–119, **108**
sociology 46–51, 108–119, **108**
souls 103–104
space decisions 57
space-time 139
spears 143
Spencer, H. 46
Spoerl, J. S. 173
stability 125
standardized currencies 165–166
status function declarations 115–116
status quo bias 124–125
steel 172–173
stereotypes 82, 122
street lighting 205–206
strong-tie networks 69
structural holes 69
sub-Saharan Africa 8
subgroups 57, 61, 68
subjective states 228
subjectivities 228
subsistence stress 161–162
subsocieties 52
surface contact 80–81, 229

surface-level diversity 235, 236
Swan, J. 177
symbolic abstractions 225
symbolic fission–fusion 231
symbolic information 233
symbolic infrastructure 161–168; crop cultivation strategies 166–167; pictograms, logograms, and alphabetic writing 162–165; standardized currencies 165–166
symbolic reasoning 20
system justification 124–125
Szathmáry, E. 41, 43, 44, 219

tangibility 136–137
task jointness 13–14
technology; diffusion of 193–194; information contained in 144
telegrams 192
telegraph, the 192
telephone, the 193
television 193
Tell Brak 197–198
Tell es-Sawwan 197
Tell Maghzaliyah 197
temperature 137–138
Tesla, N. 177, 178
Theory of Social Commitments 13, 13–14
Thomas, W. I. 48
threat bias 124
threats and threat perception 30, 54, 84–89, **86**; high 87–88; low 88; wave forms **93**, 94–98
time decisions 57
Toba, Mount, volcanic eruption of 8
Tomasello, M. 229
tools and tool use 24–25, 243–244; collective benefits 141; collective utilizability 194; complexity 195–196; definition 141–142, 173; distinction from infrastructure 141–144, **143**; in farming societies 144, 144–149; fission–fusion 142; individual benefit 141; regulation 156–157; size 159; stone 16–17
Törnberg, P. 49–51
totemization 104–105
trade 34, 51, 106–107, 111–113
transition theory 219
transportation 171, 171–172, 189
Triandis, H. 130
tribal loyalties 223
triple withouts 214
trust 70, 119–120, 166
truth-default bias 119–120
Turner, J. H. 22–23, 24

uncertainty 125, 248
undersea cables 193
unfamiliarity 82
unfocused awareness 79
uniqueness, human 2–3; biological altruism 3–10; cladistic analysis 21–25; communities 2–3; cooperative child-rearing 14–16; cooperative resource extraction 16–20, **20**, 28; entitativity 11–14, 22; eusocialness 5–7, 14; fictive kin 26; genetic similarity 3–10, 7–10, 14; hierarchies 26–28; language 20–25; reciprocal altruism 10–11; societal orientation 26; symbolic reasoning 20–21
United Nations 204
United States of America: electrical grids 180, 181; polarization 65; predominant occupations 204; railways and public transportation 189; threat perception 86; water management 183–188
urban planning 198–199
urban socialization/acclimation 212
urbanization 169, 183
US Army 104–105
US Department of Energy 180
US Energy Information Administration 180–181
US Environmental Protection Agency 187

values 52–53, 239–240
Van Alstyne, M. 70
Van Vugt, M. 36, 39
violence 32–34
virtual fission–fusion 231–232
vision 138–139
Volta, A. 139, 175–176
Voltaic Pile, the 176
volume, perception of 135–136

Wang, J. 235
warfare 33
waste management 182–184

water-lifting devices 155–156
water management and irrigation 150–157, 164, 168, 181–188
water pollution 186–187
water treatment 184
waterways 157–159
waterwheels 162, 170
wave forms: amplitude 93, 95; fission–fusion visualizations 92–100, **92, 93, 94, 96, 97**; speed 93; threat perception **93**, 94–98, **96, 97**; wavelength 93
we-ness 73–74, 78, 80–81, 90
weak-tie relationships 68–70, 72
wealth 110
Webber, M. 205–206
Weber, M. 39–40, 47–48, 202
weight 135–136, 140
Werman, D. S. 233
West, G. 202, 208, 209, 216, 220
Western Union Telegraph company 192, 193
Westinghouse, S. 178
white privilege 122
Wilson, E. O. 223
wisdom 247–248
within-group competition 234–235
within-group cultural variation 233
Wobst, H. Martin 9
World Bank 182
World Health Organization 182, 188
World Values Survey 10
worldviews 53–54, 72, 83, 126, 239–240
writing systems 162–165
Wulff, H. E. 152